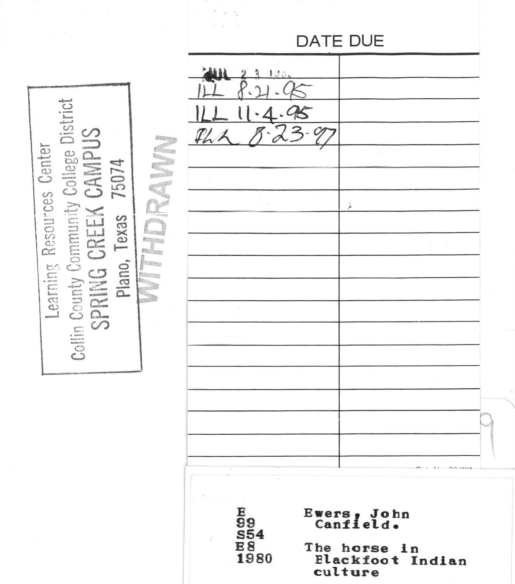

DATE DUE

JUL 23	
ILL 8·21·95	
ILL 11·4·95	
ILL 8·23·97	

The Horse in Blackfoot Indian Culture

With Comparative Material from Other Western Tribes

John C. Ewers

Smithsonian Institution Press
Washington, D.C.

Smithsonian Institution
Bureau of American Ethnology Bulletin 159
Originally published 1955; reprinted 1969

Classics of Smithsonian Anthropology Edition
Reprinted 1980
Second reprinting, with new cover, 1985

**Library of Congress
Cataloging in Publication Data**

Ewers, John Canfield.
    The horse in Blackfoot Indian culture.
    (Classics of Smithsonian Anthropology)
    Reprint of the 1955 ed. published by the
U.S. Govt. Print. Off., Washington, which was
issued as no. 159 of Bureau of American Ethnology
Bulletin.
    Bibliography: p.
    Includes index.
    1. Siksika Indians. 2. Horses—Great Plains.
3. Indians of North America—Great Plains. I. Title.
II. Series. III. Series: United States. Bureau of
American Ethnology. Bulletin; no. 159.
[E99.S54E8 1979]   970'.004'97   79-607784

ISBN 0-87474-419-9

The Smithsonian Institution began publishing important works in anthropology in 1848. Many are
still useful as primary sources of data, as documents
in the history of anthropology, and in some cases as
basic theoretical statements. Classics in Smithsonian
Anthropology is a series of reissues of these works,
as selected by the Department of Anthropology of
the Smithsonian Institution. Each volume is reproduced from the original, with concern for the clar-
ity of the illustrations. Most of the works have new
critical introductions.

CONTENTS

ILLUSTRATIONS

PLATES

(All plates follow page 358. Plate 1 deleted in reprint edition.)

FIGURES

PAGE

FOREWORD

The problem of the influence of the horse on Plains Indian culture has intrigued white men for more than a century. On April 6, 1848, Nathaniel J. Wyeth, an intelligent fur trader, wrote to Henry R. Schoolcraft, "I regret not being able to supply more facts to support a view, very strongly impressed on my mind, that the condition of the Indian of this continent has been much influenced by the introduction of Horses" (Wyeth, 1851, vol. 1, p. 208).

Modern anthropologists have recognized the acquisition and use of the European horse by the Plains Indians as a classic example of cultural diffusion. Ralph Linton (1940, p. 478), in a general discussion of processes of acculturation, mentioned the rapid changes that have taken place in Western Civilization in recent years and then added, "However, we have at least one example of almost equally rapid acceptance of a whole new complex of culture elements by a series of 'primitive' groups. This case is that of the horse among the Plains Indians. The speed with which this novelty was taken over is the more surprising in view of the revolutionary effects on many aspects of native life." Generalizations such as this are common in the anthropological literature. Yet, upon close examination, they give no hint of having been based upon a detailed factual analysis of the Plains Indian horse complex. We must conclude that these generalizations were, at best, intuitive interpretations.

For the entire Plains area there has been an appalling lack of detailed analysis of the horse complex. The nearest approach to a study of the facts relating to the functions of horses in a tribal culture is Gilbert L. Wilson's "The Horse and Dog in Hidatsa Culture" (Wilson, 1924). Some portions of that study "approach ideal completeness," as Clark Wissler, who edited it, has observed (ibid., p. 127). But this study had definite limitations. It dealt almost exclusively with the role of the horse in Hidatsa material culture. It described the use of horses by a semisedentary, horticultural tribe which was relatively poor in horses and relied heavily upon dogs for transportation of camp equipment in buffalo-hunting days. The fact remains that no analytical study of the horse complex of any nomadic Plains Indian tribe has appeared in print.

The present study was undertaken in an effort to "supply more facts" (as Wyeth stated the problem) regarding the role of the horse in a nomadic, buffalo-hunting, horse-using Plains Indian tribe, on the basis of which conclusions might be drawn regarding the important functions of the horse in the tribal culture. Selection of the Blackfoot as the Indians to be studied was an expedient one. I was stationed cn the Blackfeet Reservation in Montana for a period of 3½ years, 1941–1944, under conditions which were nearly ideal for field work with elderly Indian informants. During that period I served as the first curator of the new Museum of the Plains Indian near Browning. The Indians of that reservation as well as culturally related Blood and Piegan Indians of Alberta were intensely interested in this new museum. They visited it repeatedly. Many older Indians brought their family heirlooms to be added to the collections. As a museum man and as a year-round member of the local community I first came to know most of the elderly Indians who later served as my informants. The museum was open to the public from late spring until early fall, permitting me to devote a considerable portion of my time during the long winter period to research. Field research on this problem was inaugurated in December 1941, nine months after my arrival on the Blackfeet Reservation. It was continued until the spring of 1944, under the auspices of the Division of Education of the Office of Indian Affairs. I am grateful to Willard R. Beatty, formerly director of Indian education in Washington, to the late Freal McBride, superintendent of the Blackfeet Reservation, to William Hemsing, Reservation School Superintendent, and to his colleagues on the Blackfeet Agency staff for their active encouragement of this project. Research was interrupted by 2 years of military service, after which I transferred to the United States National Museum. The Office of Indian Affairs kindly permitted the transfer of my field notes from the Museum of the Plains Indian to the National Museum in 1946, so that I might be able to complete the project. My field investigations were completed during a summer's residence on the Blood Reserve, Alberta, and the Blackfeet Reservation, Mont., in 1947, financed by the Smithsonian Institution.

Much of the factual information on which this study is based was supplied by elderly, fullblood Piegan and Blood Indian informants, whose knowledge of the functions of horses in the late years of buffalo days was solidly grounded in personal experiences. These old people really loved horses and enjoyed talking about them. They were uniformly cooperative and interested in getting the record straight. Differences of opinion naturally arose among informants, but it was possible to iron out a number of these differences through group discussions following individual interrogations. I am indebted to the following elderly Indians for their friendly and sincere cooperation, which made this study possible. Women are indicated by asterisks.

Name:	Tribe	Life span
*Double-Victory-Calf-Robe	Blood	Ca. 1849–1951
Lazy Boy	Piegan	Ca. 1855–1948
Weasel Tail	Blood	Ca. 1859–1950
Iron	Blood-Piegan	Ca. 1859–
Green-Grass-Bull	Piegan	Ca. 1862–1951
Weasel Head	Piegan	Ca. 1863–1943
Rides-at-the-Door	Piegan	Ca. 1864–1953
Makes-Cold-Weather	Piegan	Ca. 1866–1951
Richard Sanderville	Mixblood Piegan	1866–1951
Scraping White	Blood	Ca. 1866–1948
Three Calf	Blood-Piegan	Ca. 1866–1948
*Elk-Hollering-in-the-Water-Bear-Chief	Blood-Piegan	Ca. 1867–ante-1951
Chewing-Black-Bones	Piegan	Ca. 1867–
*Deathly-Woman-Cree-Medicine	Piegan	Ca. 1868–1952
Heavy Head	Blood	Ca. 1869–1951
Mike-Day-Rider	Piegan	Ca. 1870–
Short Face	Piegan	Ca. 1870–1952
Wallace Night Gun	Piegan	Ca. 1872–1950

With the exception of Richard Sanderville, all the informants listed above are or were putative fullbloods who spoke little English. The dates of birth of Piegan and some Blood informants were computed on the basis of Blackfeet Agency census records for 1901 and 1908.

I am greatly indebted to Reuben and Cecile Black Boy for their faithful services as interpreters on the Blackfeet Reservation, Mont., where all the Piegan informants and the able Blood informant Weasel Tail were interviewed. Reuben's and Cecile's participating membership in the fullblood community, their outstanding skill in arts and crafts, their thorough knowledge of horses, and their previous experience in collecting and interpreting Blackfoot myths and stories for the Federal Writers' Project of Montana from older fullbloods made them exceptionally well prepared for their exacting task. On the Blood Reserve, Chief Percy Creighton kindly served as my interpreter.

It is not possible to mention all the English-speaking Blackfoot Indians, born since buffalo days, who provided information regarding Blackfoot horse usages in more recent times. George Bull Child, Henry Magee, John Old Chief, Jim Stingy, Jim Walters, and Mae Williamson were especially helpful members of this group.

I am indebted to Frank and Joseph Sherburne, Browning merchants, for helpful observations on Piegan horse usages based on their residence on the Blackfeet Reservation, Mont., for more than half a century; to Archdeacon Samuel K. Middleton, principal of St. Paul's Residential School, Blood Reserve, for numerous kindnesses in facilitating my field research on the Blood Reserve; and to Dr. Claude

Schaeffer, curator of the Museum of the Plains Indian since 1947, for checking a number of specific points with Piegan informants as questions arose during the writing of this work. Dr. Schaeffer also made available to me manuscript materials in the Blackfeet Agency Archives, now in the Museum of the Plains Indian.

Most of the text figures reproduced in this study are based on pencil drawings carefully prepared by Calvin Boy, a young Piegan artist. To insure their accuracy, special precautions were taken. As elderly informants described objects and/or activities I desired to have illustrated Reuben Black Boy and I made rough sketches. We showed these to Calvin Boy and explained to him the content of the desired illustrations. He then drew pictures at a very large scale so that they could be seen readily by elderly informants, many of whom had poor eyesight. The informants examined the drawings and in the presence of the artist made suggestions for any changes in detail that might be necessary. Then Calvin Boy prepared the final pencil or pen-and-ink drawings. The minority of the line illustrations were prepared by the author from his field notes and sketches.

I am indebted to the following institutions for permission to reproduce photographs of objects and scenes in this bulletin: American Museum of Natural History, New York; Brooklyn Museum; Chicago Museum of Natural History; Glacier Studio, Browning, Mont.; Great Northern Railway; Montana Historical Society, Helena; Museum of the Plains Indian; Royal Ontario Museum of Archaeology; Smithsonian Institution; and Geological Survey, United States Department of the Interior.

Throughout the period of this investigation (1941–52) I was mindful of its broader implications. I endeavored to read widely in the scattered and largely unindexed literature on the Blackfoot and other horse-using tribes of the Great Plains and Plateau. In quest of dated materials and comparative data, I examined numerous collections of specimens in museums as well as collections of early drawings, paintings, and photographs. I sought to obtain comparative data directly from elderly informants among the Flathead (1947), Oglala Dakota (1947), and Kiowa (1949) tribes as my limited opportunities for field work on their respective reservations permitted. Alice Marriott graciously supplied, through correspondence, information on Kiowa horse usages, obtained in the course of her own field work. Eugene Barrett, forester, Rosebud Reservation, S. Dak., kindly furnished some comparative data on Brule Dakota horse usages. Edith V. A. Murphy of Covelo, Calif., formerly field botanist, Office of Indian Affairs, sent me valuable comparative data on horse medicines.

In this study I approached the larger problem of the definition, origin, and history of the Plains Indian horse complex through an analysis of the Blackfoot complex and the inclusion of comparative data indicative of geographically and tribally more widespread occurrences of specific traits. The comparative data appear as footnotes or as distinct subsections of the text in pages 1–298. These data, together with my Blackfoot findings (summarized in pp. 299–322), serve as the factual basis for the conclusions set forth in the section entitled "The Plains Indian Horse Complex" (pp. 323–340).

THE HORSE IN BLACKFOOT INDIAN CULTURE

WITH COMPARATIVE MATERIAL FROM OTHER WESTERN TRIBES

By John C. Ewers

THE ACQUISITION OF THE HORSE

Clark Wissler (1927, p. 154) has named the period 1540 to 1880 in the history of the Indian tribes of the Great Plains "the Horse Culture Period." This period can be defined more accurately and meaningfully in cultural than in temporal terms. Among all the tribes of the area it began much later than 1540. With some tribes it ended before 1880. Yet for each Plains Indian tribe the Horse Culture Period spanned the years between the acquisition and first use of horses and the extermination of the economically important buffalo in the region in which that tribe lived.

Anthropologists and historians have been intrigued by the problem of the diffusion of the European horse among the Plains Indians. It is well known that many tribes began to acquire horses before their first recorded contacts with white men. Paucity of documentation has given rise to much speculation as to the sources of the horses diffused to these tribes, the date when the first Plains Indians acquired horses, the rate of diffusion from tribe to tribe, and the conditions under which the spread took place.

The three Blackfoot tribes of the northwestern Plains, the Piegan, ✳ Blood, and North Blackfoot, were among those tribes that possessed horses when first met by literate white men. To view their acquisition in proper historical and cultural perspective it is necessary to consider the larger problem of the diffusion of horses to the northern Plains and Plateau tribes. Critical study of this problem dates from Wissler's paper, entitled "The Influence of the Horse in the Development of Plains Culture," published in the American Anthropologist (Wissler, 1914). That stimulating, pioneer effort encouraged further study of the problem. Of the more recent contributions two papers by Francis Haines (1938, a and b), based to a considerable extent upon data unavailable to Wissler a quarter of a century earlier, have been most influential in revising the thinking of students of this problem.

1

THE NORTHWARD SPREAD OF HORSES

SOURCES OF THE HORSES OF THE PLAINS INDIANS

Haines' major contributions were to point out that the Plains
Indians acquired their first horses from a different source and at a
considerably later date than Wissler had considered probable.
Wissler gave credence to the theory that the first horses obtained by
Plains Indians were animals lost or abandoned by the Spanish exploring expeditions led by De Soto and Coronado in 1541 (Wissler, 1914,
pp. 9–10). The historian Walter P. Webb, in "The Great Plains," an
important regional history published 17 years later, acknowledged
his debt to Wissler in his acceptance of this theory (Webb, 1931, p. 57).
However, another historian, Morris Bishop, who had made a critical
study of early Spanish explorations, termed this theory, "a pretty
legend" (Bishop, 1933, p. 31). Haines virtually laid the old theory
to rest. After a careful review of the evidence he concluded that
"the chances of strays from the horse herds of either De Soto or
Coronado having furnished the horses of the Plains Indians is so
remote that it should be discarded" (Haines, 1938 a, p. 117).

This conclusion has been supported by more recent scholarship.
John R. Swanton, who has been a thorough student of the De Soto
Expedition over a period of years, concurred in Haines' interpretation
of the De Soto evidence (Swanton, 1939, pp. 170–171). Arthur S.
Aiton, in publishing Coronado's Compostela muster roll, commented
significantly, "Five hundred and fifty-eight horses, two of them
mares, are accounted for in the muster. The presence and separate
listing of only two mares suggests that we may have been credulous in
the belief that stray horses from the Coronado expedition stocked the
western plains with their first horses." Furthermore, he found no
record of the loss of either mare during Coronado's expedition to
the Plains (Aiton, 1939, pp. 556–570). Herbert E. Bolton, profound
student of early Spanish explorations in the Southwest, has pointed
out that even though Coronado may have taken some mares to the
Plains which had not been listed in the Compostela roll, the biological
possibility of strays from this expedition having stocked the Plains
with Spanish horses was slight. He also noted the lack of any mention of encounters with stray horses or mounted Indians in the
accounts of Spanish expeditions to the Great Plains in the later years
of the 16th and early years of the 17th century (Bolton, 1949, pp.
68–69, 400).

Exploring the alternatives, Haines found that the early 17th-century
Spanish stock-raising settlements of the Southwest, particularly those
in the neighborhood of Santa Fe, furnished "just the items necessary

to encourage the adoption of horses by the Indians to the east—
friendly contact through trade, ample supply of horses, and examples
of the advantages of the new servants" (Haines, 1938 a, p. 117).

DATING THE NORTHWARD SPREAD OF HORSES AMONG THE INDIANS

Different concepts of the sources of the horses of the Plains Indians
led to very different interpretations of the rate of their diffusion
among these tribes. Wissler's assumption that horses were available
to the Plains Indians as early as 1541, caused him to consider it pos-
sil le that they might have spread northward during the remainder of
that century so rapidly that they could have reached the Crow and
Blackfoot on the headwaters of the Missouri as early as 1600 (Wissler,
1914, p. 10). Haines, however, found "the available evidence indicates
that the Plains Indians began acquiring horses some time after 1600,
the center of distribution being Santa Fe. This development proceeded rather slowly; none of the tribes becoming horse Indians before
1630, and probably not until 1650" (Haines, 1938 a, p. 117). The
logical and historical soundness of Haines' position has been acknowledged by more recent students of the problem (Wyman, 1945, pp.
53–55; Mishkin, 1940, pp. 5–6; Denhardt, 1947, p. 103. Acceptance of
this position is also implied in Bolton, 1949, p. 400).

In tracing the northward spread of horses from the Southwest to
the Plains and Plateau tribes we must acknowledge the meagerness
of the historical data bearing on this movement. Wissler logically
assumed that "those to get them first would be the Ute, Comanche,
Apache, Kiowa and Caddo" (Wissler, 1914, p. 2). If we exclude
the Comanche, this assumption seems to be in accord with more
recent findings. Horses were first diffused northward and eastward
to those tribes on the periphery of the Spanish settlements of the
Southwest. Marvin Opler found in Southern Ute traditions a suggestion that those Indians acquired horses from the Spanish "probably
around 1640" (Linton, 1940, pp. 156–157, 171). Spanish records,
dated 1659, reported Apache raids on the ranch stock of the settlements
which continued into the next decade. The Apache carried off as many
as 300 head of livestock in a single raid. At the same time the Apache
engaged in an intermittent exchange of slaves for horses with the
Pueblo Indians (Scholes, 1937, pp. 150, 163, 398–399). The French
explorer La Salle heard that the Gattacka (Kiowa-Apache) and
Manrhoat (Kiowa) were trading horses to the Wichita or Pawnee in
1682. He believed the animals had been stolen from the Spaniards of
New Mexico (Margry, 1876–86, vol. 2, pp. 201–202). In 1690, Tonti
found the Cadodaquis on Red River in possession of about 30 horses,
which the Indians called cavalis, an apparent derivation from the

Spanish "caballos." While among the Naouadiché, another Caddoan tribe, farther south, he found horses "very common," stating "there is not a cabin which has not four or five" (Cox, 1905, pp. 44–50).

Data on the spread of the horse northward over the Plains in the late years of the 17th century are sparse. In 1680, Oto Indians who visited La Salle at Fort Crèvecoeur (near present Peoria, Ill.) brought with them a piebald horse taken from some Spaniards they had killed (Pease and Werner, 1934 a, p. 4). Deliette reported that prior to 1700 the Pawnee and Wichita obtained branded Spanish horses "of which they make use sometimes to pursue the buffalo in the hunt" (Pease and Werner, 1934 b, p. 388). In the summer of 1700, Father Gabriel Marest included Missouri, Kansa, and Ponca, along with the Pawnee and Wichita, as possessors of Spanish horses (Garraghan, 1927, p. 312). These brief references suggest that by the end of the century most and probably all Plains Indian tribes living south of the Platte River had gained some familiarity with horses. Nevertheless, testimony, of the French explorers La Harpe, Du Tisne, and Bourgmont (Margry, 1886, vol. 6) in the first quarter of the 18th century indicates that horses still were scarce among the tribes living eastward of the Apache and northward of the Caddo.

In 1705, the Comanche, an offshoot of the Wyoming Shoshoni, first were seen on the New Mexican frontier. In company with linquistically related Ute, they came to beg for peace, but on their departure stole horses from the settlements (Thomas, 1935, p. 105). In succeeding years they launched repeated bold attacks upon New Mexico, riding off with horses and with goods intended by the Spanish for trade with the Apache living northeastward of the Rio Grande Pueblos. Comanche thefts were extended to the Apache villages as well. Specific mention was made in Spanish records of one raid in which 3 Comanche and Ute Indians ran off 20 horses and a colt from an Apache rancheria in 1719. At that very time Governor Valverde was leading a punitive expedition against the troublesome Comanche (ibid., pp. 105–109, 122).

Plains tribes northeast of the Black Hills were met by white traders before they acquired horses. When La Vérendrye accompanied an Assiniboin trading party to the Mandan villages on the Missouri in 1738, those Assiniboin had no horses. La Vérendrye made no mention of any horses among the Mandan. However, he was told that the Arikara, northernmost of the Caddoan-speaking peoples, living south of the Mandan on the Missouri, owned horses, as did nomadic tribes living southwestward toward and beyond the Black Hills (La Vérendrye, 1927, pp. 108, 337). Two Frenchmen, left by La Vérendrye at the Mandan villages through the summer of 1739, witnessed the visit of horse-using tribes to the Mandan for trading purposes (ibid., pp.

366–368). These tribes cannot be identified with certainty. However, the two Frenchmen learned that they feared the "Snake" Indians. Therefore, it seems improbable these people were Shoshoni or their Comanche kinsmen. They may have been the Kiowa and Kiowa Apache, who were mentioned by La Salle as actively engaged in the northward diffusion of horses a half century earlier, and who were known to have traded horses to the horticultural peoples on the Missouri in later years.

In 1741, La Vérendrye's son took two horses with him on his return from the Mandan villages (ibid., p. 108, 387). This event seems to have marked the beginning of the trade in horses from nomadic tribes southwest of the Missouri, through the Mandan to the peoples north and east of them. Hendry (1907, pp. 334–335) traveled with an Assiniboin trading party in 1754, which employed horses for packing but not for riding. Twelve years later the elder Henry (1809, pp. 275–289) saw horses in some numbers among the Assiniboin and mentioned their use in mounted warfare. Umfreville reported (in 1789) "it is but lately that they [horses] have become common among the Nehethawa [Cree] Indians" (Umfreville, 1790, p. 189). The French trader Jacques d'Eglise, in 1792, saw horses equipped with Mexican saddles and bridles among the Mandan in the first description of that tribe after the visits of the La Vérendryes a half century earlier (Nasitir, 1927, p. 58). It is most probable that a trickle of trade in Spanish horses through the Mandan to the Assiniboin and Plains Cree existed throughout the last half of the 18th century.

The third quarter of the century witnessed a rapid expansion of the horse frontier among tribes living to the eastward of the Missouri. In 1768 Carver (1838, p. 188) found no horses among the Dakota of the Upper Mississippi, and placed the frontier of horse-using tribes some distance to the westward of them. Yet by 1773 Peter Pond saw Spanish horses among the Sauk on the Wisconsin River. Two years later he observed that the Yankton Dakota had "a Grate Number of Horses" which they used for hunting buffalo and carrying baggage (Pond, 1908, pp. 335, 353). Since the Yankton probably obtained their horses from the Teton, Hyde's 1760 estimate of the date of Teton Dakota acquisition of horses appears reasonable (Hyde, 1937, pp. 16, 18, 68). According to Teton tradition, they acquired their first horses from the Arikara on the Missouri. It was probably during the third quarter of the 18th century that the Cheyenne began to acquire horses also (Jablow, 1951, p. 10).

At the close of the 18th century the Red River marked the northeastern boundary of Plains Indian horse culture. In 1798, David Thompson noted that the Ojibwa east of that river had no horses (Thompson, 1916, p. 246). Two years thereafter Alexander Henry the younger purchased two horses from visiting Indians who lived on the Assiniboin River to the west, and commented significantly, "Those were the first and only two horses we had on Red river; the Saulteurs had none, but always used canoes" (Henry and Thompson, 1897, vol. 1, p. 47). In January, 1806, Zebulon Pike observed that traders at the Northwest Company post on Lac de Sable, near the Mississippi, had "horses they procured from Red river of the Indians" (Pike, 1810, p. 60). In the summer of that year Henry encountered nine lodges of canoe-using Ojibwa at the forks of Scratching River in present southeastern Manitoba, hunting buffalo. They owned some horses and were planning to go to the Missouri to purchase more (Henry and Thompson, 1897, vol. 1, p. 286). These were the Plains Ojibwa in process of transition from woodland canoemen to Plains Indian horsemen.

By 1805 horses had also been diffused far to the northwest in larger numbers. The Lewis and Clark Expedition established first recorded white contact with the Plateau tribes in 1805–06. On their return from the Pacific coast they were able to purchase four horses from Skilloot Indians at the Dalles, paying twice as much for them as they had paid for horses obtained from Shoshoni and Flathead on their outward journey (Coues, 1893, vol. 2, pp. 954–955). As they moved eastward they found horses more plentiful, indicating that the Dalles was near the northwestern limit of horse diffusion at that time. Lewis and Clark were impressed with the large numbers of horses owned by many Plateau tribes. Yet the Lemhi Shoshoni told them of related peoples living to the southwest of them (probably Ute) "where horses are much more abundant than they are here" (Coues, 1893, vol. 2, p. 569). The explorers found Spanish riding gear and branded mules among the Shoshoni. They believed these animals came from the Spanish settlements, which the Indians reported to be but 8 to 10 days' journey southward (Coues, 1893, vol. 2, p. 559; Ordway, 1916, p. 268).

Northern Shoshoni tradition claims that their kinsmen, the Comanche, furnished them their first horses (Clark, 1885, p. 338; Shimkin, 1938, p. 415). If we may credit this tradition, it seems possible these Shoshoni may have begun to acquire horses a few years after Comanche raids were launched on the New Mexican settlements in 1705. It is probable, too, that the Ute of western Colorado served as intermediaries through whom Spanish horses passed northward to the Shoshoni during the 18th century (Steward, 1938, p. 201). However, these movements cannot be historically documented.

Nevertheless, the sizable herds of horses seen among the Lemhi Shoshoni and their neighbors by Lewis and Clark in 1805, presuppose an extended period of horse diffusion on a considerable scale toward the Northwest prior to that date. Haines (1938 b, p. 436) has postulated a route of diffusion west of the Continental Divide from Santa

Fe to the Snake River by way of the headwaters of the Colorado, the Grand, and Green Rivers. This was the most direct route to the Northwest from New Mexico. We may note, also, that it passed through the country of Shoshonean tribes offering a peaceful highway for Comanche and Ute such as was unavailable on the western Plains, infested as that region was with hostile Apache and Kiowa. There was little incentive to divert horses westward from that route, as the Great Basin afforded inadequate pasturage for horses.

Through the Northern Shoshoni, horses were distributed to the Plateau tribes. Tribal traditions of the Flathead and Nez Percé credit the Shoshoni with furnishing them their first mounts (Turney-High, 1937, p. 106; Haines, 1939, p. 19). The Coeur d'Alene, Pend d'Orielle, Kalispel, Spokan, Colville, and Cayuse tribes of the northwestern Plateau obtained their first horses either directly from the Shoshoni or indirectly from tribes previously supplied by Shoshoni (Teit, 1930, p. 351). Although a Crow tradition recorded by Bradley (1923, p. 298) refers to their acquisition of horses from the Nez Percé, it seems more probable that the first horses obtained by the Crow came from the Comanche (Morgan, MS., bk. 9, p. 12).

THE PROCESS OF DIFFUSION

Previous writers have been more concerned with the historical problem of *when* the Plains Indians obtained horses than with the cultural problem of *how* horses were diffused. Certainly the paucity of 18th century documentation sheds little light on the diffusion process. However, when we add to this documentation the information in the literature of the first decade of the 19th century, we find much that is helpful in seeking an explanation of this process.

At the beginning of the 19th century two main routes for the diffusion of horses to the tribes of the northern Plains were observable. One route led from the Upper Yellowstone eastward to the Hidatsa and Mandan villages on the Missouri. The Crow Indians of the Middle Yellowstone served as intermediaries in a flourishing trade in horses and mules, securing large numbers of these animals from the Flathead, Shoshoni, and probably also the Nez Percé on the Upper Yellowstone in exchange for objects of European manufacture. At the Mandan and Hidatsa villages they disposed of some of these horses and mules, at double their purchase value, in exchange for the European-made objects desired for their own use and eagerly sought by the far-off Flathead and Shoshoni. Thus tribes of the Upper Yellowstone and Plateau began to receive supplies of knives, axes, brass kettles, metal awls, bracelets of iron and brass, a few buttons worn as hair ornaments, some long metal lance heads, arrowheads of iron and brass, and a few fusils of Northwest Company trade type,

before their first direct contacts with white traders in their own terri-
tories. Thus also, horn bows and possibly other products of the
western Indians reached the village tribes on the Missouri, and bridle
bits and trade blankets of Spanish origin arrived at the Mandan and
Hidatsa villages by a long and circuitous route. On their summer
trading visits to the Mandan and Hidatsa the Crow also exchanged
products of the chase (dried meat, robes, leggings, shirts, and skin
lodges) for corn, pumpkins, and tobacco of the villagers. In 1805, the
Northwest Company trader Larocque, the first white man to spend a
season with the Crow, reported that this trade was well-organized
(Larocque, 1910, pp. 22, 64, 66, 71–72). This trade was also noted by
Lewis and Clark (Coues, 1893, vol. 1, pp. 198–199; vol. 2, pp. 498, 554,
563), Henry (Henry and Thompson, 1897, vol. 1, pp. 398–399),
Mackenzie (1889, p. 346), and Tabeau (1939, pp. 160–161).[1]

We cannot be sure how long this trade was in existence before the
opening of the 19th century. However, the experienced fur trader
Robert Meldrum, who probably knew the Crow Indians better than
any other white man of his time, told Lewis Henry Morgan that when
he first went among the Crow (1827) old people of that tribe told him
they "saw the first horses ever brought into their country," and that
they obtained these horses from the Comanche. Morgan estimated,
"This would make it about 100 years ago that they first obtained the
horse," i. e. ca. 1762 (Morgan, MS., bk. 9, p. 12). Denig (1953, p. 19)
and Bradley (1896, p. 179) independently dated the separation of the
Crow from the Hidatsa about the year 1776 or a few years earlier. It is
probable that the Crow Indians did not become actively engaged in
this trade until they had acquired enough horses to make it practical
for them to leave the Hidatsa and become nomadic hunters.

The other major route by which horses were diffused northward to
the tribes of the northern Plains at the beginning of the 19th century
I assume to have been an older one, and probably the route followed
by the Comanche themselves in supplying the Crow with their first
horses. It led from the Spanish settlements of New Mexico and Texas
to the vicinity of the Black Hills in South Dakota via the western
High Plains, thence eastward and northeastward to the Arikara,
Hidatsa, and Mandan villages on the Missouri. The important middlemen in this trade at the beginning of the 19th century were the
nomadic Kiowa, Kiowa-Apache, Comanche, Arapaho, and Cheyenne.

Antoine Tabeau, a French trader from St. Louis, who was among
the Arikara in 1803–4, was told that prior to that time the Arikara
were accustomed to transport tobacco, maize, and goods of European

---

[1] Mackenzie (1889, p. 346) reported that 250 horses and 200 guns with 100 rounds of
ammunition for each were exchanged in the Crow-Hidatsa trade of June, 1805. Twelve
lodges of Shoshoni, comprising the remnant of a tribe that had been destroyed, accompanied the Crow trading party that summer (Larocque, 1910, pp. 22, 73).

manufacture "to the foot of the Black Hills" where they met the Kiowa, Kiowa-Apache, Comanche, Arapaho, and Cheyenne in a trading fair. There they secured dressed deerskins, porcupine-quill-decorated shirts of antelopeskin, moccasins, quantities of dried meat, and prairie turnip flour in exchange for their wares. Coincident with that trade was the barter of European firearms for horses, which Tabeau described:

> The horse is the most important article of their trade with the Ricaras. Most frequently it is given as a present: but, according to their manner, that is to say, it is recalled when the tender in exchange does not please. This is an understood restriction. This present is paid ordinarily with a gun, a hundred charges of powder and balls, a knife and other trifles. [Tabeau, 1939, p. 158.]

Tabeau was told that the nomadic traders obtained their horses directly from the Spaniards at "St. Antonio or Santa Fe," either buying them at low prices or stealing them, at their discretion (ibid., pp. 154–158).

Lewis and Clark made brief mention of Kiowa, Kiowa-Apache, and possibly some Comanche as wandering tribes who "raise a great number of horses, which they barter to the Ricaras, Mandans &c. for articles of European manufactory" (Coues, 1893, vol. 1, pp. 58–59). In the summer of 1806, Henry accompanied the Hidatsa on a visit to the Cheyenne to trade guns and ammunition (then scarce among the Cheyenne) for fine horses (Henry and Thompson, 1897, vol. 1, pp. 367–393).

Although this north-south trade route may have been employed for the northward diffusion of horses for several decades before the west-east trade route (previously described) was opened, it is most probable that the Arapaho and Cheyenne were not involved in it as intermediaries before their abandonment of the sedentary horticultural life in favor of a nomadic existence. Cheyenne conversion to nomadism probably began no earlier than 1750, and some villages of that tribe clung to the horticultural life until after 1790 (Strong, 1940, pp. 359, 371; Trudeau, 1921, pp. 165–167). According to Arapaho tradition that tribe also made the transition from sedentary to nomadic life (Elkin *in* Linton, 1940, p. 207). Presumably Arapaho conversion to nomadism did not long antedate that of the Cheyenne. Of the nomadic tribes actively engaged in supplying horses to the village tribes on the Missouri by the northward route in 1804, this leaves only the Kiowa-Apache, Kiowa, and Comanche as probable initiators of this trade. Since the Comanche are credited with supplying horses to their kinsmen, the Northern Shoshoni, in the 18th century, it is most probable that the Kiowa-Apache and Kiowa played more important roles in the early trade in horses with the village tribes of the Missouri.

The Arikara, Mandan, and Hidatsa villages served as foci for the further diffusion of horses to the tribes dwelling east and north of that river at the beginning of the 19th century. In late summer the nomadic Teton Dakota obtained horses, mules, corn, beans, pumpkins, and tobacco from the Arikara in exchange for products and byproducts of the hunt and European trade goods. Each spring the Teton met their Dakota relatives, the Yankton, Yanktonai, and Eastern Dakota at a great trading fair on the James River in present South Dakota, where they bartered some of the horses received from the Arikara, together with buffaloskin lodges, buffalo robes, and shirts and leggings of antelopeskin, with other Dakota tribes for the materials of the latter's country (walnut bows and red stone pipes are specifically mentioned), and European manufactured goods (guns and kettles are named) which those tribes obtained from white traders on the St. Peters (Minnesota) and Des Moines Rivers. Tabeau (1939, pp. 121, 131) reported that this Sioux trading fair sometimes attracted as many as 1,000 to 1,200 tents, housing about 3,000 men bearing arms. Lewis and Clark made repeated mention of this trade (Coues, 1893, vol. 1, pp. 95, 99, 100, 144, 217). They regarded it of special significance because it made the powerful Teton Dakota independent of white traders on the Missouri and hostile to the extension of the trade from St. Louis up the Missouri which would serve only to place deadly firearms in the hands of their enemies.

From the Mandan and Hidatsa villages horses passed to the Assiniboin, Plains Cree, and Plains Ojibwa of northern North Dakota and southern Canada. The actual trading took place at the villages of the horticultural tribes, during periodic visits from the nomadic ones. Trudeau, in 1796, told of the Assiniboin obtaining horses, corn, and tobacco from the Mandan and Hidatsa for guns and other merchandise (Trudeau, 1921, p. 173). Tabeau (1939, p. 161) and Lewis and Clark (Coues, 1893, vol. 1, p. 195) referred to the exchange of horses and agricultural products of the Mandan and Hidatsa for the "merchandise" (arms and ammunition were named) of the Assiniboin and Plains Cree.

The Mandan and Hidatsa also served as bases for the horse supply of white traders operating in the country north and east of them. Lewis and Clark's statement that Mr. Henderson of the Hudson's Bay Company came to the Hidatsa villages in December 1804, with tobacco, beads, and other merchandise to trade for furs, and "a few guns which are to be exchanged for horses" is significant of the preferred position given to both guns and horses in this trade (Coues, 1893, vol. 1, p. 207).

On the map (fig. 1) I have summarized graphically the foregoing data on trade routes employed in the diffusion of horses northward to the majority of the Plains Indian tribes dwelling north of the Platte River at the beginning of the 19th century.

A study of this map in conjunction with the preceding text seems to justify some conclusions relative to the pattern of this diffusion.

First, I am impressed with the fact that the trade in horses on the northern Plains at that time was almost without exception a trade be-

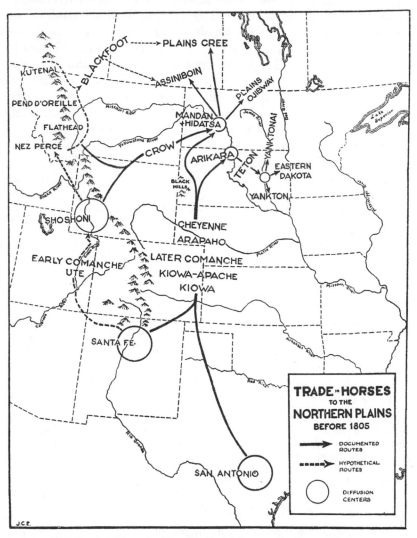

FIGURE 1.—Map showing trade in horses to the northern Plains before 1805.

tween nomadic and horticultural peoples, and that this horse trade was coincident with the exchange of products of the hunt for agricultural produce on the part of these same tribes. This barter between hunting and gardening peoples enabled each group to supplement its own economy with the products of the other's labors. There was little incentive for trade between two horticultural tribes or between two hunting peoples, as neither possessed an abundance of desirable products which the other did not have. However, the natural environment of the western Plateau yielded wild foods and other natural resources which were not found on the Plains. Therefore, the nomadic Plateau tribes stood in much the same desirable trading relationship to the Plains Indian nomads as did the gardening peoples of .he Plains. So we find that horses were diffused from the Flathead to the nomadic Crow, to the horticultural Hidatsa and Mandan, to the nomadic Assiniboin, Plains Cree, and Plains Ojibwa, with the same alternate rhythm as occurred in the northward progression of horses from the Spanish settlements to the nomadic Kiowa, Kiowa-Apache, Comanche, Arapaho, and Cheyenne, to the horticultural Arikara, to the nomadic Teton Dakota, to the horticultural Eastern Dakota.

There is good evidence that the pattern of trade in the respective products of their different economies between gardening and nomadic tribes was an old one in the Plains, and that it antedated the introduction of the horse into the area. Definite references to the trade of Plains Indians in pre-horse days reveal the pattern.

The Coronado expedition in 1541 observed that the nomadic Querechos and Teyas of the southwestern Plains—

. . . follow the cows, hunting them and tanning the skins to take to the settlements in the winter to sell, since they go there to pass the winter, each company going to those which are nearest, some to the settlement of Cicuye, others toward Quivera, and others to the settlements situated in the direction of Florida . . . . They have no other settlement or location than comes from travelling around with the cows . . . They exchange some cloaks with the natives of the river for corn. [Winship, 1896, pp. 527–528.]

In the fall of 1599, Vicente de Saldivar Mendoca met a roving band of Plains Indians not far from the Canadian River—

. . . coming from trading with the Picuries and Taos, populous pueblos of this New Mexico, where they sell meat, hides, tallow, suet, and salt in exchange for cotton blankets, pottery, maize, and some small green stones which they use. [Bolton, 1916, p. 226.]

The two Frenchmen left at the Mandan villages by La Vérendrye in 1739, reported the existence of a similar trade in words suggesting that it had been active for a period of years:

. . . every year, in the beginning of June, there arrive at the great fort on the bank of the river of the Mandan, several savage tribes which use horses and carry on trade with them; that they bring dressed skins trimmed and ornamented with plumage and porcupine quills, painted in various colors, also white buffalo skins, and that the Mandan give them in exchange grain and beans, of which they have ample supply.

Last spring two hundred lodges of them came; sometimes even more come; they are not all of the same tribe but some of them are only allies. [La Vérendrye, 1927, pp. 366–367.]

Undoubtedly some of the articles received by the Mandan in this trade were passed along to the Assiniboin. In 1738, La Vérendrye himself had found that the Mandan offered not only grains and tobacco, but also colored buffalo robes, deerskins and buckskins carefully dressed and ornamented with fur and feathers, painted feathers and furs, worked garters, headbands, and girdles to the Assiniboin in return for guns, powder, balls, axes, knives, kettles, and awls of European manufacture (ibid., pp. 323, 332). Horses do not appear to have been articles of trade at the Mandan villages at that time, but it is clear that the Assiniboin middlemen, operating far in advance of white traders, were offering to the Mandan firearms and ammunition as well as other trade goods obtained from Whites.

It is necessary to consider the diffusion of firearms to the Plains Indians as a factor related to and influencing the routes of trade followed in the northward diffusion of horses. If there was any possession as keenly sought by the historic Plains Indians as was the horse, it was the gun. As much as these Indians wanted the rapid mobility afforded by the horse, they sought the deadly firepower provided by the gun. Any tribe possessing either without the other was at a distinct disadvantage in opposition to an enemy owning both. British and French traders approaching the Plains from the north and east supplied guns to Indians. However, Spanish policy strictly prohibited the trading of firearms and ammunition to the natives. This placed those tribes in early contact with the British and French traders in an advantageous trading position. Having obtained firearms and ammunition directly from Europeans they were able to act as middlemen in bartering some of these highly desirable weapons with distant tribes that had as yet no direct contacts with white traders.

In the middle of the 18th century the village tribes of the Upper Missouri (Arikara, Mandan, and Hidatsa) were situated in a most admirable position for trading both to the northeast and the southwest. It was at those villages that the northeastward-moving frontier of the horse met the southwestward-moving frontier of the gun. Indians learned to equate guns and horses as standards of value, and a mutually profitable trade ensued by which the armed tribes of the Northeast secured mounts and the mounted tribes of the South and West secured firearms. Undoubtedly the demand for both firearms and horses far exceeded the supply. The need on the part of those Indians who received firearms for ammunition, which they could not make themselves, also helped to perpetuate this trade. At the beginning of the 19th century (as indicated by the data quoted from Tabeau) firearms still were the most desired articles sought in exchange for horses by those tribes which had access to considerable numbers of the latter, although canny horse traders then insisted that ammunition and some other articles be thrown into the scale to seal the bargain.

So it was that during the 18th century a trade in Spanish horses for French and British firearms grew up alongside the earlier pattern of exchange of products between horticultural and nomadic hunting tribes of the region. The trade in horses, therefore, appears to have been an historic elaboration of a prehistoric trade pattern among the Plains Indians.

Another aspect of this trade is worthy of note as a factor determining the direction of flow in the diffusion of horses. All other factors being equal, the nomadic tribes preferred to trade with horticultural peoples with whom they were closely related linguistically, if not biologically as well. Thus Crow traded primarily with Hidatsa, Teton with other Dakota groups, and Comanche and Ute with the Northern Shoshoni. It may well have been the attraction of European firearms that caused the Comanche to divert their trade to the unrelated horticultural peoples of the Missouri several decades after they had begun supplying horses to the Shoshoni.

Recently Denhardt has made a further significant observation:

. . . that the natives obtained their original horses, and always by far the greatest number, from the Spaniards or neighboring tribes and not from the wild herds. The Indians had mounts by the time the wild herds dotted the plains, and always preferred domesticated animals to the mestenos. Mustangs were hard to catch, and once caught, harder to tame. [Denhardt, 1947, pp. 103–104.]

Certainly the lack of references to the capture of wild horses by the Indians of the northern Plains in the literature prior to 1800, serves to support this observation and to suggest that the wild herds furnished a negligible source of horses for those tribes prior to that time.

But what of theft as a factor in the northward spread of horses? Certainly a considerable number of the horses that reached the northern tribes prior to 1800 were animals stolen from Spanish, Pueblo, or Apache settlements by intermediary nomads. It is also true that intertribal theft of horses among the northern tribes occurred prior to that time. Nevertheless, and some native traditions to the contrary, it is hardly credible that any northern tribes obtained their *first* horses by stealing the mounts of neighboring tribes who had acquired horses at a somewhat earlier date. I believe peaceful contact was a necessary condition of initial horse diffusion, in order that some members of the pedestrian tribe might learn to overcome their initial fear of horses and learn to ride and manage those lively animals. The preexisting pattern of trade furnished the most important medium of peaceful contacts and of initial diffusion of horses. The fact that such trade supplied inadequate numbers of horses to meet the needs of Indians who had gained some knowledge of handling them and a realization of the superiority of their use over foot travel and transport of camp equipment, encouraged intertribal theft. Actually there need not have been any prolonged interval between a tribe's first acquisition of horses and its initiation of horse-raiding operations. Some tribes may have begun raiding for horses within a decade after they acquired their first animals by peaceful means.

ACQUISITION OF HORSES BY THE BLACKFOOT

With this background let us consider the acquisition of the horse by the Blackfoot tribes. I have omitted these tribes from the previous discussion in order to point out the unique factors involved in Blackfoot acquisition in greater detail.

Prior to the publication of "David Thompson's Narrative" in 1916, it was the practice for students to estimate the date of Blackfoot horse acquisition. These estimates ranged from Wissler's previously mentioned and impossibly early "1600" to Grinnell's impossibly late "about the year 1800" (Hodge, 1907, pt. 1, p. 570). Burpee split the difference in his estimate of "probably the earliest years of the eighteenth century" (Hendry, 1907, p. 318). This approximated another estimate by Wissler in 1910, of "about two hundred years ago" (Wissler, 1910, p. 19).

More recent estimates have been based upon interpretations of a most remarkable account of some important events in the history of the Blackfoot during the lifetime of an aged Cree Indian, Saukamaupee (Boy) by name, who had been living with the Piegan for many years before David Thompson, Hudson's Bay Company trader, spent the winter of 1787–88 in his lodge. Thompson (1916, pp. 328–334) reckoned the old man's age at that time at "at least 75 to 80 years." Using Thompson's conservative estimate, we may consider that Saukamaupee was born no later than between 1707 and 1712. In dating the first episode of his story the old man pointed to a "lad of about sixteen years" in the camp and said that he had been about that boy's age when he went with a small group of Cree to aid the Piegan in a battle with the Snakes in which neither of the opposing forces used either guns or horses. On the basis of the above computation this must have been no later than 1723–28. Saukamaupee returned to his own people, "grew to be a man, became a skillful and fortunate hunter, and . . . procured . . . a wife." Thompson noted that Piegan "young men seldom married before they are full grown, about the age of 22 years or more." If the Cree, more than half a century earlier, followed that same custom, we may estimate that Saukamaupee was married no later than 1729–34. Saukamaupee explained that during the interval between his assistance to the Piegan and his marriage the Snakes had made use of a few horses in battle with the Piegan, "on which they dashed at the Peeagans, and with their stone Pukamoggin knocked them on the head." After his marriage he again went to the aid of the Piegan. Another battle was fought with the Snakes, but this time the enemy used no horses while the Piegan and their Cree and Assiniboin allies were armed with 10 guns. Terrified by the noise and deadly effect of this new secret weapon, the closely formed Snake battle line broke and its members fled in confusion.

Saukamaupee said that after that battle:

We pitched away in large camps with the women and children on the frontier of the Snake Indian country, hunting bison and red deer which were numerous, and we were anxious to see a horse of which we had heard so much. At last, as the leaves were falling we heard that one was killed by an arrow shot into his belly, but the Snake Indian that rode him, got away; numbers of us went to see him, and we all admired him, he put us in mind of a stag that had lost his horns; and we did not know what name to give him. But as he was a slave to Man, like the dog, which carried our things, he was named the Big Dog. [Thompson, 1916, p. 334.]

In spite of the indefiniteness of the dating of the incidents of Saukamaupee's recollections, I see no adequate reason to doubt the facts he cited. Fragments of this story have been preserved in the traditions of the Blackfoot tribes to the present time.[2] However, I do question the conclusions that have been drawn from this account by historians and ethnologists as to the date of acquisition of horses by the Blackfoot tribes.

Although Saukamaupee's description of his first sight of a *dead* horse is clear enough, nowhere in his account does he tell of the first acquisition of *live* horses by the Blackfoot. Yet J. B. Tyrrell, editor of Thompson's "Narrative," draws from the dead horse episode the unwarranted conclusion that the Blackfoot obtained their first horses from the Snake Indians in 1730. Lewis (1942, pp. 11, 60) followed

---

[2] Wissler (1910, p. 17) reported the Blackfoot tradition that before white men dominated the region the Shoshoni occupied much of the later Blackfoot country as far north as Two Medicine River. My informants of the 1940's claimed that the area of the present Blackfeet Reservation in Montana was formerly occupied by Shoshoni. Wissler (1912 a, p. 286) recorded the Piegan tradition that they received their first guns from the Cree, who taught them how to use them, and that "while some Piegan were out on the warpath they were attacked by a large number of Snake Indians. The Piegan fired on them and as they had never before seen guns they retreated." Weasel Tail, who seems to have possessed a strong interest in the historical traditions of his people, told me he understood that the Blackfoot obtained their first guns from the Cree; that the Cree joined them in a war party against the Shoshoni and Crow (?) in which the noise of the Blackfoot guns frightened the enemy so that they fled southward from their location at that time, which was near present Calgary, Alberta.

Weasel Tail volunteered that his grandfather, Talks Around, had told him the Blackfoot called the first horses they saw "big dogs." Later, because horses were about the size of elks, they began to call them "elk dogs." The change in name must have taken place before 1790, as Umfreville (1790, p. 202) recorded "Pin-ne-cho-me-tar," as the name for the horse in the first published Blackfoot vocabulary. This was certainly an attempt to render "ponokomita" (elk dog), the name still given the horse by the Blackfoot tribes.

suit with the statement "the Blackfoot received their first horses from the Shoshone in 1730." Haines (1938 b, p. 435) interpreted the Saukamaupee testimony as proof that the Blackfoot acquired their first horses between 1732 and 1737. His error in interpretation may be the more serious because he employed these Blackfoot dates as bases for backdating the prior acquisition of horses by Shoshoni and Flathead.

It seems to me that literal acceptance of Thompson's dating will justify only two proper conclusions from the Saukamaupee story: (1) that ca. 1729–34 the Northern Shoshoni, who were in conflict with the Piegan on the Canadian Plains, possessed some horses; (2) that the Piegan had no horses at that time. If we choose to be more critical of Thompson's dating, probably the most we can conclude is that the Blackfoot possessed no horses in the first quarter of the 18th century.

Wissler (1914, pp. 3–4) attributed to Saint-Pierre (1751) the first historic mention of horses among the Blackfoot. The Saint-Pierre testimony is tantalizingly indefinite. He does mention horses received in trade from Europeans (whom he termed French, but who probably were Spanish) by Indians living on the Plains beyond the French posts on the lower Saskatchewan. He did not identify these Indians by tribe (Saint-Pierre, 1886, p. clxiii.) As Roe (1939, pp. 241–242) has pointed out, it is impossible to identify these horse Indians as Blackfoot on the basis of Saint-Pierre's confused statement.

In the fall of 1754, Anthony Hendry (or Henday) of the Hudson's Bay Company journeyed westward with Cree and Assiniboin guides to seek to open trade with Indians west of those tribes, known to the Cree as "Archithinue." On the Saskatchewan Plains in October of that year he visited a camp of 200 lodges of Archithinue, and again in spring met several small bands of these Indians during his return eastward. Hendry was impressed with the fact that these Indians possessed horses and employed them skillfully in hunting buffalo. Although he gave no estimate of the number of horses owned by the Archithinue, he left the definite impression that they were better supplied than his Cree and Assiniboin companions who used horses only as pack animals. Hendry did not identify the "Archithinue natives" whom he met by any other name (Hendry, 1907, pp. 307–354). However, Mathew Cocking, sent by the Hudson's Bay Company in 1772 to try again to open trade with the Archithinue was more specific. Although he met only one small band of 22 lodges at a buffalo pound west of the Eagle Hills in present Saskatchewan, he definitely identified that band as "Waterfall Indians" (the Gros Ventres), and he stated that the general term "Archithinue" also included the Blood, Piegan, and Blackfoot (the three Blackfoot tribes) as well as the Sarsi. Furthermore, he stated that these tribes were "all Equestrian

Indians" (Cocking, 1908, pp. 110–111). This is the earliest definite statement to the effect that the Blackfoot tribes possessed horses.

Who, then, were the Archithinue Indians met by Hendry 18 years earlier? Wissler (1936, p. 5) was reasonably certain that they also were Gros Ventres. I believe we may infer with reason that the Blackfoot tribes, allies of the Gros Ventres, also possessed some horses in 1754, although they may not have been as well supplied with them as were the Gros Ventres. On the basis of the information now available, the most definite conclusion that can be drawn in dating Blackfoot horse acquisition, places this event in the interval between Saukamaupee's first sight of a dead horse and Hendry's contact with the Archithinue in 1754, or within the second quarter of the 18th century.

So it would appear that horses were acquired by the Blackfoot of the northwestern Plains at about the same time these animals reached the Mandan villages on the Missouri or very shortly thereafter. Consequently it was possible for horses to have been diffused from the Blackfoot and Gros Ventres to the Assiniboin and Plains Cree during the latter half of the 18th century. Certainly the nomadic Apache, Kiowa, Kiowa-Apache, Ute, Comanche, Shoshoni, and Flathead received horses before they reached the Blackfoot. Probably the Arikara and all of the horticultural Plains Indians south of them possessed horses before the Blackfoot obtained them. It seems most probable that the Crow, Cheyenne, and Teton Dakota obtained their first horses after the Blackfoot began to acquire them. We know so little of the early history of the Arapaho that it is impossible to estimate the period of their acquisition of horses other than to suggest that since their kinsmen the Gros Ventres possessed horses before 1754, it is most probable the Arapaho did also.

Since Blackfoot horse acquisition preceded first white contacts with these three tribes, we must rely rather heavily upon an evaluation of traditional data in determining the source of their horses. Wissler (1910, p. 19) heard Blackfoot traditions to the effect that their first horses were received from the Shoshoni and Flathead. One tradition told me stated that a Blackfoot, Shaved Head by name, went west and obtained the first horses known to his people from the Nez Percé, who told him they had taken them out of the water. Another tradition told of Sits-in-the-Night, who lived a generation later, having led a war party southward to about the location of the present Blackfeet Reservation, Mont., where they stole a number of horses from a Shoshoni or Crow camp. When the warriors mounted these horses and the animals began to walk, the riders became frightened and jumped off. They led the horses home. The people surrounded the new animals and gazed at them in wonder. If the horses began to jump about, they became frightened. After a time a woman said,

"Let's put a travois on one of these big dogs just like we do on our small dogs." They made a large travois and attached it to one of the horses. The horse did not jump or kick as it was led around camp. It seemed gentle. Later a woman mounted the horse and rode it with travois attached. According to this tradition the Blackfoot did not employ horses for riding, to hunt buffalo, or to war until after they were adapted to transport use with the travois.[3]

Interesting as this second story may be, I doubt its historicity. As previously stated, I doubt that any Plains Indian tribe learned to ride and care for horses without the advantage of the example and instruction of other Indians who had some knowledge of horses. It is improbable that the Blackfoot obtained their first horses from the Shoshoni, with whom they were at war. It is more probable that they received these animals as gifts from or in trade with the Flathead, Kutenai, Nez Percé, or Gros Ventres. Teit has reported Flathead traditions of early, peaceful trade with the Blackfoot (Teit, 1930, p. 358).

However, we can be certain that by the late years of the 18th century, theft, not trade, was the primary medium of horse acquisition exploited by the Blackfoot. Contemporary accounts of the Blackfoot during that period indicate that they were at war with their neighbors to the south and west. David Thompson observed that the Blackfoot tribes raided the Shoshoni, Flathead, and Kutenai for horses in 1787 (Thompson, 1916, p. 367). Umfreville briefly characterized the Blackfoot tribes in 1790, as "the most numerous and powerful nation we are acquainted with. War is more familiar to them than to other nations . . . In their inroads into the enemies country, they frequently bring off a number of horses, which is their principal inducement in going to war" (Umfreville, 1790, p. 200).

Thus, during the 18th century the Blackfoot developed the pattern of acquisition through capture which remained their primary method of obtaining horses from neighboring tribes throughout the first 86 years of the 19th century and until the buffalo were exterminated from their country.

---

[3] The majority of my aged Blackfoot informants when questioned regarding Blackfoot acquisition of the horse either frankly admitted they were not informed on the subject or offered a legendary explanation in reply. These mythological interpretations of a historic event which must have taken place little more than 200 years ago are given on pages 291–298.

WEALTH IN HORSES

Contemporary observers of the Plains Indians in buffalo days noted that these people reckoned their wealth in horses. Some tribes appeared to be rich in horses. Others were obviously poor. Within each tribe there were individuals who were relatively wealthy in horses. Others were desperately poor. The individual's status as an owner of horses conditioned his use of these animals and helped to determine both the nature and degree of his participation in many aspects of the life of the people of his tribe. Before proceeding with detailed consideration of the functions of horses in Blackfoot culture, it is desirable to determine as precisely as possible not only the tribal horse holdings but also the range of individual wealth in horses among the Blackfoot, and to compare Blackfoot wealth in horses with that of other horse-using tribes of the Great Plains and Plateau in order to indicate their relative standing as horse-owning people.

BLACKFOOT TRIBAL WEALTH IN HORSES

I have found no statistics on the total number of horses owned by the Blackfoot tribes prior to 1830. Three quarters of a century ago, Lt. James Bradley, who obtained much of his information on the Blackfoot from the trader, Alexander Culbertson, and other white men who had known these Indians since the 1830's, stated that "the Blackfeet had possessed horses as far back as their traditions extended but never in considerable numbers in early times, and even as late as 1833 they were poorly mounted." He estimated that "about the year 1830" the Piegan owned an average of 10 horses per lodge, while the Blood and North Blackfoot averaged but 5 horses per lodge (Bradley, 1923, pp. 256, 288).

In 1856 Blackfoot Agent Hatch estimated that the Piegan and Blood owned at least 10 horses per lodge, but the North Blackfoot had fewer horses owing to frequent raids on their herds by Cree and Assiniboin (U. S. Comm. Ind. Affairs, 1856, p. 627). Four years later, Agent Vaughan made a more detailed estimate of Blackfoot horse ownership. The ratios in the last two columns of table 1 are compiled on the basis of Vaughan's figures in the first three columns (U. S. Comm. Ind. Affairs, 1860, p. 308).

TABLE 1.—*Agent Vaughan's estimate of Blackfoot horse ownership in 1860*

Tribe	Lodges	Total population	Horses	Horse-lodge ratio	Horse-person ratio
Piegan	460	3,700	3,980	8.6	1.1
Blood	150	1,200	1,200	8.0	1.0
North Blackfoot	300	2,400	2,400	8.0	1.0

The Annual Report of the United States Commissioner of Indian Affairs for 1874 (pp. 104, 126) estimated 5,450 Blackfoot in the United States, owning 6,000 horses. This is a ratio of 1.1 horses per person. Certainly these round-number estimates of both human and horse populations are not exact. Nevertheless, they are roughly indicative of Blackfoot wealth in horses at intervals during the last half century of buffalo days. Although made by different individuals they are quite consistent. These estimates suggest that prior to 1875, the Piegan averaged about 8 to 10 horses per lodge, or a fraction over one horse per person. Majority testimony indicates that the North Blackfoot and Blood owned fewer horses than the Piegan in proportion to population. My elderly informants were in general agreement in stating that in their youth the Piegan possessed more horses than either the North Blackfoot or Blood Indians.

After the buffalo were gone and the Blackfoot tribes settled down to a more sedentary life on reservations their horse numbers grew rapidly. In 1885 the Blackfoot in Montana, whose herds had been decreased by a serious epidemic, averaged but 0.55 horses per person. By 1895 the Piegan of Montana averaged 3.8 horses per person, and by the turn of the century the proportion grew to 10.5 (U. S. Comm. Ind. Affairs, 1885, pp. 388–389; 1895, pp. 568, 585; 1900, pp. 644, 663). This growth in horse population followed the discontinuance of inter-tribal horse raiding and reflected also the encouragement of horse breeding by the United States Government. It is obvious that no correct judgment of the relative wealth in horses of the Blackfoot during buffalo days can be inferred from their much larger herds of the early Reservation Period.

In recent years the number of Indian-owned horses on the Black-feet Reservation in Montana has decreased. The agricultural extension agent, in his report of May 31, 1942, estimated that Indian-owned horses on the reservation then numbered 3,934, of which nearly half (1,822) were not work horses but unbroken range animals. He considered the large number of unbroken horses an economic liability, stating: "Grass consumed by range horses on the Blackfeet Reservation should support approximately 6,000 more cattle or 24,000 more sheep than are now grazed. Very few horses have been sold from this jurisdiction during the past three years although some changes in ownership have taken place."

WEALTH IN HORSES OF OTHER PLAINS AND PLATEAU TRIBES

I have searched the literature for comparable estimates of the number of horses owned by other Plains and Plateau Indian tribes in buffalo days. These estimates are summarized in table 2.[4] In table 3 I have summarized the information on populations and horse numbers appearing in the annual report of the Commissioner of Indian Affairs for 1874, the first year for which adequate comparative figures are available. This was a full decade before the buffalo were exterminated from the Blackfoot Country and prior to the time the majority of other tribes listed had settled down to a sedentary, Reservation existence.

In spite of the fact that the estimates appearing in tables 2 and 3 are rough calculations made by many individuals under varied circumstances, they appear, on the whole, to present remarkably consistent figures within each tribal grouping. The listing of as many estimates as could be found for each group enables us to discount some erroneous ones.[5] Furthermore, the relative wealth in horses indicated in table 2, appears to be confirmed by the data in table 3 for nearly every tribe.

These data appear to justify the conclusion that in the last half-century of buffalo days those tribes richest in horses occupied geographically marginal areas. One group of wealthy tribes (the Kiowa, Comanche, Kiowa-Apache, and Osage) lived on the southern Plains, where winters were relatively mild, in close proximity to Mexican, Texan, and later American settlements from which they could replenish their horse stock through periodic raiding. The other group of relatively wealthy tribes (Cayuse, Walla Walla, Umatilla, Nez Percé, Yakima, Paloos, Flathead, Pend d'Oreille, Northern Shoshoni and some Ute) lived west of the Rockies where they were relatively immune from the horse raids of the Plains Indians and where winters were milder and forage more plentiful than on the northern Plains. Some of this last group were noted for their attention to and skill in breeding horses.

---

[4] Such statements as "have many horses" frequently occur in early accounts of some of the Plains Indians. However, I judge these statements are not sufficiently definite to be meaningful to this study.
[5] Obviously erroneous is Catlin's claim that the Cheyenne were "richest in horses of any tribe on the Continent," Maximilian's statement that the Blackfoot had more horses than Shoshoni, and the 1871 estimate of Osage horse wealth.

The only wealthy Upper Missouri tribe was the Crow, southern neighbors of the Blackfoot, who carried on extensive trade for horses with the wealthier Plateau tribes. On the other hand, the nomadic and horticultural tribes on or near the Missouri eastward of the Blackfoot were all relatively poor in horses. The nomadic Assiniboin and Cree were so poor they were compelled to make extensive use of dogs in transporting camp equipment. The horticultural Mandan, Hidatsa, and Arikara were noted horse traders, but apparently kept few of the horses that passed through their hands for their own use. The meager evidence on the Teton Dakota, Cheyenne, and Arapaho suggests that those tribes ranked with the Blackfoot as owners of horses. In terms of 19th century wealth in horses those tribes, as well as the Blackfoot, must be considered as middle-class people. They were less well provided with horses than the nomadic southern Plainsmen and the Plateau Indians, but they were better supplied than any of the horticultural tribes (except the Osage) and all of the tribes east and northeast of the Missouri River.[6]

The information in tables 2 and 3 shows no evidence of any tribe of the Plains or Plateau having passed from poverty to wealth in horses during 19th century buffalo days. Conversely no relatively wealthy tribe was reduced to poverty during that period. It is noteworthy that the earliest estimates for the wealthy tribes (even that of 1786 for the Comanche) portrays them as owners of many horses, while the poorer tribes remained so throughout the period covered by the estimates. The assembled data suggest the probability that many if not most tribes approached their maximum numbers of horses at a relatively early date, at least as early as 1825, and possibly, in some instances, before 1800. Throughout the remainder of buffalo days tribal horse-person ratios showed few marked changes. This suggests that the increase in the number of horses owned by tribal members as the results of breeding of their own herds, capture of enemy or wild horses, gift and barter, was offset and approximately balanced by the loss of horses through capture by enemy raiding parties, gift and barter, killing of horses as grave escorts on the death of important men, killings by animal predators, and death of horses from old age, sickness, battle wounds, hunting accidents, disease, and inability to survive severe winters. In the active and dangerous life of the Plains Indians horses were expendible assets.

---

[6] The testimony of my elderly Piegan and Blood informants, who had participated in horse-stealing raids in their youth, corroborated the data in the tables regarding the horse wealth of neighboring tribes, with one exception. They claimed the Flathead and Crow had more horses than the Piegan, the Piegan more horses than the Gros Ventres, Blood, or North Blackfoot, the Assiniboin fewer horses, and the Plains Cree still smaller numbers. Table 2 credits the Gros Ventres with a higher ranking than that given them by my informants.

TABLE 2.—*Comparative data on horse population of other Plains and Plateau tribes*

Tribe	Date	Lodges	Persons	Horses	Horse-lodge ratio	Horse-person ratio	Remarks	Reference
Apache	1871		378	1,250		3.3	Apache at Fort Sill	U. S. Comm. Ind. Affairs, 1871, pp. 612,633.
Arapaho	1804						". . . independently of their chargers have many horses not laden."	Tabeau, 1939, p. 98.
Arikara	1820						"Fewer horses than Kiowa and Comanche."	Fowler, 1898, p. 65.
	1855 and ante						". . . not well provided with horses."	Denig, 1950, p. 204.
	1871		1,650	350		.2	"Arikara on Fort Berthold Reservation"	U. S. Comm. Ind. Affairs, 1871, pp. 616,626.
Assiniboin	1754						". . . horses for packing only" (Eagle band of Assiniboin).	Hendry, 1907, p. 351.
	Ca. 1800						". . . always in want of horses."	Thompson, 1916, p. 265.
	1830						"Poorest of any tribe of region in horses."	Bradley, 1923, p. 288.
	1829–55				2		"Poorest of all Upper Missouri tribes in horses."	Denig, 1930, p. 601.
	1833						". . . in comparison with other nations . . . not many horses."	Maximilian, 1906, vol. 22, p. 391.
	1845						"Forest Assiniboin of Upper Bow River—'own few horses and perform all journeys on foot.'"	De Smet, 1905, vol. 2, p. 509.
	1852	150					"few horses fit to run buffaloes."	Kurz, 1937, p. 264.
	1860						"Assiniboin camp near Fort Union—'few horses,' depending almost entirely on dogs."	Boller, 1868, p. 39.
Cheyenne	1804						". . . independently of their chargers have many horses not laden."	Tabeau, 1939, p. 98.
	1832						". . . richest in horses of any tribe on the continent."	Catlin, 1841, vol. 2, p. 2.
	1846	18		Ca. 200	11.1		"Cheyenne camp visited near Fort Bent."	Garrard, 1927, pp. 52, 55.
	1864		500	600		1.2	"Horses taken after Sand Creek Massacre, Nov. 29. Arapaho also present."	U. S. Comm. Ind. Affairs, 1867, pp. 26–68.
	1868	51		700	13.7		"Horses taken from Black Kettle's camp after Battle of the Washita."	Nye, 1943, pp. 63–69.
Comanche	1774	80		1,000	12.5		"Horses taken from Comanche village defeated by Spanish."	Thomas, 1932, pp. 62–63.
	1786	30	Ca. 330	900	30	2.7	"Smallest of 8 Comanche rancherias visited by Ortiz."	Thomas, 1932, p. 323.
	1869		2,538	7,614		3.0	"Kwahari Comanche surrendered at Fort Sill, June 2."	U. S. Comm. Ind. Affairs, 1869, pp. 384, 470.
	1875		175	700		4.0	"Fewer horses than Assiniboin."	Nye, 1943, p. 235.
Cree (Plains)	Ante-1820						". . . only a few horses."	Harmon, 1903, p. 40.
	1833						". . . many" obliged to walk when moving camp."	Maximilian, 1906, vol. 23, p. 14.
	1880							Schultz, 1907, p. 385.

Tribe	Year	Tipis	Population	Horses	Per tipi	Per capita	Remarks	Authority
Coeur d'Alene	1853		60	200		3.3	". . . a hunting camp seen by Gov. Stevens.."	Stevens, 1860, p. 131.
Crow	1805	300+		2,000+	7		". . . everybody rides—men, women and children."	Larocque, 1910, pp. 22, 64.
	1820			10,000			". . . great many mules and horses"	Chardon, 1932, Appendix E.
	1830		4,500	9,000+	22.5	2.0	"Wealthiest northwestern Plains tribe."	Bradley, 1923, p. 288.
	1833						". . . said to possess more horses than any other tribe on the Missouri."	Maximilian, 1906, vol. 22, pp. 351–352; Hodge, pt. 1, p. 368.
Flathead	1853	400			20		". . . average of 20 to a lodge" (Agent Vaughan's estimate).	U. S. Comm. Ind. Affairs, 1853, p. 355.
	1805	33		500+	15		Camp visited by Lewis and Clark in Ross's hole, Sept.	Coues, 1893, vol. 2, p. 582.
	1830				50		Greater number of horses than any northwestern Plains tribe.	Bradley, 1923, p. 288.
	1832					1.2	(With Nez Percé and Pend d'Oreille) "possess more in proportion than any other mountain tribe within buffalo range."	Irving, 1861, p. 117.
Gros Ventres	1857		400	4,000		10.0	Agent Lansdale's estimate.	U. S. Comm. Ind. Affairs, 1857, p. 379.
	1829				5		". . . at this time few ponies."	Clark, 1885, p. 198.
	1830							Bradley, 1923, p. 288.
	1833				10		". . . formerly poor, but at present more ponies."	Maximilian, 1906, vol. 23, p. 76.
	1855		2,500	3,000		1.2	Gov. Stevens' estimate.	Stevens, 1860, p. 236.
	1856						Agent Hatch's estimate.	U. S. Comm. Ind. Affairs, 1856, p. 627.
Hidatsa	1860	265	2,100	2,320	8.7	1.1	Agent Vaughan's estimate.	U. S. Comm. Ind. Affairs, 1860, p. 308.
	1833		1,500	300—		.2	Horse population.	Maximilian, 1906, vol. 23 p. 370.
	1860	30 to 60	200		3.3 to 6.6		Human population. (Wolf Chief's estimate)	Catlin, 1841, vol. 1. p. 185; Wilson, 1924, p. 174.
	1871		600	500		.8	Fort Berthold Agency.	U. S. Comm. Ind. Affairs, 1871, pp. 612, 633.
Kansa	1871		627	250		.4	Kansas Agency.	Ibid, pp. 612, 633.
Kiowa	1869		1,500	6,000		4.0		Mishkin, 1940, p. 385.
	1871		1,776	5,000		2.8	Kiowa Agency.	U. S. Comm. Ind. Affairs, 1871, pp. 612, 633.
	1875		253	475		1.9	Kiowa party surrendered at Fort Sill, Feb. 26.	Nye, 1943, p. 231.
Kiowa-Apache	1820	32	Ca. 250	Over 500	15.6	2.0	Hunting band met by Long expedition in August.	James, 1823, vol. 2, p. 108.
Mandan	1797						"Even for sole purpose of hunting their horses too few."	Thompson, 1916, p. 230.
	1833	103	1,600	300+	2.9	.2	Horse and lodge numbers.	Maximilian, 1906, vol. 23, pp. 255, 275.
	1871		450				Human population.	Hodge, 1910, pt. 2, p. 798.
	1871			150		.3	Fort Berthold Agency.	U. S. Comm. Ind. Affairs, 1871, pp. 616, 635.
Navaho	1786	700	2,800 to 3,500	1,100+	1.6	.3 to .4	Don Joseph Antonio's estimate.	Thomas, 1932, p. 350.

TABLE 2.—Comparative data on horse population of other Plains and Plateau tribes—Continued

Tribe	Date	Lodges	Persons	Horses	Horse-lodge ratio	Horse-person ratio	Remarks	Reference
Nez Percé	1830				50		(With Flathead and Pend d'Oreille) "possess more in proportion than any other mountain tribes within buffalo range."	Bradley, 1923, p. 288.
	1832		50	250+		5.0		Irving, 1851, p. 117.
	1853		2,807	9,000		3.2	Hunting camp seen by Gov. Stevens	Stevens, 1860, p. 131.
	1871						Nez Percé Reservation	U. S. Comm. Ind. Affairs, 1871, pp. 617, 635.
Omaha	1819		984	650		0.7	"...affluent chiefs and warriors owners of many horses... greater part of young men and squaws necessarily pedestrian."	James, 1823, vol. 1, p. 205.
	1871	200		3,000	15		Omaha at Omaha Agency	U. S. Comm. Ind. Affairs, 1871, pp. 610, 623.
Osage	1840						Summer hunting camp; nonhorse owners left behind.	Tixier, 1940, p. 160.
	1850		4,561	10,000		2.2	Great and Little Osage	U. S. Comm. Ind. Affairs, 1850, pp. 35, 37.
	1871		3,375	1,200		0.4	At Neosha Agency	U. S. Comm. Ind. Affairs, 1871, pp. 612, 633.
Pawnee	1820			6,000 to 8,000		0.6 to 0.8	Horse population.	James, 1823, vol. I. p. 445.
	1820		10,000				Human population.	Morse, 1822, p. 445.
	1871		2,364	1,050		0.4	Pawnee at Northern Superintendency	U. S. Comm. Ind. Affairs, 1871, pp. 610, 632.
	?		300	150		0.5	Weltfish data on Skidi only	Mishkin, 1940, p. 14.
Northern Shoshoni	1805		400	700		1.8	Lemhi camp visited by Lewis and Clark shortly after great number Lemhi horses stolen by enemy.	Coues, 1893, vol. 1, pp. 553-558.
	1826		400	Ca. 800		2.0	Camp seen by Ogden on Snake River March 30.	Ogden, 1911, pp. 356-357.
	1827	300		3,000	10	2.0	Camp seen by Ogden near Day's River in November.	Ibid., pp. 365-366.
	1833		1,500				"Not as many horses as Blackfeet"	Maximilian, 1906, vol. 23, p. 295.
	1872-76		1,500	3,000		2.0	Wind River Shoshoni data summarized	Shimkin, 1947 a, p. 266.
Teton Dakota	1871		5,000	2,000		0.4	At Whetstone Agency (Oglalla and Upper Brule).	U. S. Comm. Ind. Affairs, 1871, pp. 617, 635.
	1871		1,527	1,500		1.0	At Upper Missouri Agency (Lower Brule).	Ibid., pp. 616, 635.
	1878		2,900	3,500		1.2	Canadian Government report on Sitting Bull's camp.	Denny, 1939, p. 120.
Umatilla, Walla Walla, and Cayuse	1871		850	10,000		11.8	On Umatilla Reservation.	U. S. Comm. Ind. Affairs, 1871, pp. 607, 630.
Upper Pend d'Oreille	1857		600	3,000		5.0	(Indian Agent's estimate)	U. S. Comm. Ind. Affairs, 1857, p. 379.

Ute (Yampa, and Uintah).	1871	635	1,370	2.2	At White River Agency	U. S. Comm. Ind. Affairs, 1871, pp. 618, 636.
Wichita	1871	1,216	840	0.7		Ibid., pp. 612, 633.
Yanktonai	1871	1,020	1,000	1.0	Lower Yanktonai of Upper Mo. Agency	Ibid., pp. 616, 635.
Yankton	1871	1,947	900	0.5	At Yankton Agency	Ibid., pp. 615, 635.
Southern Plains Indians[1]	1854	1,200 to 1,500	40,000 to 50,000	27+	(Estimates of old traders in the camp)	U. S. Comm. Ind. Affairs, 1854. pp. 95-96.

[1] This was a rendezvous on the Arkansas River including entire Kiowa and Kiowa Apache, the Prairie Comanche and some Texas Comanche, 1 Arapaho band, 2 Cheyenne bands, and some Osage Indians.

TABLE 3.—*Comparative data on tribal wealth in horses, 1874*

Tribe	Agency	Population	Horses	Horse-person ratio
Cayuse, Walla Walla, and Umatilla	Umatilla	682	8,000	11.7
Nez Percé	Nez Percé	2,807	12,000	4.3
Osage (Great and Little)	Osage	2,872	12,000	4.2
Yakima, Paloos, etc	Yakima	3,500	13,000	3.7
Wichita, Caddo, Waco, Tawaconi, Kichai, Penateka Comanche, and Pawnee.	Wichita	1,897	6,099	3.2
Kiowa, Comanche, Apache, and Delaware	Kiowa	4,975	14,090	2.8
Ute	Los Pinos	2,763	6,500	2.3
Crow	Crow	4,200	8,000	1.9
Ute	White River	1,000	1,500	1.5
Cheyenne, Arapaho, and Apache	Cheyenne and Arapaho.	4,024	5,475	1.4
Flathead, Pend d'Oreille, and Kutenai	Flathead	1,829	2,590	1.4
Wind River Shoshoni	Shoshone	1,800	2,500	1.4
Bannock and Shoshoni	Fort Lemhi	600	716	1.2
Colville, Okanagon, etc	Colville	3,120	3,900	1.2
Piegan, Blood, and Blackfoot	Blackfeet	5,450	6,000	1.1
Lower Yanktonai and Lower Brule	Upper Missouri	3,000	3,275	1.1
Ute	Uintah	575	600	1.0
Navaho	Navaho	11,068	10,000	.9
Oto and Missouri	Otoe	453	400	.9
Oglalla and Miniconjou Sioux, North Cheyenne, and North Arapaho.	Red Cloud	12,103	10,000	.8
Bannock and Shoshoni	Fort Hall	1,500	1,200	.8
Brule Sioux	Spotted Tail	7,000	5,000	.7
Yankton Sioux	Yankton	2,000	1,500	.7
Omaha	Omaha	951	700	.7
Iowa, Sac, and Fox	Great Nemaha	323	236	.7
Jicarilla, Apache, etc	Abiqui	1,750	1,200	.7
Two Kettle, Miniconjou, Sans Arc, and Blackfeet Sioux.	Cheyenne River	4,982	3,100	.6
Upper and Lower Yanktonai, Hunkpapa, and Blackfeet Sioux.	Grand River	6,440	3,000	.5
Kansa	Osage	523	280	.5
Moache and Jicarilla Apache	Cimarron	750	400	.5
Assiniboin, and Santee, Sisseton, Yanktonai, Hunkpapa, and Huncpatina Sioux.	Fort Peck	7,307	3,000	.4
Santee Sioux	Santee	791	300	.4
Assiniboin and Gros Ventres	Fort Belknap	3,700	1,100	.3
Pawnee	Pawnee	1,788	600	.3
Mescalero Apache	Mescalero Apache	1,800	500	.3
Sisseton, Wahpeton, and Upper Yanktonai Sioux	Devil's Lake	1,677	383	.2
Sisseton and Wahpeton Sioux	Sisseton	1,677	383	.2
Arikara, Hidatsa, and Mandan	Fort Berthold	2,015	200	.1

It required ingenuity and effort on the part of men of these tribes to replace frequent losses once herds had been acquired.

In a later section (pp. 138–139) I shall consider the minimum number of horses needed by the average family of a nomadic Plains Indian tribe in buffalo days. Let us consider here whether there might not have been a maximum number of horses a nomadic tribe could maintain. The highest average estimate given for any Plains Indian tribe in the tables reveals a ratio of 4 horses per person in the tribal population. It seems probable that this figure approached the upper limit of the proportion of horses to tribal members that could have been cared for adequately and protected from theft by enemy raiders under the conditions of frequent camp movement and intertribal warfare prevailing among these tribes in buffalo days.

HORSE WEALTH OF INDIVIDUAL BLACKFOOT INDIANS

In the three Blackfoot tribes horses were individually owned property. Although most of the great herds of unbroken horses and the specially trained war, hunting, and race horses were the property of men, women generally owned the animals they used for riding and transport duty. Women received gifts of horses, inherited them from relatives, or obtained them in barter. These horses belonged to them, and they were free to give them away, trade them, or loan them as they saw fit. Children also owned riding horses or colts which were not disposed of without their consent.

As early as 1809, a few individuals owned large herds of horses. Alexander Henry reported that "some of the Blackfeet own 40 or 50 horses. But the Piegans have by far the greatest numbers; I heard of one man who had 300" (Henry and Thompson, 1897, p. 526). However, Maximilian's reference (1833) to a chief who owned between 4,000 and 5,000 horses appears to have been exaggerated. (See Ewers, 1943.) Indian Agent Hatch told of the visit of a Blood chief, "Chief Bird," who owned 100 horses, to Fort Benton in the fall of 1856 (Hatch MS.). Bradley described the Blood head chief, "Seen From Afar," who died in 1870, aged about 60: "He was the greatest chief Major Culbertson ever saw amongst the Blackfeet—having 10 wives and 100 horses" (Bradley, 1900, p. 258). Culbertson's appraisal of this man may have been influenced by the fact that Seen From Afar (or Far Seeing) was his brother-in-law. Nevertheless, some of my Blood informants remembered this head chief of their tribe as the wealthiest Blood Indian of his period.

The trader Charles Larpenteur, wrote of the period 1860: "It is a fine sight to see one of those big men among the Blackfeet, who has two or three lodges, five or six wives, twenty or thirty children, and fifty to a hundred horses; for his trade amounts to upward of $2,000 a year" (Larpenteur, 1898, vol. 2, p. 401). Obviously that trader was describing an important headman or chief. Schultz (1907, p. 152) told of the Piegan in the late 1870's: "Horses were the tribal wealth, and one who owned a large herd of them held a position only to be compared to that of our multi-millionaires. There were individuals who owned from one hundred to three and four hundred."

My informants agreed that the wealthiest Blackfoot Indian in buffalo days was Many Horses (Heavy Shield, Middle Sitter), principal chief of the Piegan for a short time before his death in 1866. Although my eldest informants were mere children when Many Horses died, several of them were related to him, and all had heard of him through their parents and other older Indians. Their estimates of the number of his horses ranged from "about 500" to "less than 1,000." I believe the lower figure is the more accurate one. Three Calf claimed Many Horses tried to prevent other Indians from counting his horses. If he saw someone trying to count them he brought out his medicine bag filled with deer hoofs and rattled the hoofs, causing his horses to mill around so as to make further enumeration impossible. Yet Many Horses is credited with knowing every animal in his herd. He is said to have employed 10 or more boys to care for them. When camp was moved those of his horses that were not loaned to less fortunate individuals to transport their belongings were driven in three to five large herds.

Bull Shoe (Lone Man) was the wealthiest Piegan after the death of Many Horses. He may have owned nearly 500 horses in late buffalo days. Stingy, a blind Piegan, who died in 1918, aged about 78 years, then owned between 200 and 300 horses. Many-White-Horses (ca. 1834–1905) also owned more than 100 horses at that time. Informants claimed that a man who possessed 40 or 50 horses in buffalo days was considered wealthy by his fellow tribesmen.[7] It is probable that less than a score of Piegan were entitled to that distinction at any period during buffalo days.

Certainly less than 5 percent of Piegan men were wealthy in horses in buffalo days. Probably the proportion of rich men to the total adult male populations was smaller among the Blood and North Blackfoot. The majority of the Blackfoot had a difficult time meeting the needs of their nomadic existence with a limited number of horses. A fairly large proportion of Blackfoot families, possibly as many as 25 percent, owned less than a half dozen horses in buffalo days.[8]

The traditional belief that wealth should be reckoned in horses was difficult for these Indians to forget even after horses became so plentiful in the Northwest that they could be purchased for from $2 to $5 a head (Denny, 1939, pp. 259–260). Frank Sherburne recalled with amusement that some 50 years ago, Owl Child, a Piegan who owned about 500 head of fine cattle and a great many horses, liked to brag about the size of his horse herd. His cattle had many times the monetary value of his horses, but he never mentioned them in his boasting. During the period of my residence on the Blackfeet Reservation in Montana (1941–44) there were still several older fullbloods who owned sizable horse herds. Although most of these animals were unbroken and unused, their owners had no desire to sell them. Possession of horses made those Indians feel both wealthy and important.

---

[7] Piegan remembered as wealthy horse owners in buffalo days were Water-Bull-Mountain-Chief, Big Nose (also known as Three Suns, who died in 1896, a prominent chief), Crow Feathers, Big Plume (born ca. 1826), Wolf Calf (noted leader of the horse medicine cult, born before 1800), Wolf-Comes-Over-the-Hill, Many Strikes, Wolf Tail (born ca. 1853), Middle Calf, Owl Child (born ca. 1855), Horn, Tearing Lodge (born ca. 1834), and Curlew Woman (born ca. 1823). The last named was a woman.

[8] It is important to qualify these statements with the phrase "in buffalo days," because horses became much more plentiful among the Blackfoot tribes after they settled down on reservations following the extermination of the buffalo. Not only did Stingy, Bull Shoe, Many-White-Horses, Owl Child, and other former owners of many horses greatly increase the sizes of their herds, but a number of other Indians, who had previously owned smaller herds, became rich in horses. By 1900 there were several Piegan owners of 500 to 1,000 or more horses on the Montana Reservation.

HORSE WEALTH OF INDIVIDUALS IN OTHER TRIBES

Among other horse-using tribes of the Plains and Plateau, individual ownership of horses also seems to have been the rule. Definite statements to that effect have been made regarding the Crow (Denig, 1953, p. 34) and Omaha (Fletcher and La Flesche, 1911, p. 363). In table 4 I have summarized comparative data on individual horse ownership among other Plains and Plateau tribes gleaned from the literature. Except for Henry's claim that *many* Hidatsa owned 20 to 30 horses, the data in table 4 correlates closely with those in tables 2 and 3. In the poorer tribes individual wealth in horses was reckoned in terms of relatively few horses, while among the wealthy tribes some owners possessed horses in hundreds. Compared with the Teton Dakota, another middle-class tribe, the Blackfoot exhibited greater extremes in horse ownership.

These data show that unequal distribution of horses among tribal members was the rule in the Great Plains and Plateau in buffalo days. The conception of wealth in horses differed among the tribes. While a Plains Cree owner of five horses would have been considered wealthy by his fellow tribesmen, a Crow, Nez Percé, or Comanche owner of five times that number of animals would merit no such distinction among his people. Yet even the wealthy tribes, such as the Kiowa, had members who owned very few or no horses. There must have been a greater proportion of wealthy owners among the Plateau and southern Plains tribes than among the Blackfoot. On the other hand, there were Piegan individuals who possessed more horses than the entire Hidatsa or Mandan tribes.

TABLE 4.—*Data on individual horse ownership in other Plains and Plateau tribes*

Tribe	Date	Statement	References
Assiniboin	1851	In a large Assiniboin camp "at least one third of the men have no horses they can catch."	Denig, 1930, p. 456.
Cheyenne	1806	" . . . some families had twenty or thirty horses."	Henry *in* Henry and Thompson, 1897, vol. 1, p. 377.
Comanche	1819	" . . . industrious and enterprising individuals will sometimes own from one to three hundred head of horses and mules."	Burnet, 1851, p. 232.
	1852	Most successful Comanche horse thieves owned 50 to 200 horses.	Marcy, 1937, p. 158.
Plains Cree	1840–60	" . . . it was only an occasional Cree who had a horse."	Mandelbaum, 1940, p. 195.
	Ca. 1880	It was rare for a Cree to own more than a half dozen horses.	Schultz, 1907, p. 385.
	Ca. 1880	"Most of the Cree and Assiniboin who came to visit the Piegan ca. 1880 owned no horses."	Informant, Richard Sanderville (Piegan).
Crow	1805	"He is reckoned a poor man who has not 10 horses in the spring before the trade at the Missouri takes place and many have 30 or 40, everybody rides, men, women & children."	Larocque, 1910, p. 64.
	1856	"It is not uncommon for a single family to be the owners of an hundred animals. Most middle aged men have from thirty to sixty, and an individual is said to be poor when he does not possess at least twenty."	Denig, 1953, p. 25.

TABLE 4.—*Data on individual horse ownership in other Plains and Plateau tribes*—Continued

Tribe	Date	Statement	References
Flathead and Pend d'Oreille.	1832	Many warriors and hunters of those tribes who camped with Capt. Bonneville owned "30 to 40 horses each."	Irving, 1851, p. 117.
Hidatsa_____	1806	Many Hidatsa owned from 20 to 30 horses_____	Henry *in* Henry and Thompson, 1897, vol. 1, p. 353.
Kiowa_____	Prob. ca. 1870	A few rich Kiowa counted their horses in hundreds; well-to-do owners had 20 to 50 horses; many Kiowa had 6 to 10 horses; "not a few" owned no horses at all.	Mishkin, 1940, p. 19.
Mandan_____	1797	Big White Man, the chief with whom Thompson lodged, owned but 3 horses.	Thompson, 1916, p. 230.
	1833	Sih-Chida, son of a prominent chief, "did not even possess a horse," although some Mandan owned several horses at that time.	Maximilian, 1906, vol. 23, p. 272; vol. 24, p. 16.
Nez Percé_____	1840	Some Nez Percé "have as many as 500 or 600" horses.	De Smet, 1905, vol. 3, p. 991.
	1845	Some Nez Percé and Cayuse families possessed "1,500 horses."	Ibid., vol. 2, p. 480.
Omaha_____	1819	"Those affluent chiefs and warriors who are owners of many horses, are enabled to mount their families on horseback, but the greater portion of the young men and squaws are necessarily pedestrians."	James, 1823, vol. 1, p. 205.
Pawnee_____	1820	Some Grand Pawnee individuals possessed "20 to 60 horses." (Capt. Bell.)	Bell *in* Morse, 1822, p. 237.
	1836	The "poorest families had two or three horses, many braves and chiefs had eight to twelve, one chief had 30."	Murray, 1839, p. 353.
	?	About 5 men among Skidi owned 9 to 10 horses; a larger group 4 to 6; 1 to 2 fairly common; half the people no horses at all. (Weltfish data.)	Quoted in Mishkin, 1940, p. 14.
Teton Dakota_____	1803	Black Bull, principal Brule chief, lost all his herd when Ponca raiders stole 7 horses from him.	Tabeau, 1939, p. 110.
	1833	"Many possess from 30 to 40 horses and are then reckoned to be rich."	Maximilian, 1906, vol. 22, p. 327.
	Ca. 1875	Oglala—"In my youth any man who owned 30 horses was considered well-to-do."	Eagle Bird, informant.
	Ca. 1875	Oglala—"I can recall no member of my tribe who owned more than 100 horses in buffalo days."	Maggie-No-Fat, informant.
Yankton Dakota___	_____	Those who hung around the Agency "rarely possessed more than two horses." (Inference that other Yankton had larger herds.)	Maximilian, 1906, vol. 22, p. 306.

CARE OF HORSES

The horses owned by the Blackfoot Indians in buffalo days were of smaller size and different type from those commonly seen on the several Blackfoot Reservations today. If, as Vernon (1941, p. 512) avers, any horse under 14.2 hands high at the withers is a pony, Blackfoot horses were properly ponies. Today the Indian pony is nearing extinction along with the traits of culture typical of the Blackfoot in buffalo days.

THE INDIAN PONY

No scientific study of the Indian pony based upon observation of the living animal or of skeletal materials has been made by a competent zoologist. Angel Cabrera's chapter on the Indian pony in his work "Caballos de America" (1945), is based primarily on earlier observations of that animal by 19th century traders, travelers, and Army personnel stationed in the Indian Country. These are still our best sources of information on this subject. (See Clark, 1885, p. 396; Remington, 1889, pp. 339–340; Wyman, 1945, p. 287.)

The Indian pony was close to being a type. Anthony Hendry, first to describe the horses of the Indians of the northwestern Plains in 1754, called them "fine tractible animals, about 14 hands high; lively and clean made" (Hendry, 1907, p. 338). Mathew Cocking, 18 years later, termed them "lively and clean made, generally about 14 hands high and of different colors" (Cocking, 1908, p. 106). From descriptions of contemporary observers, corroborated by the testimony of elderly informants, we gain a composite picture of the type. The adult male Indian pony averaged a little under 14 hands in height, weighed about 700 pounds, possessed a large head in proportion to its body, good eyes, "neck and head joined like the two parts of a hammer," large, round barrel, relatively heavy shoulders and hips; small, fine, strong limbs and small feet. Indian ponies exhibited a wide range of solid and mixed colors. (See plate 6.)

Robert Denhardt (1947, pp. 20–22) has traced the ancestry of the Indian pony to Barb horses introduced into Spain in the invasion of the Moors from North Africa in the 8th century. In Spain these horses were crossed with native stock. The first horses brought to America were animals collected in the southern Spanish provinces of Cordoba and Andalusia which retained the primary characteristics of the Barb horse. Introduced into the New World by Columbus in

1493, and first carried to the mainland by Cortez's expedition to Mexico in 1519, they spread northward in succeeding centuries to furnish the basic stock of the herds of the Indians of the Southwest, the Great Plains, and the northwestern Plateau.

Capt. W. P. Clark, as a cavalry officer stationed at various posts on the western frontier, had an ample opportunity to observe Indian horses. He was of the opinion that through hard usage, close inbreeding, and change in climate the Indian pony had become somewhat reduced in size from that of its Barb ancestors of North Africa (Clark, 1885, p. 306).

The Indian pony was no beautiful animal, but it was a tough, sturdy, long-winded beast that possessed great powers of endurance. My older informants stressed these qualities of Blackfoot horses in buffalo days. They were sure those small horses were fleeter of foot than the large "white man's horses" entered in the races in Browning in recent years. Frank Sherburne's statement that the fastest horse he had owned was an Indian cayuse that had been successful in competition with larger horses on the local race tracks supports the Indian contention.

The horses of the Blackfoot were of the same type as those owned by other tribes of the Great Plains and the majority of the Plateau tribes. These horses were sometimes termed "cayuses" or "squaw horses" by white residents of the Indian Country. Colonel de Trobriand, in 1867, was impressed by the superiority of the Indian pony over the horses used by the United States Army on the Plains. "The Indian pony without stopping can cover a distance of from sixty to eighty miles between sunrise and sunset, while most of our horses are tired out at the end of thirty or forty miles." He found that "the movement of Indian horsemen is lighter, swifter and longer range than that of our cavalry, which means that they always get away from us" (De Trobriand, 1951, p. 64).

The Nez Percé Appaloosa, is a larger, heavier, characteristically spotted-rump animal (Denhardt, 1947, pp. 191–193). Elderly Blackfoot informants said their people obtained a very few Appaloosa horses before the end of the Nez Percé war of 1877.

FATE OF THE INDIAN PONY

After the Blackfoot settled on reservations, Indian Service authorities recognized that their small Indian ponies would be of limited use as farm animals. As early as 1884, the Blackfoot agent in Montana reported, "Strong teams should be provided to break up the ground, for the Indian ponies are unable to do it" (U. S. Comm. Ind. Affairs, 1884, p. 152). After the land cession of 1888, the Blackfoot of Montana requested the Government to use part of the money they were to receive for this land to purchase horses for Indian use. According to Short Face, "the Blackfoot delegation to Washington was asked whether they wished heavy draught horses, medium-sized horses, or light thoroughbreds. Running Crane, who replied for the Indians, said they wanted heavy horses. That is what they got." A few large mares and a number of stallions were distributed before 1890, primarily to Indian owners of sizable herds, to breed with their Indian ponies. In 1892 the agent reported issuance of 60 more high-bred stallions, stating, "The stallions with their native mares, will soon give them a good grade of horses, instead of the small ponies they have formerly raised" (ibid., 1892, p. 172). Many of the introduced horses were Morgans. There were some Percherons and other large, heavy breeds. As a result of interbreeding, the disposal of Indian ponies, and continued replacement by larger animals, the little Indian pony has now completely disappeared from the Blackfeet Reservation in Montana. It was the opinion of both Indian Service Agricultural Extension Agents and white stock raisers on the reservation with whom I discussed this problem in the early 1940's, that no Indian ponies remained on the reservation. Some older Indians were reluctant to acknowledge the fact.

A similar replacement of Indian ponies by heavier breeds took place on the Blackfoot Reserves in Alberta. The Klondike Gold Rush of 1896 offered those Indians a good opportunity to sell many of their small horses at from 10 to 20 dollars a head, and to replace them with larger animals (MacInnes, 1930, p. 172). Blood informants stated the Canadian Government also furnished larger stallions to breed with the Indian ponies. Within the present century the usual fate of the Indian pony on the Blood Reserve has been sale to canneries in the United States, there to be made into dog meat. Nevertheless as recently as 1947, a few Indian ponies were said to be living on the Blood Reserve.

Whether the Indian pony has survived on any of the reservations in the United States is doubtful. Enoch Smoky, a Kiowa, said there were none left among the Kiowa and their neighbors of southwestern Oklahoma.

MEANS OF IDENTIFICATION

About 1790, horses with Spanish brands were seen among the Indians of the northwestern Plains (Mackenzie, 1927, p. 78). In spite of their early familiarity with branded horses the northern Plains tribes did not adopt this method of identifying these animals. Wissler (1910, p. 97) wrote of the Blackfoot, "No system of branding was used, but each person knew the individualities of his horses so that he could recognize them." This was no mean accomplishment in a Sun Dance encampment around which thousands of horses grazed. Yet informants said quarrels between owners due to inability to distinguish their respective horses were very rare.

The Blackfoot knew their horses by color, conformation, physical and action peculiarities. The wealthy Many Horses was said to have known every animal in his herd so well that he could describe a missing animal in detail to the young man he sent to search for it. Stingy, the wealthy blind man, was credited with the ability to identify many of his horses by the sound of their hoofbeats, and to know all of them by feel. Brings-Down-the-Sun, chief of the North Piegan, claimed his father could tell a horse's age by its whinny (McClintock, 1910, p. 422). These feats of recognition were exceptional. However, as a people who spent their lives in the company of horses, the Blackfoot were keenly aware of the individual peculiarities of these valuable possessions.

Owners of large herds named only those animals that were broken and in daily use in addition to a few good mares and stallions in their range herds maintained for breeding purposes. The name of each animal usually was selected to describe the horse's appearance, more rarely its peculiarities of action. As several informants recalled, "we named them by the looks of them."

Color names were most common. Common color names for horses recalled by the old people were:

White	Black	Buckskin	Sorrel
Gray	Black Pinto	Bay	Red Pinto
Mouse-colored	Blue	Dark Bay	Brown
Iron gray	Blue Roan	Roan	

Some Indians named their dun horses "Dusty." One old lady called her dark, reddish-brown horse "Burnt Bay." Localized color markings also suggested such names as "Bald Face," "Black Legs" and "Two-White-Legs." Peculiarities of size and shape gave rise to "No Mane," "Big Pinto," "Little-Gray-Horse," "Crow Foot," "Flop Ears," and "Split Ears." Other factors less commonly suggested names, such as "Gray-Horse-Crazy," "Sits Down," and "Orphan." It is not difficult to see that by employing a combination of descriptive terms, as was actually done (for example, "Black-Bald-Face" and "Bay-With-Star-on-Forehead"), it was possible to coin a great variety of names for horses. Men who owned race horses commonly called them either "Racer" or "Gambler."

When many Piegan were employed on the Blackfeet Reservation irrigation project in the early years of this century, they began to give their horses "white man names." Today the old color names are rarely heard on the Montana reservation. Even older fullbloods, who speak little English, apply English names to their horses. However, Percy Creighton said that on the Blood Reserve the old, picturesque, color names were still in vogue (1947), except for horses purchased from Whites that had been previously named.[9]

DAILY CARE OF HORSES

Among the Blackfoot daily care of family horse herds was generally entrusted to boys 8 to 12 or more years of age, except during the most inclement winter months when men of the household assumed responsibility for the task. If there were several boys in a family the father usually delegated care of the horses to the most dependable and ambitious lad. Sometimes a younger brother cared for the horses of a young married man. Otherwise the latter looked after his own horses. Owners of large herds, or owners of small herds who were sonless, commonly adopted orphan boys to care for their horses. If a young, single man went on a raiding party to steal horses from the enemy, he chose a poor but reliable and ambitious boy to look after his horses while he was away from camp, rewarding the lad with a colt for his labors. If the young warrior had elderly parents who could not obtain food for themselves, he selected a youth in his late teens to care for his horses, rustle food for his parents in the hunt, and keep them well supplied with firewood. Some poor boys got their starts as horse owners through this service.

Duties of the young herder required that he be up before daybreak each morning to go after the horses where they had been pastured the previous night and drive them to a nearby lake or stream for water. Then he drove them to good pasturage near camp and returned to his lodge for breakfast. The owner generally returned to the herd with him after the morning meal, selected the horse or horses he wished to use during the day, perhaps petted his horses a while, and gave instructions to the boy regarding pasturage for the day. At noon the lad drove the horses to water again. Toward evening he watered the horses a third time and drove them to their night pasturage, where

---

[9] The published lists of names for horses employed by the Flathead (Turney-High, 1937, p. 110); Kutenai (Turney-High, 1941, p. 71); Cree (Mandelbaum, 1940, p. 197), and Hidatsa (Wilson, 1924, pp. 194–195) show a similar preference for color names among those tribes. Eagle Bird, Oglala, and Smoky, Kiowa, told me those tribes generally named horses after their appearances. Denhart (1947, p. 232) has pointed out that it was a favorite Spanish custom to name a horse according to the impression received on first seeing the animal. Whether the Plains Indian system of descriptive horse naming was adopted from the Spanish cannot be determied from the facts available. Certainly the coincidence is most intriguing.

No Plains Indian tribe is known to have practiced branding in buffalo days. The chronicler of the Long expedition noted that the Pawnee (met in 1819) had no method of affixing distinctive marks to their horses. The many branded horses seen among the Pawnee were either stolen or traded from the Spanish (James, 1823, vol. 1, p. 439).

he hobbled the lead mare to prevent the herd's straying. When camp was not on the move the Blackfoot generally watered their horses thrice daily.[10]

At night the herd might be pastured in a coulee or valley at some distance from camp, where the animals would be concealed from possible enemy raiders. Normally, and unless clear signs of enemy raiders in the vicinity had been discovered, there was no night herding. After the boy guided his herd to night pasture he returned to camp. If it was thought an enemy party might be near, the horses were not driven to pasture until after dark. Wise herders watched their herds closely that night. Families that neglected this precaution, after they had been forewarned, sometimes awoke the next morning to find their horses gone, while those of the cautious owners remained. (A more detailed account of measures for the defense of horses appears on pp. 207–210.)

It was not the responsibility of the band or village chief to supervise daily care of the horses of his people. He selected a camp site affording good pasturage nearby, but each family looked after its own herd. During the daytime the horses of different owners frequently were pastured close together, but at night, in order to prevent the enemy from running off all the loose horses of the village, the individual herds were scattered widely.[11]

HOBBLING

When a Blackfoot herd was driven to a sheltered place at night hobbles were attached to the forelegs of the lead mare to prevent the herd from wandering to high ground where they might be seen easily by prowling enemies. When moving camp in small groups, or when a few hunters spent the night away from camp on a winter buffalo hunt, horses were night hobbled. There was no winter hobbling by the hind legs, which was a Cree practice (Mandelbaum, 1940, p. 196). The lead mare was generally an older animal of gentle disposition, and was hobbled with feet wide apart allowing freedom of movement in walk-

---

[10] Teton Dakota (Dorsey, 1891, p. 335) and Kiowa (informants) herders generally watered their horses three times each day. This was also Hidatsa practice throughout most of the year. In winter they watered their horses only twice, about noon and at sundown (Wilson, 1924, p. 178). Kroeber (1902–7, p. 148) noted that the Gros Ventres band called "Those-who-water-their-horses-once-a-day" are said to have followed this practice so that their horses would gain flesh more quickly."

[11] Most other Plains tribes also entrusted the daily care of horses to boys. This was true of the Mandan and Hidatsa, relatively poor in horses. (Maximilian, 1906, vol. 24, p. 24; Wilson, 1924, pp. 155–172.) It was also true of the horticultural Osage (Tixier, 1940, p. 160), as well as the nomadic Cheyenne (Grinnell, 1923, vol. 1, pp. 64 ff., 117), Kiowa (informants' testimony), and Teton Dakota (Dorsey, 1891, p. 335); and the northwestern marginal Wind River Shoshoni (Shimkin, 1947 b, p. 294), and Flathead (Turney-High, 1937, p. 109). However, Jenness (1938, p. 28) wrote of "young warriors" caring for Sarsi horses, and Mandelbaum (1940, p. 196) reported the care of Plains Cree horses was entirely the work of men.

ing. A more lively animal was close-hobbled so that it had to jump to move around. The hobble generally was simply constructed of a length of soft-tanned buffalo skin or rawhide. Weasel Tail demonstrated a clever hobble that would neither tighten nor slip (fig. 2). As

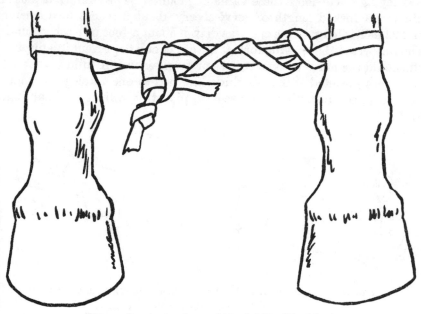

FIGURE 2.—A simple rawhide hobble, Blackfoot.

a rule hobbles were fastened loose enough to prevent chafing of the horse's legs but tight enough to prevent their slipping over the feet. In lieu of a second hobble, hunting parties sometimes tied a second horse to the leg of a hobbled animal.[12]

PICKETING

Wissler (1910, p. 97) wrote of the Blackfoot, "At night the best horses were brought into camp and picketed near the tipis of their owners." This was a precautionary measure to prevent the theft

---

[12] In 1754, Hendry (1907, p. 338) noted that the horses of the "Archithinue" of the Saskatchewan Plains were "turned out to grass, their legs being fettered." The Osage, on their summer hunt in 1840, unloaded their horses each night and set them free "after their forelegs had been fastened with enferges or horse locks" (Tixier, 1940, p. 159). Flathead (Turney-High, 1937, p. 109) and Plains Cree (Mandelbaum, 1940, p. 196) use of hide hobbles have been reported. Wilson (1924, pp. 155, 189–190) gives a detailed description and illustration of Hidatsa rawhide hobbles. W. B. Parker (1856, p. 125) noted that the Delaware Indian guides and interpreters, attached to Capt. Marcy's expedition to western Texas in 1854, hobbled their horses at night "by fastening a short loop of rawhide around both forelegs, below the knees, so that the horse could only move by a succession of jumps." He also stated that some years earlier the Army tried the experiment of "hobbling dragoon horses—when on the Plains—with iron hobbles, but had to abandon it, as the Indians invariably killed the horse when they could not get him off."

of the owners' best buffalo and war horses, and race horses (if they owned any). Women aided the men in picketing the horses. Men expected their wives to keep alert during the night for the slightest sound that might indicate a clever enemy had slipped into camp and was trying to cut loose these valuable mounts. The preferred picket pin was a forked length of serviceberry about 2 inches in diameter and 22 inches long. One end was driven about a foot into the ground. The line was tied below the fork at the upper end to prevent its slipping off should the horse become restive or frightened. A mild-mannered horse was picketed with a rawhide line tied to one foreleg. A short line with neck fastening was used for picketing a lively animal (fig. 3).[13]

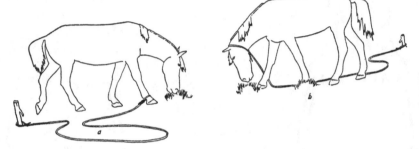

FIGURE 3.—Methods of picketing: *a*, Picketing a gentle horse; *b*, picketing a lively horse.

PASTURAGE

Before the introduction of horses the two most important requisites for campsites were adequate supplies of firewood and drinking water. The Blackfoot had knowledge of the locations of all running streams, clear lakes, and springs in and near their hunting grounds that afforded clean drinking water for themselves and their dogs. After the acquisition of horses another factor became a prime consideration in selection of campsites—adequate grass for horse feed. This did not mean thick grass. The Blackfoot were aware that horses preferred to graze

[13] In his description of the "Archithinue" camp in 1754, Hendry (1907, p. 338) wrote, "their horses . . . when wanted are fastened to a line of Buffalo skin that stretches along & is fastened to stakes in the ground." Lewis and Clark noted that each Lemhi Shoshoni warrior "has one or two (horses) tied to a stake near his hut both night and day, so as to be always prepared for action" (Coues, 1893, vol. 2, p. 558). Picketing of their best horses near their lodges at night has also been reported for the Crow (Denig, 1930, p. 547), Flathead, Pend d'Orielle, and Nez Percé (Irving, 1851, p. 119; Turney-High, 1937, pp. 108–109), Plains Cree (Mandelbaum, 1940, p. 196), Arapaho (Linderman, 1930, p. 127), and Osage (Tixier, 1940, p. 162). Arapaho, Cree, and Flathead owners sometimes took the extra precaution of sleeping with the tether of their favorite horses tied to one of their wrists. Both Blackfoot and Kutenai denied that practice. The Mandan and Hidatsa kept their best horses inside their earth lodges at night to protect them from theft by enemy raiders (Wilson, 1924, pp. 159–161).

on thinly covered side hills rather than on the luxuriant stands of the valleys. They were concerned, however, that there be sufficient grass in the neighborhood of campsites to support their herds. They also recognized that horses preferred some grasses to others.

Present-day agricultural extension agents regard the Blackfoot Reservation in Montana as one of the finest livestock ranges in the United States. However, the old-time Blackfoot preferred the area eastward of the present reservation for fall and winter pasturage. The vicinity of the Sweetgrass Hills, described by Stanley (1855, p. 447) as the favorite fall pasturage for buffalo a century ago, was a section in which the grass remained green until late fall and in which clear lakes were plentiful. In the late decades of buffalo days a favorite wintering locality of the Piegan was the valley of the Marias River from the present Shelby–Great Falls Railway crossing eastward.

Elderly informants named several range plants common along the Marias which their people regarded as excellent fall and winter forage of horses. These are: "jointed water grass" (*Equisetum arvense*), the common horsetail; "weasel grass" (*Artemisia cana*), the silver sagebrush; "blue stick grass" (probably *Chrysothannus nauseosus*), the rabbit brush; "real grass" (buffalograss, *Buchloe dactyloides*); and "jingle grass" (unidentified).[14]

On the Marias River also was found a white clay streaked with yellow that "tasted like nuts." Horses were fond of it. Some people ate it also. In fall and winter the earth around alkali sinks was peeled off, broken up, and fed to animals. Indians believed it had the same beneficial effect as salt on livestock.

Throughout the greater part of the year Blackfoot horses kept in condition on no other feed than the wild range grasses. Captain Marcy (1859, pp. 111–112) observed that "for prairie service, horses which have been raised exclusively upon grass, and never have been fed on grain, or 'range horses,' as they are called in the West, are decidedly the best, and will perform more hard labor than those that have been stabled and groomed." The Blackfoot, in buffalo days, made no efforts to put up wild hay for winter feed. Their efforts to provide grass for their horses were limited largely to the expedient of selecting camping places where the best grasses could be found.

When the grass in the vicinity of a winter camp was consumed, it was necessary to move camp. Only the severest weather conditions which made the movements of horses impossible would prevent this change of location. Some bands, whose members owned large horse

---

[14] I am indebted to Claude Schaeffer, curator, Museum of the Plains Indian, for the collection of specimens of some of these plants, and to Ellsworth P. Killip, formerly of the Department of Botany, U. S. National Museum, for the identification of these specimens.

herds, had to move camp several times in the course of each winter for no other reason than to secure adequate pasturage. This did not necessarily entail movement of any great distance. A few miles, a short day's journey, might bring them to good pasturage.[15]

WINTER CARE

The Blackfoot regarded certain actions of wild birds and animals as winter signs. If owls screamed at night, if geese flew high, if crows shifted their wings sideways in flight, or if the pelage of otter, mink, and beaver appeared heavier than usual, they knew a hard winter was approaching, and were careful to establish winter camps in the vicinity of extensive growths of cottonwood to gain protection from the cold and high winds and supplemental food for their horses.

In winter cautious owners no longer delegated care of their horses to adolescent boys. They cared for the animals themselves. In the coldest weather men donned buffalohide caps with ear flaps, buffalo robes or Hudson's Bay blanket coats, hair-lined mittens, and moccasins when leaving their lodges to tend the horses. Although they did not watch their horses all day in winter, owners watered the animals thrice daily as they did in summer. A winter camp near a spring that did not freeze was a choice location. If a spring was not handy, men chopped waterholes in the river ice near their lodges. Each man who used the waterhole broke open any new-formed ice so the hole would not freeze solid.[16]

RUSTLING

When there was snow on the ground the Blackfoot did not hobble their horses. Their front feet were left free to paw away the snow to the dry grass below. At this practice, commonly known as "rustling," Indian ponies were remarkably adept. Unless the snow was too deep to prevent them from raising their legs (i. e. over ca. 2 feet) they generally could rustle enough food in this way to gain a meager subsistence. Denny (1939, p. 53), recalled that the Canadian Northwest Mounted Police, during their first winter in Alberta, employed Indian ponies which "were hardy, serviceable animals, and would find their own food under the snow by pawing in the coldest weather." Later experience of that efficient force proved to them that eastern,

---

[15] My Kiowa informants also recalled that their winter camps had to be moved when the neighboring grass supply became inadequate for their horses. Dunbar (1880, p. 332) reported Pawnee winter camp movements due to exhaustion of grass for horses. Undoubtedly, this factor conditioned winter movements of all the nomadic Plains Indians and those horticultural tribes who spent the winter season on prolonged hunting excursions away from their more permanent villages.

[16] The Cree practice of placing alkali earth around waterholes to keep horses from straying was not mentioned by Blackfoot informants (Mandelbaum, 1940, p. 196).

stable-bred, grain-fed horses could not endure the rigors of Alberta winters as well as could western-bred, range horses (ibid., pp. 132–133).[17]

SUPPLEMENTAL WINTER HORSE FOOD

Blackfoot belief that "a horse will starve to death if it doesn't get food for four days" sharpened their watch over their horses in periods of intense cold and heavy snows. If the snow was too deep to permit rustling, the people tried to clear away an area from which they could collect grass for the horses. However, the most common supplemental feed was the inner bark of the round-leafed cottonwood. This tree was common in the valley of the Marias as well as in other river valleys in the Blackfoot Country at some distance east of the Rockies. Some owners made a practice of feeding this bark to their best mounts (buffalo runners and race horses) in winter. Others employed cottonwood bark as an emergency ration to be relied on only when grass was insufficient or unobtainable by rustling horses. Some horses "chewed like beavers" on cottonwood branches without waiting for their owners to cut them. Generally women cut cottonwood trees and limbs into sections 2 or 3 feet long, or peeled off irregular strips of the bark and gave them to the horses. For use as horse feed quantities of this bark were carried by pack horses accompanying small winter hunting parties. Older informants spoke of cottonwood bark as "better than oats." Children, too, liked to chew the bark for its sweet taste. Logs of cottonwood, from which the bark had been stripped during the winter, made a soft, easily chopped firewood for camp use the following fall.

Short Face claimed the Piegan discovered the value of cottonwood bark as winter horse feed by accident. He cited a tradition to the effect that "one winter a bridled horse was lost. Its owner, believing it had found nothing to eat, feared the horse was dead. He found it several days later with its reins caught around the trunk of a cottonwood. The horse had thrived by eating the bark of that tree. After the owner observed this he decided to feed cottonwood bark to all his horses. Soon all the Piegan who owned horses began to cut cottonwood and offer the bark to their horses." We know, however, that the practice of feeding this bark to horses in winter was both old and widespread among the Plains Indians.[18]

---

[17] The earliest reference to Plains Indian horses rustling for their winter food by pawing away the snow occurs in Henry's observations among the Assiniboin in February, 1776 (Henry, 1809, p. 289).

[18] Hendry (1907, p. 345) noted that the horses of his Cree and Assiniboin companions were "feeding on willow tops" in the winter of 1755. Lewis and Clark observed that the Mandan fed cottonwood bark to their horses in the winter of 1804–5 (Coues, 1893, vol. 1, pp. 232–233). This practice was common among the Arikara (Bradbury, 1817, p. 165) and Pawnee (Dunbar, 1880, p. 332). Capt. W. P. Clark wrote of the winter feeding of cottonwood bark to horses as a common practice among the tribes of the northern Plains (Clark, 1885, p. 307). In 1852, Capt. Marcy observed that the old winter camp sites of the Kiowa and Comanche on the Red River and its tributaries were thickly strewn with cottonwoods the bark of which had been fed to their horses (Marcy, 1937, pp. 60–61, 141–142, 168).

The St. Louis trader, William H. Ashley, in 1826, praised cotton-wood bark as a winter horse feed. "When the round leaf or sweet bark cottonwood can be had abundantly, horses may be wintered with but little inconvenience. They are fond of this bark, and, judging by the effect produced from feeding it to my horses last winter, I suppose it almost, if not quite as nutritious as timothy hay (Dale, 1918, pp. 138–139).

The practice of the horticultural tribes of feeding maize to their horses, first observed among the Mandan by David Thompson (1916, p. 230) in the winter of 1797–98, was unknown to the nomadic Blackfoot who had no access to maize.

NIGHT CARE

The Blackfoot were aware that the horticultural tribes farther down the Missouri provided stables for their horses on cold nights by taking them into compartments inside their earth-lodge dwellings.[19] Nevertheless, the Blackfoot made no effort to build covered structures to house their horses in cold weather. On very cold nights, however, Blackfoot owners drove their horses in among the trees and thickets of the river bottoms to take advantage of these natural growths as protection from wind and cold. The same precaution was taken when blizzards swept down on the camps in daytime. Often, however, the lead mare of a herd led the other animals to shelter in the timber without assistance from the owner. If the weather remained very cold, owners kept their horses in sheltered river bottoms day and night.

More as a protection against enemy raiders than against the elements the Blackfoot built night corrals within the wooded areas of the valley floor. A man who owned a large herd constructed his own corral. Owners of few horses worked together to build a corral for their animals. These generally were jerry-built, temporary fences of horizontal poles lashed with rawhide ropes to standing trees and up-ended horse travois.

WINTER LOSSES OF HORSES

Under date of February 16, 1773, while on the Saskatchewan Plains, Mathew Cocking (1908, p. 114) wrote of the death of several horses "which they say is the case at this time of the year." In February, 1832, John Work noted the death from cold of several horses belonging to his hunting party in the Blackfoot Country of present Montana (Work, 1923, pp. 131–132). These early references illustrate the ever-

---

[19] David Thompson (1916, p. 230) observed this custom among the Mandan in winter of 1797–98. It was also a practice of the Hidatsa and Arikara.

present threat of disaster to horse herds in the area of severe winters inhabited by the Blackfoot. Informants stated, however, that horse losses in most winters were light. It was only in occasional years that deep snows combined with low (20° to 40° below zero) temperatures to kill off large numbers of horses. In those years horses starved and froze to death in spite of all their owners could do for them. Present-day stockmen of the Blackfeet Reservation claim severe livestock losses may be expected, even under modern conditions, at least once a decade. There is no reason to believe winter losses were less severe or less frequent in buffalo days.

We have no complete record of winters in which large numbers of Blackfoot horses perished. McClintock (1910, p. 444; Ewers, 1943, p. 605) was told that the year 1842 brought a "hard winter when snows lay so deep that many of our horses perished." Informants remembered the winter of 1875–76, as one during which the Blood tribe and the Grease Melters Band of Piegan suffered heavy losses in horses (Ewers, 1943, pp. 605–606). The winter of 1886–87, known to the Indians as "many cattle died winter," killed so many Piegan horses that many families were forced to use dogs to travel to Old Agency for rations. More recently, severe winters were recorded in 1906–7, 1919–20, and 1949–50. In the winter of 1919–20 no less than 600 horses were lost on the Blood Reserve (Wilson, 1921, pp. 16, 18). Losses generally were heaviest in the months of January and February and in May storms.[20]

MAY STORMS

A weather peculiarity of the Blackfoot Country is the annual "May storm," usually a single storm, striking suddenly after a prolonged period of balmy spring weather, bringing a rapid and severe drop in temperature and usually heavy snow. Usually this late spring storm occurs in May. However, one year during my residence in Browning this storm arrived on June 2, bringing over a foot of snow overnight, which melted and disappeared in 2 or 3 days. These May storms struck after horses had shed their heavy, winter hair and were poorly protected from cold. The storms sometimes were fatal to

---

[20] Teton Dakota winter counts have listed a number of years during the 19th century in which many horses perished (Ewers, 1943, p. 606). Although we have no record of losses by the Assiniboin and Plains Cree, living in the notorious Red River Valley storm belt, their winter losses must have been heavy, and must have played a role of importance in keeping those tribes poor in horses. Undoubtedly milder winters favored the acquisition and maintenance of large herds by the southern Plains tribes. As early as 1820, the Long expedition noted the influence of the weather on relative tribal wealth in horses. The Kiowa and Arapaho were then trading horses to the Cheyenne. The former were able to "rear (horses), with much less difficulty than the Shiennes, whose country is cold and barren" (James, 1823, vol. 1, p. 502).

horses, especially to newborn colts. Careful owners covered their best mounts with buffalo robes or blankets made from the tops of old, skin lodge covers, when May storms struck. Tops of old lodge covers also were stretched over poles to protect mares which gave birth to colts during these storms.[21]

SPRING CONDITION

Even though few horses were lost in the average winter, that season was an ordeal for the best of them. They grew thin and weak on the food they could rustle. By spring they were a cadaverous lot. Yet most of them fattened within a month on the rich, green, spring grasses. The horses of the rich man recovered rapidly. He could afford to alternate his mounts and pack animals so as to give all of them sufficient rest to enable them to regain weight and strength. But the few horses of the poor man could not be pampered. He had to use them regularly. Consequently their chances of recovery were poor. Many of them remained thin and weak through most of the year.

In the Blackfoot Country the domesticated horse reached the northern limit of its distribution on the Plains east of the Rockies prior to white contact. The problem of maintaining horses through the winters in this region of high altitude, strong winds, heavy snows, and rapid, treacherous changes in temperature taxed Indian ingenuity. As has been shown, Indian solutions of this problem were little more than simple expedients and could not prevent heavy losses in the most severe winters. It is more of a tribute to the hardiness of the Indian pony than to the forethought of its Indian owner that this animal was able to become acclimated to the northern country in the early years of its northward migration from the more temperate climate of the Spanish settlements of the Southwest.

COMMON HORSE REMEDIES

Although there was a Blackfoot cult of specialists in the treatment of sick and injured horses, most owners were able to treat the more common horse ailments themselves, using a variety of vegetable and animal medicines.

---

[21] Maximilian, in 1833, noted a phenomenon similar to the May storm, occurring somewhat earlier in spring, in the country of the Mandan. "March and April are called by the Indians the Horse's winter, because, when the weather is warm, the horses are often driven to pasture, and then violent storms of snow sometimes occur suddenly, and destroy many of the animals" (Maximilian, 1906, vol. 23, p. 238). Lowie (1922 a, p. 435) reported the Crow practice of blanketing newborn colts in a spring storm.

TREATMENT OF SADDLE SORES

Saddle sores were a seasonal problem to the wealthy horse owner. In the spring of the year his saddle and pack horses, that had been rested during the winter months, sometimes got saddle sores from ill-fitting, improperly padded saddles used on them. Rich men could rest their afflicted mounts until they recovered. Poor men could not spare their riding horses and of necessity overloaded their pack animals. Consequently they were plagued with sore-backed horses the year round. If a wealthy man saw a likely looking but sore-backed horse belonging to a poor fellow, he might trade one of his sound horses for it.

The Blackfoot had several common remedies for saddle sores. "Snake weed" (*Yucca* sp.), if available, was boiled and applied to the sore with grass or a rag. "Dry root" (*Heuchera* sp., alumroot) mixed with buffalo fat and boiled in water, also was applied. Another remedy made use of a mixture of boiled tobacco, a bitter grass, animal fat, and commercial salt, which was rubbed on the sore and "in a month's time the sore would be healed and hair standing on it." A Blood informant said his family preferred to prick the swelling with a new arrowhead until the blood ran, then apply herb medicine.[22]

TREATMENT OF SORE FEET

To repair a worn foot that caused a horse to limp with pain, the Blackfoot owner made a rawhide protective shoe from a piece of thick hide from a freshly killed buffalo bull. He broke up horse manure and placed it in the shoe before he slipped it over the horse's foot. The shoe extended to the pastern and was held in place by a rawhide drawstring around the top. Periodically the shoe was re-

---

[22] Several observers testified to the commonness of saddle sores among Indian-owned horses of the Plains in the first decade of the 19th century. All of them attributed this to the poorly fitting saddles used by the Indians. Henry (Henry and Thompson, 1897, vol. 1, p. 47) commented upon this situation among the Cree; Tabeau (1939, pp. 88–90) among the Arikara, some of whom "more through interest than pity, cover the sores with a piece of leather or with a buffalo paunch sprinkled with ashes" to prevent magpies from picking at the raw flesh; and Lewis and Clark regarding the Lemhi Shoshoni and Walla Walla horses their expedition obtained from the Indians (Coues, 1893, vol. 2, pp. 574–575; vol. 3, p. 979). The chronicler of the Long expedition wrote of the Omaha (1819), "the backs of their horses are very often sore and ulcerated from the friction of the rude saddle . . . resting on rude saddle cloths without padding" (James, 1823, vol. 1, p. 292). Larocque (1910, p. 64) observed the care Crow owners gave their horses, stating "as soon as a horse has a sore back he is not used until he is healed." Such treatment, of course, was possible only among a people who were relatively rich in horses. Undoubtedly the great majority of Plains Indians owned too few horses to afford to rest their sore-backed animals for extended periods.

Gilmore (1919, p. 133) described Pawnee use of plant medicines in treating saddle sores. The Thompson Indians of British Columbia first washed the sore with human urine, then applied plant medicines (Teit, 1930, pp. 513–514).

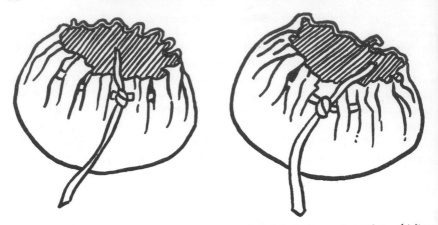

FIGURE 4.—Rawhide horseshoes similar to Blackfoot type, Arapaho. (After No. 58036, Chicago Museum of Natural History.)

moved, the hoof examined, and fresh manure inserted. When the hoof grew out, the shoe was discarded.[23]

TREATMENT OF COLIC AND DISTEMPER

The Blackfoot treated colic and distemper by the same means, i. e. by pouring plant medicine down the mouth or nose of the ailing horse. If the horse was a lively one it was held down and the medicine administered forcibly; if it was a mild-mannered animal its head

---

[23] Use of rawhide shoes to protect the feet of horses was widespread among horse-using tribes. In the middle of the 18th century Pfefferkorn (1949, p. 147) noted of the Apache in Sonora, "For want of horseshoes, they cover their horse's hoofs with thick horse or oxhide to protect them." In the summer of 1832, Captain Bonneville observed that members of a Crow war party had covered the hoofs of their horses "with shoes of buffalo hide" to protect them from the "sharp and jagged rocks among which they had to pass" (Irving, 1851, p. 53). The Plains Cree used a manure-lined shoe like that employed by the Blackfoot to cure sore-footed horses. A pair of Arapaho rawhide horseshoes, catalog No. 58,036, Chicago Museum of Natural History, collected by George Dorsey in 1905 from the Wind River Reservation, is reproduced as figure 4. This specimen is identical with descriptions of Blackfoot horseshoes. An elderly Kiowa told me his people formerly used rawhide shoes in the treatment of sore-footed horses. Chiracahua Apache employed rawhide "horse moccasins" for the same purpose (Opler, 1941, p. 396). Kutenai are said to have laughed at Flathead for making little boots to protect their dog's feet. However, the reference (Turney-High, 1941, p. 70) does not mention Flathead employment of "boots" for horses.

White traders and explorers in the northern Plains on some occasions adopted the Indian's practice of providing rawhide shoes to protect their horses' feet. Larocque used them on his journey from the Crow encampment on the Yellowstone River back to the Hidatsa villages in the fall of 1805 (Larocque, 1910, p. 49). Capt. Wm. Clark's party, eastbound down the Yellowstone Valley in July 1806, made "a sort of moccasin of green buffalo skin" to relieve their horses' worn feet (Coues, 1893, vol. 3, p. 1137). Captain Bonneville, in the fall of 1832, made buffalohide shoes for his foot-worn horses while traveling through rocky country near the Wind River Mountains (Irving, 1851, p. 234).

In the summer of 1854, Parker (1856, p. 203) saw the wife of a Southern Comanche chief "leading a horse and mule slowly backwards and forwards through a slow fire" which was "the process of hardening the hoofs by exposing them to the smoke and vapour of the wild rosemary-artemisia." I have found no other reference to this practice among Plains Indians.

was raised and the medicine poured into its mouth. A great many concoctions were tried by different individuals in this treatment. Boiled "snake weed" (*Yucca* sp.), "big turnip" (*Leptotaenia multifida*, carrotleaf), "smell foot" (*Valeriana* sp.), and bitterroot (*Lewisia rediviva*) were employed separately or in combination with still other boiled plant medicines to treat these disorders. There appears to have been much experimentation by horse owners in the concoction of foul-smelling liquids. Lazy Boy claimed none of the old-time remedies was as effective as the coal oil the Piegan used to treat colic after they settled down on the reservation.[24]

PRECAUTIONS AGAINST CHILLS

A sweaty horse that had been hard-ridden in winter was lead around for a time, then covered with a blanket made from an old lodge cover; or it was permitted to roll in snow to dry the perspiration quickly. A good horse that had been ridden hard in warmer weather was led to a lake or stream and water splashed over it. It was then allowed to run and roll in the grass.[25]

A GENERAL TONIC

Short Face said that a root having a strong odor that grows near the mountains, called "strong root" by the Indians (possibly baneberry), was smashed and fed to horses at any time of year to keep them healthy.

TREATMENT OF BROKEN BONES

A good horse with a broken leg was not shot. If the horse had been a buffalo runner, it would be no longer useful for that purpose, but it could serve as a pack animal. A wealthy owner of a prized buffalo runner which suffered a broken leg, might keep that horse as a pet. If a mare broke a leg it was kept for breeding purposes. Some owners tried to treat broken legs themselves. The leg was lanced so that the blood would flow. A splint was made of rawhide-wrapped sticks. After a long time the bones healed. But there would always be a lump where the break occurred, and the horse would always limp.

Other owners called in a horse medicine man or a specialist in the treatment of broken bones. Bear-Goes-East, a Piegan of the Blood band, was remembered as a well-known specialist. He was credited with the power to heal broken bones of animals or humans, by rubbing them with mud. The horse owner paid him well, sometimes another

---

[24] The Dakota, Omaha, Ponca, and Pawnee used the narrow-leaved comb flower (*Echinacea angustifolia*) in their treatment of distemper (Gilmore, 1919, p. 131).

[25] The Plains Cree employed these same methods for cooling off overheated horses (Mandelbaum, 1940, p. 196). Information from other tribes is lacking.

horse, for his services. Bear-Goes-East was considered a powerful doctor, but not a horse medicine man. Lazy Boy recalled that once, while on a war party, Bear-Goes-East's partner fell over a cliff and broke his leg. The Crow Indians were chasing them. Bear-Goes-East collected some mud from a nearby lake, applied it to his partner's leg, and "healed it right there." [26]

TREATMENT OF UNKNOWN ILLNESSES

In buffalo days if a horse suffered from an illness the owner was unable to diagnose, he might load a musket with powder only and fire it at the side of the horse. The horse might get well.[27] If the owner was wealthy or the horse was a valuable buffalo runner or racer the Blackfoot owner generally preferred to take no chances. He called upon one of the powerful horse medicine men to treat his mount. The horse medicine man was paid well for his services. (See pp. 270–271.)

LOSSES OF HORSES

LOSSES FROM DISEASE

Although we have no complete record of the incidence of disease among the horses of the Blackfoot in 19th century buffalo days, there are references to two epidemics during that period that caused serious losses.

On April 15, 1857, Father Adrian Hoecken wrote to Father De Smet from the Pend d'Oreille Mission:

I am distressed at learning that an epidemic is making terrible ravages among the Blackfeet. According to the last news, about 150 Indians have perished in one camp alone, near Fort Benton. When the malady had ceased scourging men it fell upon the horses. Many are dead already and many dying. We have lost five. Our hunters are forced to go to the chase on foot; for according to their account all the horses are sick. If the Nez Percés lose their horses in the war with the Government, horses will be very dear here." [De Smet, 1905, vol. 4, p. 1248.]

Well remembered by elderly informants was the epidemic of 1881–82, identified by some as mange. Their horse medicine men were powerless to cure the afflicted animals. John Young, Indian Agent for the Blackfoot stated in his Annual Report of August 11, 1882:

The wealth of these Indians lies in their ponies. During the winter they suffered serious loss. A cutaneous disease appeared among the horses for which

---

[26] A Kiowa informant stated that his people used to treat horses with broken legs by applying a rawhide-wrapped splint to the member. Crow Indians are said to have used a mud treatment for horses bitten by rattlesnakes. They bound "mud on the wound, and when the poultice dries, fresh ones are applied until all the swelling recedes" (Phinney, n. d., p. 81).

[27] This treatment was also employed by the Kutenai (Turney-High, 1941, p. 72).

no remedy could be procured, and because of it about half of the horses these Indians owned died. One chief lost sixty out of a band of eighty. The disease is again making its appearance, and by next spring most of the few horses left will probably succumb to it. [U. S. Comm. Ind. Affairs, 1882, p. 100.]

Informants' testimony indicates that Agent Young may have over-stated the case. Nevertheless, losses were severe. It came at a time when the Blackfoot had not recovered their losses of the hard winter of the mid-70's, and at a time when buffalo were becoming very scarce. It worked a great hardship on the Indians, who needed good horses as never before to locate and kill buffalo for their subsistence. Many owners, set afoot by the epidemic, redoubled their efforts to secure badly needed mounts through raiding forays on enemy tribes. At a time when horse raiding should have been an anachronism in the organized Territory of Montana, there was a resurgence of raiding activity, motivated by need rather than greed.

LOSSES FROM ANIMAL PREDATORS

Animal predators killed colts and occasionally some adult horses owned by the Blackfoot in buffalo days. Wolves were the most common colt killers. Bears and mountain lions destroyed both colts and adult animals. These losses were most common when Indian camps were pitched near the mountains. Blackfoot raiding parties returning across the Rockies with horses stolen from the Flathead or neighboring tribes also lost horses from night attacks by mountain lions.

Dogs also killed colts on those rare occasions when meat was scarce in camp, and dogs were forced to rustle for their food. Some owners protected their colts by tying dried hoofs around their necks. The rattling hoofs frightened the dogs and kept them at a distance. In normal times dogs were well fed and did not bother colts.

LOSSES FROM STOCK-POISONING PLANTS

Although my informants made no mention of horse losses from eating poisonous plants, it is probable that some horses died from this cause in buffalo days, as they have in more recent times. Stock-poisoning plants most destructive to horses on Montana ranges in 1900 were lupine and loco weed. However, the number of deaths was very small in proportion to the number of horses poisoned (Chesnut and Wilcox, 1901, p. 34).

CARE OF OLD HORSES

An old horse that had given faithful service in war, buffalo hunting, or racing was not destroyed by its grateful owner. It was cared for after its useful days were over, until it fell behind when camp moved or dropped dead in camp. A horse that died in camp was dragged away by two horses, one pulling a line tied around the dead animal's neck, the other a line attached to its tail. If the camp was a temporary one the dead horse was dragged only a short distance from the lodges. If the camp was to remain in one place for a number of weeks the dead horse was dragged a half mile or farther from the lodges and left on the prairie. Dead horses were not buried. The village chief gave the order for the removal of the dead animal and determined how far it should be dragged.

HORSE BREEDING

IMPORTANT ROLE OF HORSE BREEDING

So much emphasis has been given in the literature to the more exciting topic of horse raiding as a source of Plains Indian wealth in horses that the subject of breeding horses has been neglected. In reality animals bred from their own herds comprised a goodly proportion of the horses owned by the Blackfoot in 19th-century buffalo days. If the increase of the Indians' herds through breeding was not as great as that achieved by modern stockmen, we must remember that their herds were periodically reduced by destructive winter storms, diseases, animal predators, and other causes, as well as by theft on the part of enemy raiders. Had it not been for the breeding of their own herds, Blackfoot horse population surely would have shown a steady decrease during 19th-century buffalo days.

Blackfoot men differed markedly in the attention they gave to horse breeding and in the success they achieved in building up their herds thereby. It is noteworthy that those Piegan who were named by my informants as owners of the largest herds were also remembered as men who were especially successful in breeding horses. Stingy, the blind man, could not participate in horse raids, but he became one of the wealthiest Piegan horse owners through his skill in raising horses. Many Horses and Many-White-Horses were mentioned frequently in informants' discussions of breeding practices. The Blackfoot believed that those men who were very successful in raising horses possessed a secret power that insured their success in that enterprise.

Blackfoot efforts in breeding generally were directed toward producing one or more of three qualities in colts. These were (1) a certain color, (2) large size, and (3) swiftness of foot. Although many of their methods hardly can be considered scientific, they bear evidence of Blackfoot concern with problems of horse breeding.

SELECTION OF STUDS

There was little or no effort to mate certain stallions with selected mares. The studs were permitted to mate with any mare in a man's herd. However, the most successful breeders were careful in the choice of their stallions. A man who desired to raise colts of a certain color chose a stallion of that color for a stud. If he wished large colts he selected a stallion of greater than average size. If he wanted fast animals above all else, he employed a stallion of demonstrated swiftness. Generally men with small herds possessed a single stallion. Owners of large herds kept four or more stallions. Usually all other males were castrated. The Blackfoot recognized that some stallions were poor breeders. If, after a period of trial, a stallion failed to produce colts in the number or quality desired, a man who could afford to do so replaced that stud with another one.

Three Calf, whose father owned a fine herd of 40 pinto horses, said his father had but one stallion, a large, black pinto, bred from his own herd. Many Horses owned a number of stallions, pintos of several varieties, which he used for no other purpose than breeding and on which he lavished great care. His stallions were never broken to the saddle. Stingy, who bred for size, used a large horse for a stud. He rode it, and kept it picketed at night in the spring breeding season to prevent other Indians from making use of it. When colts dropped, he herded them with the mares and colts. The Piegan sometimes called Stingy, "White Man," because he raised such large horses. Other breeders selected their stallions for swiftness regardless of their size or coloring. All careful breeders took pains to obtain the best horses they could get of the type they most desired for studs. However, most men were too poor or too careless to devote much thought to stallion selection. They were happy just to possess a stallion. "That is why there were so many scrub, no good horses around."

If a man owned one or more mares but no stallion he might go to his neighbor's herd at night and "borrow" his stud to mate with his own mare, without the knowledge of the stallion's owner. This is said to have been a rather common practice.

Careful breeders also took pains to prevent old, broken-down stallions of their neighbors from mingling with their mares. Where so many horse herds were pastured in the neighborhood of a camp this was a difficult task. However, boys caring for the herds of cautious owners were instructed to keep their herds separate in breeding season and to drive away undesirable stallions that came near them. If a poor old stallion was found bothering their mares, the boys caught him, threw him down, and tied a large buffalo rib or hip bone to his forelock. The frightened animal left on the run. If a stray stallion persisted in bothering a man's herd, the herd owner told the stallion's owner to take better care of his horses thereafter.

MAINTENANCE OF COLOR LINES

Some men tried to build up herds of a single color. Three Calf said that after his father possessed 40 pintos he made no attempt to add to his herd except by breeding. He gave away any horses given him, and disposed of any colts bred to his herd that were not pintos. Many-

White-Horses, so named because all the horses in his herd were whites or grays, traded any dark-colored horses he obtained for white ones. Nevertheless, his horses were said to have been of rather poor quality. They were small, tender-hoofed animals. When the Government furnished large stallions to Piegan owners, Many-White-Horses refused to accept them. He feared the stallions would injure his small mares. So he continued to raise large numbers of little horses. They had more prestige than practical value.

Joseph Sherburne recalled that when he traveled the Blackfeet Reservation (in the first decade of the 20th century) making collections for his father's store, some Indian owners of large herds still specialized in horses of a particular color or conformation. He learned to recognize the peculiarities of the horses of different owners so that he could tell from a distance the ownership of many range horses by their appearance. There were 10 or 12 owners on the Blackfeet Reservation in Montana at that time whose horses were readily distinguishable by their physical appearance. Mr. Sherburne said the uniformity of these herds was maintained both by selection of studs and by swapping of horses which failed to exhibit the desired characteristics.

MAGICAL BREEDING FORMULAS

Some Blackfoot horsemen placed faith in magical formulas for insuring the birth of colts exhibiting desired qualities. If a man wanted a pinto colt he killed a magpie and tied its black and white feathered body around the neck of his mare with a buckskin string in the fall of the year, saying, "Now, I want you to have a pinto colt next spring." The magpie was worn on the mare's neck until it fell off. One informant said, "When spring came that mare would surely have a pinto colt, and thereafter all her colts would be pintos."

No other color of horse was as popular with the old-time Blackfoot as was that of the pinto. Many men were proud to be seen riding a two-colored horse.[28]

In order to get "a big colt," the Piegan Stingy is said to have made a practice of roasting a "big turnip" (*Leptotaenia multifida*, carrotleaf), slicing it with a knife, punching holes through the slices, stringing them on a buckskin cord, and tying the cord around a mare's neck. The odor of the big turnip kept the mare in fine condition all winter. In spring she would bear a "big colt." Stingy is said to have employed

---

[28] This is in contrast to the Kiowa tendency to consider pintos "women's horses" (communication from Alice Marriott). The Nez Percé (Ross, 1855, vol. 1, p. 307) preferred white and speckled (Appaloosa) horses, which they valued at two or three times the worth of other horses. Kroeber (1907, p. 424) reported Arapaho use of colored bean medicines to cause mares to produce colts of desired colors. Spotted beans produced pintos, red beans roans or bays, and white beans white or buckskin colts. My Kiowa informants had no knowledge of the use of magical breeding formulas by members of their tribe.

this formula in producing Flop Ears, considered the fastest Piegan-owned race horse of its time.

To insure the birth of a fast colt a man killed a jackrabbit, cut off its front feet and strung them with sliced "big turnip" on a buckskin cord, which he tied around his mare's neck. "That mare would have a fast colt" (color and size undetermined).

CARE OF GRAVID MARES AND COLTS

Although more colts were born in spring than in any other time of year, there were "a lot of fall colts" and some early ones. The Indians thought that it would make mares good breeders if they were used for riding or transport duty until their udders began to swell about a week before foaling. No assistance was given a mare in labor unless the weather was stormy. Then it was given the protection of an old lodge cover, if the owner possessed one.

A smart horseman paid close attention to the colt after birth. He rubbed and straightened the colt's legs and shaped its ears with his hands. If the colt appeared to him to show possibilities of becoming a valuable horse, he continued to work its legs with his hands to be sure the bones would be straight and well formed.

Most mares were put to work a few days after the birth of their colts. Poor people, who owned few horses, had no choice in the matter. Wealthier owners, however, could rest their mares for months after foaling. They might not work a mare that had foaled in spring until the following fall. Many mares owned by wealthy owners were kept solely for breeding purposes. They were neither broken to the saddle nor used as pack animals.[29]

GELDING

Although the Blackfoot practice of gelding most male horses inevitably influenced breeding by reducing the male breeding stock, "keeping them from bothering mares" was only one of three major reasons for castrating. The Blackfoot also considered gelding made their horses more tractable and fleeter of foot. In theory all males not reserved for stud purposes were castrated at between 1 and 3 years of age. Actually there were many exceptions. Some owners were negligent about having their horses gelded, which helped to account for

---

[29] The 18th-century literature on other Plains Indian tribes contains two references that suggest the Plains Indians may have been slow to learn the importance of the care of gravid mares, and that neglect of such care resulted in heavy losses of colts and limited increases in their herds through breeding. Bourgmont (in Margry, 1886, vol. 6, p. 445) observed that the Paduca (Apache), in 1724, were unable to raise colts because their mares miscarried while chasing buffalo. The increase of the herds of the little Osage was said (in 1785) to have been "entirely prevented because they load the mares too heavily and make them run too much" (Miro, 1946, p. 164). It is possible that white men, who noted these conditions, may have been influential in helping the Indians to correct them.

the number of poor quality stallions around the camps. However, Buffalo Back Fat, head chief of the Blood tribe, a keen student of horses, is known to have advised members of his family, "Don't cut your stallion too young. Wait until he is four years old. Let him have a chance to chase mares. He will be a good runner, a good feeder, and an easily managed, fancy horse."

Usually a number of horses were castrated the same day. The operation was performed by specialists. Piegan informants mentioned the names of a half dozen men of their tribe who were expert gelders. Among them were the wealthy horse owners, Stingy, Many-White-Horses, and Bull Shoe. The specialists were paid for their services. If a man had several horses castrated, he might give the surgeon a horse. If he had one or two horses gelded he made payment in less valuable articles, such as robes, blankets, saddle blankets, plain skin or cloth shirts, or arrows.

A corral was not deemed necessary for castrating. The operation was performed in the open near the lodges of the camp. The horse to be gelded was thrown down. One hind leg was drawn between the two front ones and the three legs tied securely with a rawhide rope. The other hind leg was trussed up and held by a second rope. Details of one common method of trussing are shown in figure 5. Without

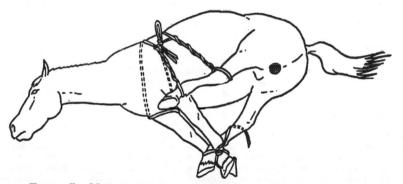

FIGURE 5.—Method of tying a stallion for castrating, Blackfoot.

prayer or ceremony of any kind the surgeon set to work. With a sharp butcher knife he cut a hole in the scrotum, squeezed out the testicles, wrapped and tied the cords by which they were suspended, then severed the testicles and threw them away. It was customary for the surgeon to ask the horse owner what material he wished used for tying, before the operation was begun. Some men insisted on the use of deer or antelope sinew, which they thought would make their horses fleet. After the operation some men picked up a testicle and tried to roll it along the horse's back, saying, "This will surely be a fast buffalo horse." This was the closest approach to ritual connected with the operation.

When the horse was untied, and rose to its feet, the castrater told the owner to whip him and make him run. The horse was watched closely for several days. If a large number of horses were gelded in the course of a few days, the band planned to remain in one place until the castrated animals were completely healed.

Gelding failures were uncommon. Short Face recalled that some men once complained that their horses swelled after Stingy had gelded them. After hearing their complaints, Stingy replied, "I shall castrate three horses. Two of them will not swell. Those horses will be no good. One horse will swell. It will be a very fast animal." It happened as he predicted, and his demonstration silenced his detractors.

Lazy Boy claimed that Black-Comes-Over-the-Hill was the most prominent and proficient castrater in late buffalo days. None of the horses he castrated died as a result of the operation. The animals he gelded never swelled. He always tied with antelope sinew. The horses he gelded were always fast horses. People said that Black-Comes Over-the-Hill possessed secret power which made him uniformly successful in his specialty. Lazy Boy could recall no other castrater among the Piegan of whom this was believed.

Informants differed in their opinions regarding the origin of the practice of gelding among the Blackfoot. Some believed that Indians, even Blackfoot Indians, originated it. Others were sure that it was learned from white men. I am inclined to agree with Wissler and Haines that the practice of gelding horses by the Plains and Plateau tribes probably was learned directly or indirectly from the Whites.[30]

---

[30] M'Gillivray (1929, p. 29) writing of the Indians in the vicinity of Fort George on the North Saskatchewan in 1794, stated, "The operation of gelding is seldom performed by the Indians as it generally diminishes the strength and vigour of the Horse, he is therefore full of fire and can with ease outrun most of the large animals on which they depend for subsistence." Possibly he was referring to the Cree Indians, who, my informants claimed, castrated their horses less commonly than did the Blackfoot. Lazy Boy cited cases of Cree stallions captured by the Piegan whose testicles had been whipped or burned but not removed. He said the Piegan gelded some of these animals successfully. However, Mandelbaum (1940, p. 196) described Plains Cree gelding practice in terms indicating that their technique was similar to that of the Blackfoot, but that "some colts died as a result of the operation," suggesting that they were not skilled surgeons. An excellent account of Hidatsa gelding practice appears in Wilson (1924, pp. 146–149, and fig. 2). That tribe gelded horses for the same reasons as did the Blackfoot. The choice of animal sinew used in tying was determined by the type of speed the owner wished for his horse. Details of trussing the animal and of the surgical operation varied from the Blackfoot procedures remembered by my informants. Usually the Hidatsa operated on 2-year-old stallions and without religious ritual. Opler (1941, pp. 259, 299) did not describe the Chiracahua Apache operation, but implied that they regarded it as a ceremony, whereas in the Northern Plains it seems to have been a secular act.

Lewis and Clark's brief account of the gelding of some of their horses by Nez Percé and by Whites stressed the fact that the animals gelded by the Nez Percé recovered quicker and suffered less than those castrated by members of their party (Coues, 1893, vol. 3, p. 1012). Haines has conjectured that the Nez Percé may have obtained a few gelded animals from the Spanish at an early date, which stimulated their curiosity, or that an Indian, who had served on one of the Spanish ranches in New Mexico, and had drifted northward as a captive or fugitive, taught the Nez Percé how to castrate (Haines, 1939, p. 23). Wissler (1910, p. 91) doubted that the practice of castrating dogs by the Blackfoot was an aboriginal custom. On the other hand Dobie (1941, p. 4) has maintained that it was Spanish custom in the Colonial Period to leave most of their male horses and cattle uncastrated. Therefore, if the Indians learned the operation from the Spanish, the former must have proceeded to make more common use of it than did the latter.

TRAINING OF HORSES AND RIDERS

CAPTURE OF WILD HORSES

The earliest reference to wild horses in or near the Blackfoot Country is an entry in Anthony Hendry's Journal for September 22, 1754, "Saw several Wild Horses" (Hendry, 1907, p. 335). At that time he was near the present Alberta-Saskatchewan border. At the beginning of the 19th century, David Thompson noted the existence of several wild herds near the Rockies, especially on the west side, and told of their horses being caught by Kutenai Indians. He also reported the escape of one of his own pack animals, which was found among a herd of wild horses. "This dull Horse took to himself all the gestures of the wild Horses, his Nostrils distended, mane erect, and tail straight; we dashed into the herd and flogged him out" (Thompson, 1916, pp. 377–378, 401).

Reconnoitering parties of the Pacific Railway Survey in 1853, saw wild horses near Milk River (Stevens, 1860, p. 91). Denny wrote of bands of wild horses ranging near the foothills toward Belly and Bow Rivers in Alberta in the eighties, which were materially augmented by strays from the ranches. He lost nearly a hundred head of his own horses to the wild herds. The best horsemen were unable to rope the wild ones. They were finally shot as nuisances (Denny, 1939, pp. 258–259).

My informants recalled that there were herds of wild horses in the Blackfoot Country in their youth. Lazy Boy attributed their origin to strays from Indian camps, domesticated horses that ran off and became wild after large numbers of Indians died in the early smallpox epidemics. In the light of the data in the preceding paragraph, this explanation appears reasonable.

Informants said that very few wild horses were caught by the Blackfoot. Most captured adults died after they reached camp. Weasel-Head claimed they could not endure the smoke from lodge fires. Some colts and yearlings were captured and raised successfully. However the taking of wild horses was confined largely to horse medicine men who had the power to attract those animals with the secret medicines

59

rubbed on their ropes. (A description of their methods appears on p. 274.) [31]

BREAKING HORSES FOR RIDING

The great majority of horses owned by the Blackfoot were put to use as riding or transport animals. Most families owned too few horses to permit the reservation of more than one stallion and young, unbroken colts as nonworking range stock. Wealthy men could afford to keep numbers of animals solely for breeding and future trading purposes. However, even those owners possessed many more well trained animals than were needed to provide an adequate supply of riding and transport horses for their immediate families, for it was common practice for rich men to loan trained horses to the less fortunate for the latter's use in hunting and moving camp. Unbroken broncos sometimes were given as presents. However, if the recipient was a poor person, a child, or an older man or woman the gift horses generally were trained ones.

Light boys in their teens broke yearling colts for their own use. Most horses broken for riding purposes were trained during their second or third year.[32] Mares as well as male horses were broken for riding. In fact some mares were used as buffalo runners and race horses.

Although it was customary for a young single or married man to break his own horses, teen-aged boys broke those belonging to the older members of their families. Boys with plenty of nerve began breaking horses at 12 or 13 years of age. Others did not try it until they

---

[31] The Plains Cree also had little success in capturing wild horses, or in keeping them alive once caught (Mandelbaum, 1940, p. 196). The apparent ineptness of the Cree and Blackfoot in this undertaking is in striking contrast to the skill of some central and southern Plains tribes. Descriptions of their well-organized horse-capturing expeditions are numerous in the literature. Two methods seem to have been much used: (1) lassoing with a running loop and (2) approaching the wild horse with the open lasso loop fixed to a long, forked stick, and dropping the noose over the running animal's head and neck. The Long expedition found that the Kaskaia (Kiowa Apache) were expert in "throwing the rope" in taking wild horses in 1820 (James, 1823, vol. 2, p. 114). Catlin fully described and pictured Comanche use of the lasso for this purpose in 1834 (Catlin, 1841, vol. 2, p. 58). Smith met members of a Cheyenne party who had successfully lassoed 200 wild horses, in 1840 (Smith, 1913, p. 273). Denig described Brule Dakota lassoing of wild horses on organized expeditions in the second quarter of the 19th century (Denig, 1951, p. 198). However, Barrett's data from Rosebud Reservation in the 1940's, indicated that the Brule employed the forked-stick method, and Grinnell (1923, vol. 1, pp. 291–295) also attributed use of that method to the Cheyenne. Perhaps some tribes employed both techniques. Dorsey (1896, p. 281) wrote of the forked-stick method in use among the Omaha.

[32] Limited comparative data suggest that it was usual Plains Indian practice to break horses for riding at an early age. The Hidatsa broke them at 1 to 2 years old (Wilson, 1924, p. 150). The Oglala, according to Eagle Bird, broke them before they were 3 years old. Enoch Smoky said the Kiowa broke their horses in their first to third years. In contrast, the Spanish-Mexicans in California in the middle 19th century allowed their horses to run wild until they were 4 or 5 years old before breaking them to the saddle. They seldom broke mares, and considered it a disgrace for a man to ride one (Denhardt, 1937, p. 13).

were in their middle or late teens. A few fellows were afraid to break horses, and never did.[33] The Blackfoot-owned horses usually were halter or hackamore broken before they were broken to ride.

Four methods of horse breaking were employed by the Blackfoot tribes. Each method was described by four or more informants.

FIGURE 6.—Breaking a bronco by riding it in a pond or stream, Blackfoot.

POND OR STREAM BREAKING

(FIG. 6)

Sometimes a group of boys went to an owner of a large herd and asked him if they could break some of his colts in the water of a nearby pond, lake, or stream. If the owner consented, he pointed out the animals they might break and warned them he would not be responsible if any of the boys were hurt. Sometimes boys took colts from a man's herd without his permission and broke them in the water. When the owner learned what they had done he gave them a good tongue lashing.

Weasel Tail described this method:

I have broken horses in a stream. It was an easy way to break them. Two boys rode double on a trained horse, leading the bronc by a rope or halter into

[33] Among the Hidatsa "colts were broken by boys fourteen to seventeen years of age" (Wilson, 1924, p. 151). Tixier, in 1840, reported that the Comanche compelled their male prisoners to train those horses that were reputed untamable (Tixier, 1940, p. 270). Of course, many Comanche prisoners were Mexicans, who were expert horsemen.

the stream. The fellow who was to ride the bronc rode behind the other one. When the bronc was in the water up to his shoulders, the front rider took hold of the lead rope near the bronc's chin, while the other boy quickly jumped on the bronc's back. As soon as the rider was seated the boy on the trained horse let go of the rope. The bronc tried to jump and buck, but as soon as his head became wet he quieted down. He tired quickly. Then the rider rode him out of the water.

At other times the technique of riding double into the water was not employed. A single boy, riding a trained horse, led the bronco. When the water came up to the top of the bronco's legs or higher he rode alongside and changed mounts, allowing the trained animal to shift for himself. Many horses were played out by the time they reached shore and could be ridden on land without fear of bucking. When a group of boys took part in breaking a high spirited horse in the water some of them roped the bronco before it reached shore and held it so that it could not get to land before it was completely tired. Horses that showed a lot of spirit after one water treatment were taken back into the pond or stream for another session. Usually one trip into the water was sufficient. After the horse came out of the water its rider rode it bareback on land for several days before it was considered ready for the saddle.

BOGGY GROUND BREAKING

This method was a variant of the pond and stream method. It could be employed when no pond, lake, or suitable stream was in the neighborhood of camp. Informants said it was less commonly used than the first method, although five of them either had employed this method themselves or had seen it used.

The bronco was led to a muddy or swampy area, and the rider jumped on its bare back. When the horse tried to buck, its feet would sink in the mire. If the rider was thrown he would not be hurt. The horse's spirit was broken before it could get out of the boggy ground. It could be led back into the area any number of times until its rider was satisfied that it would buck no more.

Lazy Boy said he went on a horse raid to the Flathead during which Morning Eagle took a fine looking colt that had never been broken. On their return journey the party came to a muddy place. Morning Eagle rode his newly acquired prize in the mud until it was played out. When he finished with it, it could be ridden on dry soil without difficulty.

SURCINGLE BREAKING
(FIG. 7)

Before a bronco could be broken on dry soil, it had to be held so as to permit the rider to mount. There were several methods of doing this. Sometimes the bronco was roped, and the lasso pulled tight around its neck while another man slipped a war bridle in his mouth, and the rider (a third person) jumped on his back. At other times the bronco was "front-footed" (both front feet roped with rawhide lasso), and the horse was thrown down. The rider took his place as the horse started to rise and the rope was loosened. Still another method was to "front-foot" the bronco, lasso one hind leg and pull it slightly forward so the horse could not kick while the rider mounted, then loosen the ropes. A fourth method called for first "front-footing"

FIGURE 7.—Breaking a bronco by riding it with a surcingle, Blackfoot.

the beast, then wrapping a rope around all four legs and blindfolding the horse with a piece of robe until the rider took his seat. Then the ropes were released and the blindfold removed.

In employing the surcingle method of breaking, the rider carried a long band of rawhide or soft buffalo skin. As he mounted the bronco he pulled this strap around the horse's belly, enclosing his own knees and shanks, and quickly tied the band in a common knot in front of him. The surcingle was tied tight enough so that by exerting pressure with his knees against the band he could keep from falling, yet loose enough so that he could extricate his legs quickly if the horse should fall. It often took three days of breaking by the surcingle method before the horse was ready for the saddle. Each day the rider stayed on the horse until it was played out.

PAD-SADDLE BREAKING

The horse was held as for the surcingle method, and a pad saddle was girthed quickly on its back, well forward. The rider mounted behind the saddle and held onto it to steady himself as the horse maneuvered in his attempts to throw him. Three Calf claimed he had seen a blind man break a bronco by riding it in this way.

My elderly Blackfoot informants were of the opinion that the pond or stream method and the boggy-ground method were the oldest ways of breaking horses known to their people. They based their opinions upon traditions as well as the belief that since these were the least dangerous methods they likely would have been the ones employed by people who had little experience in training horses. Several men said their first experiences in breaking horses were gained through use of those methods. The same men said they had employed the surcingle or pad-saddle method after they became more adept at handling unbroken horses.[34]

BREAKING HORSES FOR THE TRAVOIS

Poor people could not be choosy in selecting a horse for travois service. Wealthier families preferred to employ older, gentler horses for this work. The ideal travois horse was a large, heavily built, strong,

---

[34] Considering the bulk of Plains Indian literature and the importance many writers have attributed to the horse in the culture of those Indians, it is remarkable how little comparative material has been published on their methods of breaking horses. Wilson's elderly Hidatsa informant employed a combination of the water and boggy-ground methods in his youth (Wilson, 1924, p. 151). An Oglala informant told me the water method was an old one in his tribe. An Assiniboin, who visited the U. S. National Museum in 1950, claimed his tribe formerly employed this method. Two elderly Kiowa Indians told me they broke their first horses by this method. One said the Comanche also used it. Smoky described a Kiowa method of breaking horses in soft, muddy ground, after a hard rain, under conditions that would make bucking difficult and minimize damage to the rider if he should be thrown.

All comparative data on the surcingle method refer to peoples living west of the Rockies. George Gibbs noted and described Klikitat and Yakima use of this method in breaking horses in 1854 (Gibbs, 1855, p. 405). It is the only method mentioned for the Kutenai (Turney-High, 1941, pp. 71–72). In the mid-19th century Bartlett (1854, vol. 2, p. 237) observed Pima Indians of the southwestern desert riding bareback using a "broad girth which is passed quite loosely around the body of the horse. Into this one foot is inserted." Of still greater interest is the fact that the Spanish-Mexicans of California at that time used a surcingle in breaking horses. Although the horse was saddled, a leather girth was strapped over the saddle so as to confine the rider's knees loosely enough that he could release himself by pressing his knees to the sides of the horse (Denhardt, 1937, p. 13). This suggests the possibility of Spanish influence on this method of horse breaking, although the principle was relatively simple, and may have been independently invented by the Indians. I have found no reference to employment of the pad-saddle method by any tribe other than the Blackfoot.

My Oglala and Kiowa informants had no knowledge of the use of either the surcingle or pad-saddle methods by their respective tribes. However, they asserted that riders of those tribes broke horses on dry ground merely by riding them bareback, holding onto the mane with their hands, and maintaining a precarious toehold under the elbows of the horses' forelegs.

Both Kiowa and Blackfoot men said their people did not ride saddles in breaking horses until they obtained strong, stock saddles from the Whites in the Reservation Period.

mare over 4 years of age. Some people preferred a former saddle horse 8 or 9 years old to draw the travois.

An unbroken horse would not haul a travois. The horse had to be specially trained for this task. One common method of training employed in buffalo days was to make a simple harness, consisting of a rawhide rope around the horse's neck with a long rawhide line attached to it at each side extending backward and tied to a dry buffalo hide on the ground a few feet back of the horse's hind legs. Some people preferred a single rawhide rope tied to the horse's tail and the buffalo hide. The rope was always long enough so that the horse could not kick the hide. While one or more men led the horse by a halter, one to three men or boys rode on the hide over a selected plot of ground relatively smooth and free from stones. The horse might jump and kick at first. It might even break away from the leaders and

FIGURE 8.—Breaking a horse to the travois by training it to drag a weighted buffalo hide, Blackfoot.

spill the riders. But in time it became used to being led and to the weight drawn behind it, and quieted down. Then it would submit to the travois. (See fig. 8.)

Other Blackfoot Indians preferred to train travois horses by making them pull tipi poles crossed over their heads, as in the horse travois, or two heavy cottonwood poles similarly arranged. This makeshift travois was placed on the horse for short periods on several successive days until the horse became accustomed to the weight. Then the real travois was substituted. A horse trained to the travois readily learned to carry the additional weight of a person riding on its back. However, unless it had previously been used for riding, it would not make a good saddle horse.

TEACHING CHILDREN TO RIDE

Blackfoot children were accustomed to horses from infancy. As babies they were carried on their mother's backs on horseback when camp was moved. When they were able to sit up they rode on the travois or behind their mothers on horseback. They became familiar with the motion of a walking horse, so that by the time they were old enough to learn to ride alone their fear of horses was partially overcome. Training involved primarily teaching children to maintain their balance on horseback and to use the reins, and the proper horse commands to control the actions of their mounts.

Riding lessons were given children by their fathers or mothers near the lodges in the camp of their band. No effort was made to clear the camp of other riders or children when a child took his first lesson.

FIGURE 9.—Teaching a child to ride by tying him in a woman's saddle on a gentle horse, Blackfoot.

In fact, other children watched and sometimes made fun of the awkward efforts of the learners. The gentlest riding horse owned by the family was employed in teaching children to ride. If the horse was gentle, the mother usually served as teacher, regardless of the sex of the child. If the family owned no gentle horse, the father took charge.

My eldest informants said they learned to ride in this manner: The child was lifted into a high-horned woman's saddle and rawhide ropes were passed back and forth between the pommel and cantle on each side, and tied securely to prevent the child's falling. If afraid, the child could also hold onto the saddle horn. The parent, afoot or astride another horse, led the child's horse about camp by a hackamore. (See fig. 9.) At first the horse was led at a slow walk. As the child gained in experience and confidence, the horse was led at a swifter pace, and the child was taught to use the reins and control his mount. When camp was moved, the child was tied in the saddle and the horse on which he rode was led by an adult. About the year 1869, a fatal accident caused the Piegan to change their method of teaching children to ride. Woman Shoe was leading his little son tied in the saddle when the horse became frightened, pulled the lead rope from Woman Shoe's grasp, and ran off. The saddle girth loosened, the saddle slipped, and the child was kicked to death. Thereafter most Piegan placed their children in high-horned saddles as before, but relied upon them to keep their balance by holding the pommel, without the aid of ties.

In some families a girl was taught to ride a travois horse. A travois, unencumbered by baggage, was attached to a travois horse and the child placed on the horse's back in a woman's saddle. The mother led the horse.[35]

Informants claimed a Blackfoot child usually learned to ride alone in his fifth year. Children of other Plains Indian tribes seem to have learned to ride at an equally early age.[36]

At the age of 6 or 7 most Blackfoot boys and girls were good riders. Some youngsters rode little saddles, of the "prairie chicken snare" or pack-saddle type, which their fond mothers or grandmothers made for them. A small boy sometimes tied a short rawhide rope to his horse's mane. He employed a handhold on this rope as an aid in climbing onto his horse's back.

---

[35] In spite of the demonstrated danger of the early Blackfoot method of teaching children to ride, it was employed by many other tribes of the Plains and Plateau. Two Kiowa informants told me they had learned to ride at 4 or 5 years of age by being tied in high-horned saddles on gentle horses, led by their fathers or mothers. Numerous references in the literature to children tied in the saddle when camp was moved suggest the same method of teaching on the part of other tribes. In 1805, Larocque and Mackenzie saw that Crow children, too young to ride alone, were tied in the saddle when camp was moved (Larocque, 1910, p. 64; Mackenzie, 1889, p. 345). Gordon (Chardon, 1932. p. 347; and Denig, 1933, p. 36) also reported this Crow practice. Ferris (1940, p. 301), in his general description of Indians of the northern Rockies (period 1830–1835), noted, "Their children of three or four years of age are lashed firmly on top of their packs, and are often endangered by the horses running away with them, though I never saw one severely injured in consequence." In 1839, Farnham (1906, p. 329) saw a little Cayuse boy "but three years old" who rode alone "lashed to the horse he rode." Members of the Long Expedition (1820) observed that Kiowa-Apache children "too young to be able by their own strength to sit on a horse (were) lashed by their legs to the saddle" (James, 1823, vol. 2, p. 103). This method was reported for the Comanche in 1865 (U. S. Comm. Ind. Affairs, 1867, p. 38). Although these data would suggest that this practice was Plains-wide, Eagle Bird, an aged Oglala, told me it was not the custom of his tribe, stating that it was too dangerous.

[36] Mackenzie (1889, p. 345), in 1805, noted that Crow children above the age of 6 could manage a horse. While Gordon (Chardon, 1932. p. 347) wrote of the same tribe (period 1820), "At four or five years of age they will ride alone and guide the horse." Tixier (1940, p. 167) marveled at Osage boys who, in 1840, "were riding alone bareback, and managed their horses with skill" although they "could not have been more than five or six years old." A Southern Cheyenne woman claimed her mother told her she learned to ride at the age of 4 (Michelson, 1932, p. 1).

RIDING AND GUIDING

MOUNTING

Contrary to European practice, most Blackfoot Indians mounted from the right side and saddled their horses from that side. Older men insisted this was the "natural" way for a right-handed man to mount a barebacked horse or a horse wearing a light, weak, Indian saddle. In mounting, a man relied heavily on the pressure gained by fixing a strong right-hand grip on the horse's mane. He placed his left hand on the center of the horse's back as he jumped on to help him throw his left leg over. Lazy Boy seemed to clinch the argument for the "naturalness" of right-hand mounting when he said that in the old days a left-handed man mounted from the left side because that was easier for him. The importance of a strong saddle, which would support a man's weight in the stirrup, as a factor in mounting is indicated by the fact that after the Blackfoot obtained "white men's saddles" in the early Reservation Period, they readily changed to left-side mounting. Today all Blackfoot mount from the left side.[37]

Blackfoot women always rode astride, as did women of other Plains and Plateau Indian tribes. A Blackfoot woman mounted by placing her right foot in the stirrup and thrusting her left leg through the center of the opening between the saddle horns. She did not attempt to swing her leg over the high cantle.[38] Women's skirts were made full to permit freedom of movement afoot as well as ease in mounting and to provide a covering for the legs when mounted astride. Three Calf said that in his youth pregnant women wore an undecorated belt of rawhide, 6 inches or more in width, as a support for the abdomen in riding. It was laced in front so that it could be

---

[37] Right-side mounting formerly was the general rule among Plains Indians. Parker (1856, p. 239) observed that tribes of the southern Plains mounted from that side. Yet Opler (1941, p. 396) claimed the Chiracahua Apache mounted from the left side. Perhaps this was due to their prolonged contacts with Spanish-Mexican settlements of the Southwest. Carlos Rincon Gallardo, Duque de Regla, an authority on Mexican equitation, has informed me through Dr. Pablo Martinez Del Rio, that Mexican riders of the Colonial Period mounted from the left as a general rule. In respect to mounting, the Plains Indians seem to have followed their own conception of the easiest method, rather than Spanish-Mexican example. It is noteworthy that the Choctaw of the Southeast, ante-1775, mounted from the right side, claiming it was the more natural one from which to get on a horse (Adair, 1775, p. 426).

[38] Parker's description of Southern Comanche women's method of mounting (observed by him in 1854), shows their method was identical to that of Blackfoot women. "Drawing the left foot up, after placing the right in the stirrup, they extended it over the saddle at right angles to the right, instead of describing the arc of a circle" (Parker, 1856, p. 203. In riding astride, Plains Indian women adopted a custom that was not Spanish-Mexican practice. Carlos Rincon Gallardo, Duque de Regla, has informed me that Mexican women of the Colonial Period never rode astride. Serrano's remarks on the riding posture of Mexican women of California during the Spanish Period also indicates their preference for the side saddle. "As the saddles on which they ride have the saddle-bow and stirrups taken off, they use as a stirrup for one foot a silk band, one end being made fast at the pommel, the other at the cantle" (Bancroft, 1888, p. 447).

let out as pregnancy advanced. This belt was worn for about a month after the birth of a child. Then it was thrown away, and the mother resumed wearing the narrower, decorated woman's belt.

HORSE COMMANDS

To start his horse the Blackfoot rider repeated the sound "sh" (made with the mouth open) several times. To slow down or stop the horse he called "ka" a number of times. Both commands were nonsense sounds, having no meaning except as horse commands. "Ka" was also the command given by men to keep their horses nearby and quiet after they dismounted in war or under other conditions when it was imperative for the horse to remain still. Women trained their best mares to stand still and submit to the bridle when their owners called "ka." Elderly men, who had stolen horses from the Cree, Crow, and Flathead in their youth, said those tribes did not use the same commands. They did not recall the commands used by those tribes, but remembered that horses stolen from them by Blackfoot warriors had to be taught to respond to Blackfoot verbal commands. They said the commands "sh" and "ka" were employed by the three Blackfoot tribes and the Gros Ventres.

Today all Blackfoot, whether or not they speak much English, employ the commands "whoa" and "giddap" to stop and start their horses. They began to make use of these commands shortly after they settled on reservations after the buffalo were gone. The old commands are remembered only by members of the oldest generation. According to one Blackfoot legend, Morning Star, who made the first horse, used the commands "sh" and "ka" to control its action. (See p. 296.) [39]

The Piegan employed one other verbal horse command. A man could get his horse to drink by making a rapid clicking noise (tongue against upper teeth and release) in imitation of a drinking horse. If the horse refused to drink, but moved his head from side to side in or over the water, the rider knew the water was not good for drinking and that he must find a better watering place.

---

[39] I asked a number of middle-aged Flathead, Wind River Shoshoni, and Cree Indians, who visited the Museum of the Plains Indian in the early 1940's, about the horse commands formerly employed by their tribes. They were unfamiliar with commands used before their people adopted "whoa" and "giddap." However, elderly Oglala and Brule men recalled that members of their tribes formerly made a clicking sound (tongue against the roof of the mouth or front teeth and release) to start a horse, and the sound, "huh," repeated several times, to slow down or stop the animal. Kiowa informants claimed their people used the click and "huh" to start and stop horses in the old days. Undoubtedly Kiowa and Western Dakota use of the same nonsense sounds as horse commands was due to diffusion rather than independent invention. Perhaps if we had more complete information on the horse commands of the different Plains and Plateau Indian tribes these data would be of some significance in tracing routes of diffusion of the horse complex in this region. H. C. Bolton (1897, p. 80) found that the hiss sound "ss" was used in Mexico by halfbreed Spaniards to start a horse, while Mexicans in the Southwest used the command "check-a" to stop a horse. This suggests historic connection between Spanish and Blackfoot horse commands.

Three Calf recalled that some Crow Indians could get their horses to roll in grass after they had finished drinking by slapping the fronts of their own thighs with their hands. However, that was not a Blackfoot practice.

GUIDING

The Blackfoot employed no verbal commands to turn a horse to the right or left. The best trained buffalo and war horses, and the racers were so sensitive that they would turn to either side by pressure from the rider's knee or from his shifting weight to one side or the other. These horses could be ridden without a bridle, but they nearly always were bridled.[40]

The majority of Blackfoot riding horses were not so intelligent or so well trained. They had to be handled through use of a two-reined bridle. The rider slackened both reins in getting the horse on the run; pulled both reins in stopping it; and pulled one rein to turn the horse to the side. (Bridle types and their uses are described on pp. 75–77.)

USE OF WHIP

The Blackfoot Indians made no spurs and relatively few men employed metal spurs obtained through the fur trade in buffalo days. The best trained horses needed neither spurs nor whips to urge them to exert themselves. However, whips were commonly carried by Blackfoot riders of both sexes. A woman riding a travois struck the whip handle against one of the travois shafts as she gave the oral command to start her horse. In riding a poor or old horse many Indians kept the whip constantly in motion, raising and lowering the whip arm in time with the movement of the horse, touching the horse's rump lightly with the whip lash each time the arm descended. Frank Sherburne recalled that at the turn of the century it was a common sight to see an old Indian riding into the town of Browning, rhythmically raising and lowering his whip "every other jump of the horse." (Whip types are described on pp. 97–99.)

USE OF SHORT STIRRUPS

Both men and women among the Blackfoot tribes rode with bent knees and short stirrups when riding in the saddle. Short stirrups gave the active rider the necessary leverage to move from side to side and to rise and turn in the saddle as the need required. They enabled him to use the lance and bow and arrow more effectively when mounted,

---

[40] In 1805, Larocque (1910, p. 64) wrote of the training of Crow horses, "Most of their horses can be guided to any place without a bridle, only by leaning to one side or the other they turn immediately to the side on which you lean, and will not return until you resume a direct posture." The same sensitivity has been attributed to the best trained horses of other tribes of the Plains and Plateau by later writers.

and made it easier for him to weave his body from side to side when under fire in battle.[41]

ABILITY AS HORSEMEN

It was to be expected that people who learned to ride in early childhood and who spent much of their time on horseback would become expert riders. Blackfoot boys learned to ride double at a fast pace, to throw their bodies on one side of a running horse using it as a shield, and to shoot arrows from the bow rapidly and accurately from horseback. Girls also became excellent riders, although they had less opportunity to show their skill in dangerous or complicated maneuvers. The greatest individual feat of horsemanship remembered by Piegan informants was that of breaking a bronco while holding a baby in his arms, attributed to Dog Child, one of their fearless riders. Blood informants recalled the accomplishment of Owner-of-a-Sacred-White-Horse, a horse medicine man, who was said to have jumped his horse over a coulee more than 10 feet wide to avoid being overtaken by the enemy.

From the time of Anthony Hendry (1754) contemporary white observers have marveled at the skill of Plains Indian horsemen. Certainly no tribe or group of tribes had a monopoly on expert riders. Nevertheless, Captain Clark stated "the Comanches and Utes are considered by many Indians the best horsemen" (Clark, 1885, p. 319). This contention is supported by the writings of other competent observers. Ferris, who possessed wide, first-hand knowledge of the tribes of the northern Rockies in the 1830's, considered the Ute, "by far the most expert horsemen in the mountains, and course down their steep sides in pursuit of deer and elk at full speed, over places where a white man would dismount and lead his horse" (Ferris, 1940, p. 312). Captain Marcy, in 1852, termed the Comanche "the most expert horsemen in the world" (Marcy, 1937, p. 158). This judgment was made of Comanche horsemanship by other observers (Burnet, 1851, p. 236; Neighbors, 1852, p. 132). We need not take this praise literally to be impressed with the high regard competent American horsemen had for the riding ability of the Comanche.[42]

---

[41] The Frenchman, Tixier, was impressed by the fact that the Osage "stirrup leathers are very short" in 1840 (Tixier, 1940, p. 168). Both Captain Clark (1885, p. 319) and James Meline (1868, pp. 103, 246) reported the use of the short stirrup as characteristic of Plains Indian riders. Denhardt (1947, pp. 15–17) traced the introduction of the use of short stirrups into Spain by the Moors. The Spanish adopted the Moorish method in preference to the prevailing European practice of riding straight-legged. Spanish conquistadores brought the Moorish method of riding to America along with the horse. Probably Plains Indian use of the short stirrup was patterned after its usage by the Spanish-Mexicans. Being well suited to fast riding and ease of movement in the saddle, the short stirrup was retained by the Indians.

[42] Zebulon Pike (1810, appendix, part 3, p. 42) employed the same phrase ("the most expert horsemen in the world") in his description of the mounted Spanish troops of New Mexico, whose horsemanship he observed in 1806.

It is noteworthy that both Ute and Comanche were richer in horses in buffalo days than were the Blackfoot. Wealthy tribes had a greater selection of riding animals, and hence generally rode better mounts. If the Comanche and Ute were better riders than the Blackfoot at least part of the credit should be given to their superior horses.[43] As shown elsewhere in this study, the Blackfoot tribes were inept at capturing wild horses and at killing animals of the deer family from horseback, while the Comanche were skilled in both these difficult undertakings. This appears to me to be concrete proof of Blackfoot inferiority to the Comanche as horsemen.

---

[43] Charles Mackenzie, in 1805, observed that the Missouri Indians (Mandan and Hidatsa) "were inferior in the management of their horses" to the nomadic Crow, who, of course, not only had more and better horses but made much more common use of these animals in their daily life (Mackenzie, 1889, p. 345).

RIDING GEAR

Rawhide rope had many uses in Blackfoot horse culture. The strength, flexibility, and durability of buffalo rawhide made it preferred material for lariats, hackamores, bridles, picket lines, hobbles, saddle rigging straps, stirrup straps, travois ropes, and cords used for wrapping bundles and tying them on pack animals or the travois.

Women were the skilled leatherworkers among the Blackfoot. Although some men made rawhide rope, our older male informants acknowledged that in their youth women usually fashioned the best ropes. The tough, heavy hide of the buffalo bull was preferred material.

Three Calf recalled that his grandmother and mother, both considered clever workers in rawhide, made rawhide rope in this manner: The woman first cut one long, continuous strip from the green hide of a buffalo bull. Beginning at the outer edge, she cut a strip about 4 fingers wide all around the hide, including the leg and head projections, working in a concentric spiral, ending at the center of the hide. Then she cut a slit near one end of the strip and drove a lodge peg through this slit into the ground. She stretched the rope as tight as possible and drove another peg into the ground through a similar slit at the other end of the line. Later she pulled up one peg, stretched the strip farther, and pegged it to the ground again. After the rawhide dried, she took it off her simple stretcher and began softening it by rubbing the inner (meat side) surface of the hide with a rock. Then she doubled the strip lengthwise, hair side out, and bit it with her teeth to hold the crease. She passed one end of the strip through the eye sockets of a buffalo skull, and standing with one foot on the skull to steady it, she used both hands to saw the strip back and forth through these eye holes to rub off the hair and further soften the hide. She knocked off any hair that remained with a rock. Taking her knife again she cut the strip down the center lengthwise, dividing it into two ropes each 2 fingers wide. If these ropes were intended for bridles she allowed for a short distance of rope 4 fingers wide at each end, one end for one rope, the other for the second rope, to serve as a honda for each. She trimmed each rope very carefully to be sure that it was an even width throughout its length, except for the expanded honda end. Any short pieces trimmed off were saved for whip

73

lashes. After cutting she oiled the ropes with back fat. One buffalo-hide thus made two ropes of equal length, 17 or more feet long.

Other ropemakers employed somewhat different methods. Some cut the entire buffalo hide in a strip 2 fingers wide. They could cut one very long rope or two shorter ones this width from a hide. Some did not use a buffalo skull for dehairing, but removed all the hair with a rock. Some insisted on using coyote or badger fat to oil their ropes. Others dragged the ropes on the ground behind a horse for a time to make them soft and slick.[44]

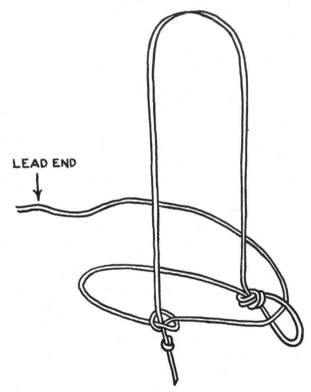

LEAD END

FIGURE 10.—A simple rawhide hackamore, Blackfoot.

HACKAMORES

The Blackfoot used a simple hackamore for halter breaking horses, breaking them to ride, and leading horses when moving camp. The hackamore was generally of a single rawhide strand 2 fingers wide. A common Blackfoot hackamore is shown in figure 10.

---

[44] Descriptions of ropemaking by the Gros Ventres, Hidatsa, and Kutenai mention minor differences in process (Kroeber, 1907, p. 150; Wilson, 1924, pp. 186–187; Turney-High 1941, pp. 75–76). We cannot be sure if these were tribal or merely individual differences in method. Kiowa informants stated that women did most of their ropemaking.

BRIDLES

Blackfoot bridles were of rawhide or buffalo-hair rope. Anthony Hendry, in the earliest description of Northwestern Plains horse culture (1754), mentioned Indian use of "hair halters" (Hendry, 1907, p. 338). Maximilian (1833) described only buffalo-hair rope in use among the Blackfoot (Maximilian, 1906, vol. 23, p. 107). Yet neither Bradley (1870's) nor Wissler mentioned buffalo-hair bridles as typical of the Blackfoot (Bradley, 1923, p. 263; Wissler, 1910, p. 95). Our informants considered the buffalo-hair bridle an old-style Blackfoot one which was little used in the time of their youth. Three Calf said his mother made ropes from the forehead and foreleg hair of the buffalo. She twisted the hair around a stick, pressed it under her bed for several nights, then retrieved it and braided it in 4 strands. This rope would not get stiff or heavy in water. It made a good bridle, but it was too light for use as a lasso on windy days. Ropes of braided horsehair were said to have been uncommon among the Blackfoot before white cowboys taught them how to make them.

Most Blackfoot bridles in use during the youth of my informants were of rawhide, single strand or braided. Single-strand rawhide bridles, usually 2 fingers wide, would not wear as long as the braided ones. Some people made a chainstitch rope of a single strand no wider than a man's little finger. After it was pounded and rolled between two flat rocks it looked much like a braided rope. When finished it had a diameter of about three-quarters of an inch. Although sometimes used for bridles, rope of this type was most commonly employed for wrapping medicine pipes and other sacred bundles.

The most popular Blackfoot bridle in those days was of three-strand braided rawhide. This rope was strong and flexible. In daily use it would last many years. Some makers braided them around a honda ring tied to the trunk of a tree. A four-strand rope was braided of green rawhide 2 fingers wide looped around a peg in the ground. All of the rope except for the short section that passed around the peg was cut in two lengthwise before braiding. After braiding it was stretched between two pegs, then the unbraided section that had been looped around the first peg was cut off. The four-strand rope was said to have been a white man's invention, first employed by the Piegan when the Blackfoot Agency was at Old Agency in the early 1880's. The Piegan then made them for themselves and sold them to cowboys for roping cattle. Some are said to have brought as much as $50 each. The Blackfoot regarded this as the best rope for lariats. It was not commonly used for bridles.

The most common form of Blackfoot bridle was that known to the Indians as "war bridle." This name probably was derived from its common use on horse-stealing raids. The Blackfoot also used it in hunting buffalo and for general riding purposes. It was a two-rein bridle formed of a single length of rope with a honda (fixed loop at the end of one rein through which the other rein passes). The end with the honda served as one rein, at the foreward part of which two half hitches were taken, placed in the horse's mouth, and tightened around his lower jaw. (Some men tied a knot in the rope below the half hitches to keep them from slipping.) The rope continued around the other side of the horse's neck (serving as a second rein), passed through the honda, and the long end remaining was carefully folded or coiled and placed under the rider's belt at one side. (See fig. 11.)

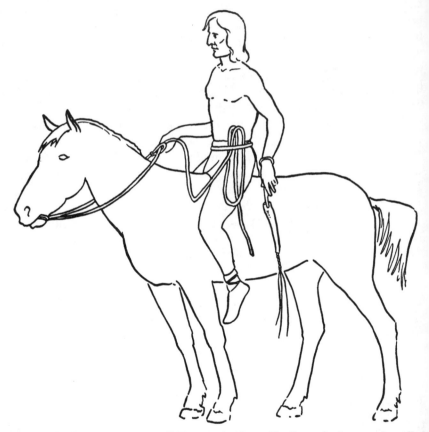

FIGURE 11.—Rider using a rawhide war bridle with the end of one rein coiled under his belt, Blackfoot.

Since these ropes were from 16 to 30 feet long, their greatest portion remained tucked under the belt. If the rider was thrown from his horse he could catch hold of the end of this rope as it payed out along the ground. There was always the danger, however, that the rope might become tangled or knotted under the belt so that when the rider was thrown or forced to dismount hurriedly from a moving horse he might be injured or killed.

Although two half hitches were most commonly used for the jaw fastening, three half hitches were employed to control a spirited horse that was difficult to handle. When the rider pulled hard on the reins the rawhide swelled in the horse's mouth and made it uncomfortable for him. For race horses a single half hitch was preferred. It left the horse's mouth freer and made him less likely to become winded.

The honda was made in several ways. Some men simply pierced the rope near the end and strengthened the loop by wrapping sinew around it. Others used a ring made from a narrow cross section of a buffalo horn. Much preferred was a small metal ring obtained from white traders. If a ring was employed, the end of the rope was passed through the ring, doubled back and securely sewn with sinew. The honda served another useful purpose. When the rider dismounted he could pass the short rein over the horse's neck, pull on the long rein, and hold his mount halter fashion. (See fig. 12.) Wissler also noted

FIGURE 12.—Use of the war bridle as a halter, Blackfoot.

this practice (Wissler, 1910, p. 96). In riding, the reins were held at the honda or slightly forward of it.

To keep a horse's head high when on parade, a long loop of the bridle rope was left pendent under the jaw. This loop would swing as the horse moved and would strike the animal on the nose if he did not keep his head up. Members of returning war parties sometimes tied scalps to the bridle under the horse's jaw for the same purpose.

COMPARATIVE DATA ON BRIDLES

Although mentions of bridles employed by other Plains and Plateau tribes are numerous in the literature, many descriptions are too fragmentary to enable us to determine exactly what the author had in mind. For example, Penicaut's description of the Caddo bridle, seen in 1714, i. e. "They have no other bit to their bridle than a hair cord which passes into the horse's mouth," may refer to a bridle of the "war bridle" type, but we cannot be sure (Penicaut in Swanton, 1942, p. 147). Hair bridles seem to have been in common use among the tribes of the northern Plains and Plateau in the early years of the 19th century. Lewis and Clark (Coues, 1893, vol. 2, p. 562) observed that the Lemhi Shoshoni used both a six- or seven-strand buffalo-hair rope and a rawhide rope but much preferred the hair one. Ross Cox (1832, pp. 84–85) said Nez Percé "bridles are merely ropes made out of hair of the horse's tail and are tied round the jaw." Maximilian (1833) noted that Assiniboin used a rope "of buffalo hair, which is fastened to the lower jaw as a bridle," and that it was like the Hidatsa bridle (Maximilian, 1906, vol. 22, p. 391). Later writers tell of the prevalence of braided horsehair ropes among the tribes of the Plateau west of the Flathead and Kutenai (Teit, 1900, p. 258; 1909, p. 535; 1930, p. 111). Perhaps their distance from the buffalo range encouraged their adoption of horsehair bridles. Yet Flathead and Kutenai used the rawhide variety, and the latter claimed both horsehair and buffalo hair bridle were recent introductions by way of the Nez Percé (Turney-High, 1937, p. 73; 1941, p. 108). The Comanche bridle ca. 1850 was "a simple rawhide noose" (Whipple, 1856, p. 28). Kiowa informants said their bridle was a two-reined buffalo rawhide rope looped around the horse's lower jaw.

The Indian "war bridle" differed markedly from the metal-bitted bridles commonly termed "Spanish bridles" by early writers. The Plains Indians became familiar with "Spanish bridles" early through capture and trade in Spanish horses. The two Frenchmen of La Vérendrye's party, who remained with the Mandan through the summer of 1739, were shown "Bridles of which the bit and curb are of one piece with very long branches, the whole finely polished," by horse-using tribes who visited the Mandan to trade (La Vérendrye, 1927, p. 371). Jacques d'Eglise observed that the Mandan had "bridles in Mexican style" in 1792 (Nasitir, 1927, p. 58). Lewis and Clark made frequent mention of "Spanish bridles" in use among the Lemhi Shoshoni in 1805, and noted that those Indians preferred them to their own simple hair or rawhide bridles when they could get them (Coues, 1893, vol. 2, pp. 559, 563, 569). Sergeant Ordway of that party saw that the Nez Percé used "Spanish bridles" as stakes in gambling in 1806.

David Thompson, in 1787, described the return of a Piegan war party from a raid far to the south, on which they had stolen directly from the Spaniards horses which still bore their Spanish trappings. "The bridles and snaffle bits, heavy and coarse as if made by a blacksmith with only his hammer. The weight and coarseness of the bits had made the Indians throw most of them away" (Thompson, 1916, pp. 371). Nevertheless, the Plains and Plateau tribes, Blackfoot included, used "Spanish bridles" when they could get them through theft or trade in the 19th century. Spanish bits were seen among the Osage in 1840 (Tixier, 1940, p. 168). In 1853, Whipple observed that the Comanche "are not averse to using both saddle and bridle, whenever in their marauding expeditions they can obtain possession of them" (Whipple, 1856, p. 28). Boller (1868, p. 65) wrote of the Mandan-Hidatsa in 1858, "Those who are so fortunate as to possess one use the heavy Spanish bit with its long iron fringes, jingling with the slightest movement of the horse." However, the simple rawhide "war bridle," with modifications to adapt it to special uses, well described by Wilson, survived in common use among the Hidatsa until the end of buffalo days (Wilson, 1924, pp. 182–185). In the paintings of George Catlin, Alfred Miller, and Rudolph Kurz the great majority of Indians pictured on horseback are shown using the "war bridle." Among the Blackfoot the metal-bitted bridle was a luxury item. The simple "war bridle" remained in common use until after buffalo were gone.

LARIATS

The long rawhide bridle served the Blackfoot as a lariat as well. Buffalo hair ropes, because of their light weight, had limited usefulness as lassos in the windy Blackfoot Country. Informants claimed the Blackfoot used lariats long before there were any American cowboys in Montana. The fixed loop was standard. Men used the lariat primarily for roping horses which they wished to cut out of their herds, for roping unpicketed horses of the enemy when on horse-stealing raids, and for roping horses for gelding or breaking to the saddle. I gained the impression that little use of the lariat was made by mounted men. Women did not use the lariat as a general rule. They trained their gentle horses to stand still when they threw one end of the long bridle line over their backs or necks and called "ka-ka-ka".[45]

---

[45] Early descriptions of the use of the lariat by northern tribes appear in the literature. Lewis and Clark (Coues, 1893, vol. 2, pp. 562–563) observed that the Lemhi Shoshoni were experts in lassoing running horses. Alfred Jacob Miller painted two watercolors of Indians lassoing wild horses (Walters Art Gallery Collection, Baltimore, Md., Nos. 80 and 137). The latter depicts a Shoshoni woman lassoing from horseback. (See also De Voto, 1947, pl. 53.) Other early references to the use of the lasso in catching wild horses by Plains Indians appear on p. 60. Pike (1810, Appendix, p. 42) marveled at the skill of Spanish cavalrymen of New Mexico in lassoing horses. There can be little doubt that the Plains Indians learned the use of the lariat from the Spanish, as Wyman (1945, p. 85) has claimed.

THE DRAGGING LINE

George Catlin described the use of a long, dragging line tied around the horse's neck, by Plains Indians in the 1830's:

The laso is a long thong of rawhide, of ten or fifteen yards in length, made of several braids or twists, and used chiefly to catch the wild horse . . . In running the buffaloes, or in time of war, the laso drags on the ground at the horse's feet, and sometimes several rods behind, so that if a man is dismounted, which is often the case, by the tripping or stumbling of the horse, he has the power of grasping to the laso, and by stubbornly holding on to it, of stopping and securing his horse, on whose back he is instantly replaced, and continuing on in the chase. [Catlin, 1841, vol. 1, p. 253.]

In his description of this item Catlin does not refer to its use by any specific tribes, but seems to infer that it was in general use among the buffalo-hunting tribes of the Plains in his time. He shows this dragging line in many of his paintings of Indians hunting buffalo on horseback.

The Blackfoot bridle, one end of which was coiled under the rider's belt, served the same purpose. This poses the question of whether the device described by Catlin might not be older than the Blackfoot one described by informants as that employed in their youth. I am inclined to believe that there were several devices employed by the Indians for the same purpose, that may have had different distributions. This is suggested by Lewis and Clark's description of the Lemhi Shoshoni halter employed in 1805—

One end of it is first tied round the neck in a knot and then brought down to the under jaw, round which it is formed into a simple noose, passing through the mouth; it is then drawn up on the right side and held by the rider in his left hand, while the rest trails after him to some distance. At other times the knot is formed at a little distance from one of the ends, so as to let that end serve as a bridle while the other trails on the ground. [Coues, 1893, vol. 2, p. 562.]

The second Shoshoni variant is the typical Blackfoot war bridle, except that the long end of one rein is allowed to drag the ground rather than tucked under the belt. Tixier, in 1840, told of Osage buffalo hunters employing a long horsehair tether, tied around the horse's neck, coiled and "passed around the rider's belt," for the same purpose (Tixier, 1940, pp. 167–168). This seems to be still another variant. Wilson's description of the Hidatsa bridle indicates clearly that it was like that of the Blackfoot, and served the same dual purpose (Wilson, 1924, p. 183). The limited data at our disposal shows that the Blackfoot variant of the dragging line was known to the Shoshoni in 1805. There is no reason to believe that the separate line, tied around the horse's neck, is an older device.

SADDLES

SADDLE MAKING

Saddle making was women's work among the Blackfoot. It was a somewhat specialized craft. Some older women who were especially skilled saddlemakers not only manufactured them for the members of their own families but also made them for trade, while other women never attempted to make saddles.[46]

Saddle making was not strictly a seasonal occupation, but Blackfoot women generally preferred to fashion them in warmer weather because of the inconvenience of working wet rawhide in winter. To a limited extent saddles were tailor-made. If the person for whom the saddle was intended was a large, heavy man or woman, the pommel and cantle were spaced a greater distance apart than was usual in frame saddles. Saddles made for children were proportionately smaller than those for adults.[47]

Saddles were highly valued, private property. A good horse was paid for with a fancy pad saddle or a high-horned woman's saddle. When a couple married their parents might give them saddles. However, some poor families owned no saddles. If a young man was ambitious, wanted to hunt and go to war, his father or another close relative had a saddle made for him. A lazy young man of poor family might never own a saddle.

At night, or in the daytime when not in use, saddles were stored inside the owner's lodge behind the beds. If a man had several wives it generally was the duty of the one who slept nearest the door to care for his saddle and other riding gear left in the lodge.

The several types of pad and frame saddles used by the Blackfoot in buffalo days were as follows:

THE PAD SADDLE

An active man's saddle, which was little more than a soft, skin pillow stuffed with hair, was known as "pad saddle." To make a pad saddle two pieces of soft tanned buffalo, deer, elk or antelope skin were cut to the same size, roughly hourglass-shaped in outline. Buffalo bull skin made the longest wearing pad saddle. Although a man might cut the pattern to suit his desire, he turned the skins over to a woman to as-

---

[46] Women were also the saddlemakers among the Wind River Shoshoni and Kiowa (Shimkin, 1947 b, p. 294; communication from Alice Marriott). Some Kiowa women were specialists to the extent that they made and traded saddles for lodge covers, dried meat, and other articles. However, Opler (1941, p. 395) found that men made the saddles of the Chiracahua Apache.

[47] The collections of the U. S. National Museum contain several small frame saddles from different Plains Indian tribes, documented as children's saddles. Kiowa informants said older women of that tribe made saddles for boys and girls.

semble the saddle. She placed one skin on top of the other so that their edges were in contact, then sewed the skins together in two nearly parallel lines of soft skin or rawhide cord extending lengthwise of the center. She then began to sew the edges of the top and bottom skins together with sinew thread, leaving sufficient openings at each side to stuff the saddle before completely closing the edges. Buffalo or deer hair were preferred for stuffing, although some women used grass for that purpose.

The pad saddle illustrated in plate 2, *a*, shows the basic pattern and decoration. This specimen (U. S. N. M. No. 2656) was collected by Capt. Howard Stansbury in 1849, and labeled "Black Feet Indians of the Rocky Mountains." It measures 16⅜ inches long and 14 inches wide through the center and weighs 1 pound 5 ounces. In 1947, I showed photographs of this specimen to elderly Blackfoot Indians. They pronounced it typical of pad saddles used by Blood and Piegan men in their youth. This specimen is decorated with porcupine-quill rosettes and quilled lozenges in each corner. Pendent from the lower border of the saddle near each corner are two quilled skin pieces separated by quill-wrapped skin thongs. The edge seam joining the bottom and top skins is covered with quillwork. Informants recognized this as the usual pattern of decoration of old Blackfoot pad saddles. However, in their youth the same pattern was worked out more frequently in beadwork. [48]

From the center of each side extend U-shaped tabs used for fastening the girth to the saddle. The most common girth was a rawhide strap 2 to 4 fingers wide, doubled over the tab on the left side of the saddle and sewn with sinew, passed under the barrel of the horse and secured to the tab on the right side of the saddle with a rawhide latigo strap. Less common girthing was obtained by suspending soft skin straps from each tab and tying them under the horse's belly. Informants believed the saddle illustrated was either ridden without stirrups or the stirrups were suspended from the same tabs as the girth. In their youth most pad saddle riders used stirrups. Some Blackfoot pad saddles were equipped with a second pair of small tabs, located forward of the girth tabs, from which the stirrup straps were suspended. Many pad saddles had a rectangular, transverse piece of rawhide 4 inches or more in width across the center of the saddle and sewn to the skin base. This piece hung down at the sides far enough to conceal the girth tabs. In some cases holes

---

[48] A Piegan "sattel mit quill," collected by Maximilian in 1833, formerly in the Museum für Völkerkunde, Berlin (No. IV B 110) may have been of the pad-saddle type. Edward Harris, who accompanied Audubon to the Upper Missouri in 1843, collected a Blackfoot pad saddle, which is now in the Museum of the Alabama State Department of Archives and History, Montgomery, Ala. It is similar in pattern and decoration to the specimen collected by Captain Stansbury.

were made near the ends of these rawhide strips from which the stirrup straps were hung.

Fully rigged, with stirrups and girth, the pad saddle weighed less than 3 pounds. It was no heavier than a modern American racing saddle. The experienced Indian trader, W. T. Hamilton, claimed a horse could travel 20 miles farther in a day under a pad than under a frame saddle (Hamilton, 1905, p. 37). The pad saddle provided a light, elastic, soft seat. It was used primarily by active young men in buffalo hunting, fighting on horseback, horse racing, and general riding. Its specialized use in breaking broncos has been described (p. 64). Children, older men, and women rarely rode pad saddles, unless they did not have access to a frame saddle.

DISTRIBUTION OF THE PAD SADDLE

The pad saddle is an old type among the Blackfoot and their neighbors. In his tantalizingly brief description of "Archithinue" riding gear seen in 1754, Hendry stated, "They have . . . Buffalo skin pads, & stirrups of the same" (Hendry, 1907, p. 338). Presumably he referred to the pad saddle described above. Certainly Alexander Henry described the use of the pad saddle by the Blackfoot, Assiniboin, and Cree prior to 1809 (Henry and Thompson, 1897, vol. 2, pp. 526–527). The artists Paul Kane (1847) and Frederich Kurz (1852) pictured Blackfoot ponies bearing pad saddles (Bushnell, 1940, fig. 8; Kurz, 1937, pl. 22). Elderly Blackfoot said the pad saddle went out of use soon after they settled on reservations and obtained ample numbers of white men's stock saddles which were sturdier and were equipped with pommels needed for working cattle. Reuben Black Boy (born 1883) recalled having seen but one pad saddle in use among the Piegan. That was before the Agency was moved to Browning in the mid-90's.

West of the Blackfoot the pad saddle was ridden by younger men in buffalo days. Lewis and Clark saw young Lemhi Shoshoni men riding pad saddles without stirrups in 1805 (Coues, 1893, vol. 2, p. 562). In 1812, Ross Cox noted Nez Percé use of the pad saddle with stirrups (Cox, 1832, p. 84). Later writers reported the use of this saddle by the Klikatat, Yakima, Shuswap, Thompson, Couer d'Alene, Flathead, and Sanpoil (U. S. Comm. Ind. Affairs, 1854, p. 227; Teit, 1909, p. 534; 1930, pp. 110, 353; Ray, 1932, p. 117). Pierre Pichette told me the Flathead seldom used stirrups with the pad saddle. A variant of the pad saddle from the Klamath of Oregon is in the United States National Museum. This specimen (U. S. N. M. No. 24108) was collected in 1876.

The fur trader, Daniel Harmon, described the pad saddle of the Assiniboin, Atsina, Blackfoot, and Mandan and their neighbors in the first quarter of the 19th century, "On the back of the horse, they put a dressed buffalo skin, on the top of which they place a pad, from which are suspended stirrups, made of wood and covered with the skin of the testicles of the buffalo" (Harmon, 1903, p. 291). Kurz observed and illustrated Crow pad saddles in midcentury (Kurz, 1937, p. 260, pl. 9). Later writers described pad saddle use by Hidatsa and Mandan (Mathews, 1877, p. 19; Boller, 1868, p. 225; Wilson, 1924, p. 190), and Cheyenne (Grinnell, 1923, vol. 1, pp. 206, 208; vol. 2, p. 17). There are four Teton Dakota pad saddles in the collections of the United States National Museum. These collections also contain a pad saddle from the Yanktonai (No. 8415) collected in 1869, and one from the Sisseton (No. 9062) received that same year. Two Winnebago pad saddles have been illustrated (Radin, 1923, p. 29).

The pad saddle is well represented in the works of white artists who pictured the life of the Indians of the northern Plains in buffalo days. Probably the first published illustration of this saddle type was Peter Rindisbacher's "Sioux Warrior Charging," which appeared in the "American Turf Register and Sporting Magazine" for October 1829 (opp. p. 73). Sketchy renderings of pad saddles appear in several of George Catlin's tribally unidentified hunting scenes and in his painting of a grizzly bear hunt on horseback. Bodmer's lithograph of a buffalo hunt on horseback (1833) shows the pad saddle in use. Kurz drew a number of fine sketches of pad-saddled horses seen among the Upper Missouri tribes in 1851–52. Charles Wimar's original sketch books from the period of his trip up the Missouri and Yellowstone in 1858 (now in the City Art Museum, St. Louis) contain drawings of pad saddles. Study of the most detailed of these early illustrations and of museum specimens indicates that tribal differences in construction and decoration of the pad saddle among the Upper Missouri tribes were negligible.

I have seen a single pad saddle specimen from a southern Plains tribe. It was collected by Jarvis prior to September 1848, and was labeled "Comanche" in Jarvis' own hand (Acc. No. 1848, 67, New York Hist. Soc., now in the Brooklyn Museum). This specimen is identical with northern Plains pad saddles. Three Kiowa informants claimed men of their tribe did not use pad saddles in the late years of buffalo hunting. Tixier's description of the equipment of Osage buffalo hunters seen in 1840 mentions only the frame saddle (Tixier, 1940, p. 168). Nevertheless, fragmentary descriptions indicate that the pad saddle may have been in general use in that region in earlier times. Pénicaut described Caddo riding gear in 1714, "their stirrups are suspended by a cord . . . of hair which is fastened to doe skin doubled into four thicknesses and serving them as a saddle" (Swanton, 1942, p. 147). Apache warriors, in 1744, were said to have ridden with a "skin serving them for a saddle" (Whipple, 1856, p. 117).

These early references, in addition to those referring to the northern tribes, suggest that the pad saddle may have been virtually Plainswide in its distribution in the 18th century. As Wissler (1915, p. 36) has suggested, the pad saddle, of basically simple construction, may have been diffused over the Plains with the horse, while the more complex frame saddle passed northward at a slower rate. Although the origin of the pad saddle cannot be determined with certainty on the basis of data available, it is possible that it was derived from the Spanish-Mexican pack saddle. Pfefferkorn (1949, p. 95), who saw that saddle in use in Sonora in the middle 18th century, described it as two cushions of tanned cowhide, four-cornered and stuffed with hay, attached to one another in the middle. This may have been the prototype of the active young man's saddle of the Plains Indians.

PAD-SADDLE VARIANTS AMONG THE BLACKFOOT

Two variants of the pad saddle were described by aged Blackfoot informants. A very simple saddle was made from a single thickness of hide from a buffalo bull's neck. The hide was placed on the horse, hair side down, and held in place by straps pendent from each side, tied under the horse's belly. A rawhide cord, sewn together at the ends to make a continuous belt was suspended over the top of the pad so that the loop ends served as stirrups. Men returning from horse raids sometimes made saddles of this type if they had time and opportunity to kill buffalo en route. The saddle could be quickly fashioned from untanned buffalo hide. Its use was preferred to riding bareback for days over rough country. This type also served the poor or lazy fellow who could afford no better saddle.

The second variant of the pad saddle was composed of a pair of horizontal, cottonwood sideboards, like those used for frame saddles, joined by flexible skin pads stuffed with grass in front and back in lieu of pommel and cantle. This made a light saddle that could be folded easily and carried under the owner's arm when not in use. It was an uncommon saddle type.

THE "WOOD SADDLE"

The typical woman's saddle was a frame of cottonwood covered with rawhide, known to the Blackfoot as "wood saddle." The type is illustrated by a Blood Indian specimen in the Chicago Museum of Natural History, collected by R. N. Wilson prior to 1897 (cat. No. 51,752). Sideboards measure 19 inches long. The cantle rises to a height of 12.8 inches. (Pl. 2, b.) This type was described by Alexander Henry in 1809, as "made of wood well joined, and covered with raw buffalo hide, which in drying binds every part tight. This frame rises about ten inches before and behind; the tops are bent over horizontally and spread out, forming a flat piece about six inches in diameter." He believed this saddle type was older than the pad saddle (Henry and Thompson, 1897, vol. 2, p. 527). In 1833, Maximilian observed this saddle and noted that both pommel and cantle "frequently has a leather fringe hanging from it" (Maximilian, 1906, vol. 23, p. 107). Gustavus Sohon shows this type of saddle ridden by the two women in the left background of his field sketch, "The Bloods Come in Council," drawn in 1855. The men in the foreground appear to be riding pad saddles. (Pl. 4.)

In making a wood saddle a woman split a green cottonwood log and trimmed two pieces to equal size about one-half inch thick, 16 to

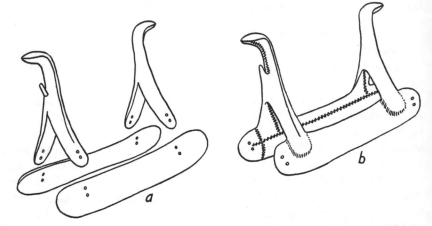

FIGURE 13.—Construction of a woman's "wood saddle," Blackfoot. a, Wooden pommel and cantle ready for assembly; b, rawhide-covered assembled saddle.

20 inches long, and 3 or 4 inches wide, for the sideboards. Three Calf said his mother bent the sideboards slightly by pressure over the shaft of a travois while the wood was still green. Two forks of green cottonwood were carefully selected for pommel and cantle. Care was taken that they should be approximately the same size and that both prongs of each fork should be of equal thickness. The top of each fork was bent and trimmed with a knife to a flat disk shape and the ends of the prongs were curved. A small hole was burned in the front of the piece to be used for the pommel just above the junction of the prongs and a straight wooden spike tightly fitted into the hole. With a redhot iron rod two pairs of holes were burned in the sideboards at both sides of each prong, the outer surfaces of the lower portions of the prongs were grooved, and were tied to the sideboards by buckskin thongs passed through the grooves and the sideboard holes.

The buffalo rawhide used for covering the frame was first soaked in a pond or stream for several days until it became green and foul smelling. It was then stretched on the ground, hair side up, boiling water was thrown upon it, and the hair was taken off with a rock. The woman then turned the hide over and scraped the flesh from the underside with a hide scraper. The hair side was not scraped, as that would have made the hide too thin. The hide was then stretched over the saddle frame, fitted, cut and finally sewn with rawhide cord. The stitches were placed on the inside of the saddle where they would not be seen when the saddle was in use. (Fig. 13.)

Care had to be taken that the saddle did not warp as the tough rawhide dried and shrunk. Two methods of preventing warping were described. Three Calf said his grandmother placed a newly sewn saddle over a log about the size of a horse's back and tied it down until the rawhide dried. Lazy Boy's mother rolled up an old lodge cover tightly and forced it between the side bars of the saddle, then she wrapped a cord around the saddle and cover to bind them securely until the rawhide saddle covering dried.[49]

After the saddle cover dried, two holes were burned near each end of both sideboards used for tying: (1) the grass-stuffed soft skin pads which ran parallel and underneath the sideboards and (2) the rawhide rigging straps fastened to the outside of the sideboards. A fully rigged saddle is shown in figure 14. The rigging straps on the left side of the saddle looped about the cinch ring, which was commonly of rawhide. The ring shown in figure 14 was considered a very strong one. It was made by coiling narrow rawhide cord, wrapping the coils with more rawhide cord, and covering the circle thus formed with a tubing of rawhide. Another type of ring was of two rawhide disks of the same size sewn together. It was not considered as strong as the first type. Informants regarded this as the most important link in the girthing. It had to be as strong as possible. Lazy Boy said that about the year 1860 (i. e. "when the first steamboat came to Fort Benton") the Piegan began to obtain metal girth rings from traders. A metal girth ring was expensive, being worth, at that time, a coyote or fox skin in trade. Only rich people could afford them. But the Blackfoot recognized their superior strength. Before the buffalo disappeared the metal rings declined in value and most Blackfoot women procured them for their saddles. About the time these metal girth

---

[49] George Catlin's illustration of a Crow lodge shows a saddle drying beside the lodge. The saddle is staked to the ground to hold it in shape (Catlin, 1841, vol. 1, pl. 20). Another Catlin illustration (reproduced in Wissler, 1915, fig. 1) shows this same drying method. A Kiowa informant said women of his tribe staked their frame saddles out to dry. However, Blackfoot informants, when told of that method, thought it would be a very good way to dry saddles, but said they had never heard of Blackfoot women making use of it.

rings were introduced smaller metal rings useful for hondas also began to be offered in trade.

The cinch was a band of rawhide about 4 inches wide. One end was doubled and tied around the girth ring on the left side of the saddle. The band passed under the horse's belly and was fastened to the rawhide or metal ring suspended from the rigging straps on the right side of the saddle. Several methods of fastening were

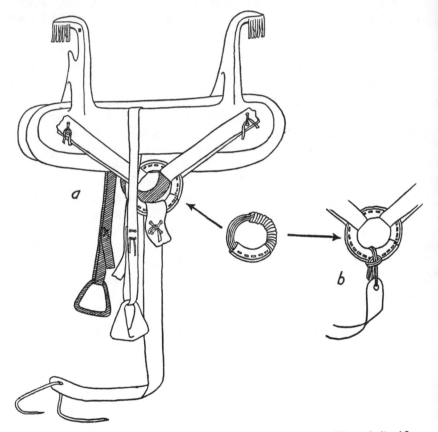

FIGURE 14.—Rigging of a woman's saddle, Blackfoot. *a*, View, left side; *b*, detail of latigo tie on right side.

employed. The simplest method was to punch a hole near the loose end of the girth, pass a rawhide latigo cord through it and tie the cord to the right-side ring. Some people preferred to fold the end of the girth and sew it to give the added strength of two thicknesses of rawhide at the point of strain. Another common method of securing the girth was to sew a rawhide or metal ring in the end of the girth band, and tie this ring to the right-side ring suspended from the rigging straps with a rawhide cord. Some people used a half hitch to make this tie, leaving the end tucked back so that it could be pulled out quickly in taking off the saddle. Horses always were saddled from the right side.[50]

A feature of the wood saddle that puzzled some informants was the spike in the front of the pommel. Double-Victory-Calf-Robe said this spike was "Crow style" taken over by the Blackfoot. She had heard that Blackfoot women's saddles of the early 19th century did not have this feature. Mrs. Cree Medicine claimed the spike served solely as a hook on which to hang the whip. Three Calf thought its main purpose was to indicate which end was the front of the saddle. Wissler has explained the use of the hook for the suspension of a rawhide seat which was attached at the back of the cantle by a wooden pin passed through a loop in the rawhide cover. He said "the hook has apparently become conventional, because it is found on saddles where the support is not used and the eye is wanting, though these are said to be degenerate forms" (Wissler, 1910, p. 94). Judging from the differences of opinion among my older informants regarding the function of the hook and the absence of any mention of the eye or seat, it would appear that the suspended seat was uncommon among the Blackfoot in the last two decades of buffalo days.[51]

Wood saddles were decorated with buckskin fringes pendent from the disks of both pommel and cantle, or with long, triangular beaded or quilled flaps suspended from the outer margins of these disks. Some women decorated their saddles by driving round-headed brass tacks into the pommel and cantle.

Blackfoot and Blood informants regarded the wood saddle as a woman's saddle. It was used on the travois, and sometimes on pack horses, as well as on riding horses. However, men did not ride the wood saddle, unless they had no pad or "prairie chicken snare" saddle.

DISTRIBUTION OF THE "WOOD SADDLE"

The distinguishing characteristics of the "wood saddle" are found in the pommel and cantle. They are of carved wood, and are of the same design, the cantle being the same form as the pommel in reverse. A characteristic of the Blackfoot "wood saddle," the large, flattened disk-shaped, horizontal projections of the pommel and cantle, is also found in the "wood saddles" of other northern Plains

---

[50] An examination of the Plains Indian saddles in the collections of the U. S. National Museum to which the rigging is attached shows that this was a widespread Plains Indian custom.

[51] With this feature in mind, I have examined the saddles in the collections of the U. S. National Museum known to have been made and collected before the buffalo disappeared. The majority of these Plains Indian saddles have neither suspended seats nor provisions for the pins in the backs of the cantles necessary for their use, although nearly all the wood saddles have hook projections on the pommels. Since Indian women generally placed a buffalo robe over their saddles before mounting, the need for a suspended rawhide seat seems questionable.

and Plateau tribes. Lewis and Clark's description of Lemhi Shoshoni women's saddles seen in 1805, mentioned the high pommels and cantles as "ending sometimes in a flat point extending outward" (Coues, 1893, vol. 2, p. 562). Miller's illustrations of Shoshoni women's saddles in the 1830's, show that characteristic. Gustavus Sohon pictured the "wood saddle" type in use among the Flathead in the 1850's (pl. 4). In the United States National Museum is a fine old example of this type marked "Columbia River" collected prior to 1867 (No. 2541). These collections also include examples of this type from the Ute (Nos. 11035 and 11036, collected by Powell in 1872), and Paiute in southern Utah (No. 14637, collected by Powell in 1874). The earliest dated specimen of this type I have seen from the Plains, is the Sioux saddle collected by Jarvis, probably in the period 1833–36. This saddle, termed a "pack saddle" in the collector's handwriting, is now in the Brooklyn Museum (Acc. No. 50–67–52) (see pl. 3, b). There are two Crow saddles of this type in the United States National Museum collected prior to 1870 (Nos. 6468 and 8521).

Women's saddles from the southern Plains tribes are of somewhat different design. Their pommels and cantles curve outward near the tops, which are concave in section. A Comanche saddle of that type was collected by Dr. E. Palmer in 1868 (U. S. N. M. No. 6916). Mooney obtained a number of saddles of this type from the Kiowa in 1891. I have also seen Cheyenne and Osage saddles of this type in museum collections. An elderly Kiowa Apache woman told me this was the traditional woman's saddle of her tribe.

This appears to have been a southern Plains variant of the wood saddle. It would appear proper to distinguish the Blackfoot type as a northwestern one in view of its distribution in the northern Plains and Plateau.

The origin of the "wood saddle" is difficult to determine. Wissler (1915, p. 33) has pointed out the difficulty of tracing Indian saddles to Mexican or Spanish prototypes because "while we have a fine series of specimens from the Indians we have very little of the kind from the period of Spanish colonization." Perhaps he should have added that we have no really early Plains Indian saddles either. The oldest dated "wood saddle" (the Sioux saddle, pl. 3, b) was collected in the 1830's, nearly two centuries after the Plains Indians began to obtain horses. By that time the Plains tribes had been subjected to French, English, and American influences, through the fur trade, as well as to influences from Mexico. It is significant also that Mexican saddlery changed after the period of the conquistadores. In fact Mexican historians have claimed that by the period of the second Viceroy of New Spain, Don Luis de Velasco (1550–64), the "silla mexicana," a saddle distinct from that introduced by Cortez, was already in use in Mexico

(Rangel, 1924, pp. 13 ff.; Villar, 1941, p. 278). Yet I have seen no specimen or illustration of a specimen of a well-documented Mexican frame saddle dating prior to the third decade of the 19th century. I have found no reference to a Mexican saddle exhibiting the distinctive characteristic of the Plains and Plateau Indian woman's saddle (i. e. pommel and cantle of like shape, reversed). Unless and until proof can be found that this general feature of Indian women's saddles was also characteristic of some of the saddles ridden by Mexicans, French, English, or Americans prior to 1800, I shall be of the opinion that the design of the Indian "wood saddle" was not copied directly from Whites, but was a remodeled adaptation of the white man's wooden frame saddle in the construction of which the Indians exercised considerable ingenuity.

THE "PRAIRIE CHICKEN SNARE SADDLE"

A frame saddle with low-arched horn pommel and cantle was known to the Blackfoot as a "prairie chicken snare saddle." The sideboards and girthing of this saddle were like those of the "wood saddle." It differed only in the material and form of the pommel and cantle. Plate 3, a, illustrates a "prairie chicken snare saddle" of Blackfoot origin from the collections of the Museum of the Plains Indian (Cat. No. 1871). The sideboards measure 19 inches long. The pommel is 8½ inches high, and cantle 8¼ inches.

In the manufacture of the "prairie chicken snare saddle" two sections of fresh-killed elk or black-tailed deer antler were softened in warm water to make them pliable. Then they were bent and cut to the desired shape. One piece served for the cantle, the other, of like size and shape, for the pommel. In tying the antlers to the sideboards some women burned holes through the antlers near their ends for the buckskin tie strings. Others grooved the antlers horizontally and passed the tie strings through these grooves and holes burned in the sideboards at the ends of the grooves (fig. 15). Mrs. Cree Medicine considered the second method the stronger one. The saddle was then covered with green rawhide and protected from warping while the rawhide dried and set by the same methods employed in the making of "wood saddles."

In my older informants' youth the "prairie chicken snare saddle" was the nearest approach to an all-purpose saddle known to the Blackfoot. Older men, children, and some women used it for a riding saddle. Young men preferred it to the pad saddle for riding on long journeys. It was used on the travois and as a pack saddle in moving camp. It was the favorite saddle employed in packing butchered buffalo. When used for packing, some people sewed V-shaped raw-

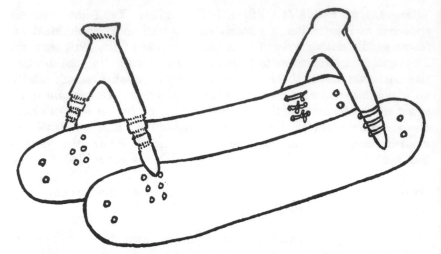

FIGURE 15.—Construction of a "prairie chicken snare saddle," Blackfoot.

hide flaps to the centers of pommel and cantle. Holes were punched in the flaps and, after the load was in place, a rawhide line was passed back and forth over the pack and through these holes and tied to hold the load securely and prevent its shifting. This saddle was never decorated. It could be made with less time and effort than either the pad or wood saddle. Thus it was less valuable. These factors undoubtedly encouraged its wide use.

DISTRIBUTION OF THE "PRAIRIE CHICKEN SNARE SADDLE"

There is every reason to believe that the "prairie chicken snare saddle" is not an old type among the Plains Indians. Alexander Henry made no mention of it in his description of Blackfoot saddles in 1809. Bradley, writing in the 1870's, was the first to mention the use of elkhorn in Blackfoot saddle construction. This saddle type does not appear in the works of artists who interpreted the Plains Indians from personal observations in the field prior to 1850. Kurz did not illustrate it in his many representations of saddles seen by him among the Upper Missouri tribes in 1851-52. In his description of the Cheyenne use of this saddle type, Grinnell (1923, vol. 1, p. 207) termed it a comparatively modern invention of the Kiowa, from whom the Cheyenne learned how to make it.

If we may credit this explanation of the origin of the "prairie chicken snare saddle," we must recognize that the type spread rapidly over the Plains and deep into the Plateau as far as the Sanpoil and Thompson (Ray, 1932, p. 118; Wissler, 1915, fig. 20). Its use by Coeur d'Alene, Plains Cree, and Teton Dakota has been reported

(Teit, 1930, p. 110; Mandelbaum, 1940, p. 196; Densmore, 1948, p. 204). The collections of the United States National Museum contain examples of this saddle type from the Crow, Northern and Southern Cheyenne, and Kiowa. Kiowa informants spoke of its use by that tribe both as a man's riding saddle and pack saddle. Pierre Pichette said the Flathead commonly used this type as a pack saddle.

Certainly the type differed markedly from the pack saddle with crossed wooden pommel and cantle commonly employed by American fur traders on the Plains and in the Rockies in the period 1837–51 (see Miller's sketch, pl. 85, Ross, 1951; Kurz, 1937, pl. 32).

STIRRUPS

All types of Blackfoot saddles were equipped with stirrups when used for riding. In 1809, Alexander Henry observed that the Blackfoot "stirrup attached to the frame by a leather thong, is a piece of bent wood, over which is stretched raw buffalo hide, making it firm and strong" (Henry and Thompson, 1897, vol. 2, p. 527). Informants said stirrups were made of green, flat strips of cottonwood or poplar that could be bent without heating. They were covered with wet buffalo rawhide or scrotum sewn with rawhide cord. Stirrup straps were of rawhide about 1 finger wide, looped over the side bars of frame saddles and through the centre openings in the stirrups. Generally these straps were simply tied at the ends to the desired length. The use of toggle or buckle fastenings was not common.

USE OF WHITE MEN'S SADDLES AND ACCESSORIES

Aged Blackfoot informants readily admitted that "white men's saddles" were stronger and better fitting than the ones the Indians made themselves. Apparently their ancestors held the same belief. We know the Piegan were familiar with Spanish saddles at least as early as 1787, when David Thompson saw a number of saddles a Piegan war party had brought back from a raid on a Spanish party far to the south (Thompson, 1916, p. 371). In 1856, Denig (1952, p. 148) reported "the Blackfoot and Crow Nations perceive at once the convenience and utility of European articles, especially portions of clothing, horse gears and other things . . . [they] will pay well for a good saddle." In 1858, the Blackfoot requested Agent Hatch for a few strong saddles, at least enough for their chiefs, to be included in their annuity goods received under the terms of their 1855 treaty with the United States (U. S. Comm. Ind. Affairs, 1858, p. 438). Lazy Boy said that some wealthy Piegan purchased saddles from Joe Kipp's trading post on the Marias before 1880. However, the majority of the members of the tribe continued to use native-made saddles until stock saddles were issued to them by the Government in the early Reservation Period.[52]

SADDLE BLANKETS

Blackfoot riders placed blankets of skin under all types of saddles to prevent their saddles from chafing the horses' backs. In 1809, Alexander Henry reported, "Under each kind of saddle are placed two or three folds of soft dressed buffalo skin, to keep the horse from getting a sore back" (Henry and Thompson, 1897, vol. 2, p. 527). In my informants' youth the Blackfoot preferred a saddle blanket made from the shoulders of a buffalo where the hair was long, or the breast where the hide was thickest. Most people used an undecorated hide with the hair on, rectangular in shape. The blanket was either doubled, hair side out, with the fold at the front of the saddle, or single thickness with the hair side next to the horse. Usually the blanket extended 2 or 3 inches beyond the saddle at front and back. Blankets placed under pack saddles were longer, in order to prevent the horse's back from being rubbed by any part of the load. The doubled blanket sometimes was ridden without a saddle. Some saddle blankets of single thickness were decorated with red-flannel edging all around, or a double edging comprising an outer border of red flannel about 3 fingers wide and an inner border of white cloth 1 finger wide.[53]

---

[52] Other Plains and Plateau tribes appear to have followed the practice of using Spanish or American saddles whenever they could procure them. Lewis and Clark found some Spanish saddles among the Lemhi Shoshoni in 1805 (Coues, 1893, vol. 2, pp. 520, 569). Jacques d'Eglise reported "saddles . . . in Mexican style" used by the Mandan in 1792 (Nasitir, 1927, p. 58). Scattered through the records of the American Fur Co. (papers in the N. Y. Historical Society) are listings of saddles bought by Pratte, Chouteau & Co. of St. Louis. Sufficient quantities are listed to indicate that the saddles were purchased for the Indian trade and not merely for the use of field employees of the company. Maximilian (1833) said that the Mandan "sometimes obtain saddles from the whites, which they line and ornament with red and blue cloth" (Maximilian, 1906, vol. 23, p. 345). These may have been of the California saddle type, which Marcy termed the favorite of the mountain men (Marcy, 1859, pp. 118–120), and which seems to have been pictured in a number of Kurz' drawings of fur traders and a few Indians of the Upper Missouri in 1851–52 (Kurz, 1937). One of the most interesting saddles in the collections of the U. S. National Museum is a U. S. Cavalry saddle reported to have been taken from Indians who had participated in the Custer Massacre, 2 weeks after that event. The Indians had stripped it of its commercial leather rigging and equipped it with Indian-made stirrup straps, stirrups, and cinch (Cat. No. 59,741). However, many Plains Indian saddles obtained in the field before the end of buffalo days have parts (rigging straps, stirrup straps, and/or girths) of commercial leather or cloth, in addition to metal girth rings, obtained from Whites. Some of the saddles bearing the earliest dates of collecton have the most commercial leather used in their rigging. It seems apparent that Indians tried to adopt as much of the white man's saddlery as they could afford. If they had not the means to obtain a trade saddle, perhaps they could at least acquire, strong, long wearing, trade materials for rigging their native saddles. In view of these circumstances it is impossible to date Indian saddles on the basis of the degree of acculturation shown by their rigging. Some of the specimens employing only native materials probably are of more recent manufacture than many specimens using trade materials in their construction.

[53] The Blackfoot did not make the fancy saddle cloth of soft skin or canvas with heavily beaded borders such as were used by the Teton Dakota, Crow, Cheyenne, Ute, and Shoshoni

SADDLE HOUSINGS

"When an Indian is going to mount he throws his buffalo robe over the saddle, and rides on it," wrote Alexander Henry of the Blackfoot in 1809 (Henry and Thompson, 1897, vol. 2, p. 526). This practice was continued until the end of buffalo days. A buffalo robe was folded and placed over the center of the "prairie chicken snare saddle" or the "wood saddle" before the rider mounted. By the time this thick padding was added to the wood saddle the lofty pommel and cantle did not appear so high. The buffalo robe seems to have been the most common housing for frame saddles among the Plains tribes. In recent years Blackfoot women riding the wood saddle or even the stock saddle in Fourth of July parades have thrown a large, trade blanket over the saddle and modestly tucked the pendent ends around their legs to conceal them.

In my informants' youth young men liked to drape a mountain-lion skin over their pad saddles as a housing. This showy skin was arranged so that the animal head fell over one side, the tail the other. Maximilian (1833) observed Blackfoot fondness for mountain-lion skin saddle housings. He noted that the skin was edged with a broad band of scarlet cloth, and that the Blackfoot valued it at a good horse or seldom less than $60. Bodmer's excellent lithograph of a Blackfoot man on horseback illustrates the use of the mountain-lion skin housing at that time (Maximilian, 1906, vol. 23, p. 107, and Atlas, pl. 19).[54]

MARTINGALES AND CRUPPERS

Martingales and cruppers had both practical and ostentatious value for the Blackfoot. They were used on the travois or pack horse to keep the load from slipping. Men generally used cruppers on riding horses only when traveling in mountainous country to hold the saddle in place. When moving camp or when on parade the favorite wives of wealthy men liked to dress up their horses with showy martingales and cruppers. The prevalence of elaborately decorated martingales and cruppers in the Fourth of July parade at Browning and at the Calgary Stampede in recent years is no indication of their com-

---

(Wissler, 1915, fig. 18, p. 17). However, I have found no description of the use of such cloths in the early accounts of those tribes. Those elaborately decorated cloths probably were late 19th century developments. The buffalo-skin saddle blanket seems to have been the most common type among the Plains tribes. However, the Plateau tribes, who had less access to buffalo, used saddle blankets of deer, bear, or mountain goat skin, or of woven matting (Teit, 1900, p. 258; 1909, p. 534; 1930, p. 111; Ray, 1932, p. 118; Turney-High, 1941, p. 72).

[54] Maximilian said the Crow followed the same custom (ibid., vol. 22, p. 349). Opler (1941, p. 396) was told that the Chiricahua Apache liked to drape a mountain-lion skin over the saddle bag to make it look nice, and that they followed Mexican example in this practice. Whether the Mexican custom goes back to the Colonial Period has not been determined.

monness in buffalo days. In former times those objects were indices of their owner's wealth and status.

Bodmer illustrated a fancy crupper on a Blackfoot man's horse in 1833 (Maximilian, 1906, Atlas, pl. 19). However, the earliest pictorial representation of the elaborately decorated martingale and crupper combination I have seen appears in Sohon's 1855 field sketch, "The Bloods Come in Council" (pl. 4). In size and shape the pieces portrayed by Bodmer and Sohon resemble specimens collected in more recent years. Bradley (1870's) stated that the Blackfoot woman's ornamental crupper had a fringe of horsehair to the lower ends of which little bells were attached. In my informants' youth cut buckskin fringes were also used. The ornamental crupper had a soft skin or trade flannel base. It was decorated with beadwork or (if of skin) in angular painted designs "something like a parfleche design." In more recent times (since ca. 1875) floral designs, combined with the double-curve have been employed commonly. Martingales were similarly ornamented (Wissler, 1915, fig. 15; Ewers, 1945 b, figs. 61–63).

Much more common in buffalo days were martingales and cruppers of narrow bands of rawhide, used on the riding horses of both sexes and on pack animals. The martingale was a rawhide band about 3 fingers wide, tied to the prongs of the pommel of the wood saddle by rawhide cords. The crupper was a single or double strip about the same width throughout most of its length, extended by means of a grass-padded loop, strengthened with soft skin binding, under the horse's tail. It was tied to the front or rear horn prongs of the frame saddle with buckskin cord (fig. 16). Some women painted the sur-

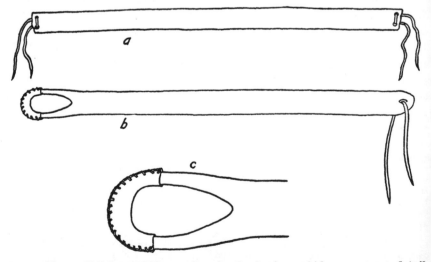

FIGURE 16.—*a*, Simple rawhide martingale; *b*, simple rawhide crupper; *c*, detail of crupper tail pad, Blackfoot.

faces of these rawhide martingales and cruppers in geometric designs. Weasel Tail said the first crupper he used as a young man (ca. 1875) was a white man's harness crupper obtained in trade.[55]

WHIPS

Maximilian (1833) observed, "In general every Blackfoot carries a whip as well as weapons in his hand" (Maximilian, 1906, vol. 23, p. 103). Bradley (1870's) wrote, "They were unacquainted with spurs, but used a whip consisting of a wood, bone or horn handle, some fifteen inches long, and a double lash of rawhide, from twenty to twenty-four inches long. A loop of skin was attached to the handle of the whip, by which it was suspended to the wrist" (Bradley, 1923, p. 263). These measurements agree closely with Wissler's measurements of Blackfoot handles and lashes on specimens collected a half century ago (Wissler, 1910, p. 96).

Informants pointed out that whips were kept in the possession of mounted Indians at all times. They might serve as weapons in a fight. Men also found their whips useful implements for beating their wives if they misbehaved.

Generally men and women made their own whips. Thoughtful makers permitted the leather of the wrist hanger to extend farther

---

[55] The elaborately beaded horse collar made by the Crow and some Plateau tribes in the late years of the 19th century (Douglas, 1937; Lowie, 1922 b, p. 314, fig. 12; Teit, 1930, p. 354, fig. 37) probably was a late development. Catlin's illustration of a Crow man mounted for participation in a sham battle at the Hidatsa villages in 1832, portrays a fancy martingale similar to the Blackfoot type. The same illustration shows an elaborate crupper, which the author described as "embossed and fringed with rows of beautiful shells and porcupine quills of various colors (Catlin, 1841, vol. 1, pl. 76, p. 192). Alfred Jacob Miller depicted a fancy crupper decorated with quills and beadwork in his illustration of a Sioux woman on horseback in 1837 (Ross, 1951, pl. 72). He portrayed elaborately fringed cruppers on women's horses in other illustrations of the same year (ibid., pls. 9, 96, 131, 188). In 1851, Kurz (1937) drew decorated cruppers on horses belonging to Potawatomi, Omaha, Iowa, and Crow. Hillers' 1873 photograph of a Uintah Ute woman on horseback shows an elaborate crupper and martingale similar to ones used by Blackfoot women (Steward, 1939, pl. 30). An Omaha decorated crupper of the period 1855, is illustrated in Fletcher and La Flesche, 1911, pl. 48. Mooney collected a painted and beaded skin crupper from the Kiowa (Cat. No. 152,829, U. S. N. M.). However, my Kiowa informants said the most common crupper in their tribe was of rawhide 2 inches wide.

Undoubtedly the greater attractiveness of decorated cruppers of elaborate design caused collectors to secure them in preference to the simple rawhide ones for museum collections. Fortunately, however, the series of Plains Indian saddles in the U. S. National Museum includes many cruppers that were attached to saddles obtained prior to 1880. The majority of these cruppers are of rawhide, painted or unpainted, much like the common form of Blackfoot crupper described above. A few are of commercial leather, including a Teton Dakota specimen obtained after the Slim Buttes Battle in 1876, which is obviously a white man's harness crupper complete with metal buckles (Cat. No. 276,607).

It seems unlikely that the use of martingales and cruppers was an Indian invention. The elaborate ones may be adaptations of Spanish-Mexican pieces such as the ones illustrated in the Codex Baranda (Wissler, 1915, p. 33). The more simple, rawhide ones may have been adapted from those in use among the fur traders in the Plains and Rockies in the second quarter of the 19th century. Miller's (1837) illustrations show the simple crupper in place on the horses of many fur traders as well as a few Indian-owned horses (Ross, 1951). Kurz (1937, pl. 32) shows the simple crupper on a trader's horse sketched August 28, 1951.

than necessary so that if the front of the handle cracked they could turn the whip around and use the hanger end for the lash until they had an opportunity to make a new whip. Women generally made whip handles of serviceberry. A hole was burned through the handle about 2 inches from the lash end, and shallow channels were cut in each side leading from this hole to the lash end of the handle. A narrow rawhide lash was pushed through the hole and passed through a longitudinal slit in the rawhide at the end of the handle. The two ends were then braided a few times. The remainder of the lashing hung loose. One or two inches from the other end of the handle another hole was burned through which the rawhide wrist hanger was passed.

Elkhorn-handled whips were made while the horn was green. The honeycomb center at the front end of the handle was burned out with a hot wire. A small hole was then burned at one side of the handle about 2 inches from the front. The rawhide lashing was then doubled and the folded end pushed into the front hole far enough so that a wooden or antler plug could be driven into the side hole to hold the rawhide in place. The wrist hanger was attached as was that of the wooden-handled whip. Some wooden-handled ones also used the plug method of lash attachment (fig. 17).

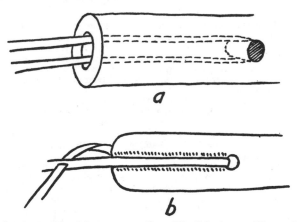

Figure 17.—Methods of whip construction, Blackfoot. *a*, Plug attachment of lash in an elkhorn-handled whip; *b*, channel attachment of lash in a wooden-handled whip.

These were the most common Blackfoot whip types. However, other forms were made occasionally. A unique specimen is the whip with a wooden handle carved in the form of a horse's head, in the collections of the Museum of the Plains Indian. This whip was used by the medicine women during the ritualized preliminary marches to the Sun Dance encampment. However, the whip employed in the

Horse Dance, the cult ceremony of the horse medicine men, was of conventional type (pl. 16, *B*, *e*).[56]

HORSE DECORATION

Some young men among the Blackfoot roached the manes or split the ears of their favorite mounts "just to make them look pretty." However, most horse decorations were of a more temporary character, employed on special occasions. These occasions were: (1) in the "riding big dance" preliminary to a raid for scalps, (2) in battle, (3) on return to camp from a successful horse raid, (4) on visiting other tribes, (5) in sham battles honoring visitors, and (6) in the ritual camp movements immediately preceding the establishment of the Sun Dance encampment in late summer.

In the 1870's, Bradley mentioned the main types of Blackfoot horse decoration. "On occasion of ceremony the horses were ornamented with dashes of paint on the face and body and with feathers fastened to the mane and tail and sometimes by a mask made of the head of the buffalo, the horns attached, the eyes of the horse appearing through the original eye holes of the skin" (Bradley, 1923, p. 263). The limited comparative data available is sufficient to show that none of these methods of ornamentation was peculiar to the Blackfoot.

HEAD ORNAMENTS

Among the valuable possessions of the second chief of the North Blackfoot, Old Sun, seen by Wilson in 1887, was—

a very elaborate headgear for a horse to wear when going into battle. One part of it covered the head like a mask, holes being left for the eyes, and was fitted with a pair of horns; the other part was a sort of banner, to be suspended to the

---

[56] The common Blackfoot types of elkhorn and wooden-handled whips were widely diffused in the Plains and Plateau. Maximilian (1833) mentioned both wood and elkhorn-handled whips in use among the Assiniboin. However, he claimed the Mandan whip handles were of wood only, and mentioned only elkhorn-handled whips among the Crow (Maximilian, 1906, vol. 22, pp. 349, 391; vol. 23, pp. 10, 345). However, Larocque, while traveling with the Crow in the summer of 1805, noted that they stopped on the Little Horn to procure whip handles. "There is plenty of ash here. There were few persons in the Camp that were not employed in making themselves horse whip handles with that wood; it was with that design that they came here, as that wood is seldom found elsewhere" (Larocque, 1910, p. 38). Omaha used both wood and "bone" whip handles (Dorsey, 1896, p. 280). Both types were employed by the Plateau tribes (Teit, 1930, pp. 111, 354. Kiowa informants spoke only of wooden-handled whips, cedar preferred, in use among their people. However I have seen elkhorn-handled whips collected from that tribe. A whip said to have been used by the Sac and Fox chief Keokuk, in 1832, is in the U. S. National Museum collections (No. 167, 149). The handle is of horn, the lash of rawhide. Were it not for its elaborately beaded wrist hanger, this specimen could be lost in Blackfoot collections.

Trade whips were furnished the Indians at an early date. In February 1835, Pratte, Chouteau & Co. of St. Louis ordered "4 dozen Riding whips for Indians, Showy, and not high priced" from the American Fur Co., in New York (American Fur Co. Pap., N. Y. Hist. Soc., Orders Inward, book 1, p. 59). However, the Mexican braided-horsehair quirt does not appear to have been common among the Plains Indians.

lower jaw; both parts were profusely decorated with red, yellow, and blue feathers. We were told that such a headdress as this was, in Indian estimation, worth a couple of horses. [Wilson, 1887, p. 190.]

In the eighties, Frederic Remington, the artist, saw "the equipment of a Blackfoot war pony, composed of a mask and bonnet gorgeous with red flannel, brass tack heads, silver plates and feathers . . . " (Remington, 1889, p. 340). Wissler (1913, p. 457, fig. 29) reproduced native drawings of masks employed in the "riding big dance" by the Piegan.[57]

I have seen a single example of Blackfoot horse headgear. It was a beautiful mask made of a single piece of skin entirely covered with porcupine-quill work, which fitted over the forehead and face of a horse. Holes were cut for the eyes. This specimen, which was probably not over 50 years old, was said to have been used by the Piegan in dress parades. It was owned by the late Mrs. John B. Monteith of Glacier Park Station, who showed it to me in 1942.

BODY PAINT

The Blackfoot favored red paint for decorating the bodies of their horses. Some young men daubed round spots on both hips of their horses solely for ornament. If a man ran over an enemy while riding in battle he was privileged to paint a hand on both shoulders of his war horse. Just before a returning horse-raiding party entered their home camp, its members stopped to paint red, horizontal lines across the foreheads of their stolen horses. Wissler (1913, p. 457, fig. 29) has described and reproduced native drawings of body painting on horses in the "riding big dance." [58]

MANE AND TAIL ORNAMENTS

A Blackfoot on the warpath braided the tail of his horse part way, tied the end of the tail in a knot, and fastened a feather in it with a buckskin cord. Weasel Tail claimed the three Blackfoot tribes, the Gros Ventres, and Sarsi all followed this practice so they could tell their horses from those of their enemies. In the summer of 1942,

---

[57] In 1806 Alexander Henry accompanied an Hidatsa trading party to a Cheyenne village. When they neared their destination some of the Cheyenne rode out to meet them on fine horses some of which "were masked in a very singular manner, to imitate the head of a buffalo, red deer, or cabbrie with horns, the mouth and nostrils—even the eyes—trimmed with red cloth. This ornamentation gave them a very fierce appearance (Henry and Thompson, 1897, vol. 1, p. 377). Whether the elaborate Blackfoot and Cheyenne horse headgear was in any way influenced by Spanish horse armor is problematical. Certainly the horned feature appears to have been a native invention.

[58] Lewis and Clark noted that among the Lemhi Shoshoni visited in 1805, "a favorite (horse) is frequently painted" (Coues, 1893, vol. 2, p. 563). Teit claimed Flathead "horses were often painted" (Teit 1930, p. 353). An Omaha man "frequently painted his horse to represent a valorous act . . . or in a manner intended as a representation of a vision" (Fletcher and La Flesche, 1911, pp. 352–353.)

I saw an elderly Piegan tie two feathers in the tail of the horse of a middle-aged man which was to be ridden in the Fourth of July parade at Browning. (This ornament is now in the Denver Art Museum, Cat. No. FB1–95–G.) The old man then said a short prayer that the horse might not fall or throw its rider. This also is said to have been an old Blackfoot custom.[59]

DECORATION OF WOMEN'S HORSES

A wealthy Blackfoot took pride in providing his favorite wife with fancy trappings for her riding horse, to be employed when visiting neighboring camps or other friendly tribes, and when moving to the Sun Dance encampment. These trappings, including decorated bridles, martingales, cruppers, saddlebags, and the finest painted rawhide containers obtainable, were thought to enhance the woman's appearance on horseback.

---

[59] Lewis and Clark (1805) noted Lemhi Shoshoni practice of decorating the manes and tails of their horses with feathers (Coues, 1893, vol. 2, p. 563.) The Crow claimed they tied up their horses' tails to make them run faster (Marquis, 1928, p. 114). Omaha young men occasionally "decked the manes and tails of their horses with bright ribbons or bands painted in gay colors" (Fletcher and La Flesche, 1911, p. 358).

THE TRAVOIS AND TRANSPORT GEAR

In addition to their riding gear, described in the previous section, the Blackfoot Indians employed a variety of specialized horse gear for transporting their lodges and other possessions. This equipment was ingeniously adapted to the needs of a nomadic people.

THE HORSE TRAVOIS

Blackfoot tradition claims that their ancestors employed the A-shaped dog travois before they acquired horses. The horse travois, therefore, appears to have been an adaptation of the earlier dog travois to use with a larger and stronger animal. Some informants claimed the Blackfoot originated the horse travois. This contention cannot be proved or disproved at this late date, but it is a possibility. The earliest apparent reference to the use of the horse travois refers to its employment by tribes of the northwestern Plains. On December 8, 1754, the fur trader Anthony Hendry noted that the men of his little trading party of Cree and Assiniboin were "employed making Sleds of Birch for the Women and Horses." Again on March 8, 1755, he stated "Men and Women repairing Snow Shoes and Sleds" (Hendry, 1907, pp. 343, 348). Although the devices drawn by the horses may actually have been sleds, it appears more probable that they were travois. I have found no later description of the Indian use of sleds with horses in this area. On the other hand, informants recalled that the Blackfoot used travois in winter in their youth. Certainly Maximilian's reference to "loaded dog sledges" seen among the Blackfoot in the summer of 1833, was a short description of the travois (Maximilian, 1906, vol. 23, pp. 104, 141). Apparently the French name "travois" did not come into general use among the Whites of the region until a later date. Earlier writers, at a loss for a short descriptive name, resorted to such misleading words as "sled" or "sledge."

The earliest illustration of a Blackfoot horse travois I have seen appears in Sohon's 1855 sketch (pl. 4). Charles Wimar's painting, "Indians Approaching Fort Benton," executed 4 years later portrays a distant view of a number of loaded horse travois (Rathbone, 1946, pl. 20). Photographs of Blackfoot horse travois appeared in Grinnell (1895, opp. p. 156) and Wissler (1910, pl. 8).

102

HORSE TRAVOIS CONSTRUCTION

Wissler (1910, pp. 88–91, fig. 56) has described and figured the Blackfoot dog travois, made with ladder or net type loading platform. Informants claimed the ladder-type platform was preferred for both dog and horse travois by the Blackfoot. They considered the netted platform a Cree type. The dog and horse travois differed primarily in size, apex construction, and the hitch.

Among the Blackfoot the horse travois was made and owned by women. If a man had several wives, all worked together in making travois. Generally each family made its own. However, the wealthy husband of a woman who was not skilled at this work would get her one in trade. He might give a horse for a travois. Poorer people would pay no more than 4 robes.

The travois was made entirely of wood and rawhide. Figure 18 illustrates the construction, and the travois in place on the horse's back. The shafts (a and a') were two stout poles of lodgepole pine. Generally they were obtained from the eastern slope of the Rockies or from the Bear Paw Mountains. They were generally about 4 to 5 inches in diameter at the base, a little larger than lodgepoles, although the Blackfoot referred to these shafts as "lodgepoles." Usually the shafts were made a little longer than necessary to allow for shortening through wear at the base. However, Weasel Tail said the travois would ride better if the distance forward of the tie (b) was relatively short. Shafts with long frontal projections (over 3 feet beyond the tie) had little spring. The tie (b) generally was made with a wet tendon from the back of the buffalo's neck wrapped with soft-tanned skin rope. The hitch was composed of a flat strip of rawhide (c) about 4 fingers wide. Each end of this strip was wrapped under and around one of the shafts, doubled back upon itself and sewn with rawhide cord. Through transverse slits in the center of this rawhide piece was passed a long rawhide line about 2 fingers wide (d). One end of this line was carefully and tightly wrapped around each shaft as far down as the bottom edge of the loading platform, where these lines were tied, leaving sufficient length of line to permit the ends to be used for tying the load on the platform. This rawhide line played an important role in the construction of the travois. Actually it carried the weight of the pull in transport and also kept the shafts from splitting. Three Calf pointed out that one could tell the maker's pride in craftsmanship by examining her pole wrapping line. If she had been careful to remove all the buffalo hair from the rawhide with a rock, if she had made the line in one continuous strip, and if she had cut it an even width throughout its length, she was a skilled craftsman. However, if she left bits of buffalo hair clinging to the surface, if she cut the line in uneven width, or if she had tied two or more lines to-

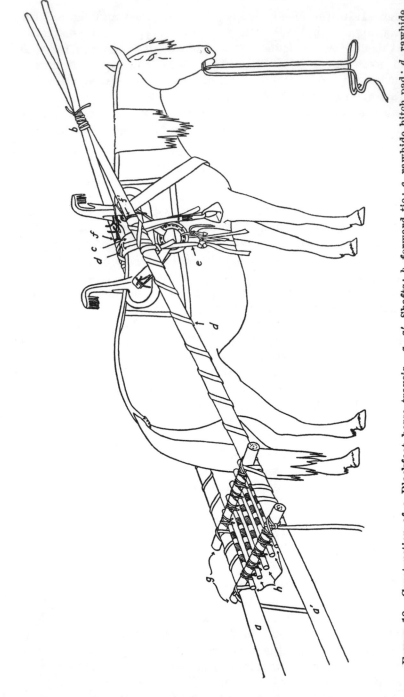

FIGURE 18.—Construction of a Blackfoot horse travois. *a*, *a'*, Shafts; *b*, forward tie; *c*, rawhide hitch pad; *d*, rawhide hitch and pole wrapping line; *e*, girth strap; *f*, *f'*, rawhide cord saddle ties; *g*, primary struts, loading platform; *h*, secondary struts, loading platform.

gether she was a lazy or incompetent worker. The Blackfoot referred
to the hitch as "my load." In addition to the rawhide pad and pole
wrapping line, the hitch included a cinch (e) of narrow rawhide rope
tied to one shaft, passed under the horse's belly and tied to the shaft
on the other side. This cinch was tight enough to hold the load but not
too tight to be uncomfortable to the horse. Two rawhide cords (f and
f') were wrapped around the shafts, forward of the hitch and tied
to the prongs of the saddle to complete the securing of the shafts.

The Blackfoot spoke of the loading platform as "my broad road."
It was composed of 2 transverse primary struts made of lodgepole
pine, spaced about 20 inches apart (g). These struts were notched
near each end, fitted over the shafts, and lashed in place with rawhide
line. Secondary struts (h) of birch or serviceberry were placed
about 5 inches apart at right angles to the primary struts. They were
lashed underneath the primary struts, by wet tendons from the neck of
a buffalo. These secondary struts in many cases were made of pieces
of wood in the bark, from which evenly spaced bands of bark were
peeled for decorative purposes. The front end of the loading platform generally was less than 2 feet from the horse's tail when the
travois was in place.

TRAVOIS ACCESSORIES

The basic travois described above weighed about 50 pounds. Sometimes a cage of bent willows was added to give protection to children,
the aged, or puppies carried on the loading platform on hot, sunny
days. These willows were arched and tied to the loading platform
at the ends and sides. The willow framework was covered with buffalo
robes to keep out the sun.

Either a "wood saddle" or "prairie chicken snare saddle" was used
on the travois horse. A martingale and crupper were employed to
hold the saddle in place. The former was a plain strip of rawhide 3
fingers wide, tied at each end to the pommel prongs. The crupper
was also most commonly of plain rawhide, 3 fingers wide, with padded
tailpiece. Its forward portion passed under the rear horn of the
saddle and tied to the prongs of the front horn (fig. 18).

TRAVOIS ADJUSTMENT AND REPAIR

Generally a travois lasted about a year in service over rough ground.
If conditions did not permit making a new travois the loading platform could be loosened and moved forward, or the worn butt ends
could be lengthened by taking two shorter pieces of pine or cottonwood, notching each in two places and lashing them to the underside
of the travois platform at the primary strut crossings. Each short
piece thus served as an extension to one of the old shafts. A make-

shift travois could be constructed of cottonwood poles if no lodgepole pine was handy. However, cottonwood generally was considered too easily split to make good travois shafts. It is noteworthy that the Blackfoot never developed any method of capping or binding the base ends of travois shafts to prevent wear and splintering.

CARE OF THE TRAVOIS IN CAMP

Horse travois, like dog travois, sometimes were piled together in conical piles, base ends down, to keep dogs from chewing at the leather parts. More commonly, each travois was propped at an angle, base end down, by a single long pole support. It could then be used as a stage for drying meat, or as a sun shelter covered with buffalo robes or skins, that could be turned with the daily movement of the sun. Beaver and medicine pipe bundle owners generally leaned their travois against the back of the lodge in order to hang their sacred bundles upon them during the day. The travois served women as a step-ladder in the erection and taking down of the lodge. A woman leaned it against the front of the lodge and climbed upon the loading plat-form to place or extract the topmost pins used to hold the lodge cover together.

SURVIVAL OF THE HORSE TRAVOIS

The Government began to issue wagons to the Montana Black-foot prior to 1893. In that year Agent Steele reported the issuance of 35 wagons, and added that about 300 were then in use by the In-dians of that reservation (U. S. Comm. Ind. Affairs, 1893, p. 172). In the following year Captain Cooke, the new agent, issued 150 wagons, believing that all heads of families were then provided with these vehicles. However, he stated that the wagons issued were not suitable for the service required of them (U. S. Comm. Ind. Affairs, 1894, p. 160). My informants recalled that those early Government issue wagons were narrow gage, with thin spokes like a buggy and of rather weak construction. They would not stand the hard treatment the Indians gave them. The inadequacy of these wagons, combined with poor roads, often muddy and deeply rutted, encouraged the retention of the travois until the 20th century. Wissler (1910, pp. 88–91) mentioned travois use in the first decade of this century for hauling wood. Joseph Sherburne recalled that the Indians brought travois to Browning to haul food and supplies from the traders' stores until 1902 or 1904. Ceremonial use by the medicine woman in the Piegan Sun Dance survived until at least 1909 (personal communication from the late Walter McClintock). In recent years horse travois have been made for display in the Fourth of July parade at Browning and have occasionally been employed for hauling wood in rough country where wagons could not be used. Reuben and Cecile

Black Boy made a horse travois for the permanent collections of the Museum of the Plains Indian in 1942.[60]

THE LODGEPOLE HITCH

A specialized gear, which I shall term the lodgepole hitch, was employed by the Blackfoot for transporting lodgepoles in moving camp. An equal number of poles was dragged at each side of the horse or

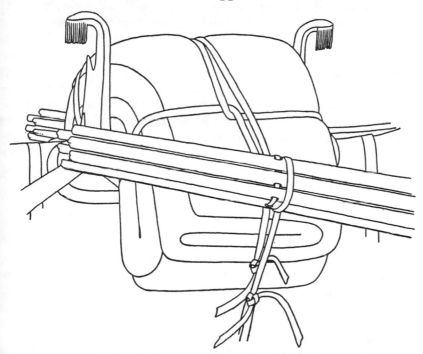

FIGURE 19.—The Blackfoot lodgepole hitch.

mule, the number varying with the size and weight of the poles employed in the owner's lodge and with the strength of the transport animal. A small hole about one-half inch in diameter was burned through each pole about 18 inches from its upper end with a hot iron rod. The poles to be dragged by each animal were laid on the ground in two piles. A rawhide line was then threaded through each group of poles. They were then lifted to the sides of the animal and the two rawhide lines were tied together over the center of the horse's back. In some instances the poles were further secured by a rawhide line connecting the two groups of poles and passing under the animal's belly (fig. 19). However, many women omitted this line, pre-

---

[60] The Blackfoot experience with Government issue wagons was paralleled on the Crow Reservation. Although they began to receive wagons as early as 1874, the Crow had little use for the light-weight, narrow-gage vehicles. They traded them to white men for more useful articles until the Indian Service forbade Whites to accept these ID-marked vehicles. Meanwhile the Crow continued to use "lodgepole transports" (Marquis, 1928, pp. 147, 126–127). Enoch Smoky claimed the Kiowa made little use of wagons before ca. 1890.

ferring to let the poles joggle with the movement of the horse as camp moved. Short Face said it was important that the holes bored in the poles should be of small diameter, as wear during transport enlarged them. If the owner made the holes too large the poles would crack at those points. At best, lodgepoles lasted but 1 year owing to wear of the butt ends trailed on the ground as well as the friction at the holes.

Poor people, who owned few horses and small lodges with short, light poles, sometimes tied their poles in two bundles to the loading platform of travois, one bundle at each side, secured by rawhide cords. An improvised travois was also easily constructed by tying two or more crosspieces, similar to the primary struts of the travois loading platform, to the bundles of poles dragged by a horse. These crosspieces were placed in the approximate position of the loading platform of the true travois. Buffalo robes and bedding generally were transported on this makeshift travois, but children, the aged, and miscellaneous camp equipment also could be carried upon it. Too heavy a load, however, would spring the poles and render them useless as foundation supports for lodge covers.

DISTRIBUTION OF THE TRAVOIS AND METHODS OF POLE TRANSPORT

It is well to consider these methods of transportation together in discussing the distribution of the travois, as the two have been confused in the literature, even in the writings of professional ethnologists. For example, Bushnell (1922, fig. 3, p. 66) reproduces an old woodcut portraying a Dakota horse dragging lodgepoles after the fashion described above for the Blackfoot. The caption under the illustration reads "Horse Travois."

In reality the true travois, which can be defined as an A-shaped drag, comprising two shafts, a loading platform which is an integral part of the whole structure, and a hitch for attachment of the travois to the horse, had a relatively limited use among many tribes of the Plains and Plateau. The improvised travois made by tying a temporary loading platform between dragging bundles of lodgepoles was more common. While the method of dragging lodgepoles in moving camp, erroneously labeled "travois" by Bushnell, was virtually universal among these tribes.

Undoubtedly all of the tribes of the Plains were familiar with the true travois. It seems to have been most widely used as a litter for transporting the sick and injured rather than as a means of carrying camp equipment. Blackfoot informants mentioned use of the travois in moving those handicapped persons. In the 1830's Ferris observed that the Flathead conveyed the wounded "on litters consisting of two lodgepoles fastened on either side of a packhorse with skins stretched on cross bars so as to form a bed for each of the sufferers" (Ferris, 1940, p. 334). In 1854, W. B. Parker (1856, p. 193) saw a Southern Comanche chief, crippled with rheumatism and disease of the spine, transported in the same manner. The Wind River Shoshoni and Crow used the travois for transporting wounded (Lowie, 1922 a, p. 220, 1924 b, p. 249). A photograph, believed to have been taken before 1900, illustrates the Crow method of transporting an injured man on a travois (pl. 5, *b*). This specialized use of the travois penetrated northwestward as far as the Sanpoil of northeastern Oregon (Ray, 1932, p. 117).

The use of the true travois for transporting household goods in moving camp seems to have had a more limited distribution. Because of lack of detail in most early descriptions it is difficult to trace this distribution with certainty. The travois was little used by the Plateau tribes. Teit (1930, p. 112) reported that the travois was well known to the Coeur d'Alene but they did not use it, deeming packing better adapted to rough mountainous country than hauling. He said the Flathead seldom used the travois even when hunting on the Plains for prolonged periods (ibid., p. 354). Turney-High (1937, p. 105) and my Flathead informant, Pierre Pichette, claimed that tribe never used the travois. Spinden said it was unknown to the Nez Percé (Spinden, 1908, p. 224). Wind River Shoshoni, according to Lowie (1924 b, p. 249) rarely used the travois. Colonel Brackett's brief mention of Washakie's band seen by him on the move, June 15, 1869, "dragging their property with them on lodge poles which are strapped to the saddles of their ponies in a manner peculiar to themselves" may refer to the improvised rather than the true travois (Brackett, 1917, p. 338).

Crow use of the travois for moving camp equipment has been vigorously denied by both Lowie (1922 a, p. 220) and Curtis (1909, vol. 4, p. 21). That they did use a makeshift "drag" of lodgepoles "on which they place their furniture" was observed by the trader Zenas Leonard (1904, p. 258) who spent 6 months among the Crow in 1834–35. Le Forge, who lived with the Crow in the 1870's, used the word "travois" in describing the Crow vehicle familiar to him (Marquis, 1928, pp. 127, 147). The Crow case must remain questionable.

Judging from modern examples of the Sarsi travois seen by the writer in the parade preceding the Calgary Stampede in 1941, that tribe's travois was like that of the Blackfoot. The Plains Cree horse travois varied in details of construction. Although the shafts crossed at the front and were tied together with thongs and sinew, and the loading platform had primary struts of transverse "sticks," leather thongs took the place of secondary wooden struts. A rawhide line around the horse's belly tied to the shafts served as a hitch (Mandelbaum, 1940, p. 197). Henry (1897, vol. 2, p. 518) in 1808, called the Assiniboin horse travois like their dog travois, which he said had a netted hoop loading platform.

Haupt's drawing of a Dakota horse travois (reproduced in Winchell, 1911, p. 434) shows the shafts crossed and tied, a loading platform of five primary struts only, while the hitch is made simply by wrapping and tying the shafts to the base of the saddle pommel with skin cord. There is no shaft wrapping such as was typical of the Blackfoot hitch. A photograph of a Teton travois in the Bureau of American Ethnology (neg. No. 3, 711–K) portrays long shafts and a platform of the netted hoop type, similar to that of the Blackfoot dog travois illustrated in Wissler (1910, fig. 56a). Another Teton photograph in the same collections (neg. No. 3, 169–6–13) shows still another variant. The shafts are short and do not cross. The platform is like the one in Haupt's drawing. Seth Eastman's painting, "Sioux Breaking Camp," in the Boston Museum of Fine Arts, shows an Eastern Dakota horse travois which combines short shafts with a netted hoop-type platform. These examples show a considerable range of variation in the details of Dakota horse travois construction. There are brief contemporary descriptions of Teton Dakota horse travois used in buffalo days (Stansbury, 1852, p. 46; Boller, 1868, p. 30; Prince Paul in Butscher, 1942, p. 209.)

Probably the best comparative description of a horse travois is that of the Hidatsa by Wilson (1924, pp. 275–276, figs. 98–101). This is a much simpler contrivance than that of the Blackfoot. The shafts are short, extending only 8 inches forward of the hitch, which is simply a rawhide line wrapped around one shaft, carried over the animal's back and tied to the other shaft. The platform is an oval hoop. This type of travois is also credited to the Mandan (ibid., p. 283).

Kroeber mentioned but did not describe the Arapaho horse travois (Kroeber, 1902–7, pp. 23–24). Journalist Evans of Colonel Dodge's expedition of 1835, observed that the Arapaho travois was made "by tying their lodge poles together, one on each side of a horse with cross pieces" (Evans, 1927, p. 210). A photograph entitled "Arapaho Ration Issue 1870" (Bureau of American Ethnology neg. No. 49–b) shows a number of true travois with platforms of the netted hoop type. In the Smithsonian Institution Anthropology Archives there is an excellent old photograph of a Cheyenne true travois which shows short shafts and netted hoop platform. This type of travois appears in the native Cheyenne drawing, plate 5, a.

My Kiowa informants explained that the Kiowa made relatively little use of the travois for carrying camp equipment. The shafts were short and did not cross in front. They were made of cottonwood or cedar. The platform was composed of primary struts only laid transversely of the shafts and parallel to one another. The hitch was two rawhide cords. Each was passed through a hole burned in a shaft, similar to the holes burned in Blackfoot lodgepoles, and tied to the saddle pommel.

Positive information on the occurrence of the true travois among other Plains tribes is lacking. The scattered data mentioned above, however, are sufficient to show clearly that this vehicle was not standardized throughout the area. Variants in shafts, hitch, and loading platform occurred. Even among related Dakota tribes several variants were present. The simplest construction involved the use of a few primary struts for a loading platform and a hitch achieved by tying the shafts to the prongs of the saddle pommel. The Blackfoot type gives the impression of being the strongest and most carefully planned travois. Its hitch and loading platform were relatively complex. Its use apparently was shared by the Sarsi. Curiously enough a photograph of a Gros Ventres horse travois, taken by Dan Dutro on Milk River in 1890 (in Montana Historical Society Library) resembles the Hidatsa type in its short shafts and netted hoop platform, although its pole wrappings suggest the use of the Blackfoot type hitch. In the light of the wider distribution of the simpler variants of the travois the Blackfoot type appears to have been a specialized one, presumably of later development. It is possible that the Blackfoot themselves may have used a simpler form of travois prior to the middle of the 19th century.

The simplest form of true travois seems to have been only slightly more specialized as a transport vehicle than the improvised travois composed of a temporary platform tied between bundles of lodgepoles on which children and/or camp equipment were carried. Catlin's painting of a Teton Dakota camp on the move, executed in 1832, shows the improvised type in use (U. S. N. M. No. 386460). It also appears in his painting of a Comanche camp on the move, done 2 years later (U. S. N. M. No. 386447). Lieutenant Albert apparently saw the improvised travois with a "basket" fixed between the lodgepoles in use by an Apache camp seen near Fort Bent in the summer of 1845 (Abert, 1846, p. 10). In the next year Garrard observed Southern Cheyenne moving camp near Fort Bent. A "tray shaped basket or hoop, latticed with hide thongs" was tied between the two bundles of trailing lodgepoles for carrying children and household articles (Garrard, 1927, p. 52). Although Skinner (1926, p. 280) claimed the Iowa had the travois, his description of their vehicle as a means of moving "tipis bundled on their own poles" suggests that it was of the improvised variety. Wilson (1924, p. 197) described the use of the improvised travois among the Hidatsa and pointed out the danger of springing the lodgepoles if too heavy loads were carried on them. These data indicate that the improvised travois probably had a wider distribution than the true travois, and that a number of tribes used both, just as the Blackfoot did.

The dome-shaped, willow frame, sunshade placed on the platform of either the true or improvised travois had a wide distribution. It is shown in the illustrations of Cheyenne and Dakota travois previously mentioned. It was mentioned in Parker's description of the litter employed in transporting the Comanche chief. Maximilian, in 1833, saw these "semi-globular, transparent wickerpanniers" in use among the Yankton Dakota (Maximilian, 1906, vol. 22, p. 309). Stansbury saw this "Light wicker canopy" on Teton Dakota travois in 1849 (Stansbury, 1852, p. 46). Kiowa informants said women of their tribe made these frames of dogwood. Apparently this accessory was almost as widely used as was the improvised travois.

The practice of dragging lodgepoles, divided into equal bundles suspended at the sides of a horse or mule, their butt ends dragging on the ground, appears to have been universal among tipi-using tribes of the Plains. My limited field data suggest that even the hitch was similar to that of the Blackfoot. Both Oglala and Kiowa informants stated that their tribes burned holes near the small ends of the poles, through which they were strung with rawhide lines. The Hidatsa used a red-hot iron about the size of a lead pencil to burn the holes about 2 feet from the ends of the poles (Wilson, 1924, pp. 193, 278–279, figs. 35, 105, 108).[61]

PRINCIPAL ITEMS OF LUGGAGE CARRIED BY PACK ANIMALS

THE PARFLECHE

The parfleche was much used as a container for carrying possessions on packhorses. This folded envelope of tough, long-wearing, waterproof rawhide was capable of considerable expansion when packed. Its construction and decoration by the Blackfoot have been described in detail (Wissler, 1910, pp. 79–82; Ewers, 1945 b, pp. 16–18). Its general form and method of folding is shown in figure 20.

Although some parfleches were carried on the travois when camp was moved they were most commonly transported in matched pairs, one each side of a packhorse. Hence they were generally made in

---

[61] A number of early illustrations have been published showing horses or mules dragging lodgepoles in this general manner. (See Bushnell, 1922, fig. 3, for Teton; Ross, 1951, pl. 66 for Pawnee, and pl. 128 for Shoshoni; and Whipple, 1856, p. 21, for Kiowa.) An old stereopticon view in the files of the Division of Ethnology, U. S. National Museum, depicts Omaha use of this method. The picture is corroborated by the description in Fletcher and La Flesche (1911, p. 275). Curtis (1909, vol. 4, p. 226) described this method of transport as used by the Cheyenne. Pierre Pichette said the Flathead moved their lodgepoles in this manner while on prolonged winter hunts east of the Rockies.

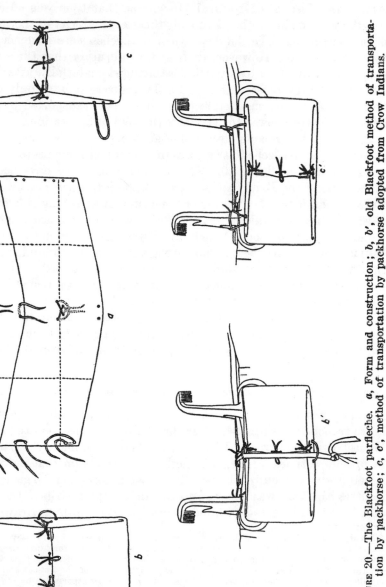

FIGURE 20.—The Blackfoot parfleche. *a*, Form and construction; *b*, *b'*, old Blackfoot method of transportation by packhorse; *c*, *c'*, method of transportation by packhorse adopted from Crow Indians.

pairs, identical in size and decoration. Wissler (1910, p. 81) found that the average size of Blackfoot parfleches in the collections of the American Museum of Natural History at that time was 60 cm. in length by 38 cm. in width. Probably the great majority of those specimens were made since the days when parfleches were in general use in moving camp. However, there is no indication that the sizes or proportions of Blackfoot parfleches changed materially after these Indians settled on reservations. Parfleches were painted only on the flaps, the only portions visible when they were transported by packhorse. Thus use served to determine the field of decoration.

Blackfoot informants declared that there were two methods of attaching the parfleche to the horse in use among their people. They are illustrated in figure 20. The method claimed to have been the oldest among the Blackfoot is shown at the left (b, b'). Two holes were burned with a hot iron near the center of each long side of each parfleche, through which short cords of rawhide were passed and tied. A band of rawhide about 1 inch broad was passed around the horse's belly outside the parfleches and through these loops to bind the cases tight to the sides of the animal. Then the topmost cord loops of the two parfleches were tied together to prevent the cases from slipping. The other method was one that Weasel Tail said was adopted from the Crow, although he could not give the time of its adoption. In this method two sets of holes were burned in one long side of the parfleche, longer rawhide cords were passed through them an ʻ over the horn of the saddle (fig. 20, c, c').[62]

ANTIQUITY OF THE PARFLECHE

It appears probable that the parfleche, so admirably adapted to horse transport, originated after the Plains Indians acquired horses. Weasel Tail was sure the Blackfoot tribes did not make the parfleche in pre-horse times. His grandmother had told him that before the Blood Indians acquired horses they used a container termed "Gros Ventres bag." It was made of a soft-tanned buffaloskin in the shape of a shallow globe (when filled), closed at the top by a drawstring,

---

[62] The photograph in pl. 5, b, definitely shows the use of this second method by the Crow. Maggie No Fat told me this was the Oglala method, and Kiowa informants described its use by that tribe also, although they said a rawhide rope was commonly passed around the barrel of the horse also to confine the cases to the sides of the animal and prevent joggling. Granville Stuart's general statement on parfleche transportation by the Indians of Montana in 1865, mentions, "Two loops of small cord are fastened on each side near the ends, which are used to hang over the forks of the packsaddle, a rope is then passed around and lashed tight, which binds the parfleches firmly and enables the horse to carry them easily" (Stuart, 1865, p. 78). The Flathead, Coeur d'Alene, and Okanagon are reported to have used the method of parfleche suspension by loops over the saddle horns (Teit, 1930, pp. 112, 221, 352). In 1819, the Omaha transported their dried meat in "quadrangular packages, each of a suitable size to attach conveniently to one side of the packsaddle of a horse" (James, 1823, vol. 1, p. 212). This appears to be the earliest reference to the use of parfleches as luggage by any Plains Indian tribe.

and carried on the platform of the dog travois. He said his mother still owned a Gros Ventres bag when he was a boy. She used it for transporting pemmican on the travois.

Wilson obtained a description and a native drawing of a large buffaloskin bag of similar shape, although the top was folded over and tied rather than closed by a drawstring. In the youth of his informants the Hidatsa used this bag for transporting ripe corn on the ear and dried squash. It was also carried on the dog travois platform as a general packing case (Wilson, 1924, fig. 95, pp. 272, 283–284). The Plains Cree, who never adopted the parfleche, used both rawhide bags with flap covers and soft skin drawstring bags, "averaging perhaps two feet wide and one foot deep" (Mandelbaum, 1940, p. 213). These two Cree types are suggestive of the early Blackfoot and the Hidatsa ones previously described. Possibly the drawstring one is a survival among the conservative Plains Cree from pre-horse days.

To the west of the Blackfoot, the Flathead claimed "a sack to be folded and laced was in use before the advent of the horse for carrying purposes" and that the parfleche "came into vogue with the introduction of the horse" (Teit, 1930, p. 354). Both Okanagon and Coeur d'Alene had traditions to the effect that their respective tribes did not use the parfleche until after the acquisition of horses (ibid., pp. 50, 221). The Wind River Shoshoni had a similar tradition (Lowie, 1924 b, p. 309).

This evidence from several tribes regarding the absence of the parfleche in the northern Plains and Plateau in pre-horse times is bolstered by the lack of any detailed descriptions of this very useful and handy container in 18th-century accounts of the Plains Indians. Frederic H. Douglas has kindly shown me a colored drawing of an original parfleche in the Musée de l'Homme, Paris, dated ante-1789. This specimen is slightly larger than most 19th century parfleches in Museum collections (75 cm. × 38 cm.), but falls well within the extremes represented in those collections. Its construction and painted decoration is like that of later parfleches. It is not tribally identified. This specimen demonstrates that this type of rawhide container was made in the Plains before 1790. However, it is probable that the parfleche, considered by Wissler (1938, p. 222) to be one of the material traits typical of Plains Indian culture, was not widely used in the Plains before 1800. The earliest illustration of the parfleche I have seen is Bodmer's accurate rendering in Maximilian's Atlas, pl. 81 (1906). In later years the use of the parfleche spread far into the northwest even to tribes that did not make them but secured them in trade. Spier (1925, p. 96) and Douglas (1942, pp. 107–108) have listed its breadth of tribal distribution at its greatest extent.

Weasel Tail also argued the relative lateness of the parfleche among the Blackfoot on technological grounds. He claimed it would have been an arduous task to cut and trim large areas of tough rawhide with the stone knives used by the Indians prior to trade contacts with Europeans. It is probable that the metal knife stimulated the invention of the parfleche and/or encouraged its wide use. The maker of the early parfleche in the Musée de l'Homme undoubtedly was acquainted with both metal knives and horses.

In Maximilian's time (1833) the Blackfoot were making and using "many kinds of painted parchment bags, some of them in semicircular form, with leather strings and fringes" (Maximilian, 1906, vol. 23, p. 104, and illus. p. 105). By that time the Blackfoot had been using metal knives for more than a half century.

THE DOUBLE-BAG

Wissler collected and briefly described a buffalohide container composed of two deep pockets connected by a broad hide band, known to the Blackfoot as a "double-bag." He found this type was "once in general use" by women as "a general carrying bag" (Wissler, 1910, p. 74). This specimen (No. 50/5381, Amer. Mus. Nat. History) is shown in plate 9, *b*. Each pouch is 14 inches deep and 9 inches wide at the bottom.

Elderly Blackfoot informants described this type of bag to me as a container used in transporting foods and domestic articles on a pack horse. Such a bag was often made from the bottom of an old buffalo cowskin lodge cover. It was placed over the top of a pack animal's load, one pocket suspended on each side of the horse. In the pockets were placed one large or two small buffalo calfskins filled with berries. The calfskins (complete except for the heads) were closed at the necks by skin cords (fig. 21). The bag also was a handy container for transporting miscellaneous articles such as lunches to be eaten en route, and tin plates, and iron frying pans which were in rather common use among the Blackfoot in the late years of their nomadic existence.[63]

Like such other once common articles as the digging stick and the native-made wooden bowl this double-bag has become exceedingly rare. I have seen no specimen other than the one collected by Wissler. Since it was in general use among the Blackfoot and Hidatsa I should

---

[63] Wilson's aged Hidatsa informant described the use of this type of bag by that tribe in transporting shelled corn. The Hidatsa also termed this container "double-bag." It was about 15 inches wide at the bottoms of the pockets, tapering to the tops (Wilson, 1924, p. 273, fig. 96). In his next paragraph Wilson describes in detail the manufacture of the buffalo calfskin bag used by the Hidatsa for transporting corn. Although it is in every respect like the Blackfoot berry bag, Wilson makes no mention of Hidatsa carrying this bag in the pockets of the double-bag.

suspect that it had a wider distribution in the northern Plains. I described the double-bag to Kiowa informants. They were entirely unfamiliar with it.

In view of the limited data available on the double-bag it is impossible to determine either its origin or antiquity. It may have been an Indian invention, or it may have been adapted from saddlebags employed by trappers and traders in the Indian Country.

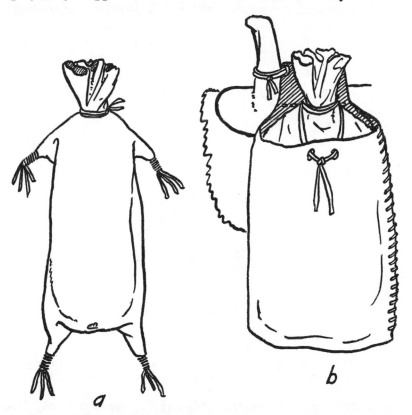

FIGURE 21.—a, Buffalo calfskin berry bag; b, berry bag transported in the pocket of a double-bag on saddle of a packhorse, Blackfoot.

PRINCIPAL ITEMS OF LUGGAGE TRANSPORTED BY RIDING HORSES

The Blackfoot commonly used three types of luggage in carrying articles on riding horses. Generally these were placed on the horse ridden by a woman of the household when camp was moved. Items carried in these containers are listed on pages 136–137.

THE DOUBLE SADDLEBAG

The double saddlebag (illustrated in Wissler, 1910, p. 95, and Ewers, 1945 b, p. 57) was made from a rectangular piece of soft dressed skin about 60 inches long by 24 inches wide. This piece was doubled on the long dimension and the edges sewn together. A longitudinal slit, cut in the center of its length, served as the opening of the bag. Long, cut fringes (15 inches or more in length) were sewn to the ends of the bag. According to the Blackfoot ideal these fringes should be long enough to fall below the horse's belly when the bag is in place across the horse's back. In earlier times, probably before 1870, these bags were decorated with panels of painted or quilled de-

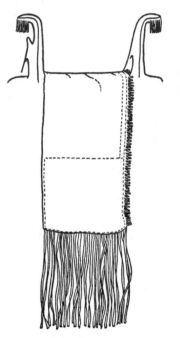

FIGURE 22.—Double saddlebag thrown over a woman's saddle for transportation, Blackfoot.

signs in rectangular areas the width of the pendent sides. Specimens of more recent manufacture have these panels in beadwork over a background of red or black flannel.

Double saddlebags were transported in either of two ways. Most commonly they seem to have been thrown over the center of the woman's saddle, hanging an equal distance at each side (fig. 22). The rider threw a buffalo robe over the bag then mounted on top of it. Thus the distance between the pommel and cantle of the woman's saddle determined the proper width of the saddlebag (about 12 inches). Less commonly the saddlebag was placed over the cantle of the saddle through the slit opening at the center of the bag. A little over half its width then rested on the horse's back behind the saddle. The Blackfoot considered the double saddlebag a woman's piece of luggage. Men did not carry these bags on their horses.[64]

RECTANGULAR RAWHIDE SADDLEBAGS

Single saddlebags of rawhide were commonly transported on women's horses. The rectangular bag was made from a single piece of rawhide, folded at the bottom and laced together along the sides. It was closed by a flap at the top. The side exposed to view (when the case was hung over a saddle horn, by a skin cord passed through two holes burned in the back a short distance below the top flap) generally was painted in geometric design. Some of these cases had long, cut-skin fringes pendent from the side seams. The construction and decoration of this type of bag is described and illustrated by Wissler (1910, pp. 76–78) and Ewers (1945 b, p. 18).[65] (See fig. 23, b.)

CYLINDRICAL RAWHIDE SADDLEBAGS

The cylindrical container is made of three pieces of rawhide. The largest piece was rolled into a tube and the overlapping long edges laced together. The other two pieces were rawhide disks which served as covers for the tube, one tied over each end of the tube by buckskin cords. Many cylindrical cases of this type have long, cut-skin fringes pendent from the long side seam. (See illus. in Wissler, 1910, pp. 78–79, and Ewers, 1945 b, p. 18). This tubular case was suspended from the saddle horn in traveling. Two holes were burned in the tube at a point opposite the seam, and a skin cord was passed through them and over the saddle horn. Painted, geometric designs were used in the decoration of this case. As this type of case was used primarily for carrying ceremonial objects it was less common than the rectangular form [66] (fig. 23, a).

If the rawhide parfleche was a post-metal-knife development among the Plains tribes, as has been suggested (p. 116), it is probable that

---

[64] This type of container is well represented in Museum collections from the northern Plains. Some specimens from the Teton Dakota are exquisitely beaded. Teit (1930, pp. 111, 354) recorded its use by the Couer d'Alene and Flathead. The double saddlebags of the Apache are distinguished by the use of cut-leather decoration. However, Kiowa informants said that tribe did not make this type of bag in their youth, although they obtained some of them in trade from other tribes. The fur trader, Charles Larpenteur, implied that the form of this saddlebag was copied from the Whites, although it was in common use among the Upper Missouri tribes in his time (i. e. ante-1850) (Larpenteur, 1898, p. 67).

[65] Wissler (1910, pp. 77–78) has recorded the occurrence of this type of bag among the Sarsi, Gros Ventres, Kutenai, Yakima, Nez Percé, Arapaho, Dakota, and Thompson. Teit has described and illustrated them from the Flathead and Coeur d'Alene (Teit, 1930, pp. 111, 354).

[66] Similar cases were employed by other Plains and Plateau tribes. Wissler (1910, p. 79) reports them from such widely separated tribes as the Nez Percé, Ute, Assiniboin, and Comanche. Kiowa informants told me members of that tribe formerly used the cylindrical rawhide case for storing and transporting feather bonnets exclusively.

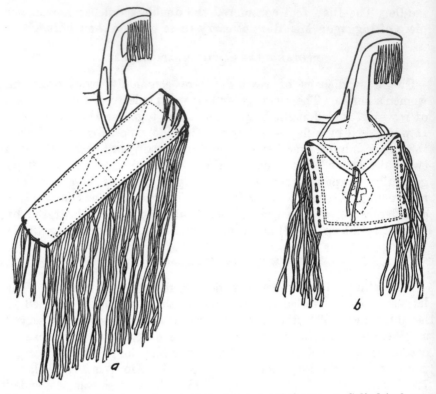

FIGURE 23.—Rawhide cases transported on a woman's horse. *a*, Cylindrical case with rawhide strap hanger; *b*, fringed, rectangular case with rawhide strap hanger.

these rawhide saddlebags were also. It is likely, therefore, that their form, and especially their decoration were adapted to the conditions of horse transportation. Certainly the long cut fringes, which present such a handsome picture blowing in the wind or trailing by the side of the riding horse would have been an impractical nuisance if placed on a dog or carried on the low-slung dog travois. Even in the late years of their nomadic existence it was the wealthly families among the Blackfoot who owned the most elaborately decorated luggage. The saddlebags and rawhide cases carried on the riding horses of favorite wives were thought to dress up the horse and make the women look well on horseback.

THE HORSE IN CAMP MOVEMENTS

Many factors other than the possession of horses conditioned Blackfoot nomadism in historic times. These factors were geographic, climatic, and bionomic as well as cultural. Before considering in detail the functions of horses in camp movements let us survey briefly the influence of these other factors on the Blackfoot yearly round.

THE BLACKFOOT COUNTRY

At its largest extent, prior to the first Blackfoot treaty with the United States Government in 1855, the territory of the three Blackfoot tribes extended from the North Saskatchewan River in Canada southward to the present Yellowstone National Park. The Rocky Mountains formed its western boundary. The mouth of Milk River, some 300 miles eastward, marked its easternmost limit. (See map, fig. 24.)

Within this area lie the headwaters of both the Missouri and the Saskatchewan Rivers, comprising numerous swift-flowing streams. From the base of the Rockies the land slopes toward the east, dropping from an elevation of 4,366 feet at present Browning, near the mountains, to about 2,150 feet at the mouth of Milk River. Isolated uplifts east of the Rockies (the Sweetgrass Hills, Cypress Hills, Bearpaw Mountains, Little Rocky Mountains, Little Belt Mountains, and Big Belt Mountains) served as landmarks to the Indians and furnished timber, found elsewhere only in the stream valleys and on the slopes of the Rockies. Near the mountains the surface is more broken than Plains-like, yet there, as farther east, rich grasses afford excellent grazing for buffalo and horses.

Wild life abounded in this region. Great herds of buffalo blackened the Plains. Antelope, deer, elk, bighorn, bear (both black and grizzly), beaver, otter, mink, muskrat, wolves, foxes, badgers, weasels, and rabbits offered a variety of animal foods and materials for use in Indian handicrafts. Recently Schaeffer (1950, pp. 37–46) listed some 80 bird species (in some cases families) recognized by the Blackfoot as residents of their territory, including several species of game birds. Although fish were abundant in the streams and lakes, they were rarely eaten by the Blackfoot. Edible plant foods of primary importance to the Indians were the spring roots of the prairie turnip, bitterroot and camass, and the fall berries of the chokecherry, buf-

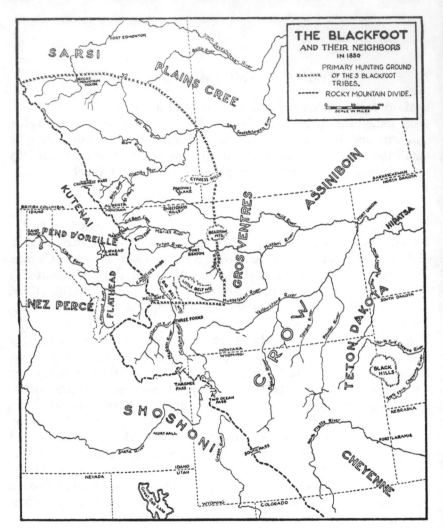

FIGURE 24.—Map showing the Blackfoot and their neighbors in 1850.

faloberry (bullberry), and sarvisberry. Of these plants only bitterroot and camass (found near the mountains) were not characteristic
of a much wider area of the northern Plains.

While these rich natural resources favored a hunting and collecting economy, climatic factors discouraged agricultural pursuits.
Throughout most of the Blackfoot country the growing season was
too short and too dry to make corn cultivation practical under aboriginal conditions. Summers in the area are short with cool nights.
Winters are long, cold, and frequently severe, during which rapid
changes in temperature of as much as 50 degrees, strong winds, heavy

snows and blinding blizzards occur. Temperatures of 20 to 40 degrees below zero are not uncommon in severe winters.

The known movement of the Blackfoot in early historic times was southwestward from the vicinity of the Eagle Hills in present Saskatchewan toward the Rockies and the valley of the Missouri. Pressure from Cree and Assiniboin moving westward in their rear and the attraction of fine buffalo hunting grounds to the southwest probably were important factors influencing this late 18th and early 19th century movement. However, it should be noted that the Blackfoot also moved in the direction of their best sources of horses and *away* from the white men's trading posts on the Saskatchewan. It is probable that establishment of American trading posts on the Missouri near the mouth of the Marias in 1831 and subsequent years tended to encourage most of the Piegan and many Blood Indian bands to range south of the international line. Prior to 1831, Blackfoot war parties traveled far south of the Missouri, but it is doubtful whether their hunting camps often crossed that river before then.

In the mid-19th century and earlier the friendly Sarsi and Gros Ventres occupied part of the country claimed by the Blackfoot in the far north and east, while hostile tribes disputed their right to hunt in portions of their claim. The Cree and Assiniboin impinged on Blackfoot territory in the northeast, the Crow in the southeast. Several trans-Rockies tribes pressed their right to hunt buffalo on lands claimed by the Blackfoot east of the mountains, and especially south of the Missouri. The rights of these western Indians were recognized by the Government in the Blackfoot Treaty of 1855, which set aside the southern portion of the Blackfoot claim, south of the Musselshell River, as a common hunting ground for the western tribes and the Blackfoot, in which none of the tribes might establish permanent villages. That treaty also recognized the right of the Assiniboin to hunt in the easternmost portion of the Blackfoot claim west of the mouth of Milk River. Thus the movements of Blackfoot hunting bands were much more restricted than the boundaries of their claim. It was rare for any Piegan, Blood, or North Blackfoot band to hunt east of the Bearpaw Mountains, south of the Musselshell River, or north of the Red Deer River. I have indicated the common hunting territory of the Blackfoot tribes on the map (fig. 24). This was the region within which the three Blackfoot tribes actually made their living in the mid-19th century.

THE BLACKFOOT YEARLY ROUND

The annual movements of the Blackfoot tribes may be considered in terms of four seasons of unequal length: (1) the season of the winter camp, (2) the spring hunting and root-gathering season, (3) the summer hunting and Sun-Dance season, and (4) the fall hunting and berry-collecting season.

THE WINTER CAMP

A century ago (1853) Gov. Isaac I. Stevens wrote of the Blackfoot: "It is the custom of the several bands of this tribe to locate in sheltered and otherwise eligible places, in the vicinity of wood, water, and grass, in the early winter, where they remain as inert as possible until the melting of the snow" (Stevens, 1860, vol. 12, p. 102). This course was dictated by the treacherous and frequently severe winter weather of the region in which they lived. For a Blackfoot camp to have remained on the open plains in winter would have been suicidal. Informants stated that the separate bands generally moved into winter camp in late October or early November, well in advance of the period of intense cold and heavy snows which usually did not set in until near the end of December. Winter camps were established in broad, timbered river valleys offering shelter from winds and snows. Important requisites for a winter camp site were an adequate supply of firewood and of cottonwood for feeding horses, a good water supply for humans and horses, and sufficient wild grass for horse pasturage. In later buffalo days the nearness of temporary or small trading posts also proved a factor in winter campsite selections.

When the band arrived at the site chosen for winter camp they usually pitched their lodges in the open for a few weeks. As the weather grew colder, around the end of November or early December, the chief gave orders to move the lodges in among the thick timber of the valley. With axes and knives men and women cut out the underbrush and sufficient timber to permit their placement of lodges among the trees, leaving enough timber surrounding the group of lodges to serve as a windbreak and snow fence. Some of the brush cleared away was piled around the bases of the lodges to give additional weather protection. The remainder of the brush and felled trees was used for firewood. The lodges were not alined in a camp circle but were huddled rather closely together in no particular order.

Usually each band remained in the selected locality all winter, or as long as there remained sufficient wood for fuel and grass within easy access of the horses. Exhaustion of either supply, or absence of game in the neighborhood for an extended period, would necessitate camp movement. However, a short journey of less than a day's march might bring them to a new site possessing adequate resources for another winter camp. Green Grass Bull said that bands whose members owned large horse herds had to move camp several times each winter. Informants stressed the fact that fuel and grass needs made it imperative that the bands of each Blackfoot tribe winter separately.

Demands on these resources were too great to allow all the members of a tribe to winter in one large village.

The bands wintered in different localities in different years. The winter count of Elk Horn, a Piegan (reproduced in Wissler, 1911, pp. 45–46), lists the winter camps of his band for 12 successive years beginning ca. 1849. During that period these camps ranged from the Sweetgrass Hills, near the International Boundary, to "south of the Missouri," yet more than half of the winters were spent on the Marias. The valley of the Marias was a favorite winter camp ground for Piegan bands from ca. 1848 to 1880. In 1848 the American Fur Co. established winter trading posts, occupied from October to March, for the convenience of the Blackfoot on both the Marias and Milk Rivers. They were occupied annually until 1856 (Bradley, 1900, p. 258). In 1853 Governor Stevens mentioned these posts and added, "the winter homes of the Blackfeet, some six to seven thousand strong are on the Teton, the Marias, and Milk Rivers (Stevens, 1860, vol. 12, p. 239). The trader W. T. Hamilton found the camp of the Piegan head chief, Little Dog, on the Marias in October 1858 (Hamilton, 1900, p. 58). In the late seventies James Kipp and James Willard Schultz operated Fort Conrad near the present Great Northern Railway bridge over the Marias. At that time some Blood and even North Blackfoot bands, as well as the Piegan, wintered on that river (Schultz, 1907, pp. 60, 105). Schultz wrote that "the Marias was a favorite stream with the Blackfeet for their winter encampments, for its wide and by no means deep valley was well timbered. In the shelter of the cottonwood grove the lodges were protected from the occasional north blizzards, there was an ample supply of fuel, and there was fine grass for the horses. There were also great numbers of deer, elk, and mountain sheep in the valley and its breaks" (ibid., p. 37). My elderly Piegan informants recalled the Marias valley as a favorite winter location. They said the several bands were spread out, at distances of several miles apart, from near the junction of Cut Bank and Two Medicine Creeks forming the Marias to the big bend of the Marias.

The vicinity known to the Indians as Willow Rounds, located some 5 miles down the Marias from the junction of Cut Bank and Two Medicine Creeks, is portrayed in plate 7. The Willow Rounds locality was nearly ideal as a winter campsite. There the valley floor is broad, affording several square miles of grassland for horses. The river banks are still well timbered with cottonwoods, as they were in buffalo days. The steep embankment on the north side of the valley rises more than 100 feet, shutting off cold north winds, while Abbott Coulee to the southwest affords a gentle ascent to the grassy plains beyond. This area was occupied by Piegan winter camps during the third quarter of the 19th century. It also was the site of a winter trading post operated by Baker and Bro. of Fort Benton, licensed Indian traders in 1868–69 (Bradley, 1923, pp. 346–347).[67]

Bradley, on the basis of information furnished by Alexander Culbertson, stated that in earlier times (ca. 1833) the Piegan wintered on Sun and Teton Rivers and sometimes as far south as the Three Forks of the Missouri. At that time the Blood Indians wintered on the Marias or on Belly River, and the North Blackfoot on Belly and Bow Rivers (Bradley, MSS., Mont. Hist. Soc., book A, p. 179). There is no indication that the Piegan wintered as far south as the Three Forks after 1850.

When geese were seen flying north the Blackfoot knew it was time to leave their winter camps. Beaver bundle owners kept a sort of calendar on notched sticks, one notch representing each day, by means of which they could predict the day on which geese would be sighted in the spring. When the river ice broke up, and before leaving winter camp, the beaver ceremony was held. The approach of spring also was determined by the band chief through observation of the development of embryos taken from buffalo cows killed by hunters. When he noted that the unborn calves began to develop hair he knew spring was near and calves would soon drop. Breakup of the winter camp usually occurred in late March or early April, depending upon the severity of the winter. Thus the nomadic Blackfoot spent at least 5 months of the year in relatively fixed residences.

SPRING HUNTING AND COLLECTING SEASON

March was remembered by elderly Indians as a difficult month during which the buffalo began to drift eastward and northeastward away from the Indians' winter villages. The bands would be forced to subsist on smaller game or go hungry unless they packed and moved after the buffalo. Each band went its separate way in pursuit of buffalo. Buffalo calves generally were born in the period between the end of winter and the annual May storm. Numerous calves were killed for children's robes and soft skin bags. The medicine pipe ceremony, held on the occasion of the first thunder in spring, generally was observed in April or May. It was also the season for making willow back rests, construction and repair of riding gear, and fashioning of warm-weather clothing. During this season the

---

[67] In October, 1859, Snowden's detached party of Raynolds' Expedition saw a locality on the South Fork of Cheyenne River, S. Dak., in the Teton Dakota country which was much used by Indians for winter camps because of its natural advantages: "A bottom enclosed and protected by hills, filled with large cottonwood, and young groves that would furnish sustenance to almost any number of horses; good grass covers the bottom and neighboring hills" (Raynolds, 1868, pp. 158–159).

horses, thinned and weakened by winter, fattened on the spring grasses. Toward the end of spring women and children dug prairie turnips and sometimes bitterroot and camass with fire-hardened, birch digging sticks. These roots provided a welcome change in diet after a winter of eating meat and dried foods.

This spring season, during which the separate bands hunted and collected plant foods, may be regarded as a transitional period of relatively short duration between the breakup of the long winter camps and the formation of the tribal summer encampment. Generally it lasted little more than 2 months, during which frequent moves were made. In bionomic terms it may be characterized as the period between the drift of buffalo eastward from the winter camps shortly before the birth of calves in spring and the time when buffalo bulls became prime in June.

SUMMER HUNTING AND SUN DANCE SEASON

Informants claimed the longest time the Blackfoot tribes remained in one place, except for the period of the winter camps, was during the period the scattered bands assembled for the tribal summer hunt. During the spring season a woman who had vowed to give the Sun Dance that summer told the chief of her band of her vow. He dispatched a messenger with pipe and tobacco and the message to the chief of another band of his tribe. That chief notified another band chief in the same way, and the process continued until all of the scattered bands received the word. The first invitation usually was sent out when the berries were in blossom in late spring. Generally the bands began to assemble to form the great tribal camp circle around early June. The bands had been scattered over a wide area. Some Piegan bands, for example, may have traveled north or east of the Sweetgrass Hills, some bands to the lower Marias or south of the Missouri, while others may have been westward on Sun River or near the mountains digging camass and/or bitterroot. It required several weeks for all of the bands to come together at the appointed place and take their assigned places in the tribal camp circle.

When all the bands had come in, the organized tribal summer hunt began, under the leadership of the tribal head chief and strictly regulated by society police. This hunt provided hides for the construction of new lodge covers, meat, and especially tongues needed by the medicine woman for use in the Sun Dance ceremony. Only bull tongues were collected for this purpose and as many as 300 tongues might be required. After the tongues were received they were prepared and dried by the medicine woman's female helpers. Then the head chief sent two experienced warriors to search for a site for the

Sun Dance encampment. The neighborhood of the Sweetgrass Hills was a favorite site for the Piegan Sun Dance in late buffalo days, but it was often held at other locations within their range.

When the site was selected, usually at no great distance from where camp was located at the time of selection, the whole camp made four moves on 4 successive days. On the fourth day the site of the Sun Dance encampment was reached. These daily moves were in the nature of dress parades. The Indians wore their finest clothes, decorated their horses with their best trappings, and the men rode with their weapons and shields exposed to view. The medicine woman who had vowed the ceremony rode a travois horse. She was careful not to hang anything on the saddle in front of her. The natoas bundle was carried behind her. The sacred tongues were packed on her travois and on top of them was placed a fringed, rawhide bag holding her ceremonial paints, badger skins, and pipe. The three sticks used later to support her ceremonial bonnet (a part of the bundle) were tied alongside one of the travois shafts.

The Sun Dance was timed to coincide with the ripening of the sarvisberries, or dogfootberries farther east. This was in the month of August. The first sarvisberries were served to dancers in the Sun Dance lodge. Sun Dance ceremonies consumed 8 to 10 days, at the end of which the camp circle was dissolved and the bands separated for the fall hunt.

This summer season usually occupied 2 or 3 months from some time in June to about the beginning of September. It was the only season of the year in which the bands of the tribe camped in one village in the form of a circle of lodges. (See pl. 8.) At other seasons the separate bands did not use the camp circle arrangement of lodges.

FALL HUNTING AND COLLECTING SEASON

In the fall, buffalo cows, whose meat was much preferred to that of bulls, were prime. This was the great buffalo hunting season, when large numbers of animals were killed and quantities of meat were obtained, and when berries were collected and mixed with meat and tallow to make pemmican. Each family endeavored to put up as much dried meat, berries, and pemmican as their winter needs or their means of transportation would permit. It was an active season, during which the number of camp moves was determined largely by the available supply of meat. Obviously camp could not be moved while women were busy drying meat and berries, and making pemmican. During a successful fall hunt stops of a week or longer in one locality were not uncommon. On the other hand, if a band failed to come upon buffalo in sizable herds, more frequent moves were necessary. Generally, the more successful the hunting, the fewer camp movements were required during the fall season. Although the fall hunting season may be considered as ending with the establishment of the winter camp, the Blackfoot continued to hunt buffalo and prepare meat for eating in the severe winter months during the months of November and December or until heavy snows and bitter cold restricted this activity. In the years prior to about 1850 they employed drives over cliffs or into pounds constructed in the vicinity of the winter camp in this early winter hunting.

This summary of the Blackfoot yearly round suggests that the Blackfoot were less "nomadic" than a literal interpretation of that word would imply. Blackfoot nomadism varied with the seasons and was conditioned by the food supply, the weather, and the Sun Dance ceremony. Some five months were spent in winter quarters. Nearly a month was required for assembly of the tribal encampment in early summer during which the bands that arrived early remained in one locality for several weeks (if the food supply permitted). Eight or ten days were spent in the Sun Dance encampment in late summer. The Blackfoot were most "nomadic" in spring, mid-summer, and fall.[68]

MOVEMENT OF A BLACKFOOT BAND CAMP

PREPARATION FOR MOVEMENT

Preparations for movement of a Blockfoot band camp were similar but on a smaller scale and less complicated than those undertaken for the movement of an entire tribe during the summer hunting season preceding the tribal Sun Dance. In the latter case the band chiefs met the night before the camp was to be moved and reached a decision as to the direction and destination of the next day's journey. The head chief called the leaders of four men's societies and delegated to each of them responsibilities for guarding the camp en route. Members of one society were told to scout ahead of the main body, those of a second society were instructed to guard it on the left, those of a third society were told to guard it on the right, and those of the fourth society were asked to remain in camp until all of the others had moved off and to bring up the rear as rear guards. The decision of the head chief, reached after consultation with the band chiefs, was announced to the people of the large camp by the chief's herald on the night before the

---

[68] Jenness' description of the Sarsi yearly round during "the early nineteenth century" divides the year into 5 seasons, although the rhythm of relatively active and passive nomadism appears very like that of the Blackfoot (Jenness, 1938, pp. 11–12).

move was to be made so that everyone would be in readiness to make an early start the next morning.[69]

In planning the movement of a Blackfoot band, the band chief consulted other prominent men of the band before announcing the move. He called upon certain individuals in the band to act as scouts, side, and rear guards.

Among the Blackfoot the medicine pipe owner played an important role in camp movement. In dismantling his lodge on the morning of the move he placed his bundle at some distance from it if the move was to be a long one; he left it standing on its tripod near the lodge if the move was to be a short one. He took pains to point his pipe in the direction the camp was to go. Before he set out, the medicine pipe owner made a smudge and prayed for the safe journey of the camp, that no accident would befall any member and that no enemies would be encountered en route. The medicine pipe man led the main body when camp moved.[70]

PACKING UP

Experience made the Blackfoot efficient in packing their belongings quickly on the morning camp was to move. Except for the lodge and bedding most items were packed ready for transportation before the morning of the move. They needed only to be tied in their proper places on horses or travois. This greatly expedited last-minute preparations. J. M. Stanley (1855, p. 448), who accompanied Low Horn's Piegan village of 90 lodges on its move southward to Fort Benton in the fall of 1853, wrote that "in less than an hour the whole camp was under way".[71]

As among other Plains Indian tribes Blackfoot packing of lodges and furnishings was women's work. In a household of several wives the husband's favorite wife served as job foreman, supervising the work of the other wives, the aged women, and grown girls of the

---

[69] Larocque's description of movements of the entire Crow camp in the summer of 1805, reveals that Crow custom was similar to that described by living Blackfoot informants, at that early date. He observed that the principal chief consulted the other chiefs before deciding upon a move, then issued the order. That chief's lodge was the first to be taken down on the morning of the move (Larocque, 1910). Tixier (1940, p. 179) noted that heralds announced breaking of camp the night before the Osage hunting camp made a move during the summer of 1940. As early as 1776, the elder Henry (1809, p. 310) observed the Assiniboin chief's practice of notifying the camp of the next day's march in advance. My Kiowa informants stated that in that tribe the principal chief's decision was made known to tribal members through his announcer the night before camp movement, and that this chief led the procession when camp was under way.

[70] Perhaps the Mandan and Hidatsa had a very similar custom. Alexander Henry (1897, vol. 1, p. 369), who accompanied these tribes on a visit to the Cheyenne in 1806, observed that Le Borgne's "grand pipe of ceremony" was carried at the head of the procession. Boller (1868, p. 277) noted that Poor Wolf "carried the pipe" and led the line of march when the Mandan-Hidatsa moved camp ca. 1860.

[71] Denig (1953, p. 86) credited the Crow with being able to pack and start on the march in "less than 20 minutes."

household engaged in the task. Each family was responsible for its own belongings. Every article had its assigned place and means of transportation.

PACKING THE LODGE

The lodge was the bulkiest, heaviest, and most complex possession transported by the Blackfoot in moving camp. A century ago Denig (1930, p. 578) wrote that among the Upper Missouri tribes the size of the lodge was determined "by the number of persons to be accommodated or their means of transporting it." Two decades later Bradley (1923, p. 258) stated that Blackfoot lodge size varied according to the size "desired or the wealth of the occupants." Informants claimed the latter factor was of primary importance, for the larger the lodge the greater were the number of skins required for construction of its cover and the number, length, and basal thickness of the lodge poles necessary for its foundation. Consequently the larger the lodge, the greater the number of horses required to transport it.

Before the skin cover was replaced by the canvas one during the period 1870–85, Blackfoot lodges were sized according to the number of buffalo cowskins employed in the construction of the cover. The smallest lodge had 6 skins, the largest about 40 skins. Alexander Culbertson (in 1848) saw a lodge of 40 skins owned by the Blood chief, Seen-from-Afar, a wealthy owner of 100 horses and husband of 10 wives (Bradley, 1900, p. 258). None of my informants claimed to have seen a lodge larger than 30 skins. Weasel Tail said the average Blackfoot lodge numbered 12 to 14 skins, figures also cited by Wissler (1910, p. 100). A lodge of that size was 14 to 16 feet in diameter at the base and provided sleeping accommodations for a family of 8, with their baggage.

Informants said that skin lodges had less lodgepoles in proportion to their size than the more recent canvas lodges. Weasel Tail said 19 poles were used for support of a 14-skin lodge (4 main poles, 5 secondary ones on each side, 2 near the door, 1 at the center of the back, and 2 ear-support poles). Modern Blackfoot who set up canvas-covered lodges in their Sun Dance encampments take pride in the length of their lodgepoles. In many lodges the poles extend 4 or more feet above the crossing. They criticize shorter poles, saying they look "like a crop-eared horse." However, in buffalo days only the wealthy could afford the extravagance of poles much longer than were needed to support their covers.[72]

Wealthy families among the Blackfoot made new lodges every summer, before the Sun Dance encampment. Cowskins collected during

---

[72] Palliser (1863, p. 138) observed that Blackfoot lodges generally were larger and better furnished than those of the Cree, a tribe poor in horses. On the other hand, the horse-wealthy Crow tribe was renowned for having the finest lodges among the Upper Missouri tribes in buffalo days (Catlin, 1841, vol. 1, pp. 43–44; Lowie, 1922 a, pp. 222–223).

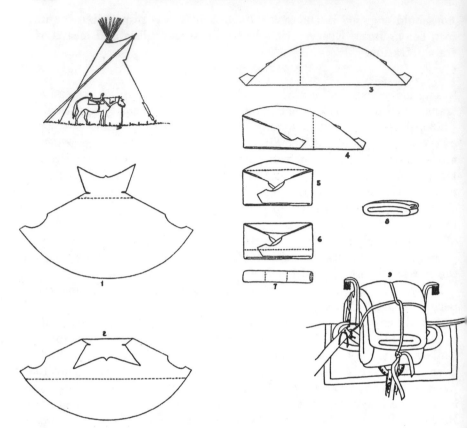

FIGURE 25.—A common method of folding a lodge cover for transportation by pack horse, Blackfoot.

the summer months, when buffalo hair was short, were easier to dress than those obtained during cooler weather. Near Fort McKenzie, August 9, 1833, Maximilian saw a Piegan camp of "old dirty brown leather tents" (Maximilian, 1906, vol. 23, p. 123). Apparently the covers had not been renewed at that date. Middle-class families generally renewed their lodge covers every other year, while poor families often were content to rely upon the kindness of wealthy men to give them old lodge covers after they had made new ones. The rich family's large cover was cut down to meet the needs of the poor one by trimming several feet off the base of it to make a much smaller cone.

The lodge cover was folded neatly and carefully to pack it for transport. One of several methods of folding employed by the Piegan is illustrated in figure 25. Some women preferred to begin by rolling the sides of the lodge toward the center, then folded over the ear flaps, folding up a portion of the bottom and providing a somewhat larger pack. Others first made a fold along the vertical axis at the center and continued to fold the skin on this axis until the package was the width of the saddle, then folded or rolled up the top and bottom ends. Figure 19 shows the lodge cover in place on the pack or woman's saddle. The tie rope encircling the horse's belly prevented shifting of the load.[73]

The cover of a 12- to 14-hide lodge weighed from about 90 to 105 pounds. It required the services of two women to lift it onto the horse or travois. Generally the Blackfoot transported the cover on the back of a packhorse. In winter they preferred to place the cover on the travois, especially if there was snow on the ground.[74]

The lodgepoles, after being taken down, were divided into equal bundles and tied to the sides of packhorses, through holes burned near the upper ends of the poles, by the hitch described on page 107 and illustrated in figure 19. The average-size lodge had 19 poles, each 18 feet to 22 feet long, weighing approximately 20 pounds each. The dragging ends of the poles provided considerable friction in traveling over rough country, limiting the number of poles each horse could transport to 5 or 6 each side, or a total of 10 or 12. Consequently it required two horses to transport the poles of the average lodge.[75]

Larger lodges, requiring a greater number of longer and heavier poles, needed more than two horses to move them. Schultz (1919 a, p. 50) claimed one horse could transport only 2 of the 36-foot lodgepoles required for the 28-skin lodge of the Piegan chief Lone Walker. Since that lodge was said to have used 30 poles, 15 horses would have been needed merely to transport them, according to Schultz' calculations. This figure seems excessive. However, it is obvious that the wealthy owner of one or even two large lodges needed more horses to move his lodgepoles than did the average Blackfoot. Rich men also employed mules for pole transport because they were stronger than Indian ponies. (See Appendix.) In many families certain horses were selected and reserved for the sole service of hauling the lodge-

---

[73] The method of folding the cover employed by Wilson's Hidatsa informant and illustrated by him (Wilson, 1924, figs. 106, 107) was not described by my Blackfoot informants. There is no reason to believe that all Hidatsa women folded their lodges in that manner. My Blackfoot data indicate that the method of folding followed individual rather than tribal preference.

[74] My Oglala and Kiowa informants also stated that those tribes preferred to transport lodge covers on pack horses. Wilson (1924, p. 193, fig. 35) indicated that was also Hidatsa practice, and Grinnell (1889, p. 279) stated that it was the Pawnee custom. The Omaha, in 1819, were reported to have carried their conic lodge covers of skin "neatly folded up, and suspended to the pack-saddle" (James, 1823, vol. 1, p. 206). Denig (1953, p. 36) noted Crow practice of transporting the lodge cover on horseback in the mid-19th century.

[75] On page 112 I have cited references to show that other Plains Indians transported their lodgepoles in the same manner as did the Blackfoot. Grinnell (1923, vol. 1, p. 226) and Wilson (1924, pp. 193, 272) described Cheyenne and Hidatsa use of two horses to transport the poles of one lodge, although in the latter case some of the poles were attached to the horse carrying the cover.

poles. During camp movement pole-dragging horses generally were led by ropes held by women riding travois horses ahead of them.

The poor in horses were forced to adopt ingenious expedients for transporting the short poles for their small lodges, unless they could borrow a horse or horses to help them move camp. Sometimes they attached poles to the sides of travois beds. Sometimes they employed dogs to drag their poles, each dog dragging two to four poles.[76]

Necessary accessories of each lodge were the wooden pegs driven into the ground around the lower edge of the cover to anchor it, and wooden pins used to fasten the cover together at the front. The Blackfoot generally carried these accessories in two rawhide bags (either scraped clean or with the hair left on) tied together over the saddle, one each side of a pole-dragging horse or the cover-carrying animal. Draught screens or lodge linings of skins were folded and packed on top of the lodge cover on the packhorse or placed on travois.

The estimated load of the average Blackfoot lodge accessories may be itemized:

	Pounds
Cover (12 or 14 skins)	90–105
Poles (19 at 20 lbs. each)	380
Lining (8 skins at ca. 7½ lbs.)	60
Pegs and pins	30–40
Total	560–585

It required three horses to transport the lodge and its accessories when camp was moved. If a family possessed a painted lodge, its accompanying sacred bundle generally was carried in a rectangular fringed rawhide case over the rear horn of the wife's (or favorite wife's) saddle. Some families transported these bundles on the travois.

PACKING HOUSEHOLD FURNITURE

Buffalo robes used for bedding and decorated willow backrests were carried on the travois. Sometimes, especially during the ritual moves prior to the establishment of the Sun Dance camp, women placed backrests on the travois so that one end would hang down at the back of

---

[76] Boller (ca. 1860) observed a camp of Canoe Assiniboin: "Owing to the scarcity of horses among this band . . . and the necessity of using dogs as their beasts of burden, most of the lodges consisted of from six to ten skins only" (Boller, 1868, pp. 134–135). However, Pierre Pichette claimed that the relatively wealthy Flathead employed rather small skin lodges on their prolonged winter buffalo hunts on the Plains due to the difficulty of hauling heavy loads over the Rockies. Many Flathead hunting lodges, he claimed, were not over 10 skins. Tribes of wealth nearly equal to that of the Blackfoot seem to have used lodges of about the same size. In 1833 Maximilian (1906, vol. 22, p. 327) found that Teton Dakota tipis were "generally composed of 14 skins." However, Denig (1930, p. 578) said that prominent Teton leaders owned lodges of as many as 36 skins in the second quarter of the 19th century. Teton lodge covers of that large size were taken apart in the center of the back. Half of the cover was transported by each of two horses.

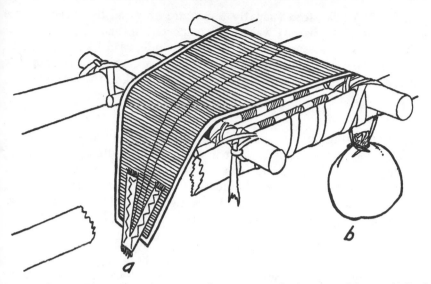

FIGURE 26.—*a*, Placement of a willow backrest on the bottom of a travois load to enhance the appearance of the travois from the rear; *b*, method of transporting water in a paunch container.

the load making it "look pretty" (fig. 26, *a*). [77] All of the items placed on a travois sometimes were wrapped in an old lodge cover and tied securely with rawhide rope 2 to 3 fingers wide, to protect them from dust, rain, or snow. If a family owned a great many buffalo robes they sometimes transported them on a makeshift platform of two crosspieces tied to the bundles of lodgepoles trailed by a pole-dragging horse.

PACKING FOOD

Dry meat, tallow, and pemmican in quantity were transported in parfleches, either in pairs suspended from each side of a pack horse (fig. 20) or on the travois platform. Small quantities of meat or pemmican to be eaten for lunch en route were carried in rectangular rawhide bags hung from the horn of a woman's saddle. [78]

Chokecherries, serviceberries, gooseberries, and bullberries collected in the fall and dried for winter use were transported in buffalo calfskin bags in the pockets of "double-bags" on pack horses. (See p. 116

---

[77] Grinnell (1923, vol. 1, p. 243), who considered willow backrests luxury items unknown to the Indians before the acquisition of horses, said the Cheyenne carried them rolled in compact bundles on horseback. A Kiowa informant said that tribe generally carried bedding on top of a pack horse's load.

[78] The Kiowa also employed the parfleche primarily as a meat-carrying case. The Cheyenne (Grinnell, 1923, vol. 1, p. 244) used them primarily for meat, berries, and roots. James (1823, vol. 1, p. 212) wrote of the Omaha, "The meat, in its dried state is closely condensed together in quadrangular packages, each of a suitable size, to attach conveniently to one side of the pack saddle of a horse," suggesting that the parfleche was used by that tribe for transporting meat in 1819.

and fig. 21.) Tobacco (usually a mixture of dried bearberry leaves and commercial tobacco) was also transported in that way.

The white underscrapings of buffalo rawhide, used like flour to mix with dried berries in making berry cakes, were carried in rectangular rawhide bags hung over the saddle horn or placed on the travois.

CLOTHING

Dress clothing and extra articles of ordinary wear not worn on the day's journey were carried either in the double saddlebag (see p. 117 and fig. 22) or in parfleches on the travois, with the exception of those articles included in medicine bundles. [79] Paints, combs, looking glasses, and other toilet articles were carried in small rectangular rawhide cases over front or rear horns of women's saddles.

HOUSEHOLD UTENSILS

According to Blackfoot tradition, pottery cooking vessels were formerly carried on horseback, in specially constructed rawhide containers tied on the top of a packhorse's load (Ewers, 1945 a, p. 295). Metal trade kettles were placed in skin sacks, often made from parts of old lodge covers, and tied on the top of the packhorse's load.[80]

The Blackfoot transported tin plates, frying pans, and metal spoons and knives in "double-bags" thrown over the backs of pack animals in late buffalo days. Small tools and utensils, such as arrow-making equipment, pipe-making tools, pemmican mauls, and skin-dressing tools were transported in plain, rectangular rawhide cases, usually on horse or dog travois. Even owners of a considerable number of horses sometimes carried these articles on dog travois. Carrying relatively light loads, the dogs could keep up with the horses in the moving camp.[81]

SOCIETY AND MEDICINE PARAPHERNALIA

All society and sacred paraphernalia among the Blackfoot were individually owned and were transported by the family of the owner. A society leader, in whose lodge the ceremonies of the group were held, had that lodge moved in the same way as other lodges of the camp. Ceremonial rattles were carried in fringed, rectangular, rawhide cases

---

[79] Kiowa informants claimed their people always carried extra clothing in parfleches.

[80] I have seen no Blackfoot kettle cases; however, there is a Crow specimen in the U. S. National Museum, which is illustrated in plate 9, a. Denig (1953, p. 36) reported that in the mid-19th century the Crow carried kettles, pots, pans, etc. in individual sacks with cords attached by which they were tied to a horse's pack. Frank Bosin said the Kiowa wrapped their kettles in soft buckskin, then tied them to packhorse loads when moving camp.

[81] In 1846, Garrard (1927, p. 52) saw Southern Cheyenne transporting stone hammers, skin-dressing tools, wooden bowls, and horn spoons in "square" rawhide bags slung on each side of pack mules.

over the saddle horn of a wife's saddle. Drums usually were wrapped in the bedding on the travois to prevent damage to them.

War bonnets and small medicine bundles were carried in cylindrical rawhide cases (p. 119 and fig. 23, *a*), over the rear horn of a woman's saddle by the wife of the owner.[82] Larger bundles, such as the natoas and beaver bundles were carried on the travois, led by the principal wife of the owner. The medicine pipe bundle, according to tradition, was carried in its special, fringed rawhide case over the back of the medicine pipe man. However, in my informant's youth it was carried on a separate horse led by the pipe owner, or even on the travois, on top of bedding, led by the owner's wife.

WEAPONS

Women carried knives in rawhide sheaths at their belts while moving camp. These were their only defensive weapons. Men, unencumbered by any baggage, carried their fighting weapons and ammunition, ready to meet any unexpected attack.[83]

CHILDREN

The elaborately decorated cradle was a luxury item among the Blackfoot in buffalo days. Women who were lucky enough to own them carried their infants in cradles hung from the front horns of their saddles. Most women carried their babies on their backs, wrapped in part of an old lodge cover and inside the mother's buffalo robe. Toddlers often rode on the travois. A family with several children might fold a large buffalo hide like a box, its sides held upright by parfleches, and place the children in the center. When tired of riding the children got off the travois and ran for a while. The willow sunshade also was employed on the travois to transport children and puppies. Boys and girls 5 years of age or older rode horseback alone, the less experienced riders tied in the saddle to prevent their falling. If a family owned few horses the children might ride double, or even triple on a single horse.[84]

---

[82] Frank Bosin said the Kiowa used tubular rawhide cases for holding war bonnets only. They preferred rawhide cases of the rectangular type for other sacred objects.

[83] Denig (1953, p. 36) said the Crow wife carried her husband's medicine bag and shield, as well as his sword, if he owned one. Her husband carried his gun and accouterments. Grinnell (1923, vol. 1, p. 128) reported that Cheyenne men carried only their arms when camp was on the move. La Vérendrye (1927, p. 317) observed that when the horseless Assiniboin moved camp in 1738, the men carried "only their arms."

[84] All of these methods of transporting children were used by other tribes. Their practice of tying young children in the saddle or on a packhorse's load has been cited (p. 67). Miller in 1837, depicted a cradle hung to the saddle bow of a woman's horse. The watercolor is not tribally identified (Ross, 1951, pl. 9, and description on opposite page). Garrard (1927, p. 52) did not mention use of baby cradles by the Southern Cheyenne camp whose movement he witnessed in 1846. Rather he said mothers carried their infants on their backs, inside their robes. The travois (true or makeshift) was used for transporting children by the Eastern Apache (Abert, 1846, p. 10), Hidatsa-Mandan (Boller, 1868, p. 177), Iowa (Skinner, 1926, p. 280), Teton (Prince Paul *in* Butscher, 1942, p. 209), Yankton (Maximilian, 1906, vol. 21, pp. 309–310), Southern Arapaho (Michelson, 1933, p. 597), and Southern Cheyenne (Garrard, 1927, p. 52).

The travois also served the Blackfoot as a vehicle for transporting the aged, too feeble to ride horseback, as well as the sick and wounded.[85]

WEIGHTS AND LOADS

In 1908, H. W. Daly, chief packer, Office of the Quartermaster-- General, recommended a load of 250 pounds for an Army pack mule weighing not less than 850 pounds, traveling 20 to 25 miles a day under ordinary conditions or 10 to 15 miles a day over rough and mountainous country (Daly, 1908, pp. 134, 136). I estimate that a fair load for an Indian pony, weighing approximately 700 pounds, would have been about 200 pounds under similar conditions.

Boller (1868, p. 30), an experienced trader, said the Teton Dakota carried "from 250 to 300 pounds" on the travois. Stanley (1855, p. 449) observed that the Piegan transported "often three hundred pounds" on their travois. The limit for the travois load dragged by the small Indian pony must have been about 300 pounds. I estimate that the lodgepole-dragging horse could pull a load of poles weighing a little more than that of the packhorse but less than that of the travois load. The awkwardness of the load and the friction of the many dragging poles combined to restrict the transport capacity of the pole-dragging animal.

HORSE NEEDS FOR THE AVERAGE FAMILY

We are now in a position to estimate the number of horses required by an average Blackfoot family in the mid-19th century. Our hypothetical average family would number 2 grown males, 3 grown females, and 3 children.[86]

After discussing the horse needs for a family of this size with a half dozen elderly informants (separately), I concluded that a family "should have had" 12 horses, as follows: 1 horse to carry the lodge cover and its accessories; 2 horses to drag the lodgepoles; 2 horses for packing meat, miscellaneous foods, and equipment; 3 horses to carry the women and infants (at least 2 of which would pull travois); 2 common riding horses for the men; and 2 trained buffalo runners for the men. None of these horses would then have to pull or carry heavier loads than those indicated above as fair loads for Indian ponies. However, this estimate makes no allowance for additional horses to

---

[85] Probably this was widespread Plains Indian practice. Prince Paul (in Butscher, 1942, p. 209) noted Teton Dakota use of the travois to transport "ancient squaws" a century ago. Comparative data on travois use in carrying sick and wounded have been cited (p. 108).

[86] I have derived these figures from Indian Agent Vaughan's estimate of an average of 8 persons to the lodge among the three Blackfoot tribes in 1860. His figures also estimated that women somewhat outnumbered men, and children comprised roughly 40 percent of the Blackfoot population at that time (U. S. Comm. Ind. Affairs, 1860, p. 308).

replace any of the active animals in case of their death, injury, or theft. A well-balanced herd would require 4 or 5 additional animals, which could be pressed into service to replace future losses, in order to give the family a sense of security.[87]

When we compare the number of horses informants thought the average family of 8 "should have" with the best estimates of the number of horses per lodge among the Blackfoot tribes in the mid-19th century (see p. 21), we find a noticeable discrepancy. In the year 1860 the person-horse ratio was nearer 1:1 rather than the 1:1½ an average family "should have had." Consequently the average family had to cut corners to get by with a smaller number of horses. This was done in a number of ways: (1) by overloading a smaller number of pack animals (2) by employing a smaller number of common riding horses (3) by making use of a single buffalo horse, and/or (4) utilizing dog travois to carry meat and light equipment. By employing a smaller number of transport and buffalo hunting horses the family restricted its possibilities of obtaining meat and of transporting food surpluses, something of special importance in the fall of the year in the period preceding the establishment of winter camp.

Informants indicated that a young married couple with a baby or no children could make out with as few as 5 horses: 1 common saddle horse and 1 buffalo runner for the husband, 2 pack horses to transport the cover, poles, and accessories of a small lodge, and 1 travois horse for the wife.[88]

However, a large family, comprising more than 5 adults and growing children "should have had" 15 to 20 or more horses.

My information indicates that in the average family all horses except buffalo runners were pressed into service when camp was moved. In the well-regulated household animals used for transporting the lodge and pack and travois horses were regularly assigned to those duties each time camp was moved.

MOVING CAMP ON THE PART OF A WEALTHY FAMILY

A wealthy family of average size owning 30, 50, or more horses encountered little difficulty in moving camp. The favorite wife directed packing of the household equipment. She generally rode a saddle horse carrying her husband's toilet articles, feather bonnet and/or other small medicine bundles over the horns of her fancy

---

[87] Mishkin (1940, p. 20) estimated that a "well balanced herd of ideal size" for a Kiowa family of five adults would comprise 10 pack animals, 5 riding animals, and 2 to 5 buffalo horses. Differences between his figures and my Blackfoot estimates are apparent in transport, riding, and buffalo horse categories. Perhaps the relatively wealthy Kiowa thought 5 buffalo horses were desirable. It is doubtful if they were necessary.

[88] Elkin (1940, p. 208) regarded "four or five horses" as "the indispensible minimum for a man and wife; two for riding and the rest for packing," among the Northern Arapaho.

saddle. His dress clothing was packed in her double saddlebag. Her horse was richly decorated with fine crupper and martingale. If the family possessed a large or important medicine bundle she transported it on a travois, leading the travois horse behind her. Each of the other wives had a travois which she rode or led behind her from a saddle horse. Packhorses were available to transport large quantities of meat and plant foods when moving to winter camp. Horses assigned to lodge transport duties needed not to be heavily loaded. Additional horses were available to relieve sick or injured horses of their duties.

The loose horses not needed for transport duty were driven by boys in the rear of the family group. Informants said the loose horses of a wealthy man sometimes were "spread out as wide as the town of Browning" when camp was on the move. If the owner had no boys of his own or had not adopted a young man to help him with his horses he would give boys of other families colts in return for their assistance in driving his horses when camp moved.[89]

MOVING CAMP ON THE PART OF A POOR FAMILY

Weasel Tail cited the case of a poor Blood Indian who owned but one horse. His lodge cover was the upper part of a rich man's discarded cover. His lodge was so small there was no room to hang a tripod and kettle inside it. When camp moved he and his wife walked. She led the horse with a travois attached to it, on which were packed the lodge cover and scanty family baggage. Their children rode on the back of the travois horse on top of other baggage. The small, short lodgepoles of the dwelling were dragged by dogs. The family owned no willow backrests, no dress clothing, and transported very little food. Informants indicated that this case was not unique.

However, most poor families tried to borrow horses from wealthy relatives, chiefs, or men ambitious of becoming leaders and interested in adding to the number of their supporters in return for favors granted. If the prospective borrower was known to be a lazy fellow, who remained in camp and would not join horse raids or attempt to better his condition through his own efforts, his request might be refused with some such comment as "Let him walk." The rebuke was intended to shock him out of his laziness. Those who were poor through misfortune rather than inertia (because their horses had been stolen by the enemy or lost through diseases or winter storms, or because of the death or injury of a hunter) generally could get a loan

---

[89] The Nez Percé (Haines, 1939, p. 288) and Southern Cheyenne (Garrard, 1927, p. 53) also drove the loose horses of each family in a separate band when camp moved.

of horses for moving camp. Wealthy horse owners among the Piegan, such as Many Horses and Stingy, were well remembered for their generosity in loaning horses to the poor. According to a family tradition, Buffalo Back Fat, head chief of the Blood Indians, sometimes told those who had borrowed horses from him to keep them when they sought to return the animals.[90]

In the period of the serious mange epidemic among the Piegan (ca. 1881) the loss of horses was so great that camp movements were seriously handicapped. Short Face said that the chief and other wealthy men of his band then went ahead with some other families of the camp and, about noon, sent their horses back to transport the possessions of those left behind. In those difficult days dogs were extensively used for transport duties and many people walked.[91]

COMPARATIVE DATA ON THE POOR IN HORSES

The early literature contains several striking descriptions of the methods employed by the poor in horses among other tribes in moving camp.

Lewis and Clark wrote of the Lemhi Shoshoni in 1805:

. . . were he [the husband] so poor as to possess only two horses, he would ride the best of them, and leave the other for his wives and children and their baggage; if he had too many wives or too much baggage for the horse, the wives would have no other alternative but to follow him on foot; they are not, however, often reduced to these extremities, for the stock of horses is very ample. [Coues, 1893, vol. 2, p. 558.]

Ferris described in greater detail the lot of the poor among the Rocky Mountain Indians in general in 1832:

Those who are not so fortunate or wealthy as to possess the number of horses requisite, are obliged to walk or put enormous loads upon such as they may own. In one instance, in the year 1832, I saw a mare loaded with, first—two large bales containing meat, skins, etc., on opposite sides of the animal, attached securely to the saddle by strong cords; secondly—a lodge, with the necessary poles dragging on each side of her; thirdly—a kettle, axe, and sundry other articles of domestic economy; fourthly—a colt too young to bear the fatigue of travelling was lashed to one side; and finally—this enormous load was surmounted by a woman with three young children; making in all sufficient to have fully loaded three horses, in the ordinary manner. Though this rather exceeds anything of the kind I ever saw, yet large loads, in like manner surmounted by women and children, colts and puppies, are often observed on their moving jaunts. [Ferris, 1940, p. 299.]

---

[90] Frank Bosin said the loaning of horses to the poor for use in moving camp was a common practice among wealthy Kiowa.

[91] In 1819 the Long expedition reported a similar procedure among the Omaha, a tribe relatively poor in horses. "They are sometimes so successful . . . in the accumulation of meat, as to be obliged to make double trips, returning after midday for half the whole quantity, which was left in the morning" (James, 1823, vol. 1, p. 212).

Boller (1868, pp. 124–125) was a member of a camp of Hidatsa which traveled on a visit to the Assiniboin in the sixties. He observed that one of the party was an old, lame Assiniboin returning to his people. He "had one horse and a travee, upon which his three children and all his worldly goods were transported. His squaw led the wretched animal" while the old man walked in the rear. They were finally left behind the rest of the moving camp and did not catch up until the day after the others had reached their destination. Boller noted that a squaw with three small children was also left; she carried one on her back and another in her arms, while the eldest trotted along by her side. Some time after, a young Indian who had loitered behind came up and reported that the squaw had just killed the youngest "because it was too small to travel."

Abandonment of the aged poor was common practice among many of the nomadic tribes of the Upper Missouri (Denig, 1930, pp. 576–577). However, both Denig (1953, p. 38) and Larocque (1910, p. 57) claimed the Crow were a notable exception to this rule. Both writers credited the Crow custom of transporting the aged when camp was moved to their relative wealth in horses. Among the Pawnee (Dunbar, 1880, p. 328), Osage (Tixier, 1940, p. 140), and Sauk and Fox (Forsyth in Blair, 1912, vol. 2, pp. 233–234), the aged and the poor were left behind when the great majority of their tribesmen embarked on prolonged buffalo hunts on horseback. Of the Plains Indian tribes in general it may be safely stated that the aged were the first to suffer from a shortage of horses.

Next to suffer were the women. There can be no doubt that the horse proved a great boon to women. The transport horse replaced the pedestrian woman burden bearer as well as the dog travois. The statements quoted below support and underscore Phillip St. George Cooke's generalization regarding the Plains Indians. "The husband strives to obtain wealth in horses to relieve his family of travelling on foot and carrying burdens" (Cooke, 1857, p. 117).[92]

---

[92] La Vérendrye noted that "the women and dogs carry all the baggage" among the horseless Assiniboin whom he accompanied to visit the Mandan in 1738 (La Vérendrye, 1927, p. 317). Later traders who met horse-using tribes of the western Plains commented on the improvement in the status of women due to possession of horses. In 1772 Cocking (1908, p. 111) stated that the Gros Ventres "use pack-Horses, which give their Women a great advantage over other Women who are either carrying or hauling sledges every day in the year." Of the Crow, in 1805, Larocque (1910, p. 59) said, "The women are indebted solely to their having horses for the ease they enjoy more than their neighbors." Bourgmont, in 1724, noted the heavy loads carried by Kansa women as well as their dogs and said they had difficulty marching because of the weight of their baggage. At the Padouca (Apache) village a Skidi Pawnee chief told Bourgmont he was eager to make peace with the Padouca "to obtain horses which will help us to carry our belongings when we move to our winter grounds, because our wives and children die under the burden when

FORMATIONS ON THE MARCH

John Mix Stanley (1855, pp. 448–449) observed that Low Horn's Piegan village of 90 lodges en route to Fort Benton in September 1853, was "drawn out in two parallel lines on the plains." The "chiefs and braves rode in front, flank and rear, ever ready for the chase or defense against the foe." Informants claimed the use of advance guards scouting for signs of game and the enemy, and of side and rear pickets was common in the movement of tribal and band camps among Blackfoot tribes in their youth. Scouts sometimes traveled as far as 3 miles ahead of the main body, and flanking and rear guards sometimes were nearly as far distant from it. Scouts ascended hills and rising ground the better to look out for game and foes. The main body was led by the medicine pipe man and the chief or chiefs with their families. Other camp members fell in behind them in family groups (including travois, pack animals, riding animals, and loose horses). Sometimes the main body moved in single file, at other times with two or more families abreast, depending to some extent on the character of the country traversed. Men not assigned to guard duty traveled with their families and assisted the women in retrieving any baggage that might become untied and fall to the ground. Not infrequently lodgepoles wore through their suspension holes and had to be retied.

However, Weasel Tail stated that the ideal formation was not always employed in band movements. Sometimes, when the band felt secure from enemy attack, the side pickets were eliminated. The history of Blackfoot warfare, however, suggests that it was at such times the enemy sometimes attacked with disastrous losses to the defenders. Brings-Down-the-Sun, the North Piegan chief, told McClintock (1910, p. 473 ff.) of a case when the camp was protected by front and rear guards only while passing through hilly country. The Crow Indians attacked on the unprotected flanks and killed or captured many Piegan. On another occasion the Crow suffered a serious defeat

we return" (Margry, 1876–86, vol. 6, pp. 414, 425). Forsyth (in Blair, vol. 2, p. 236) said of the Sauk and Fox in 1827, "if any carrying is obliged to be done for want of horses, the women have to shoulder it." Omaha women (in 1819) loaded their horses and dogs, then took "as great a weight upon their own backs as they can conveniently transport." Among the horse-poor Omaha at that time "the greater portion of the young men and squaws were necessarily pedestrian" (James, 1823, vol. 1, p. 205). In 1834 Zenas Leonard visited a horseless "Bannock" village which journeyed to the Plains once a year to hunt buffalo, where they remained "until they jerk as much meat as their females can lug home on their backs" (Leonard, 1904, p. 148). Miller's watercolor of Pawnee Indians moving camp (1837) portrays a number of women carrying heavy loads on their backs, as well as loaded horses and dog travois (Ross, 1951, p. 66). The Pawnee, of course, were poor in horses.

at the hands of the Blackfoot as a result of neglect of adequate scouting precautions (Denig, 1953, p. 48).[93]

THE NOON STOP FOR LUNCH

On days when camp was to move the Blackfoot usually were up at dawn, packed, and on the march before 8 o'clock. They breakfasted before getting underway. At noon the chief called a stop for a short rest and lunch. Lunch generally was not a cooked meal but consisted of prepared meat, pemmican, or dried plant foods carried in rawhide cases by the women, suspended from the horns of their saddles. If possible, the stop was made near water. Otherwise drinking water was carried along in paunch containers. The flanking guard parties carried their own lunches and stopped to eat, holding their repective positions in relation to the main body. However, it was customary for the leader of each guard group to ride in to the main body to consult with the chief during the noon stop.[94]

CROSSING STREAMS EN ROUTE

Blackfoot bands carried no bull boats or other watercraft for use in crossing rivers and deep streams while on the march. In the 1870's Bradley (1923, p. 257) described their method of crossing streams:

. . . they made a kind of float from the skin covering of the lodges, upon or within which their effects were placed, men, women, and children swimming, the warriors towing the floats by a cord held in the mouth. Such horses as were fit for that service were also made to do duty in transporting their riders. By these means a village of 500 lodges would cross a considerable stream within an hour's time.

---

[93] The guarding of a moving camp by advance scouts, side pickets, and rear guard seems to have antedated the acquisition of horses by the northern Plains tribes. La Vérendrye wrote of the formation employed by the horseless Assiniboin with whom he journeyed to the Mandan villages in 1738, "The marching order of the Assiniboin villagers, especially when they are numerous, is in three columns, the scouts in front, the wings (extending back) to a good rearguard ; the old and disabled march in the main body which is in the middle" (La Vérendrye, 1927, p. 317). The elder Henry's description of an Assiniboin movement in 1776, involving a camp of about 200 lodges and over 500 dog travois, however, makes no mention of side pickets (Henry, 1809, p. 309). Larocque's earliest description of the Crow (1805) mentioned their employment of advance scouts and rear guard, but no side pickets. Possibly the use of flanking pickets became more necessary after the introduction of horses increased the mobility of potential attackers. In earlier times, when enemies of necessity approached more slowly on foot, there may have been less need for flank protection. Nevertheless, flankers were employed to protect large camps on the move, even in La Vérendrye's time.

In the 19th century, use of side, advance, and rear guards was common to both nomadic and horticultural Plains tribes as well as to the Plateau peoples when moving camp on buffalo-hunting expeditions. The younger Henry (Henry and Thompson, 1897, vol. 1, pp. 369, 393) noted that the Hidatsa-Mandan employed this formation en route to and returning from their visit to the Cheyenne in the summer of 1806. This formation has also been reported as characteristic of the Crow (Marquis, 1928, p. 144), Pawnee (Dunbar, 1880, p. 328), Osage (Tixier, 1940, p. 166), Kiowa (Battey, 1875, pp. 185–186), and Flathead (Turney-High, 1937, p. 117).

[94] Larocque's excellent description of Crow camp movement in 1805, points out that the Crow usually made a midday stop for lunch (Larocque, 1910).

Informants added details to this description by stating that the lodge covers were rolled up at the sides, baggage and children placed in them, and the women swam along behind pushing the covers while men towed them from in front by ropes. The lodgepoles were placed under the travois and bound to them to form crude rafts on which backrests and other luggage were transported over the water. Horses towed these improvised rafts. Crossing a wide river, such as the Missouri, provided the Indians a noisy time. Horses whinnied, dogs yelped, people shouted. When the camp safely reached the other side its members generally stopped for the day to dry their clothes and gear and to feast. In the absence of any contemporary drawing of Blackfoot methods of stream crossing I have reproduced Sohon's original sketch of Flathead Indians traversing a stream as plate 10. The Flathead method was essentially the same as that employed by the Blackfoot.[95]

The problem of management of horses in water must have confronted the Indians soon after they acquired their first horses. Hendry (1907, p. 351) observed that the "Archithinue" of the Saskatchewan Plains were adept in the employment of horses in "swimming broad and deep rivers," in 1755. Yet Weasel Tail stated that in his youth a man was careful to choose a horse known to behave well in water, if he attempted to ride across a stream. Otherwise he preferred to swim or to let his horse tow him across by holding on to the animal's tail. Kane (1925, p. 76) observed this method of river crossing employed by Blackfoot in 1848.[96]

STOPS EN ROUTE BECAUSE OF RAIN

If the moving camp was overtaken by a hard, sudden rainstorm en route, they sought shelter in brush if any was near, built makeshift shelters of a few bent willow branches in the generalized sweat-lodge pattern, covered them with buffalo robes, and remained inside until the storm moved on. If, however, the rain continued through the day they would be forced to set up their lodges at or near that place.

ARRIVAL AT NIGHT CAMP

Usually the site for the night's camp was determined in advance by the band chief on the basis of its known distance from the previous

---

[95] Father Mengarini (1938, pp. 16–17), and Major Owen (1927, vol. 1, p. 37) described Flathead methods of crossing streams as employed in the mid-19th century. Mandelbaum (1940, p. 196) found that Plains Cree horses were trained to pull "rafts" tied to their tails, but he did not describe the rafts. Lowie (1922 a, p. 219) said the Crow made rafts of parallel tipi poles, spread hides over them, and placed the cargo on top.

[96] In 1806 the younger Henry (Henry and Thompson, 1897, vol. 1, p. 331) observed Mandan young men swimming horses across the Missouri. "They fastened a line to the horse's mouth, the end of which one of them took in his teeth, and swam ahead, whilst others swam on each side and in the rear, driving the animal very expeditiously."

day's camp, and availability of wood, water, and wild grass. When the chief reached this locality he selected a spot for his lodge or lodges. His women folk began unpacking and setting up his lodge.[97] Other families pitched their lodges around his, being careful not to scatter too widely because of the danger of attack. Lodges in a band camp were not aligned in a circle, but were placed within a distance of about 10 to 12 feet of one another in an otherwise unplanned cluster.

The medicine pipe man placed his bundle on its tripod behind his lodge. The men smoked and conversed as the women unpacked, set up the lodges and prepared the evening meal. Boys who cared for the horses were given their instructions by family heads. If there were signs of the enemy a horse corral was built for their protection at night. Generally the day's march ended in the middle or late afternoon so that there was ample time before dark to erect the lodges and make preparations for the night.

MAKING CAMP WITHOUT WOOD OR WATER

Sometimes it was known in advance that night camp would have to be made without wood or water. If no wood was available dried buffalo chips were substituted for firewood. Buck brush or dried grass were employed to start the chips burning.

If a dry camp was anticipated water was carried along in buffalo paunches, about the necks of which willow sticks were woven to keep the vessels round. Each vessel was closed at the top by tie strings or by a fitted rawhide cover. These vessels were transported tied to the outer ends of travois platforms where the primary struts crossed the shafts (fig. 26, b). Each family carried four or more paunches, depending upon its size and the number of dogs and horses owned.[98] Horses and dogs were watered by pouring the liquid into basin-shaped troughs of rawhide. In the spring of the year large ponds of water, formed from melting snows, appeared in depressions in the Blackfoot country, affording a ready supply of water in localities normally dry through the summer and fall months. Little difficulty was experienced in obtaining water in spring.

---

[97] Larocque's (1910, p. 61) description of Crow movements states that the principal chief "pitches his tent the first, all the others encamp about him." Frank Bosin said this was also Kiowa practice.

[98] Use of buffalo-paunch containers for carrying water on the march was common among the Plains Indians. In 1820, the Kiowa Apache were seen carrying water in buffalo paunches of 6 to 8 gallons capacity, closed at the tops by sticks passed through their margins. In camp the paunches were suspended from tripods of light poles (James, 1823, vol. 2, pp. 103, 108). The Hidatsa carried water for dogs in wood-skewered buffalo paunches, on dog travois (Wilson, 1924, p. 225, fig. 58). A Kiowa buffalo-paunch water vessel is on exhibition in the Southern Plains Indian Museum, Anadarko, Okla. Specimens from the Gros Ventres and Mandan are on exhibition in the American Museum of Natural History, New York City. A drawing by a Southern Cheyenne artist, showing a paunch vessel tied to a travois for transport in the manner employed by the Blackfoot is reproduced on plate 6, b. This drawing (U. S. N. M. No. 166,032) was collected by H. R. Voth in 1889.

DISTANCES TRAVELED PER DAY

Many factors determined the distance of the day's march. Weather conditions, the terrain traversed (whether hilly or relatively level, and the number and sizes of watercourses to be crossed), availability of game, relative fear of enemies in the neighborhood, as well as the Indians' relative desire for hurry, all influenced the speed of movement and distance covered. Informants said that on some days band camps made no more than 5 miles, stopping for the day at noon. A normal day's march was about 10 to 15 miles. Yet in the spring of the year, when the Indians were eager to leave their winter camps on the Marias to obtain fresh buffalo meat, they made as far as the Sweetgrass Hills in a day, a distance of at least 18 miles. Mrs. Cree Medicine recalled that her band, in a hurry to obtain rations at Old Agency, traveled from the site of the earlier Agency north of Choteau to Old Agency on Badger Creek in 1 day and about 6 hours. The country traversed is hilly and crossed by several small streams. Yet they made this journey of nearly 50 miles in less than 2 days. If a band believed there was danger from the enemy they traveled rapidly, continued after dark, and made 25 or more miles a day.[99]

---

[99] Although Turney-High (1937, p. 116) reported that the Flathead traveled 30 miles a day, average estimates for the Crow (Denig, 1953, p. 36), Nez Percé (Haines, 1939, p. 68), and Kiowa (informants) were given as 10 to 15 miles in a day's travel. Dunbar (1880, pp. 328–329) estimated the daily marches of the Pawnee on their buffalo hunts at "from eight to twenty miles," explaining that in winter they did not begin their march as early as in warmer weather, when they set out at dawn, or sooner. They ended the day's march between noon and nightfall "as circumstances dictated." By comparison it is noteworthy that Coronado, in his final march to Quivera with 30 picked men, averaged 10 miles per day (Bolton, 1949, p. 286). White muleteers on the old Santa Fe Trail considered a *jornado* (day's march) about 12 to 15 miles (Inman, 1899, p. 57).

The most valuable comparative description of camp movements by a nomadic Plains Indian tribe is contained in Laroque's journal of his 2½ months' travels with the Crow from the Hidatsa villages on the Missouri, via the eastern base of the Big Horns, to their medicine lodge site on the Yellowstone near present Billings, Mont., June to September, 1805. In 76 days camp was moved 47 times (roughly 2 of every 3 days). The greatest daily distance recorded was 24 miles, the smallest 3 miles. The median distance traversed on days camp moved was 9½ miles. On most travel days the Crow started early in the morning and traveled until afternoon, stopping at noon for lunch. Night camps were made beside streams, and most of the days' travels were along or between watercourses. With one or two exceptions the Crow did not move camp during rain. On several days rain either delayed the start or caused an early stop. Delays of a day or more en route were caused by inclement weather (rain), serious illness in camp, stops to hunt (although parties of men frequently hunted at a distance while the main body moved), to dry meat, to tan hides after a hunt, and to dry tongues for the medicine lodge; to rest in security while scouts reconnoitered ahead fearing the presence of enemies; to cut ash whips; and to settle a disagreement among leaders as to the route to be followed. Another day's stop was made to rest the horses as soon as they reached a locality offering good pasture after 2 days' march across barren country. Laroque's journal probably affords a better understanding of the day-to-day rhythm of camp movement and the factors conditioning this movement than any other known document on the nomadic tribes of the Plains (Larocque, 1910).

THE HORSE IN HUNTING

BUFFALO IN THE BLACKFOOT COUNTRY

From the time of the first explorations of the Blackfoot Country by Whites until the decade of the 1870's this region was abundantly stocked with buffalo. Anthony Hendry, the first white man known to have visited the Saskatchewan Plains, made frequent mention of the "Great Plenty of Buffalo" he saw there in the fall of 1754 (Hendry, 1907, pp. 329–337). Lewis and Clark, the first American explorers of the Blackfoot Country, marveled at the "vast quantities of buffalo" seen by them on their westward journey from the Great Falls of the Missouri to the Gates of the Mountains in June and July, 1805 (Coues, 1893, vol. 2, pp. 364–418). Captain Lewis passed "such immense quantities of buffalo that the whole seemed a single herd" on his quick trip northward to the vicinity of the present Blackfeet Reservation in July 1806. A few days earlier he had seen buffalo on Sun River "in such numbers that there could not have been fewer than 10,000 within a circuit of two miles" (ibid., vol. 3, pp. 1081, 1088). In 1855 Governor Stevens claimed "the quantity of buffalo" between Fort Union and the Rockies was "almost inconceivable" (Stevens, 1860, p. 239). In September of that year Lieutenant Mullens reported that "innumerable herds of buffalo" were feeding in the Judith Basin, while at the same time John Mix Stanley saw "numerous herds" grazing near the Sweetgrass Hills and northward to Milk River (Stevens, 1860, p. 123; Stanley, 1855, p. 447). While traveling from the Musselshell River to Fort Browning on Milk River in March, 1870, Peter Koch noted that "for a distance of forty miles I do not think we were ever out of easy rifle shot of buffalo" (Koch, 1896, p. 302). In the summer of 1874, W. J. Twining, chief astronomer and surveyor for the International Boundary Survey, observed that the Plains between the Sweetgrass Hills and the Rockies and southward to Fort Benton was "literally black" with buffalo. He considered the Sweetgrass Hills to have been the center of the feeding ground of the great northern buffalo herd at that time. He believed this great herd then ranged from the Missouri River north to the Saskatchewan (Twining, 1878, pp. 63–64, 282).

Yet by the fall of 1879, only 5 years later, the buffalo had been exterminated in the Canadian portion of the Blackfoot Country except for a few small bands of stragglers (Denny, 1939, pp. 130–131, 142–143). That winter the Blackfoot made their last great buffalo hunt

148

south of the Missouri in the Judith Basin. The next winter's hunt was unsuccessful. Richard Sanderville claimed the last wild buffalo in the Blackfoot Country were killed by a party of Piegan hunters near the Sweetgrass Hills in 1884.

The contemporary observations (quoted above) confirm the claims of my aged informants that buffalo were plentiful in the Blackfoot Country in their youth (the late 1860's and early 1870's). As Hornaday's historical map of the extermination of the buffalo graphically illustrates, the Blackfoot Country was the last buffalo hunting ground of the Plains Indians (Hornaday, 1889).

BLACKFOOT USES OF THE BUFFALO

Nearly a century ago Indian Agent Vaughan wrote that the buffalo was "the staff of life" of the Blackfoot (U. S. Comm. Ind. Affairs, 1858, p. 435). Frequent repetition of this phrase has not dulled its essential truth. Throughout their known history the Blackfoot have shown a striking preference for the meat of a single animal. Their current desire for beef, almost to the exclusion of any other meat, probably is a survival from the days when the buffalo was their common food. Not only did they consume it in great quantities but a number of the parts were avidly devoured during butchering, without benefit of cookery. These were the liver, brains, kidneys, the soft gristle of the nose, the blood, and the marrow from leg bones. Older men ate the testicles raw, claiming they made them healthy and virile. The contents of the intestines of newborn calves were considered delicacies for the aged of both sexes. An informant spoke of this food as "the Indians' cheese." All fleshy parts of the buffalo were cooked, although the Blackfoot showed a decided preference for the tongue and ribs. Buffalo figured prominently in the diet of Blackfoot Indians of all ages. As Maximilian (1906, vol. 23, p. 133) noted in 1833, Blackfoot mothers gave infants choice pieces of buffalo meat to suck. Toothless old people sucked the juices in the same way. Quantities of dried meat and pemmican were pounded for winter use. In times of food scarcity even the grease-soaked bags which had contained fat or pemmican were eaten to stave off starvation.

The nonfood uses of the buffalo in Blackfoot material culture were more numerous than any previously published list of the many uses of this animal by Indians of the Plains would indicate. Therefore, I have listed these uses below. This list includes only items mentioned by informants in the course of my specialized field studies of aspects of Blackfoot material culture. A more exhaustive search for rare usages probably would increase this list of some 87 items to more than 100. This list serves to illustrate not only Blackfoot dependence upon the buffalo but also their ingenuity in utilizing buffalo products.

In a sense many of the materials employed were byproducts of the chase. The Blackfoot hunted buffalo primarily for food and hides. Animals killed for those purposes offered ample amounts of the other bodily parts utilized. Considerable ingenuity was employed in reusing old lodge covers (especially the upper portions that had become softened and rendered rain resistant from the smoke of lodge fires).

Nonfood uses of the buffalo in Blackfoot material culture

Clothing:
  Winter robes, for both sexes (hair lined).
  Winter caps, with earlaps, for both sexes (hide with the hair).
  Winter moccasins, for both sexes (hair lined).
  Winter leggings, for both sexes (skin, tops of old lodges).
  Winter mittens, for both sexes (hair lined).
  Winter shirts, for boys and men (skin, tops of old lodges).
  Winter coats, for boys and men (hide with the hair).
  Winter dress, girls and women (skin, tops of old lodges).
  Short winter cape, for girls and women (hair inside).
  Winter "underpants" for girls and women (calfskin).
  Spring moccasins, for both sexes (tops of old lodges).
  Hock moccasins (from rear legs, worn by war party members whose supply of moccasins were worn out).
  Moccasin soles, both sexes (rawhide, used especially for repairing soft-soled moccasins).
  Belts, both sexes (rawhide).
  Breechclothes, males (tops of old lodges).
  Headdress ornaments (hair and horns).
Lodge and furnishings:
  Lodge covers (cowskin).
  Lodge doors (cowskin).
  Lodge linings (cowskins).
  Bed covers (robes, with the hair).
  Lodge ornaments (hair and tail).
Weapons:
  Shields (rawhide, from bull's neck).
  Bow backings (twisted bull sinew).
  Bow strings (twisted bull sinew).
  Arrowhead and feather wrappings (sinew).
  Powder flasks (horn).
  Cover and hafting of stone-headed warclubs (rawhide).
  Ornaments for clubs (hair or beard).
  Knife sheaths (rawhide).
Tools, utensils, and crafts media:
  Arrow straighteners (boss rib).
  Fleshing tools (tibia and part of femur).
  Meat and berry pounders' hafting (rawhide).
  Mauls' hafting (rawhide).
  Emergency kettles (rawhide).
  Water buckets (paunch).
  Spoons (horn).
  Cups (horn).
  Ladles (horn).

Tools, utensils, and crafts media—Continued
  Fuel (dung).
  Fly brushes (tail on stick).
  Glue, used in arrow making (boiled phallus).
  Skin softening agents (brains, fat, and liver).
  Thread (sinew, occasionally rawhide).
  Pipe-polishing medium (fat).
  Paint-mixing medium (fat).
  Paint brushes (hip bone or shoulder blade).
  Quill flattener (horn).
  Tool for dehairing rope, (skull).
Riding and transport gear:
  Frame-saddle covering (rawhide).
  Pad-saddle covering (soft skin).
  Pad-saddle stuffing (hair).
  Saddle-rigging straps (rawhide).
  Stirrup coverings (scrotum or rawhide).
  Martingales, simple form (rawhide).
  Cruppers, simple form (rawhide).
  Parfleches (rawhide).
  Rectangular saddlebags (rawhide).
  Cylindrical saddlebags (rawhide).
  Dougle-bags (rawhide).
  "Gros Ventres bags" (soft skin).
  Tobacco pouches (calfskin).
  Berry bags (unborn calfskin).
  Bridles (rawhide or hair).
  Honda ring (horn).
  Hackamores (rawhide).
  Lariats (rawhide).
  Picket ropes (rawhide).
  Hobbles (rawhide).
  Saddle blankets (skin or robe).
  Saddle housings (robe).
  Travois hitches (rawhide).
  Pole hitches (rawhide).
  Miscellaneous tie strings (rawhide).
  Horse blankets (robe, or top of old lodge).
  Horse-watering troughs (rawhide).
  Horseshoes (rawhide).
Recreational equipment:
  Boys' sleds (rib runners, skin seat).
  Girls' sleds (large pieces rawhide).
  Ball stuffing (hair).
  Hoop and pole game hoop netting (rawhide).
Ceremonial and religious paraphernalia:
  Sun Dance altars (skull).
  Bindings for Sun Dance lodge rafters (strips of hide with hair).
  Rattles (hoofs and rawhide).
  Horse masks (skin and horn).
  Winding sheets for dead (skin or robe).
  Beaver bundle headdress (hide with hair).
  Matoki (Woman's Society) headdresses (hide with hair).

BUFFALO HUNTING SEASONS

Although buffalo were considered fair game by the Blackfoot throughout the year, these Indians recognized seasonal differences in the quality of meat and the utility of hides. Throughout most of the year the meat of bulls was tough and unpalatable compared with that of cows. For that reason the Indians showed a marked preference for killing cows save in the early summer when bulls were prime. They recognized the approach of the bull hunting season when they saw the yellow flowers of so-called "tooth grass" (probably *Thermopsis montana*, the mountain-goldenpea). In the warm summer months, when buffalo hair was short, skins were taken for lodge covers and the numerous other articles made from soft-dressed skins or rawhide. Cows were at their best in fall, when "spear grass" (probably *Stipa comata*, needle-and-thread) was spread out. This was the period of intensive hunting to secure winter meat supplies, ending in the impounding of buffalo at sites near winter camps shortly before the approach of heavy winter (i. e., in November and December). It was only during the cold months, November through February, that buffalo hair was long. That was the season for killing buffalo to obtain robes for the fur trade and for Indian use in making cold weather garments and bedding. Calves, generally born in May, were hunted shortly thereafter.

Attention was partially diverted from hunting for two short periods in spring and fall. In spring and early summer roots were dug; in fall berries were collected. These seasons coincided with the ones during which the horticultural tribes of the Plains also were concerned primarily with plant foods. During the winter months the horticultural Oto, Omaha, Pawnee, Kansa, Osage, and Sauk and Fox of the 19th century were absent from their permanent villages, hunting buffalo as did the nomadic tribes. In spring they returned to their semipermanent villages to plant their crops. In summer they again resorted to the chase, returning to their villages in fall to harvest their crops and again set out on the long winter hunt. These tribes' practice of agriculture and seasonal occupation of semipermanent villages distinguished them from the nomadic tribes of the Plains. Nevertheless, throughout the greater part of the year they lived in portable dwellings as nomadic buffalo hunters like their non-horticultural neighbors.[1]

---

[1] The following sources describe the seasonal movements of these tribes: Oto (Dodge, 1836, p. 5; Whitman, 1937, p. 7) ; Omaha (James, 1823, vol. 1, pp. 201–202; Fletcher and La Flesche, 1911, pp. 270–271) ; Pawnee (James, 1823, vol. 1, pp. 445–446; Dunbar, 1880, pp. 276–277) ; Kansa (Wedel, 1946, p. 18), Osage (Morse, 1822, p. 205; Cooke, 1857, pp. 121–122) ; Sauk and Fox (Morse, 1822, pp. 126–127; Forsyth *in* Blair, 1912, vol. 2, pp.

THE BUFFALO HORSE

Great care was taken by the Blackfoot in selecting and training a buffalo hunting horse. This animal was the man's primary charger, ridden only in hunting, to war, and on dress occasions. Informants named five qualities sought in a buffalo runner: (1) enduring speed (the ability to retain speed over a distance of several miles); (2) intelligence (the ability to respond instantly to commands or to act properly on its own initiative); (3) agility (ability to move quickly alongside a buffalo, to avoid contact with the larger animal, and to keep clear of its horns); (4) sure-footedness (ability to run swiftly over uneven ground without stumbling); and (5) courage (lack of fear of buffalo). Usually a man selected the horse he wished to train as a buffalo hunter on the basis of its demonstrated swiftness and alertness. A 4-year-old was preferred, but a man who owned few horses might select a horse a year younger. The horse's courage could be determined only through experience in chasing buffalo. Some horses never overcame their fear of those large, shaggy beasts, and could not be trained as hunters. It took patient practice and use of the whip to train a horse to run close beside a buffalo.[2] The courageous horse, through experience, learned to follow the buffalo, move in close and "do its work" with little urging from its owner, so that the latter could concentrate upon making his kill. A well-trained buffalo horse would turn as the rider shifted his weight to one side, or in response to pressure from the rider's knee. Most buffalo runners were males, although some mares made good hunting horses.

Many Blackfoot men regarded their buffalo horses as priceless possessions. They would not trade them or give them away. In trade a buffalo runner of known ability would bring several common riding

233–234). It is most probable that this seasonal hunting-cultivating rhythm of the horticultural tribes of the Plains antedated their acquisition of horses. Before 1700 Nicholas Perrot (Blair, 1912, vol. 1, p. 119) reported that the tribes of the northern Prairies set out on buffalo-hunting expeditions each autumn after they had harvested their crops, returned to their villages in March to plant "the grain," then embarked on a hunting trip. The De Gannes Memoir (Pease and Werner, 1934 b, p. 339–344) described the same seasonal rhythm among the horticultural Illinois in 1688.

The Mandan of the Upper Missouri were more sedentary, not because they did not observe the same seasonal rhythm, but because buffalo were numerous near their winter villages making prolonged hunting trips at that season unnecessary (Maximilian, 1906, vol. 23, p. 345).

[2] In writing of the Coronado expedition to the Plains in 1541, Castenada noted, "there was not one of the horses that did not take fright when he saw them (buffalo) first" (Winship, 1896, p. 542). Yet M'Gillivray (1929, p. 29) wrote of the Indian-trained buffalo horse of the North Saskatchewan in 1794, "he delights in the pleasure of the chace, and is so animated at the sight of a Band of animals that he can scarcely be restrained from pursuing them." During Captain Clark's journey down the Yellowstone in the fall of 1805, the loose horses driven by Sergeant Pryor sighted a herd of buffalo, and "having been trained by the Indians to hunt, immediately set off in pursuit of them, and surrounded the herd with almost as much skill as their riders could have done" (Coues, 1893, vol. 3, p. 1148).

horses or transport animals. Only a race horse of tested speed would have greater value than a well-trained buffalo horse.[3]

Buffalo runners of the Blackfoot were given special care. Three Calf recalled that his father, who owned several buffalo horses, would not permit boys to catch, ride, or play with any of them. After a chase a buffalo horse was taken to a stream, water was thrown on it, and it was rubbed down. Some men made a practice of throwing water on their buffalo horses every morning and evening to toughen them and prepare them for hard winters. Before setting out on a chase the hunter's wife carefully prepared his mount for him. She met him on his return, took his horse from him and cared for it.[4]

METHODS OF BUFFALO HUNTING ON HORSEBACK

Two general methods of hunting buffalo on horseback were employed by the Blackfoot; the surround, and the chase (referred to in some accounts as "running buffalo").

The surround method employed a considerable number of horsemen to encircle a herd of buffalo, start them milling in a circle, and shoot down the frightened and confused animals as they rode around them. Wissler (1910, p. 37) reported Blackfoot use of the surround. The classic description and illustration of this method are from the hand of George Catlin (Catlin, 1841, vol. 1, pp. 199–201, and pl. 79). His original painting of a Hidatsa surround is in the United States National Museum (No. 386,394).[5]

The chase was a straightaway rush by mounted men, each hunter singling out an animal from the herd, riding alongside it and killing it at close quarters, then moving on to another animal and killing it in like manner. The Blackfoot seem to have virtually abandoned the surround in favor of the chase around the middle of the 19th century. During the last two decades of buffalo hunting (i. e. in the youth of my older informants) the chase alone was employed as a method of

---

[3] In 1806 Henry wrote that among the Hidatsa "first-rate horses, such as are trained for war, or noted for running, can hardly be had for any quantity of goods. The only article that will induce them to part with a horse of this kind is a white buffalo hide" (Henry and Thompson, 1897, vol. 1, p. 353). Marcy (1937, pp. 156, 158) found the Comanche refused to part with their buffalo horses. Frank Bosin told me the Kiowa rarely would trade a buffalo horse. He stressed the point that such horses were necessary to their livelihood and pointed out that horses not specially trained for buffalo hunting were incapable of that activity.

[4] This seems to have been common Plains Indian practice. It was reported of the Crow as early as 1805 (Larocque, 1910, p. 59), of the Hidatsa-Mandan (Boller, 1868, p. 232), Osage (Tixier, 1940, p. 170), and Comanche (Marcy, 1937, p. 157). Assiniboin women rubbed down the returning buffalo horse with sage before it was allowed to graze (Long, 1942, p. 171).

[5] As early as 1750, Father Vivier briefly described the Pawnee surround on horseback. "They hunt on horseback with arrows and spears; they surround a herd of cattle, and but few escape" (Jesuit Relations, vol. 69, p. 227). Wissler reported the use of the surround by the Mandan, Arikara, Arapaho, Omaha, and Cheyenne also (Wissler, 1910, p. 50). He said it was employed by "the southern tribes generally."

killing buffalo from horseback. The tendency toward the abandonment of the surround may have been plainswide. Certainly the best contemporary descriptions of that method are found in writings of the period ante-1850.[6]
The chase had definite advantages over the surround. It was certainly less dangerous. It made it easier for the hunter to single out a buffalo for the kill and to get an unobstructed shot at that animal. It could also be practiced by any number of hunters, from a single rider to the able male population of a large village. Apparently the chase was practiced at an early date in the northwestern Plains. Anthony Hendry, while visiting the "Archithinue" (probably Gros Ventres) village of 200 lodges, entered in his diary under the date October 16, 1754, "with the Leader's permission, I rode a hunting with twenty of his young men. They killed 8 Buffalo, excellent sport. They are so expert that with one or two arrows they will drop a Buffalo. As for me I had sufficient employ to manage my horse" (Hendry, 1907, p. 350). This earliest description of buffalo hunting on horseback by northwestern Plains Indians suggests the employment of the chase. Since my Blackfoot informants stated that it frequently required three or more arrows to kill a buffalo in their time, we may judge that the "Archithinue" were very skilled in killing buffalo from horseback at that early date. By the period of the 1830's the chase seems to have been the preferred method of buffalo hunting throughout the Plains.[7]
A detailed description of the chase, the favored Blackfoot method of hunting buffalo in the youth of my informants, follows.

THE BUFFALO CHASE ON HORSEBACK

PREPARATIONS

Before a chase the principal chief (of a tribal summer camp) or the chief (of a band camp) invited all the chiefs or leading men of his village to his lodge to discuss plans for the hunt. Often this meeting took place the night before a large hunt. Then the chief (through his announcer) told the people to catch their buffalo horses and extra pack animals to be used to bring in the meat. If the camp was a tribal one, the chief at that time proclaimed that the prohibition against individual hunting was in force. I gained the impression that this regulation was less common in the smaller band camps. Women who were

---

[6] Dunbar, writing of Pawnee culture of the period of the 1830's, stated, "The Pawnees seldom resorted to a surround, attacking from all sides at once. This method was more tedious and dangerous, and was regarded as less huntsmanlike" (than the chase) (Dunbar, 1880, p. 330).

[7] With the exception of the single surround mentioned, all of George Catlin's numerous paintings of Indian buffalo hunts on horseback by tribes of both the northern and southern Plains depict the chase. Contemporary descriptions of Plains Indian employment of the chase are legion.

not to accompany the hunters to aid in butchering and packing meat back to camp were left in camp. Sometimes they were instructed to move camp while the hunt was in progress.

EQUIPMENT

In leaving camp for the hunt each hunter rode a common horse (to be later used for packing meat, if his horses were few) and led his buffalo horse in order to save its strength for the chase.[8] Women and boys followed with the pack animals.

Although some Blackfoot preferred to ride bareback in hunting buffalo, many used the pad saddle. Weasel Tail said he always rode a pad saddle when hunting buffalo because it added little weight to his mount while providing him with a firm seat with feet braced in the stirrups to permit a steadier aim. A few hunters rode "prairie chicken snare saddles."

Generally hunters wore leggings, a breechcloth and moccasins, and a shirt with short sleeves which would not get in their way or become bloodied in butchering. These were either skin or old cloth garments without any decoration. Old clothes were desirable for the bloody business of killing and especially of butchering.

Before the introduction of the breechloader among the Blackfoot in 1870, firearms were rarely employed in the buffalo chase. It was too difficult to reload a muzzle-loading musket on a fast-moving horse to make its use practical. Most men would have had to stop their horses each time they reloaded, thus losing ground on the running herd. Kurz (1937, p. 195) described the use of muzzle-loaders by white hunters attached to Fort Union in 1851, who were skilled in reloading on the run. However, the very great majority of Blackfoot Indian hunters preferred the bow and arrow for the buffalo chase. This bow was short, often not more than 3 feet in length, so as to be easily managed on horseback. It was of ash, chokecherry or sarvis berry. The quiver, slung at the rider's back, contained 20 to 30 iron-headed arrows. The stone-headed arrow went out of use among the Blackfoot long before the time of my informants. Some men preferred to use a short, metal-headed, ash-poled lance. However, the use of the lance in buffalo hunting was on the wane among the Blackfoot even before the introduction of breech-loading rifles. Lazy Boy, my eldest Piegan informant, could not recall ever having seen the lance carried by a buffalo hunter of his tribe. Even as early as 1833, Maximilian (1906, vol. 23, p. 119) remarked, "I saw few

---

[8] This seems to have been a common Plains Indian practice, reported for the Cheyenne (Hamilton, 1905, p. 28), Plains Cree (Mandelbaum, 1940, p. 191), Plains Ojibwa (Skinner, 1914, p. 494), and Hidatsa-Mandan (Boller, 1868, p. 77).

lances among the Blackfeet." [9]   As soon as Blackfoot Indians could acquire breechloading firearms they discarded the bow and arrow as a buffalo-hunting weapon.   However, the new guns were expensive, and poor people of necessity continued to employ the bow and arrow. Among all the buffalo-hunting tribes the bow and arrow seems to have been the favorite hunting weapon in use before ca. 1870.

THE APPROACH

Through scouts the location of the buffalo herd which was to be the object of attack became well known in advance.   The hunting party moved cautiously, trying to keep out of sight of the buffalo, and always approaching from down wind of the herd to prevent them from catching human scent.   If the terrain permitted, the approach was from behind a hill or from the mouth of a coulee where the hunters could be concealed from sight of the buffalo until they were nearly upon them.   When the hunting party got as close to the buffalo as they could approach without alarming their prey the hunters dismounted, mounted their buffalo horses, and left their common riding animals in the hands of the women and boys who remained with the pack animals in concealment.   The leader of the hunters lined them up to give them all an equal chance.[10]   At a signal from him, they whipped their buffalo runners into a run, each hunter being eager to be the first to make a kill.   Sometimes they approached the game in two groups according to preconceived plan, some of the men riding along the right of the herd, others (including the lancers and left-handed bowmen) riding on the left.   This approach may have been understood by some writers as an employment of the surround. Actually it was not.   It was running the buffalo by two parallel groups of hunters.[11]

THE RUN

(PL. 14)

No time could be lost once the buffalo became aware of the approaching hunters and started to run in the opposite direction.   Healthy cows could run faster than bulls.   In a small running herd the cows generally took the lead, followed by the bulls, which were in turn trailed by the calves.   Except in the summer season when bulls were prime, Blackfoot hunters, confident of the speed and ability of their

[9] The former use of the lance in buffalo hunting has been reported for the Nez Percé (Spinden, 1908, p. 213), Cheyenne (Grinnell, 1923, vol. 1, p. 263), Osage (Tixier, 1940, p. 192), and Kansa (Farnham, 1906, p. 85).

[10] This practice of lining up the hunters to give them an equal opportunity has been reported as common among the Plains Cree (Mandelbaum, 1940, p. 191), Osage (Tixier, 1940, p. 191), Pawnee (Dunbar, 1880, vol. 5, p. 330).

[11] Hamilton (1905, pp. 28–30) witnessed the employment of this approach in two divisions of hunters by the Cheyenne in the 1840's.

horses, generally by-passed the running bulls to get to the cows. Unless he was left-handed, the bowman approached the buffalo he had singled out for slaughter from the right side, brought his horse close alongside, fixed an arrow to his bow and aimed at the fatal spot, which Hornaday (1889, p. 471) described as "from 12 to 18 inches in circumference, and lies immediately back of the foreleg with its lowest point on a line with the elbow." The arrow was shot without sighting, generally with the bow held a little off vertical, the top tilted to the right. However, each hunter used the position easiest for him. Informants insisted that all Blackfoot hunters did not learn to shoot in the same way, nor did they all employ the same method of arrow release. As the arrow left the bow the trained buffalo horse swerved away from its quarry, running in close again to permit additional shots if required.

Informants were familiar with the common stories of men who had shot arrows completely through buffalo. Weasel Tail claimed he had twice done this in killing young cows. Nevertheless, they stated that it usually required three or more arrows to bring down a running cow. The quiver was carried on the back with the opening behind the hunter's left shoulder (if he was right-handed), so he could easily and quickly take another arrow from it with his right hand, fit it to the bow held in his left hand, and shoot rapidly.

On the run the hunter carried the long end of his bridle rope coiled and tucked under his belt (fig. 11), so that should he be thrown but not hurt or badly shaken up, he could grab the free end of this line as it paid out and retrieve his horse, possibly in time to mount and continue the chase (p. 76).

Blackfoot lancers usually approached buffalo from the left side.[12] They delivered their blows in powerful overhand chops.

The run usually continued until the herd outdistanced the pursuing hunters.

NUMBER OF BUFFALO KILLED IN A SINGLE CHASE

Testimony of my Blackfoot informants supported the generalization of Tixier (1940, p. 191), written more than a century ago, that in the buffalo chase the "best beast belongs to the best horse, and for this reason they say on the prairie 'My horse has killed many buffalo.' " Boller (1868, p. 232) told of an expert Hidatsa hunter, The Last Stone, of whom it was said, "He could kill on any kind of horse," a high tribute to his ability as a marksman to bring down his game at a long distance. However, the very great majority of the Blackfoot, and of the Hidatsa as well, relied upon the speed and courage of their mounts to bring them close beside the buffalo before shooting.

[12] Osage lancers also killed buffalo from the left side of that animal (Tixier, 1940, p. 192).

Four or five buffalo cows were the most informants could recall having been killed on a single chase by the best Blackfoot marksman with the best horse under him. Most hunters rarely killed more than one or two buffalo at a chase. Men with inferior buffalo horses had to be satisfied with killing the slower running bulls. The owner of a poorly trained or short-winded horse could not hope to kill any buffalo via the chase.[13]

BOYS' HUNTING OF BUFFALO CALVES

Boys 10 years of age or older gained their first experience in buffalo hunting on the fair weather hunts from spring through fall. After the men started a herd and rode after it the boys, on 1- or 2-year-old colts, followed after the calves left in the wake of the running herd. They imitated the actions of their elders, riding in close and shooting the calves with bows and arrows. In this way they gained skill and confidence so that in their middle teens they could begin hunting adult buffalo.[14] Nearly all my elderly, male Blackfoot informants had chased buffalo calves. Only the oldest of them had had opportunities to kill adult buffalo before these animals were exterminated from the Blackfoot Country.

Three Calf said that as a boy he helped hunters pack meat to camp and was also given the task of cleaning buffalo intestines. Boys were not taken on winter hunts on horseback.

HUNTING ACCIDENTS

Accidents were not infrequent in hunting buffalo. Horses stumbled on uneven ground, stepped in badger holes, or were gored by wounded bulls. Riders were thrown and injured or killed. Lazy Boy recalled that Lame Bull, the Piegan head chief at the time of the 1855 treaty, was killed while running buffalo 3 years later. Amid the dust of the chase Lame Bull's horse did not move adroitly enough to avoid an old bull that attacked him. The horse fell on Lame Bull breaking his neck and crushing his ribs. Generally the less intelligent and well-trained the horse, the greater was the chance of serious accident in the chase.[15]

---

[13] Contemporary statements regarding other tribes give similar maximum figures. Tixier (1940, p. 193) among the Osage found that "a good horse can overtake three or four cows in one hunt." Boller (1868, p. 227) noted that among the Mandan-Hidatsa "the more expert hunters will kill from three to five cows in a chase."

[14] Grinnell (1923, vol. 1, p. 118) reported Cheyenne boys' practice of hunting buffalo calves. He wrote that "if on his first chase a boy killed a calf, his father was greatly pleased, and if a well-to-do man, he might present a good horse to some poor man, and in addition might give a feast and invite poor people to come and eat with him."

[15] Writers on the Cheyenne (Hamilton, 1905, p. 29), Hidatsa-Mandan (Boller, 1868, p. 234), and Pawnee (Dunbar, 1880, p. 331) have mentioned the frequency and seriousness of accidents that occurred among those tribes while running buffalo.

BUTCHERING AND PACKING

When the men had finished their killing their leader waved to the women to come out with the pack animals. Meanwhile the men located the buffalo they had killed by the marks on their arrows in the fallen beasts. A woman who was not lazy would help her husband in butchering. Together they could complete the task of butchering a buffalo in about an hour. Wissler (1910, p. 42) was told of Blackfoot men who could butcher 5 to 12 animals in a day. A common butcher knife was used, and a hind leg was cut off to employ as a hatchet in breaking the ribs.

Wissler (1910, p. 41–42) has properly distinguished two types of butchering, "heavy butchering," and "light butchering." In the former the animal was utilized to the fullest extent. In the latter only the best parts of the animal were taken. "Light butchering" was common when meat was relatively plentiful and/or killing was far from camp and few pack animals were available. In times of scarcity "heavy butchering" was the rule.

Informants claimed it required two pack animals to carry the meat of a buffalo cow that had been subjected to "heavy butchering." Mrs. Cree Medicine described the method of packing employed by members of her family. One pack animal carried only the four quarters of the animal. The tendons of the forequarters were tied together with a piece of rawhide and they were thrown over the pack saddle so that one quarter fell at each side of the pack animal. The hind quarters were slung in the same way. The hide was thrown over the back of a second pack horse, the two slabs of back fat were folded over this, and the ribs were tied with rawhide cord and added to the load. Then the two flanks were tied together and placed on the horse. A hole was punched in the boss ribs through which a cord was passed and tied to the pack. Next the hipbones were packed, and the neck was cut away from the head, split open from the bottom, and spread out over the top of the load. Finally the edges of the robe (at the bottom of the pack) were raised and tied together to hold the pack securely. The woman generally wrapped the entrails in a separate bundle and carried it herself. A buffalo cow averaged 400 pounds of meat produce. Thus it would have been too great a burden to consign this entire weight to a single Indian pony. However, informants said that when "light butchering" was resorted to a single packhorse could carry the load. Thus the number of pack animals available to the hunter often was the determining factor in the choice of method of butchering and the total amount of food that he could salvage from a single chase.[16]

---

[16] The literature contains a number of references to Indian horses belonging to other tribes packing the meat of an entire buffalo, and Alexander Henry wrote of a returning

The Blackfoot hunter returned to camp riding his buffalo horse while his wife took charge of the pack animals. There was a strong belief among the Blackfoot that the buffalo horse should never have meat packed on it. However, poor people sometimes had little choice. The Blackfoot never packed meat on a race horse.[17]

LOANING OF BUFFALO HORSES FOR HUNTING

Owners of few horses among the Blackfoot rarely possessed a good buffalo runner. They tried to borrow trained buffalo horses from wealthy relatives or band chiefs. The loan of buffalo horses not only improved the opportunities of the poor but enhanced the prestige of the loaner and proved his right to leadership. Some wealthy men owned as many as 10 or more trained buffalo horses, some of which they loaned the poor for hunting. Some men of wealth gave their wives buffalo horses, which they might loan to poor relatives. However, if a man found that his wife had loaned one of his buffalo runners without his knowledge, he might give her a sound beating. Horses were loaned for the duration of a chase. If the hunt was near camp they would be returned within the day.

Three Calf said his father loaned horses for buffalo hunting in this way:

A man asked my father for the loan of a horse. Father told him, "Yes, get that pinto (pointing out a buffalo runner in his herd), and another horse to pack with if you need it." There was no agreement in advance for any payment to be made on the loan. If the borrower was appreciative he gave a lot of the best meat from the buffalo he killed to my father. If the man was selfish and offered my father no meat, the next time he wished to borrow horses, father told him, "No."

If the buffalo runner met with an accident (suffered a broken leg or a rupture) while hunting on loan, and the borrower was known to be a reliable, earnest fellow, father told him, "That was nothing to be ashamed of. It was an accident. Young man, your body is worth more than the horse. Let's have no hard feelings." But if the borrower was an irresponsible fellow, father gave him a rough talking to, and made him replace the lost horse.

Informants agreed that there were no standardized repayments for the loan of buffalo horses. Payments depended upon a number of factors, including (1) whether meat was plentiful or scarce in the

---

party of Mandan hunters seen by him in 1806 in which each horse was loaded with about half a buffalo plus the weight of a rider (Henry and Thompson, 1897, vol. 1, p. 336). Either such references referred to instances of "light butchering" or the pack animals must have been greatly overloaded. In the Mandan case just cited the latter certainly was the case.

[17] Other Plains Indian tribes seem to have shared the taboo against carrying meat on a buffalo horse. James (1823, vol. 1, p. 210) wrote that the Omaha (in 1819) "rarely subjected" buffalo runners "to the drudgery of carrying burdens." Tixier (1940, p. 193) observed among the Osage that "when a pack animal follows the hunter, the hunting horse returns to camp without any other burden but its rider." Turney-High (1937, p. 117) specifically mentioned the Flathead taboo against packing meat on a buffalo horse.

home of the horse owner at the time of the hunt, (2) whether the owner himself hunted and whether he was successful in this particular hunt, (3) the size and food needs of both the owner's and borrower's families, and (4) the generosity of owner and borrower. Some owners were themselves able hunters and generally would not accept meat or hides from the borrower. On the other hand, men who were too old to hunt or were physically handicapped (such as the wealthy Piegan blind man, Stingy), were forced to rely upon the buffalo killed by other men while riding their horses. If game was scarce the loaner expected a share of the meat killed by riders of his horses. However, it usually was not necessary for the borrower to give him as much as half the kill.

The loaning of buffalo horses was a widespread Plains Indian custom.[18]

FEEDING THE POOR

Poor families which either were unable to borrow buffalo horses or possessed no able-bodied hunter in their lodges were forced to rely upon the charity of the wealthy for their buffalo meat. Some poor people took their dogs or poor horses out where buffalo were butchered, when the animals were killed near camp. There they could generally find successful hunters who would give them meat to carry home for their consumption. However, Weasel Tail recalled that hunters were loathe to give away the meat of fat cows. They generally preferred to give lean meat to the poor.

Mrs. Cree Medicine told the story of a young man who was found lying beside a partly butchered buffalo by an old couple who had gone out from camp hoping to receive some meat from the kill. The old couple thought he was dead. They threw water on him and he did not move. Then they started back to camp to tell the people of his death. When they had gone a short distance they turned around and saw

---

[18] Tixier (1940, p. 184) wrote of the Osage, "The more horses that are owned by a savage, the more hunters he can send to the buffalo hunt." Llewellyn and Hoebel (1941, p. 229) told of a Cheyenne woman who loaned a horse to young men for hunting and received a hide or two in exchange. Kiowa men of wealth loaned horses for hunting, but Frank Bosin claimed the lender generally did not expect payment in meat. Elkin (1940, p. 224) described the Northern Arapaho practice in words that indicate that payments varied much as they did among the Blackfoot. Boller noted that a wealthy Hidatsa-Mandan "could always command the services of a good hunter." He also observed that a man who had lost his horses "will usually act as a hunter for some relative rich in horses, who by giving him a few robes now and then, in payment as it were for his services, affords him an opportunity to regain his former position" (Boller, 1868, pp. 52, 195). Mandelbaum (1940, p. 195) reported that among the Plains Cree, notoriously poor in horses, only about 1 lodge in 10 owned a good buffalo horse. "A number of families would attach themselves to the owner of such a horse and followed him wherever he moved his camp. They shared in the buffalo he was able to secure by means of his horse. Since these families were dependent on the horse owner for food, they were naturally quick to carry out his wishes or orders." This is an extreme example of the correlation between buffalo horse ownership and leadership among Plains Indians. Yet even among the wealthier tribes the rich man's generous use of horses to benefit the poor served to pave his way to social and political distinction and helped him to maintain that position once attained.

the young man, standing up, butchering the buffalo. After he returned to camp they told him they had brought him back to life. He then reluctantly gave them some of the best parts of his meat. Other people claimed the young man had deliberately played dead to avoid giving any of his meat to the aged couple. He became known by the name Playing-Dead-beside-the-Buffalo. As David Thompson observed a century and a half ago, stinginess was a trait detested by the Blackfoot. He noted that the "tent of a sick man is well supplied" after a chase, and that deaths from hunger were very rare (Thompson, 1916, pp. 355–356). One of the recognized responsibilities of band leadership among the Blackfoot was that of feeding the poor.

REGULATION OF THE SUMMER BUFFALO HUNT

In summer, when all of the bands of a tribe gathered prior to the Sun Dance encampment, the head chief, through his announcer, declared the hunting regulation in force. All tribal members understood this meant that anyone who sought to kill buffalo on his own before the tribal hunt was organized would be severely punished by society members selected to act as policemen. A century ago Mitchell (1855, pp. 686–687) explained, "This policy is obvious, as one individual might frighten off a herd of buffalo sufficient to feed the whole camp." Piegan regulation of buffalo hunting was observed by David Thompson (1916, pp. 358–359) prior to 1800:

> The same evening a Chief walked through the camp informing them that as the Bisons were too far off for hunting they had given orders to the Soldiers to allow no person to hunt until further notice. Such an order is sure to find some tents ill provided. While we were there, hunting was forbidden on this account. Two tents which had gambled away their things, even to dried provisions, had to steal a march on the Soldiers under pretence of looking after their horses; but finding they did not return were watched. In the evening of the second day, they approached the camp, with their horses loaded with meat which the Soldiers seized, and the owners quickly gave up; the former distributed the Meat to the tents that had many women and children, and left nothing to the owners; but those that had received the Meat, in the night sent them a portion of it. Not a murmur was heard, every one said they had acted right.

The punishment in that instance was much less severe than that described by Mountain Chief as Piegan punishment about 1850. The culprit's weapons were broken, his clothes torn, his saddle broken to pieces, his rope and whip cut into small bits, and his horse's tail bobbed (Dixon, 1913, pp. 109–110). Informants recalled that in their youth the disobedient man's meat was taken from him, his weapons were broken, and his clothing was torn by the police. My data suggest that the punishment was not standardized, but varied in proportion to the disturbance to the buffalo herd on the part of the culprit and the supply of meat in the camp.

Strict regulation of the tribal buffalo hunt by society policemen was customary among other Plains Indian tribes. In table 5, I have summarized the punishments exacted by different tribes as reported in the literature. In all probability, however, their punishments were no more standardized than among the Blackfoot. Physical punishment by flogging the offender seems to have been widely employed. The principal object of all punishments for this offense seems to have been to teach the culprit a lesson that would discourage his repetition of the antisocial act. By and large, punishment seems to have been lightest among the wealthy Comanche and most severe among the poor Ponca and Plains Cree. The wholesale destruction of the culprit's property by Ponca and Plains Cree policemen, and the later restitution of his losses seems to have been a prodigal waste of limited tribal resources. Undoubtedly, the offense was more harmful to the welfare of a tribe poor in horses that would have difficulty in catching up with the disturbed herd than to a tribe possessing larger numbers of horses and much greater mobility.[19]

TABLE 5.—*Penalties for premature hunting in tribal buffalo hunts*

Tribe	Penalty	Reference
Plains Cree	Offender's lodge and all possessions destroyed; generally given gifts to compensate his losses at later date.	Mandelbaum, 1940, p. 227.
Plains Ojibwa	Offender flogged. His shirt cut to shreds.	Skinner, 1914, p. 494.
Crow	Offender beaten; arms broken or lodge cut to pieces	Larocque, 1910, p. 60.
Cheyenne	Offender whipped. If persisted in disobedience, his lodge cover and poles destroyed, and perhaps his horses killed.	Grinnell, 1923, vol. 1, p. 262.
Wind River Shoshoni	Offender's horse whipped over the head; all hides taken destroyed.	Lowie, 1915, p. 819.
Flathead	Offender received severe whip lashing at hands of chief.	Turney-High, 1937, p. 118.
Omaha	Offender knocked down and flogged	James, 1823, vol. 1, p. 208.
Ponca	Offender beaten, his horses and dogs destroyed. Next day presents given him to restore his losses.	Skinner, 1915, pp. 796–797.
Pawnee	Offender given merciless flogging	Dunbar, 1880, p. 330.
Kansa	Offender severely whipped, but property not destroyed.	Skinner, 1915, p. 819.
Osage	Offender flogged with whips	Tixier, 1940, p. 189.
Kiowa	Offender's horse shot	Battey, 1875, pp. 185–186.
Comanche	"Only punishment meted out to offenders was to reprove them."	Lowie, 1915, p. 812.

EARLY WINTER BUFFALO DRIVES

Although the earliest description of the impounding of buffalo in or near the Blackfoot Country appears in Cocking's account of his visit to a Gros Ventres pound in November and December, 1772, it is probable that the communal buffalo hunt by means of pounds was employed by the Blackfoot before they obtained horses (Cocking, 1908, pp. 109–

---

[19] The Red River halfbreeds on their organized buffalo hunts adopted a prohibition of individual hunting like that of the Plains Indians. Sibley noted that "when the halfbreeds have no acknowledged leader, those possessed of fleet horses advance at full speed, leaving the others no chance to secure a portion of the prey, there arise discord, quarrels, hatred, and all their train of evils" (Sibley, 1854, p. 104).

113). Three types of buffalo drives were employed by the Blackfoot within the historic period: (1) driving buffalo into corrals on the level Plains, (2) driving buffalo down steep slopes or over relatively low embankments into corrals, and (3) driving them over high cliffs so that the animals would be killed or maimed by their fall. No corrals were needed at the bases of these cliffs to prevent the animals' escape. Probably all three Blackfoot tribes employed the first method in prehistoric times. In the historic period it was used only by the North Blackfoot. The second and third methods were then employed by the Blood and Piegan. Blackfoot drives have been described by Henry (Henry and Thompson, 1897, pp. 576–577) ; Maximilian (1906, vol. 23, p. 108) ; Bradley (1923, p. 256) ; Grinnell (1892, pp. 228–232) ; Wissler (1910, pp. 34–38) ; and Barrett (1922, pp. 22–27). These writers considered the drive a winter method of buffalo hunting among the Blackfoot. As Barrett (1922, p. 23) stated, the drives were employed most frequently in the early winter period immediately following the establishment of winter camps (i. e., in November and December).

In historic times the Blackfoot employed mounted men to drive buffalo toward the V-shaped approaches to the pounds (Bradley, 1923, p. 256; Wissler, 1910, p. 37; Ewers, 1949, p. 359). Wissler claimed that Blackfoot use of horses and guns caused the drives to fall into disuse (Wissler, 1910, p. 37). Inasmuch as firearms were little used by the Blackfoot in buffalo hunting, I suggest that the popularity of the chase on horseback was the primary cause of the abandonment of the traditional drives. The last Piegan drive occurred in the early 1850's, while the North Blackfoot used this technique as late as ca. 1872 (Ewers, 1949, pp. 358–360). However, it is probable that drives were uncommon among both those tribes for some years prior to their last recorded employment.

The relationship between poverty in horse ownership and continued use of buffalo drives is borne out by the fact that the only tribes of the northern Plains to make extensive use of this hunting technique after about 1850 were the horse-poor Assiniboin and Plains Cree.[20]

The midwinter season, comprising the months of January and February, provided the most severe test of Blackfoot ability to keep their food supply abreast of their needs. Indian ingenuity devised a number of methods of hunting under cold weather conditions which, in combination, were usually adequate to supply necessary subsistence.

---

[20] Denig wrote in 1854, "We know of no nation now except the Assiniboin and Cree who practice it [the drive], because all the rest are well supplied with horses that can catch the buffalo, therefore, they are not compelled to resort to these means to entrap them" (Denig, 1930, p. 532). The Plains Cree even employed the drive in the summer months in the mid-19th century (Kane, 1925, pp. 80–82; Hind, 1860, vol. 1, pp. 355–359). The Sarsi, poor allies of the Blackfoot, are also reported to have made summer drives (Jenness, 1938, p. 17).

WINTER HUNTING ON HORSEBACK

In open winters, with little snow or heavy ice, it was possible to send out hunting parties on horseback. When buffalo were not found near the band camp, a few lodges of men, sometimes accompanied by a woman or two to do the cooking, went out on short hunting expeditions of less than a week's duration, or until they located and killed as many buffalo as they could pack back to camp. Possibility of these small groups being overtaken and massacred by enemy war parties made prosecution of these expeditions dangerous. Schultz (1907, pp. 62–63) witnessed these small winter hunting excursions during his residence among the Piegan prior to 1880.

THE WINTER HUNTING HORSE

Some Blackfoot Indians owned horses which were specially valued as winter hunting animals. The ideal winter buffalo runner was a male, at least 8 years of age, fully developed, solidly built, broad backed, long winded, and sure footed. It had to be a horse that did not mind the strong, cold, west wind, as the hunting approach was always against the wind. Many horses tended to duck their heads when running against the fierce winter blasts and so were of little value for hunting at that season. A colt that would break the ice of a stream and go into the water to drink was thought to be one that would later become a good winter hunting horse.

Winter hunting horses generally were fed on cottonwood bark and received special care during the cold months. In spring, when most other horses were weak and thin, these horses were strong. As soon as other buffalo runners fattened, the owner of a winter hunter let that horse run. It was not commonly ridden or used for hunting in summer or fall. I gained the impression that good winter hunting horses were rare and that they were owned by wealthy Indians only.

WINTER HUNTING ON FOOT

In some years the snow was so deep for extended periods it was impossible to use horses in hunting. Lazy Boy said that if the snow was over 4 inches deep it was useless to try to hunt buffalo on horseback. He recalled one winter when a rapid thaw was followed by a quick freeze. "Everything was ice. The only way we could hunt buffalo was to sneak up on them on foot."

There were a number of methods of stalking buffalo in winter. At that season the cold winds sweeping over the Plains drove wild game to shelter in timbered river valleys. Buffalo, deer, or antelope often could be found in the river bottoms near winter camps and killed without difficulty with bows and arrows or guns. Firearms were very useful to the Blackfoot in hunting buffalo on foot in winter.[21]

Hunters sometimes covered their heads and bodies with buffalo-skins or wolfskins in stalking buffalo afoot. Paul Kane (1925, p. 267) saw both skins worn by Indian buffalo hunters near Fort Edmonton in the severe winter of 1847–48. Weasel Tail recalled a Blood Indian method in which two men inside a buffalo robe shaped much like a buffalo in form moved close to a herd. When they came within arrow range a third man, who had followed close behind them, hidden from view of the grazing herd, stepped quickly aside and shot the buffalo. Paul Kane both observed and practiced a more fatiguing method of winter hunting at Fort Edmonton. A group of hunters crawled on their bellies, one behind another, in a winding course simulating the movement of a great snake. Approaching from leeward, they got within a few yards of a buffalo herd before rising and opening fire (ibid., p. 268).

FOOD RATIONING

Even the ingenious methods of hunting just described were of no avail if the buffalo drifted away from camp and beyond range of footmen during weather unfavorable to hunting on horseback. If game disappeared in an open winter the Indians could move camp, but under heavy snow conditions their horses were a handicap. Yet Lazy Boy, my eldest Piegan informant, could recall only one winter when buffalo disappeared at a time when the weather was too bad to use horses. His band, the Skunks, remembered that year as "when we ate dogs winter." A number of dogs were killed for food before buffalo drifted in from the north and meat again could be obtained. Mrs. Cree Medicine, of the Lone Eaters Band, could also remember but a single winter when members of her band were forced to eat dogs to avert starvation.

However, periods of reduced food consumption due to lack of game were more common. The poor people were the first to suffer. Then the wealthy, who had put up extensive winter supplies the previous fall, had to share their food with the poor. Meals were reduced to one a day to conserve the dwindling supply. Then, if a hunter or group of hunters managed to kill one or two buffalo and/or several smaller animals, they brought the meat to the band chief. He had it cut up and divided so that each family head in the camp received nearly the same amount, regardless of the number of persons in his family. When game became more plentiful this primitive form of

---

[21] Denig (1953, p. 37) reported that the Crow seldom used guns in hunting "except on foot when the snow is too deep for horses to catch the buffalos."

food rationing was discontinued. The chief relinquished his authority in food distribution. Each family again procured its meat according to its ability and its needs.[22]

MEAT CONSUMPTION OF THE BLACKFOOT

In 1881, the United States Government allowed the Indians of Blackfeet Agency 1½ pounds of beef per person per day in rations. Smaller quantities of other foods were included in the ration issues at that time (Ewers, 1944 c, p. 77). Informants claimed that in buffalo days the Indians "needed" more meat than that. An average daily consumption of 3 pounds per person in those days appears to be a conservative estimate.

In 1806, the fur trader, Alexander Henry (Henry and Thompson, 1897, vol. 2, p. 446) weighed 150 buffalo cows, killed from September 1 to February 1, and found they averaged 400 pounds exclusive of the offals. Bulls in the same period averaged 550 pounds exclusive of waste. The total eatable meat of one full-grown bull weighed as much as 800 pounds. Since the Blackfoot showed a decided preference for cow meat except during the early summer when bulls were prime, we may conservatively estimate the meat furnished by the average buffalo killed by them the year round at 400 pounds.

On the basis of the figures presented in the two paragraphs above we can estimate that one buffalo would furnish enough meat to feed our hypothetical average Blackfoot family for a period of 16 days, provided none of the meat was wasted, and the meat could be transported until it was all consumed. Carrying this line of reasoning further, it would appear, on purely mathematical grounds, that two dozen buffalo would have adequately supplied the meat needs of the family for a whole year.

However, such neat mathematical formulas bear little relationship to actual Blackfoot buffalo consumption. The abundance of buffalo in the Blackfoot Country, the relative ease with which they could be killed by mounted hunters, the limited facilities of the average family for transporting meat surpluses, and the demands of the fur trade for buffalo robes encouraged the wasteful slaughter of these animals during the 19th century. [23]

---

[22] The tendency to share equally the limited food returns of difficult periods has been noted among other Plains Indian tribes. Lewis and Clark observed that nearly one-half the Mandan passed down river in the dead of winter 1805–6, to hunt for several days. On their return "the game was equally divided among the families of the tribe" (Coues, 1893, vol. 1, p. 224). Boller (1868, p. 298) visited a camp of Arikara, a large part of whose horses had been stolen, which was reduced to sharing the limited proceeds of the hunt at the rate of one meal per person per day.

[23] That the fur trade encouraged the slaughter of many more animals than the Blackfoot needed for food can be illustrated with some precision. In 1857, 23,000 buffalo robes were traded by Indians at Fort Benton (Bradley, 1910, p. 156). The Indians trading there

Abundance of buffalo, coupled with the efficient method of hunting them provided by the use of horses, encouraged prodigal waste of meat. As early as 1754, Anthony Hendry observed that when buffalo were plentiful the "Archithinue" of the Saskatchewan Plains took only the tongues and other choice pieces, leaving the rest to the wolves (Hendry, 1907, pp. 334, 336, 338). Two Blackfoot hunters on horseback could kill enough buffalo to provide over a ton of meat in a matter of minutes on a single chase. Yet the average family possessed only enough pack animals to transport about a quarter of that weight in meat, in addition to household equipment, when camp moved. These factors encouraged "Light butchering" and use of only the choice parts of the buffalo in good times. Then feasting and the consumption of enormous quantities of meat within a short period of time were common. Then there was plenty of meat for rich and poor alike. Yet at other times, especially in late winter, when buffalo were scarce the Indians were reduced to strict rationing of limited food supplies on the basis of one meal a day.

IMPROVIDENT FOOD HABITS OF OTHER PLAINS TRIBES

Examples of the wastefulness of buffalo resources by other Plains tribes are numerous in the literature. A few selected observations from fur traders' accounts show that such improvidence was common to wealthy and poor tribes alike. Larocque (1910, p. 60) wrote of the wealthy Crow, with whom he traveled in the summer of 1805:

> They are the most improvident with regard to provision. It is amazing what numbers of Buffaloes or other quadrupeds they destroy—yet 2 or 3 days after a successful hunt the beef is gone. When hunting they take the fattest and cut part of an animal and leave the remainder; but it is no wonder that in a country abounding so much in Deer of all kind and Buffaloes and where the inhabitants kill it with so much ease to themselves, being always on horseback, that their love of good eating should expose them to the danger of a temporary fast.

In 1804, Tabeau (1939, p. 208) said the Arikara "would always have more provisions than would be needed to sustain them, if they were not prodigal in times of abundance." Yet the Arikara were relatively poor in horses. Tabeau cited the consumption of more than 100 boned cows, providing in excess of 30,000 pounds of meat, by an Arikara village of about 200 people in 4 days. This would average a buffalo a day for a family of 8 Arikara during the period of this

---

were the Blackfoot tribes and the Gros Ventres, having a combined population of about ?,400 (Vaughan in U. S. Comm. Ind. Affairs, 1858, p. 432). Probably the robes were all aken during the 4 cold months when buffalo hair was long, making their robes acceptable o the traders. We may compute that the meat of the animals killed to supply the robes raded would have furnished a daily average of over 8 pounds per person over the 4-month period. In addition, the Indians killed buffalo to obtain robes for their own use as bedding, winter garments, etc. necessitating a still greater slaughter of buffalo.

feast. Even allowing for the voracious appetites of the Arikara there must have been much more meat wasted than eaten.

Boller (1868, p. 229) observed of the relatively poor Hidatsa-Mandan, "When there is plenty of meat, the large bones and coarse pieces are always thrown aside, but in times of scarcity there is absolutely nothing left but the head."

This feast or famine economy quite likely existed among the Plains Indians before the introduction of horses. Nevertheless, their employment of horses, by making buffalo much easier to kill, encouraged greater squandering of buffalo resources, hastened the extermination of the buffalo, and thus contributed to the disintegration of their traditional culture based upon buffalo hunting.

HUNTING OF OTHER MAMMALS ON HORSEBACK

The hides of deer, elk, and antelope were very useful to the Blackfoot in the manufacture of summer and dress clothing. These animals were formerly numerous in the Blackfoot country. Although David Thompson (1916, p. 359) wrote of Piegan "bets between individuals upon hunting in running down animals, and the Red and Jumping Deer" from horseback in the period ca. 1800, both the more recent literature and the testimony of my informants claim that these animals were hunted by footmen. Denig (1930, pp. 535-537) said it was the general practice of all the Upper Missouri tribes to hunt deer, elk, and antelope on foot.[24] My Blackfoot informants said that not only was there no communal hunting of deer, elk, or antelope by mounted men, but it was rare for a lone horseman to ride one of those animals down. Weasel Tail said few Blackfoot-owned horses were swift enough to chase them. Lazy Boy referred to a colt, born from a mare stolen from the Shoshoni, that was able to catch up with an antelope herd as a rare and unusually speedy horse.

Nevertheless the literature indicates that deer and antelope hunting by mounted Indians of the southern Plains and Plateau was not uncommon.[25] Their skill and ability in this activity may be considered proof of the greater speed of their horses as well as their superiority as horsemen over the Blackfoot and other Upper Missouri tribes.

---

[24] However, Raynolds (1868, p. 62) witnessed two Crow Indians chase an elk on horseback and bring it down, in the fall of 1859.

[25] The Nez Percé preferred to hunt deer from horseback "wherever the ground would permit," in Lewis and Clark's time (Coues, 1893, vol. 3, p. 1013). Teit (1930, p. 103) credited Coeur d'Alene horsemen with running down antelope on open ground, although "this kind of hunting was not always successful." In 1840, Tixier (1940, p. 169) witnessed an Osage deer hunt by relays of mounted men. Twelve years later Marcy (1937 p. 156) saw two young Comanche women ride after antelope, and rope them. Enoch Smoky told me the Kiowa formerly hunted deer, elk, and antelope from horseback.

THE HORSE IN WAR

BRIEF HISTORY OF BLACKFOOT INTERTRIBAL WARFARE

American fur traders recognized the Blackfoot as the most potent and aggressive military power in the northwestern Plains in the 19th century. Collectively the three Blackfoot tribes comprised one of the three strongest military powers of the Great Plains. The other two great powers of the Plains were the Teton Dakota (allied with the Northern Arapaho and Northern Cheyenne), and the Comanche (allied with the Kiowa and Kiowa-Apache). Allies of the Blackfoot were the Sarsi and (until 1861) the Gros Ventres.

Blackfoot war parties operated in a vast theater of warfare extending far beyond the limits of the area over which they hunted (fig. 24). In 1787, David Thompson reported a Piegan raid from the vicinity of present Edmonton, Alberta, southward as far as "about 32 degrees north latitude." Members of that party returned with spoils in horses and riding gear captured directly from the Spanish (Thompson, 1916, pp. 370–371). That was by all odds the most distant Blackfoot raid that has been reported. Against the Assiniboin and Cree the Blackfoot raided eastward beyond the South Saskatchewan and beyond Fort Union at the mouth of the Yellowstone. They raided westward as far as Sand Point, in present Idaho, against the Salishan tribes (Teit, 1930, p. 364). They repeatedly attacked the Flathead in their Bitterroot Valley homeland west of the Rockies, and frequently warred upon the Kutenai of Tobacco Plains (Hamilton, 1900, p. 103). Their raids against Shoshonean enemies carried them westward to Fort Hall and the Boise Valley on Snake River and as far southwestward as Utah Lake, in present Utah (Stuart, 1896, p. 119; Steward, 1938, p. 208). Gregg (1905, vol. 19, pp. 221–239) reported "'Blackfeet" parties raiding along the Santa Fe Trail in the southern Plains in 1829–31. These were members of a group of "Blackfeet" and Gros Ventres who joined the Cheyenne and Arapaho near the Black Hills some time prior to 1826, and moved south of the Platte River with them (Grinnel, 1923, vol. 1, pp. 39–40). Colonel Dodge found "a small band of Blackfeet proper, consisting of about fifty" living with the Cheyenne in the fall of 1835 (Dodge, 1836, p. 25). Some of these Blackfoot may not have returned to their own people, for Major Culbertson met 10 lodges of Blood Indians living with the Arapaho at the Laramie Treaty Council 16 years later (Bradley MS.; bk. A, p. 184).

Blackfoot traditions claim that the Shoshoni were their only enemies in pre-horse times. According to Saukamappee's account some Cree and Assiniboin warriors aided the Piegan in fighting the Shoshoni in the period preceding Blackfoot acquisition of horses (Thompson, 1916, pp. 328–338). This indicates that those eastern neighbors of the Blackfoot were friendly at that time. Yet James Isham, in 1743, reported that "the Sinne-poets and other Indians" were going to war against the "Earchethinues" (perhaps both Gros Ventres and Blackfoot), while Graham recorded Assiniboin raiding of "Archithenue" horses in 1775 (Isham, 1949, pp. 113, 311). Probably Blackfoot-Cree warfare also was initiated soon after the Blackfoot acquired horses. Assiniboin and Cree, well armed by white traders and covetous of Blackfoot horses and hunting grounds, continued to exert pressure on the Blackfoot from the northeast. Those tribes continued at war with the Blackfoot until the middle 1880's, although occasional short-lived periods of peace interrupted the prolonged hostility.

After the Blackfoot tribes acquired both horses and firearms they pushed the Shoshoni southward and westward and forced the Flathead and Kutenai from their hunting grounds on the Plains immediately east of the Rockies to sanctuary in the wooded valleys west of the mountains (Ferris, 1940, pp. 90–92; Thompson, 1916, pp. 304, 327–44, 463; Teit, 1930, pp. 316–321). Lacking firearms the Shoshoni and Salishan tribes were inadequately equipped to oppose the aggressive and numerous Blackfoot. By the end of the first decade of the 19th century the Salishan tribes and the Nez Percé began to acquire firearms. They united in buffalo-hunting expeditions onto the Plains which were strongly opposed by the Blackfoot (Ewers, 1948, pp. 14–17). The Salishan tribes and the Shoshoni remained enemies of the Blackfoot until the end of buffalo days. Blackfoot-Nez Percé conflicts were rare after about 1855.

Contemporary white observers of the Blackfoot did not mention any conflicts with the Crow Indians prior to 1800. It is probable these tribes seldom met prior to that date. Yet, in 1811 Henry (Henry and Thompson, 1897, vol. 2, p. 726) found that the Crow were the only tribe to venture northward against the Blackfoot. Blackfoot-Crow hostility continued, with few brief peaceful intervals, until 1885.

In the middle of the 19th century the Blackfoot were at the height of their power. Their frequent raids over the Rockies endangered the Catholic Mission to the Flathead and were an important cause of its abandonment in 1850. Three years later they forced the temporary abandonment of John Owen's trading post among the Flathead. On the south, Blackfoot raids forced the American Fur Co. to abandon its post among the Crow in 1855. Midcentury also witnessed the retreat of the Cree from their eastern borders. In 1845, De Smet reported that the Cree were continually encroaching on Blackfoot territory (De Smet, 1905, vol. 2, p. 519). But before 1865 the region around Fort Edmonton, once the scene of many battles, became peaceful, due to Cree withdrawal eastward (Mandelbaum, 1940, p. 185). So successful were the Blackfoot in their wars on all fronts that in 1861 the Piegan did not hesitate to accept the challenge of their old friends the Gros Ventres, and added them to their list of enemies.

A number of the more distant tribes which came in less frequent contact with the Blackfoot than those mentioned above, considered the Blackfoot enemies. Maximilian found the Hidatsa, Mandan, and Arikara referred to the Blackfoot as enemies in 1833 (Maximilian, 1906, vol. 23, pp. 383, 553; vol. 24, p. 15). Teton Dakota hostility toward the Blackfoot increased as the extermination of buffalo east of the Missouri forced them to move westward in the middle of the century. When Sitting Bull and his followers fled to Canada in the spring of 1877, their nearness to the Blackfoot increased the incidence of small-scale conflicts between Teton and Blackfoot until those Sioux returned to the United States in 1881. Blackfoot relations with the Cheyenne and Arapaho were generally friendly during the first half of the 19th century. However, Blackfoot raids on Cheyenne and Arapaho horse herds were reported in 1858 (U. S. Comm. Ind. Affairs, 1858, p. 447).

In the youth and young manhood of my informants (ca. 1865–85) the Blackfoot tribes raided the Flathead, Pend d'Oreille, and Kutenai west of the Rockies, the Cree, Assiniboin, Gros Ventres, and Teton Dakota on the east, and the Crow on the south. Raids against the Shoshoni and other more distant tribes were infrequent. The Piegan, Mountain Chief (born ca. 1846), claimed to have counted coup on members of seven or eight different tribes: Cree, Sioux (perhaps including both Assiniboin and Teton), Plains Ojibwa, Gros Ventres, Flathead, Nez Percé, and Crow. The last great battle, involving large forces on both sides, was fought with the Cree near present Lethbridge, Alberta, in 1870. However, raiding for horses continued until 1885–86.

THE HORSE AS A CAUSE OF INTERTRIBAL CONFLICTS

The Blackfoot and neighboring tribes regarded the horse raid as an overt warlike act and a proper and important part of their war complex. It is true the ideal horse raid was aimed at the capture of enemy horses by stealth, without the knowledge of their owners and without bloodshed. It was not directed toward the conquest of enemy territory nor toward the extermination of the fighting force of an enemy tribe. Nevertheless, a horse raid consituted an intertribal incident recognized by the Indians as an act of aggression. Warriors were expected to respect the property rights in horses of individuals of other tribes with whom their own tribe was at peace. A horse raid directed against a tribe previously at peace with that of the raiders was recognized as a legitimate cause for retaliation in kind or in force against the aggressors' tribe. If the raid was carried out against a tribe previously hostile, the raid tended to prolong war between the tribes involved and to nullify any peace negotiations that might be planned or in progress between chiefs of those tribes. Indians who lost horses through capture by a small party of raiders invariably blamed not only the members of that party but their entire tribe.

The causes of intertribal wars in which the Blackfoot engaged, and which were initiated prior to 1810, cannot be specifically documented from historical records. Nevertheless, the prominent part played by horse raiding in the intertribal warfare of the late 18th and early 19th century as emphasized in fur traders' accounts suggests that the Indians' need for horses to use in hunting buffalo and transporting food and domestic articles furnished a major motive for that early warfare. Our knowledge of the direction of flow in the distribution of horses among the tribes of this region in the 18th century and of the relative wealth in horses of these tribes at a somewhat later date would suggest that the Blackfoot were the aggressors in their early wars with the tribes to the south and west, while the horse-poor Cree and Assiniboin were the aggressors in their conflicts with the Blackfoot.

The origin of only one intertribal war involving the Blackfoot has been adequately documented. Its cause can be traced directly to the practice of raiding for horses. Prior to 1861 the Blackfoot and Gros Ventres had been allies. In the fall of that year a Pend d'Oreille raiding party stole horses from the Gros Ventres on the Missouri below Fort Benton. To throw their pursuers off their track the clever Pend d'Oreille left some of the stolen horses in the vicinity of a Piegan camp on the Marias. The Gros Ventres, in hot pursuit, found some of their horses near the Piegan, concluded that a party of that tribe had stolen them, and attacked the Piegan camp. In this action a Piegan chief is said to have been killed, and the Piegan were roused to retaliation against the Gros Ventres. Thereafter, despite a record of more than a century of peaceful relations prior to the misunderstanding, the Piegan and Gros Ventres were at war. Their warfare continued sporadically, with considerable loss of life on both sides, until the middle 1880's, in spite of repeated Government attempts to negotiate a peace between these former allies (Bradley, 1923, pp. 313–315; Curtis, 1928, vol. 18, p. 177; and informants).

The influence of horse raiding as an obstacle to the making and maintenance of peace between warring tribes can be documented from the literature. Accounts of the Blackfoot written in the 19th century tell of at least a dozen truces negotiated between Blackfoot tribes and one or more of the neighboring tribes with whom they had been at war. The longest peaceful period was the Kutenai-Piegan peace noted by Thompson (1916, pp. 389–382). He claimed it endured for 10 years prior to 1808. In the spring of 1808, a Piegan war party crossed the Rockies, stole 35 Kutenai horses and killed a Kutenai in the action. Thompson (ibid., p. 389) commented significantly, "thus is war continued for want of the old Men being able to govern the young Men." The shortest recorded peace was that between the Crow and Blackfoot attested at the 1855 Blackfoot Treaty Council. Agent Hatch reported that a Blood Indian war party went against the Crow less than 10 days after that treaty was signed (U. S. Comm. Ind. Affairs, 1856, p. 626). That same treaty proclaimed peace between the Blackfoot tribes and Flathead by common agreement among the chiefs in attendance. Apparently that peace was effective for more than 18 months. Father Hoecken, writing from the Flathead country in April 1857, expressed fear that it would not last (De Smet, 1905, vol. 4, pp. 1247–1248). In the early summer of 1860, Major Owen, trader among the Flathead, stated flatly, "since the treaty of '55 the Blackfoot have made frequent predatory excursions to the different Camps from (on) this Side and have run off many horses" (Owen, 1927, vol. 2, p. 215). In 1858 Cree and Blackfoot leaders tried to arrange a truce in their long warfare. Their efforts were nipped in the bud by Cree young men who could not resist the temptation to run off Blackfoot horses (Hind, 1860, pp. 253–262).

Throughout the century prior to 1885, peace between the Blackfoot tribes and their neighbors (other than Sarsi and Gros Ventres) was the exception, war the rule. Peaceful periods were brief interludes between hostilities. They were always of uncertain duration and usually short lived. Older and wiser men, tired of continual warfare, sought peace in good faith. But ambitious young men, needing horses to gain a degree of economic security, social prestige, and political recognition, negated the best efforts of their peace-minded chiefs through resumption of raiding. Enduring peace with neighboring tribes was impossible until after the Blackfoot passed from a mobile, buffalo-hunting economy to a sedentary life based primarily upon the issuance of Government rations and secondarily upon the raising of livestock other than horses. This change did not take place until after the buffalo was exterminated.

THE HORSE RAID

TRIBAL PREFERENCES OF BLACKFOOT HORSE RAIDERS

Maximilian (1906, vol. 23, pp. 96, 112) claimed that the Blackfoot were "all great adepts at stealing horses" and that "horse stealing is an eminent art among them." Their skill in capturing horses was acknowledged by their bitterest enemies, the Crow and the Flathead (Marquis, 1928, p. 205; Teit, 1930, p. 326).

These skilled horse thieves possessed knowledge of the quality of the horses of their enemies which encouraged them to be selective in their thievery. Informants agreed that most horses owned by the Assiniboin and Cree were relatively poor. Consequently many raids against those tribes were made in retaliation for their raids on the Blackfoot rather than for the purpose of obtaining fine mounts. The Gros Ventres, they said, owned some fine and some poor horses, as did the Piegan themselves. Their nearness to the Piegan made Gros Ventres camps a frequent target of Piegan horse raiders after 1861. The Teton Dakota were said to have owned horses of relatively high quality before the Government took most of their best ones from them in 1877. However, the distance between Blackfoot and Teton villages tended to make raiding of the latter's camps less tempting to the Blackfoot than would have been the case had the tribes lived nearer each other. Informants considered that the best horses were owned by enemy tribes living south and west of the Piegan. Most of them credited the tribes west of the Rockies—the Flathead, Kutenai, Pend d'Oreille, Nez Percé, and Shoshoni—with ownership of the best horses. A century ago a Blackfoot Indian told Governor Stevens, "he stole the first Flathead horse he came across—it was sure to be a good one" (Stevens, 1860, p. 148). My informants said the Crow Indians had better horses than any other Plains tribe known to them, although their horses generally were not as fleet as those of the over-the-mountain tribes. Leforge, who lived many years among the Crow, also regarded the horses of tribes to the westward as swifter ones (Marquis, 1928, pp. 48–49).

In the youth and young manhood of my informants the tribes of the Rockies and the Crow, possessing both more and better horses than neighboring tribes to the east, were the principal targets of Blackfoot raiding parties. Horse raids across the mountains by means of the passes favored by Blackfoot war parties (Cadotte's Pass, Marias Pass, and Crow's Nest Pass) necessitated strenuous and prolonged expeditions, rarely undertaken except during the warmer months when the mountains were relatively free from snow. However, travel over the Plains to the Crow was both easier and quicker. There was no closed season on raiding the Crow horse herds.

ORGANIZATION OF THE HORSE RAID

Members of Blackfoot raiding parties always were volunteers. Some young men were lazy, cowardly fellows who never joined these parties. Some favored sons of wealthy families were discouraged from joining these expeditions. But the horse raid offered young men of poor parents their best opportunity for economic security and social advancement. Consequently many of the most active raiders were poor fellows. Most participants in horse raids were young men in their upper teens and early twenties. On rare occasions men in their forties led these expeditions. Weasel Tail said he had no recollection of any man over 50 years of age participating in this activity. Most commonly raiding parties comprised from 4 to 12 men. Occasional expeditions of 50 or more members were reported, and daring thefts of enemy horses by a lone Blackfoot also occurred. But they were rare.[26]

The key figure in any Blackfoot horse-raiding party was the leader, an experienced man whose past successes inspired confidence in his ability to lead a group to the enemy, capture horses, and return without loss of party members. Often the leader himself organized a raiding party, inviting certain of his young friends to join him. At other times young men desirous of making up a party requested an acknowledged leader to lead it. It was common practice for members of a horse-raiding party to drum on a piece of buffalo rawhide in accompaniment to their war songs the night before setting out. Other young men of the camp, upon hearing their performance and wishing to volunteer to accompany them, would join in the singing. There were many war songs appropriate for this occasion. A song especially liked by Weasel Tail had the words, "Girl I love don't worry about me. I'll be eating berries coming home." As the singers moved about camp, friends and relatives gave them presents of food and moccasins for their journey. The members might disperse to meet at a spot agreed upon outside the camp and set out that night, or they might decide to wait until the following morning to get under way.[27]

PREPARATIONS

A war party might have been planned for several days or it might have been organized within a few hours. In either case it required

---

[26] The small horse-raiding party seems to have been preferred by the Upper Missouri tribes. Opler (1936, p. 209) stated that Jicarilla Apache horse-raiding expeditions seldom numbered more than 10 men. However, Comanche and Kiowa raids against Mexican settlements frequently were large-scale operations.

[27] The custom of horse-raiding party members drumming and singing war songs before embarking on a raid has been reported as typical of the Kiowa, Comanche, Lemhi and Wind River Shoshoni, Nez Percé, and Crow (Lowie, 1915, pp. 811, 820; 1916, p. 851).

preparations involving the assembling of necessary sacred and secular equipment for the journey.

WAR MEDICINES

Not only the leader but each participant carried his own sacred war medicine to protect him from harm and bring him luck in his undertaking. These medicines were obtained through the dreams of the individuals themselves in which they received instructions for the preparation and ritual manipulation of these medicines, or they were received from older men who had been successful in war and whose medicines were highly respected by their juniors. In my informants' youth the first type was uncommon. Weasel Tail alone of my informants claimed to have used a war medicine originating in his own dream. He had a vision of a wolf cap and wolf robe and a song having the words, "I am a wolf. I am going to eat a person." He always wore the cap and robe and sang this song before he went into an enemy camp to take horses. He was but 15 years old when he dreamed this medicine.

It was much more common for a young man to go to an old man before he embarked on his first raid and ask him for some of his power. Usually, but not always, the older man was a relative of the younger one. The request was preceded by the offering of a pipe and gifts. Usually the young man also made a sweat bath for the older one. Some Blackfoot elders were frequently called upon for assistance because of their known success in war and/or because younger men who had obtained their help had achieved remarkable success. The Piegan elders On-Lucky-Trail and Under Bull were such men. The former was also considered to possess the power to tell young men of the location of fine horses owned by enemy tribes. The latter possessed the Arapaho medicine pipe bundle. Feathers from that bundle brought success to many raiders. The elder man commonly prayed for the young warrior who sought his aid and gave him a war song and a medicine object to carry on his expedition. It was common practice for the recipient of a war medicine to give the donor one or more horses after a safe return from a successful raid. Some young men were eclectic in assembling their war medicines, obtaining sacred objects from two or more older men in whose powers they had great faith.

I have knowledge of some 40 Blackfoot war medicines. Fourteen have been described in the literature: 11 by Wissler (1912 a, pp. 92–95), 2 by McClintock (1930, pp. 12, 29), and 1 by Uhlenbeck (1911, p. 67). From informants I obtained the information on 21 war medicines summarized in table 6. Although in theory there were no limitations upon the types of objects that could be used as war medicines, an analysis of these 40 medicines reveals that variety was limited and the great majority of them tended to follow a definite pattern. The majority of war medicines consisted simply of a feather or bunch of feathers worn in the hair. Undoubtedly the lightness and compactness of feathers made them practical objects for carrying on long journeys afoot into enemy country. The data in the table also indicate the conservatism of the Blackfoot in placing their trust in tried and proved medicines obtained from successful elderly warriors in preference to originating new medicines.

TABLE 6.—*Some war medicines of Blackfoot warriors*

Owner	Tribe	Origin of medicine	Description
Weasel Tail	Blood	Own dream	Wolf cap and wolf robe.
Lazy Boy	Piegan	Three Suns	"He gave me an owl feather for my hair. Even if you hit me with gun fire you could not hurt me while I wore that plume."
		Tail Feathers	"He gave me a coyote skin painted red to wear around my neck. A coyote sees a long ways and never misses what he goes after."
		On-Lucky-Trail	"He gave me sacred paint for my face."
		Red Eagle	"He gave me a red paint from his medicine pipe bundle."
Rides-at-the-Door	do	White Quiver	"He gave me a plume from the Under Bull medicine pipe bundle to wear in my hair."
		Many-Tail-Feathers	"He gave me an eagle tail feather, with a metal ring attached representing the sun, and horse hair tied to the ring."
Iron	Blood	Moon	"He (my father) gave me a song given him in a dream, also an otter skin bandolier and a tuft of owl and prairie chicken feathers for my hair."
Scraping White	do	Striped Calf	"He (my father) gave me a song and the skin of a blackbird which I tied on my head. My father dreamed these medicines and used them himself on the war path."
White Quiver	Piegan	Under Bull	A plume from Under Bull's medicine pipe bundle.
Bear Chief	do	do	Do.
Arrow Top	do	Striped Dog	A plume from the medicine pipe bundle of Striped Dog.
Heavy-Turns-Over	do	Little Dog	An owl head to be tied in the hair.
Jim Blood	do	Wolf-Crop-Ears	A plume worn in the hair.
Coat	do	Many-Tail-Feathers	A buffalo necklace with buffalo tail in center.
Duckling	Blood	Makes Fire	A coyote tail worn on the head.
Spotted Bull	do	(?)	A bunch of feathers, with brass tack decorated rawhide disk fastened to it, worn in the hair.
Middle Bull	do	A horse medicine man (name unknown).	A rawhide rope, short whip, and piece of white horse's mane worn as necklace.
Striped Calf	do	Head Robe	A skunkskin bandolier.
Little Dog	Piegan	Big Lake	A bunch of owl feathers worn in the hair. "When an enemy shoots a man wearing these feathers he will not hit him."
Double Gun	do	do	Bunch of owl feathers worn in the hair (obtained from his father, Big Lake).
Big Crow	do	Crow Flag	Two striped eagle feathers worn in back of his head, from Crow Flag, a North Blackfoot.
Sacred-Turning-Bull	N. Piegan	(?)	A buckskin shirt with round brass buttons ("moon disks") upon it.
Three Eagles	do	Brings-Down-the-Sun	An owl's head.
Running Wolf	do	do	A necklace, consisting of a brass piece in moon shape with figure of horse incised on it and plumes hanging from ends. "He sprinkled water on it before going into an enemy camp to capture horses. In a short time clouds covered the moon, making it easier to take horses from the enemy."

Medicine songs also were intended to protect their possessors as well as to bring them luck in taking horses. Uhlenback (1911, pp. 66–67) mentioned three songs employed by the Piegan, Bear Chief. One, known as "the song of the horse-stealing" was actually a prayer to the sun, "Sun look at us, have pity on us, help us." Another, sung while in sight of the enemy camp, was intended to pacify the enemies' dogs, "In the night I am not seen, the dogs are my partners." A third song, rendered when the sound of enemy firing was heard, had the words, "The guns can see me, I can see the bullets, they are like birds, they curve."

Rides-at-the-Door explained the use of his own war medicine:

When I went to the enemy to steal horses I carried my war medicine in a small, cylindrical rawhide case. This medicine could never be put down. In a lodge it always had to be hung up. When my party got near the enemy camp, I made a little fire, took charcoal and sweetgrass and made a smudge. I sang the song given me with my medicine and prayed before donning my medicine plume. In my prayers I asked Sun for horses, to get away safely and not to have to return on foot. Sometimes I prayed to the sun, "See me. The rain is holy and the wind is holy." Then it was bound to blow, and the sleeping enemy would not hear us when we went into their camp and took their horses.

It was not uncommon for an inexperienced young man, doubtful of the potency of his own war medicine to "call a help" on an older man of the war party just prior to the rush for enemy horses. The more experienced man would give him a feather from his own medicine or other token of his own medicine power. A fearful young warrior might make a vow before the other men of his party to feast the owner of some powerful medicine bundle on his return home, should he pull through safely. Vows to undergo self-torture at the next tribal Sun Dance were also made before entering the enemy camp to take horses (Ewers, 1948 b, pp. 167–168). These last-minute petitions for supernatural aid helped to bolster the wavering courage of inexperienced raiders.

Informants' testimony revealed the Blackfoot belief that reliance upon the protective power of war medicine was no justification for reckless exposure in battle. Lazy Boy cited the case of Calf Shield, whose power came from Big Lake, a noted Piegan chief. On the way to take horses from the Sioux, Calf Shield's entire party was wiped out. Although no one survived to tell of that action the Piegan generally claimed the party must have taken too great chances. "It was not the fault of the medicine or its giver if the recipient took too great a risk." Thus repeated losses of possessors of renowned war medicines in combat failed to shake Blackfoot faith in the power of these medicines. There were always a number of brave warriors able to testify to the potency of their medicines in preserving them from almost certain death on the warpath.

Some men were credited with the power to predict the outcome of horse raids. Weasel Tail said Takes-a-Gun, a Piegan, had a formula for such prediction. When he joined a raiding party he called upon the sun, "Sun, tell us if we are going to get horses." Then he explained to others of the party, "If you see sun dogs on both sides of the sun we shall get many horses. If there are sun dogs on one side only, we shall get only a few." In dreams any member of an outgoing party might be warned of disaster ahead. When he told his fears to the others, some or all of them might turn back. There was no stigma attached to desertion of a raiding party as a result of supernatural warning. Indeed should some of the men persist in the enterprise and meet loss of personnel or failure to capture horses, the medicine of the man who had turned back in response to his warning was recognized as powerful by his fellow tribesmen.[28]

CLOTHING

During the warmer months members of horse-raiding parties generally wore undecorated, soft-soled moccasins, leggings, breechclouts, and shirts. Shirts were needed even in summer to protect their wearers from sunburn by day and chill by night. In winter, raiders wore Hudson's Bay Company's blanket coats with capotes, as overcoats. These coats were predominantly white, which served as a camouflage against a background of snow and overcast sky. Blankets had black, red, or yellow stripes. Makes-Cold-Weather said he used to prefer red or yellow stripes, as they could be seen less easily from a distance than black ones. Other specialized winter garments were mittens of buffalo hide, hair inside, which were tied together by a skin cord passing from wrist to wrist over the wearer's shoulders and underneath his blanket coat; and a pair of soft-soled, hair-lined, buffalohide moccasins. The moccasins sometimes were stuffed

---

[28] The Blackfoot concept of war medicine had its counterpart among other Plains Indian tribes. Larocque (1910, p. 66) wrote of the Crow in 1805: "When they go to war they take their medicine bags, at least the Chief of the party does, when they have found out their enemies and on the point of beginning the attack the bag of medicine is opened, they sing a few airs but very shortly smoke and then attack." Zenas Leonard (1904, p. 256) briefly described Crow war medicines of which he learned during 6 months' residence among that tribe in 1934–35; Boller (1868, p. 324) told of an Hidatsa chief who gave a young Crow warrior half his medicine, after which the young man was very successful in stealing horses. It was common practice among the Plains Cree for a young man to obtain his war medicine with accompanying songs and ritual from an older successful warrior (Mandelbaum, 1940, pp. 258–259). Grinnell (1923, vol. 2, pp. 108–125) stressed the use of bird feathers and skins as war medicines by the Cheyenne. Certain Cheyennes were also credited with the power to prophesy the outcome of war adventures. Enoch Smoky told me of a Kiowa who, by the screeching of owls, could predict the success or failure of horse raids. On one occasion he predicted that several members of his party would be killed, but none wounded. The party suffered just as he said it would. Smoky claimed the Kiowa did not carry war medicines on horse-raiding expeditions, limiting their use to raids for enemy scalps.

with grass to give greater warmth to the feet. Figures 27 and 28 illustrate the summer and winter costumes of Blackfoot horse raiders.[29]

Summer or winter, horse-raiding parties setting out on foot were careful to carry along supplies of extra moccasins. Each man was responsible for his own footgear. Blackfoot moccasins of buffalo days were of the soft-soled variety, which usually withstood but 2

FIGURE 27.—Blackfoot horse raiders in warm-weather dress.

days of walking over rough country before they needed repair or replacement. Female relatives generally gave each warrior several extra pairs of moccasins, as well as awls, sinew thread, and extra pieces of skin with which to make repairs en route.

---

[29] The blanket coat was a favorite winter garment of warriors among neighboring Upper Missouri tribes. Boller (1868, p. 299) mentioned Hidatsa-Mandan preference for white blanket coats. Kurz (1937, pl. 34 lower, and pl. 46 lower) illustrated the blanket coat worn by Assiniboin and Chippewa (?). The original sketchbooks of Charles Wimar, in the City Art Museum, St. Louis, include several good representations of this garment, as seen by that artist among Indians of the Upper Missouri in 1858.

FIGURE 28.—Blackfoot horse raider in winter dress.

WEAPONS

Members of horse-raiding parties carried no shields, lances, or war clubs. Their weapons were bows and arrows, guns, and knives. The knives, carried at the waist in rawhide sheaths, were sharp and heavy enough to cut firewood and timber for temporary shelters. They served as axes as well as knives, useful in skinning and cutting up animals for food, cutting loose picketed horses from the enemy camp, and as weapons for hand-to-hand fighting if necessity required.

THE PACK

Each Blackfoot warrior carried a pack containing: (1) extra moccasins, an awl, and sinew for moccasin repair; (2) one or two rawhide ropes, each about 20 feet or longer, with a honda in one end, for use in catching, riding, and leading enemy horses; (3) a small pipe and tobacco; and (4) the man's personal war medicine. Some men also carried whips in their packs. Scouts carried wolfskins in their packs or wore them over their other clothing. The contents of the pack were wrapped in the top of an old lodge cover, a large piece of rawhide, or a trade blanket, rolled like a blanket roll, tied with rawhide rope and carried on the owner's back by a rawhide strap over his upper arms and chest. (See fig. 27.) Pieces of rawhide wrapping could be cut off for use in moccasin repair as the need arose.[30]

FOOD

Blackfoot raiders generally carried their food in separate containers rather than in the pack. Many men favored a rectangular, unfringed, rawhide case, carried by a strap over one shoulder or on top of the main pack on the back. Dried meat and pemmican were the favored foods.[31]

THE OUTWARD JOURNEY

W. T. Hamilton (1905, p. 52) writing of the Blackfoot of the period ca. 1842, said they "almost always went to war on foot." Informants said that in their young manhood there were both foot and mounted horse-raiding expeditions. They acknowledged that it was easier for men to conceal themselves from the enemy when afoot than when mounted. However, in the last decade of horse raiding the

---

[30] Horse-raiding parties of other tribes carried their equipment in similar packs. Catlin's painting of a foot war party of an unidentified Upper Missouri tribe (U. S. N. M. No. 386352) shows each member carrying a pack on his back. In the summer of 1833, Maximilian (1906, vol. 23, p. 204) met an Assiniboin war party at Fort Union, the members of which carried "small bundles" on their backs containing meat, moccasins, and tobacco. Mead (1908, p. 106) described the equipment of Pawnee horse raiders of the period ca. 1860: "They went lightly armed, each had a very serviceable bow and quiver of arrows and a knife, a few carried a light gun. Each Indian carried tucked under his belt, from four to six extra pairs of new moccasins and one or more lariats ; a pack weighing twenty pounds or more containing dried meat, both fat and lean ; some pieces and straps of tanned skins to repair their moccasins and clothing and useful for bridles. The above mentioned articles, with a pipe and tobacco, an occasional light squaw axe, and a few trifles, comprised all that was necessary for a thousand mile journey." Informants stated that Blackfoot raiders not infrequently carried extra moccasins tucked under the belt rather than in the pack. Some Blackfoot men carried 1 or 2 pairs of moccasins under the belt or sewn to the shirt at the back of the shoulders in addition to those in the pack, as a precautionary measure in case their pack might become lost in a surprise attack by the enemy en route.

[31] Catlin's portrait of Red Thunder, son of a Hidatsa chief, "in the costume of a warrior" depicts a rawhide case like that used by Blackfoot horse raiders hanging at his side from a strap over his shoulder (U. S. N. M. No. 386172).

mounted party gained in popularity, especially in expeditions directed against the Crow. The mounted party could travel much faster and could more easily evade white authorities who at that time were seeking to put an end to intertribal horse raiding. It required 16 to 28 days' travel afoot from the vicinity of the Piegan Old Agency on Badger Creek to the Crow camps south of the Yellowstone; whereas a mounted party could make the journey in 8 to 12 days. Weasel Tail said, "Usually on the eighth day our scouts saw the Crow camp. On the ninth day we took their horses." While foot war parties averaged about 25 miles a day in good weather, mounted parties traveled more than twice that distance in the same time.[32]

In the initial stages of the outward journey, when danger of encountering the enemy was at a minimum, raiding parties usually traveled by day, moving at a steady pace, in no particular order, and stopping occasionally to rest and smoke. But as they neared the enemy country they moved more cautiously, traveling at night and hiding out during the daylight hours. A party nearing enemy country halted to kill game for food enough to subsist them for the remainder of their journey. They built one or more war lodges in a heavily timbered bottom or on a thickly wooded height. The war lodge usually had a framework of fallen or cut timbers covered with brush or bark, set in a conical form with an angular covered entranceway. (See Ewers, 1944 a, pp. 183–186 and plate.) It served a fivefold purpose, as a protection against the enemy (concealing the fire from view and serving as a fort in case of surprise attack), as protection from the weather (especially in winter or rainy weather), as a base for scouting operations, as a supply base, and as an information center to which members of homeward-bound parties could return and leave pictographic messages to others of their party telling of their actions and movements (ibid., pp. 189–190).[33]

From the war lodge the leader sent ahead a small number of picked men as scouts to locate the enemy camp. Wearing wolfskins, they moved cautiously, fearful of encountering enemy war or hunting parties. From high ground they surveyed the surrounding territory, concealed by their wolfskins, before advancing. They were suspicious of any sudden movements of game, and they examined burned-

---

[32] Lieutenant Carleton (1943, p. 276) reported that Teton Dakota parties customarily went on foot against the Crow and Blackfoot in 1845. Denig (1930, p. 545) claimed it was usual for horse raiders of all the Upper Missouri tribes to leave camp afoot in the period ante-1854. This was the common practice among the Cheyenne (Grinnell, 1923, vol. 2, p. 7), Pawnee (Dunbar, 1880, p. 335), and Jicarilla Apache (Opler, 1936, p. 210). However, the Comanche even as early as 1820, appear to have preferred mounted raids for horses (Burnet, 1851, p. 236). Alice Marriott has informed me that Kiowa parties frequently rode in quest of enemy horses, but if the group was composed largely of poor young men seeking to obtain animals to start their own herds, they walked.

[33] War lodges also were constructed by Plains Cree, Crow, Teton, Gros Ventres, Assiniboin, and Cheyenne horse raiders (ibid., p. 190).

out fires and tracks made by horses, travois, and footmen and noted their relative recency and direction of movement.

While the scouts were gone members of the party left at the war lodge hunted for buffalo, deer, elk, or other game, killing only enough to provide dried meat for the remainder of their journey. They dried the meat and filled the provision bags. Sometimes they made up additional packets of meat for each member. These were small, skin or rawhide containers that could be carried at the belt holding quantities of meat sufficient only for an occasional quick lunch on horseback while hastening homeward with captured horses.

When the scouts located the enemy camp they watched it from a concealed position long and closely enough to determine its size, and numbers of men, horses, etc. Then they returned to the war lodge as rapidly as possible. As they came in sight of their fellows they approached in a zigzag course, indicating they had found the enemy. While their leader went out to meet the scouts, the other members of the party set up a pile of sticks near the war lodge. Returning with the scouts the leader kicked over the pile of sticks and all party members scrambled for them. Each stick a member retrieved was an augury of a horse he would take from the enemy.

Guided by the scouts, the whole party moved cautiously, traveling only by night and hiding out by day, until they reached a well concealed position overlooking or in sight of the enemy camp. After the leader had an opportunity to observe the camp, he outlined his plan of attack to the other members of his party.

THE ATTACK

Shortly before the time of attack arrived, the party members opened their packs, took out their personal war medicines, sang their sacred war songs, prayed for success, painted and donned their medicine gear. Usually the rush for horses was made at daybreak. Generally the leader selected only a few of the bravest and most experienced men to enter the enemy camp with him, and cut loose the picketed horses and lead them out. Usually they carried no weapons other than their knives as they stealthily entered the enemy village. They sought out the picketed horses previously spotted as the most likely looking ones. When each man cut picket lines and led horses away he was careful to stay close to the horse he believed to be the fastest so he could jump on it and make a quick getaway should someone in the camp become aware of the theft and rouse the enemy. Sometimes these men left picketed horses with the younger, inexperienced party members outside the camp and returned again for more of the choice animals. At other times the men outside the camp drove off some of the range herds while the leader and his assistants took the picketed animals. It was a common practice for men who went after the picketed horses to rub cottonwood sap on their bodies and hands. The cottonwood odor would tend to quiet the horses and make them willing to follow the strangers who led them away.

THE HOMEWARD JOURNEY

Whether or not the enemy became aware of the actions of the raiding party, a quick getaway was important in order to get as much head start on their pursuers as possible. It was not unusual for a successful Blackfoot raiding party to take as many as 40 to 60 horses on a single raid. However, the great majority of my informants who had participated in horse raids denied that any Blackfoot party returned home with as many as 100 animals. They acknowledged that over 100 horses had been run off on raids known to them, but stated that the difficulty of driving that number of animals homeward at a fast pace, over uneven country, through timber and across streams for hundreds of miles resulted in the loss through straying or abandonment of some of the animals. It was unsafe to be too greedy. The enemy might overtake the captors of many horses, whose homeward progress was slowed by the necessity for driving an unwieldy herd in front of them.[34]

On the first portion of the homeward journey the raiders generally rode without breechcloths, to prevent blistering of their skin from the steady friction of their horses' backs in riding over rough, uneven ground at a fast clip. Yet sometimes men became so sore and blistered during this part of the journey they had to dismount and walk. This not only slowed their progress but increased the danger of being overtaken by the enemy.

The return journey was made at a much faster pace than the outward one. Rides-at-the-Door said that 4 days and nights after he took horses from the Crow south of the Yellowstone he was home (i. e., in the vicinity of the present Blackfeet Reservation, Montana). For the first 2 or 3 days and nights raiders rode steadily, switching from one mount to another as their horses tired. If a horse played out so that it could not keep up with the rest, it was usually turned loose. If it was a very good horse, the raiders might shoot it, to prevent the enemy from retaking it. Usually a party returning from the Crow reached the vicinity of present Belt, Mont., 200 miles north of the Yellowstone River, on the second night or third day. There they

---

[34] The literature mentions raids by southern Plains tribes resulting in the theft of far greater numbers of horses. Gregg (1941, pp. 337–338) told of about 500 Comanche, who, according to Mexican papers of 1841, "were then driving off about 28,000 head of stock— horses, mules and cattle." This may have referred to a series of carefully organized raids in which the number of Indian participants far exceeded the numbers commonly active in individual raids by the Blackfoot and neighboring Upper Missouri tribes.

stopped to rest, overnight, and continued homeward at a more lei-
surely pace.

DISTRIBUTION OF CAPTURED HORSES

At the first resting place after leaving the enemy camp the horses
taken on the raid were distributed among party members. This distribution was a sore test of the character of the leader and his more
experienced men. It was the leaders' responsibility to supervise distribution. Yet the Blackfoot recognized the right of each individual
to any picketed horses he had taken from the enemy camp. They also
recognized the right of the man or men to range horses they had run
off. It often happened that there were party members who had neither captured picketed horses nor run off range stock. Those who had
recognized claims to horses were then expected to give up some of
them to the less fortunate. After pointing out the animals they
wished to retain (usually the best ones), they called upon members
of the party who could claim no horses to divide the remaining animals. There was a strong element of enlightened self-interest in
this practice. Raiders who had taken horses knew that if they were
not liberally inclined toward those who had taken none, the latter
would desert the party and would leave them the task of driving all
the horses home. It was still more important that the leader of the
party should act generously. If he was unfair or stingy in distrib-
uting horses, warriors would not follow him in the future.

Nevertheless, informants who had been on numerous raids said that
arguments over possession of horses were common, especially among
groups of men who had jointly run off range horses. A man might
have his heart set on possessing a certain animal that appealed to him.
He became angry if another man received that horse in the distribution. The story was told of two men who argued over the possession
of a captured horse. In the end the man who did not receive it drew
his knife, plunged it into the disputed horse and killed it, saying,
"If I can't have that horse, no one will enjoy it."

The system of distribution just described brought the greatest rewards to the men who had taken the greatest risks. They received
both the most and the best horses. To avoid trouble and ill-feeling at
the time of distribution, party members sometimes agreed in advance
upon an equal division of the captured animals. In that case the
leader took first choice, then called upon each man in turn to make
his selection. If the number of captured horses was not equally di-
visible by the number of party members the leader decided what was
to be done with the horses remaining after each man had made his
choice.[35]

---

[35] Denig (1930, p. 475) described the frequent quarrels among Assiniboin horse raiders
over division of their spoils, sometimes resulting in the killing or running off in the night

RETURN TO CAMP

Upon nearing the home village, members of a successful Blackfoot raiding party halted, painted themselves just as they were when they raided the enemy camp, decorated their horses, and moved toward camp shooting in the air to notify their tribesmen of their return. All the people of the camp came out to greet them. If an old woman came to a successful raider and told him she had prayed for him during his absence he might give her a horse, whether or not she was a relative. It was common practice to give horses to relatives, especially to fathers-in-law or brothers-in-law, after a raid. Then the raider would tell his wife to bring to his lodge the old man who had given him war medicine and prayed for his welfare. He fed the old man and gave him one or more of the horses captured on the recent raid.

Generous giving of horses, secured at great risk from enemy camps, was regarded as a praiseworthy act. He who, in the intoxication of success, gave away all the horses he had taken without thought for himself, was remembered for his generosity long after the gifts were distributed. Action of that kind served as a steppingstone to leadership. It was customary for a person who had received a captured horse as a gift to aid the donor in preparing for future raids through presents of moccasins, food, ammunition, or even a gun, if the young man did not possess one.[36]

ACCUSTOMING CAPTURED HORSES TO ONE'S HERD

To prevent a captured horse from straying from its new herd the Blackfoot owner tied it neck and neck with a gentle mare in his herd. After 4 or 5 nights of this treatment the new horse could be released without fear of straying. If the stolen horse was the only one owned by an individual he initiated it into the herd of one of his relatives by the same method. Some men tried to hasten the process by trimming off pieces of the hocks of the two animals necked together, mixing

---

of horses in dispute by men who received few horses. He claimed men of large families or of "force in camp," able to back up their claims received the most horses. According to Llewellyn and Hoebel (1941, p. 223) the Cheyenne often agreed upon equal distribution of horses taken on a raid, although their usual system recognized the claim of each man to the horse or horses he was first to count coup upon. Smoky claimed the Kiowa commonly followed the system of equal distribution. The leader called upon each man in turn, beginning with his closest friend or relative. If a man chose a mare any colts that followed that mare were his also. The leader was the last to make a selection. If a few animals were left after each man had a like number the leader drove them home and gave them away. The Kiowa also recognized a man's right to make his selection and then describe another horse in the herd not previously claimed, stating, "Don't pick that horse. I am going to give it to [name], a poor old man [or woman] when I get back." That horse was reserved for the gift indicated.

[36] Other writers have reported liberal giving of horses by members of returning raiding parties among the Mandan (Maximilian, 1906, vol. 23, pp. 352–353) ; Cheyenne (Grinnell, 1923, vol. 2, p. 15) ; and Crow (Marquis, 1928, pp. 175–176). The motivation for and honor accorded such gifts were the same as among the Blackfoot.

the trimming with dirt and water, and rubbing the strong-odored concoction on the noses of both animals. Other owners mixed some manure of the gentle mare with grass and rubbed it on the nose of the new horse. Then in a couple of days the two animals would stay together without tying. This treatment also was employed to accustom a horse obtained as a gift or in trade to the new owner's herd.[37]

WOMEN ON HORSE-RAIDING EXPEDITIONS

It was not uncommon for a childless young woman to accompany her husband on a horse raid. Weasel Tail explained, "My wife said she loved me, and if I was to be killed on a war party she wanted to be killed too. I took her with me on five raids. Some of them I led, and my wife was not required to perform the cooking or other chores. She carried a six-shooter. On one occasion she stole a horse with a saddle, ammunition bag and war club." He recalled three married women who had taken guns from the enemy while on war parties with their husbands. Two of these women were Piegan, one Blood. Elk-Hollering-in-the-Water, a short woman of very slight build, told me she had taken objects from the enemy while on raiding parties with her husband, Bear Chief, a Piegan. The most famous Piegan woman warrior of the 19th century was Running Eagle, subject of J. Willard Schultz' book, "Running Eagle the Warrior Girl" (1919). She was known to some of my informants as a leader of many successful horse raids who was killed while attempting to take horses from the Flathead.[38]

BOYS ON HORSE-RAIDING EXPEDITIONS

James Doty (1854, p. 7), in a brief description of Blackfoot horse raiding, written a century ago, stated, "In one of these parties are generally found 3 or 4 young men, or mere boys, who are apprentices. They go without the expectation of receiving a horse, carry extra moccasins and tobacco for the party, do all the camp drudgery, and consider themselves amply paid in being permitted to learn the science of horse stealing from such experienced hands." According to informants these boys were 14 or 15 years of age. Younger boys were considered too great a risk. They might, through carelessness, endanger the lives of the entire party. The boys performed the duties

---

[37] The Puyallup-Nisqually introduced a new horse into a herd by dampening "scales from above the first joint of its leg" and rubbing on the leg of a horse to which it was tied for the night. "After that the new horse would not wander" (Smith, 1940, p. 30). I have found no comparative data on this point from other tribes.

[38] Denig (1953, pp. 64–68) has recorded the biography of Woman Chief, the outstanding woman warrior of the Upper Missouri. Gros Ventres by birth, she was captured by the Crow as a child. She led a number of successful Crow war parties before she was killed while on a visit to her own people, the Gros Ventres, in the early 1850's.

of cooking, carrying wood and water, and carrying the men's (or at least the leaders') packs. Sometimes they were permitted to hold the horses cut loose from pickets when the warriors brought them out of camp. Sometimes they assisted in running off grazing horses outside the camp. Experienced men took pains to point out to them how the raids should be conducted and why they employed the tactics followed on these expeditions. The boys gained much valuable information by watching the skilled actions of their elders. If a raid was successful the older men might give a horse to a boy who accompanied them. Through this on-the-job training boys learned the arts of war.

FREQUENCY OF HORSE RAIDS

All evidence from the literature and informants indicates that the horse raid was by far the most common type of Blackfoot war expedition. Father De Smet claimed the Blackfoot made 20 horse raids against the Flathead alone in the year preceding February 1842 (De Smet, 1905, vol. 1, p. 363). There may have been years in which the three Blackfoot tribes sent out more than 50 horse-raiding parties. As a rule horse raids were less common during the cold, snowy, winter months. However, Weasel Tail said he used to prefer raiding in winter. If the attack on an enemy camp was made before or during a snow storm the tracks of the fleeing raiders would become covered, making it impossible for them to be closely followed by the enemy.

Participation in these raids differed markedly on the part of individuals. Some young men never joined them. Others made repeated raids. Of my elderly, fullblood, male informants there was none who had not been on several raids, but only one, Weasel Tail, known as a youth of poor family, participated in more than a dozen horse raids. In the generation of the fathers of my elderly informants his record would not have been remarkable. The late White Quiver, of Weasel Tail's own generation, was regarded by my informants as the most active and successful horse raider of whom they had knowledge. White Quiver was the Blackfoot horse thief par excellence.

WHITE QUIVER, THE MOST SUCCESSFUL BLACKFOOT HORSE RAIDER

In 1921 Superintendent Campbell of the Blackfeet Reservation, Mont., wrote, "White Quiver was formerly considered the most successful horse thief among all these Indians" (Campbell, MS., 1921). Not only did my Piegan informants unanimously endorse this statement, but all elderly Blood Indians questioned on the point said their tribe possessed no member whose record as a horse raider compared with that of White Quiver, the Piegan. (See pl. 11.)

White Quiver, of the Bugs Band, was born about the year 1858. When he was a small boy his father, Trails War Bonnet, was killed by the Crow. White Quiver vowed vengeance against that tribe. In later years he led many raids on their horse herds. White Quiver started going on war parties while still a boy. He grew to be a tall, strong man of remarkable physical stamina, who could ride 3 days and nights without food while driving captured horses homeward from an enemy camp. Rides-at-the-Door, who went on eight horse raids under White Quiver's leadership, remembered him as a generous, easy-going, fun-loving man. He described White Quiver's appearance as "tall, very dark, and ugly." The Crow Indians, who suffered most from his thievery, dubbed him "the big Negro." Crow mothers are said to have disciplined their crying children by saying, "Keep quiet. The big Negro is out there. He will get you if you don't stop crying."

White Quiver told Rides-at-the-Door he had gone to the enemy 40 times to steal horses, yet his career as a horse raider ended before he was 30 years of age. He raided the Crow more than any other tribe. Superintendent Campbell claimed White Quiver had made 11 trips to the Crow and each time came home with horses. He also took horses from the Gros Ventres, Cree, Assiniboin, and Sioux. White Quiver considered the Flathead his friends. Informants could recall 15 distinct raids led by White Quiver.

White Quiver's war medicine was a plume from the medicine pipe bundle owned by Under Bull, and known as the Arapaho pipe. In the 1940's this medicine pipe bundle was owned by my interpreter, Reuben Black Boy. When White Quiver returned with horses he usually gave one or more of them to Under Bull.

White Quiver's tactics were unorthodox but extremely successful. Usually he traveled to the enemy on horseback rather than on foot. (Rides-at-the-Door said every time he accompanied White Quiver on a raid he went mounted.) White Quiver was always the party leader and insisted on taking the greatest risks himself. Often he left the others of his party in a secluded spot some distance from the enemy camp, entered the camp alone, and brought horses out to them. Rather than follow the usual Piegan practice of taking horses at night or at daybreak, White Quiver preferred to boldly walk into the enemy camp at dusk, just as the people were settling down for the night. When he brought horses out he told each member of the party to take a good one to ride. When a stop was made on the return journey, he told each man he might keep the horse he was riding. Then he distributed the driven horses equally among the party members.

White Quiver's war parties generally were small ones. Informants could recall only 2 parties led by him which numbered more than 11 men. One of these raids was against the Sioux, on which 30 men killed all the enemy of 5 lodges and took all their horses. The other, comprising 17 men, was a raid on the Gros Ventres during which the enemy discovered their presence and only White Quiver got away with a horse. Among his successful raids against the Crow were: 38 horses and 6 mules taken by 11 men; 80 horses taken by 10 men; 48 horses captured by 6 men; 34 horses taken by 4 men; and about 20 horses captured by 4 men. No less than 62 men were named who had been on horse raids under White Quiver's leadership. Several of them accompanied him four or more times. White Quiver's last raid was made at a time when white authorities in both Montana and Alberta were actively trying to put an end to intertribal horse raiding. Leading a party of 8 men to the Crow, White Quiver made off with over 50 horses. On the return journey authorities from Fort Benton apprehended the party and took the stolen horses from them. White Quiver restole the horses from the authorities and drove them to Canada. There the Mounted Police again took the horses from him. But White Quiver managed to recapture at least a part of the herd and succeeded in bringing them to the Blackfeet Reservation in Montana. This was a whirlwind finish to an extraordinary raiding career.

White Quiver preferred the excitment of raiding to the business of building up and managing a large herd of his own. Many of the horses received as his share of the loot he gave away to relatives or poor people after his party reached the home camp. He never became a wealthy horse owner. In the spring of 1921, not long before his death, White Quiver owned but 7 horses. There were many Indians then living in his section of the Blackfeet Reservation, the Heart Butte district, who owned much larger herds.

A complex of factors help to explain White Quiver's preeminence as a horse raider. His father's murder gave him an initial motivation of the strongest kind. His physical strength and stamina enabled him to lead the hyperactive and strenuous life of almost continuous raiding. His unorthodox dusk attacks seem to have caught the enemy off guard time after time. His willingness to perform the most dangerous tasks himself, coupled with his reputation for success and generosity in distribution of captured horses, made him a popular war party leader who never wanted for followers. Finally, his generosity in giving away horses, and his lack of either social or political ambition, made him a popular hero whose deeds have been remembered by the many beneficiaries of his liberality and by their relatives.[39]

---

[39] If there were Blackfoot men of earlier generations whose achievements as horse raiders equaled or surpassed those of White Quiver, their deeds have been forgotten. However, Thaddeus Culbertson, (1851, p. 122) met a halfbreed Crow Indian at Fort Union in the summer of 1850, whose record approached that of White Quiver. Although not yet 30 years of age this man, Horse Guard, was said to have "engaged in about thirty expeditions, always returning with hair (scalps) or horses, and getting his party back safely." In 1855 Horse Guard was chief of a band of some 50 lodges (McDonnell, 1940, p. 113). In 1874 "Horseguard" was "the head chief of the River Crows," one of the two major divisions of the Crow Indians (Koch, 1944, p. 422).

THE RAID FOR SCALPS

Denig (1930, pp. 548–551) and Wissler (1910, p. 155) have properly distinguished another type of raiding party from that of the horse raid. Denig described the "war parties for battle" of the Upper Missouri tribes in general. Wissler referred to Blackfoot "expeditions for scalps and revenge." Since these expeditions were directed toward killing the enemy and taking scalps rather than horses, I shall term them "scalp raids." Scalp raids differed markedly from horse raids in motivation, organization (size and leadership), preliminary ceremonies, equipment, tactics, and postraid ceremonies.

The scalp raid most commonly was motivated by desire for revenge against an enemy who had (1) recently defeated a portion of the Blackfoot in battle or (2) killed a Blackfoot chief or several prominent warriors. Scalp raids generally were prosecuted by relatively large forces, often recruited from several of the Blackfoot and allied tribes and led by one or more prominent chiefs. David Thompson (1916, p. 347) observed (ca. 1800) that Kootenae Appe, the Piegan war chief, "was utterly averse to small parties, except for horse stealing . . . He seldom took the field with less than two hundred warriors but frequently with many more." In the summer of 1848, Paul Kane (1925, p. 303) met an expedition moving against the Cree comprising warriors of the North Blackfoot, Blood, Piegan, Gros Ventres, and Sarsi, which he claimed numbered 1,500 men. This is the largest Blackfoot war expedition that has been reported. Its numbers may have been somewhat exaggerated. A review of the contemporary literature on the Blackfoot covering the period 1800–70 reveals numerous references to war parties of more than 100 members, and to battles involving several hundred warriors.

Table 7 lists 17 intertribal battles in which relatively large forces of Blackfoot Indians engaged during the period 1808–70, which have been reported by reputable authorities. Undoubtedly the Blackfoot were involved in other battles of equal or greater size during that period which were not reported. The estimates of the numbers and casualties in some of these conflicts may be exaggerated. Most of the contemporary writers had direct contact with only one of the tribes engaged, and Indians notoriously exaggerated both the total numbers and the losses of their enemies. Nevertheless, I believe the data of this table give a relatively accurate idea of the frequency, the scale, and the heavy casualties resulting from the major intertribal conflicts in which the Blackfoot participated in the 19th century.

My information indicates that scalp raiding was more common among the Blackfoot and their enemies of the Upper Missouri prior to 1855 than after that year, even though two of the greatest Blackfoot victories occurred as late as 1866 and 1870, respectively. Prior to

TABLE 7.—*Large-scale battles in which the Blackfoot participated, 1808–1870*

Date	Location	Blackfoot force	Opponent's force	Action	Casualties	Reference
1808	Near Three Forks, Missouri River.	1,500 "Blackfeet".	Ca. 800 Flathead and Crow.	Blackfoot attacked, but forced to retire in order after heavy fighting.	Many killed (no numbers listed).	James, 1916, pp. 52–53.
Summer 1810	Near eastern approach to Marias Pass.	170 Piegan.	150 "Selish".	Blackfoot attacked on horseback, forced to retreat.	7 to 16 Piegan killed; 5 "Selish" killed.	Thompson, 1916, pp. 423–425; Henry and Thompson, 1897, vol. 2, p. 713.
August 1812	The Plains.	Ca. 350 Piegan.	Ca. 350 Flathead.	Piegan attacked afoot, forced to withdraw.	"Several slain and wounded each side."	Thompson, 1916 pp. 551–562; Cox, 1832, p. 167.
Ante-1835	...do	Blackfeet.	Crow.	Blackfoot ambushed by Crow.	"70 Blackfoot scalps taken."	Ferris, 1940, pp. 245–246.
Aug. 28, 1833	Outside Fort McKenzie.	Ca. 2,000 Piegan.	Ca. 500 Assiniboin and 100 Cree.	Enemy attacked detached party of ca. 30 Piegan lodges near fort; entire Piegan camp came to rescue and forced enemy withdrawal.	Over 40 Piegan scalps and 6 or 8 enemy ones taken.	Maximilian, 1906, vol. 23, pp. 146–153; Audubon, 1897, vol. 2, pp. 133–136; Bradley, 1900, pp. 207–210.
1834	The Plains.	69 Piegan.	Entire Crow camp.	Piegan forted, attacked by Crow on horseback.	All Piegan killed.	Leonard, 1904, pp. 262–272.
1840	(?)	200 "Blackfeet".	60 Flathead.	Lasted 5 days.	50 Blackfoot killed.	De Smet, 1905, vol. 1, pp. 220–221.
1845	U. S. Plains.	50 lodges, Small Robes band of Piegan.	Large Crow force.	Piegan defeated.	Ca. half Piegan men killed, ca. 200 taken prisoner.	Ewers, 1946, pp. 398.
Spring 1846	...do	A "Blackfeet" camp.	Ca. 30 Flathead and 40 Pend d' Oreille.	Blackfoot defeated.	24 Blackfoot killed, 40 wounded; 4 Flathead killed.	Mengarini, 1938, pp. 17–18.
Summer 1848	Canadian Plains.	1,500 Blackfoot, Blood, Piegan, Gros Ventres, and Sarsi warriors.	90 lodges of Cree.	Only Sarsi, Blood and N. Blackfoot portion of force engaged enemy; Cree escaped.	10 Blackfoot lost; 19 Cree killed and 40 wounded.	Kane, 1925, pp. 303–305.
1849	Marias River.	Piegan or Gros Ventres.	2 bands of Assiniboin.		26 Blackfoot killed; 52 Assiniboin killed.	Denig letter of Dec. 1, 1849, in Mo. Hist. Soc. Library.
Oct. 27, 1858	East slope of Rockies.	Ca. 200 "Blackfeet".	300 Kutenai.	Blackfoot attacked on horseback but repulsed.	35 Blackfoot scalps taken; 4 Kutenal killed, 20 wounded.	Hamilton, 1900, pp. 82–84.
Oct. 28, 1858	Near Rocky Mountain Divide.	Ca. 350 "Blackfeet".	...do	Blackfoot attacked on horseback and afoot; repulsed.	9 Kutenai killed; Blackfoot losses greater.	Hamilton, 1900, pp. 90–96.
Nov. 5, 1858	Tobacco Plains.	Ca. 300–400 "Blackfeet".	...do	Blackfoot attacked but retreated to a grove; burned out by Kutenai and forced to flee.	Not given.	Hamilton, 1900, pp. 107–112.
Dec. 4, 1865	Canadian Plains.	Ca. 50 lodges N. Blackfoot.	Cree.	Cree attacked at night, destroyed 25 Blackfoot lodges; later driven off.	Ca. 12 Blackfoot killed, 15 wounded; ca. 10 Cree killed, over 15 wounded.	Hughes, 1911, pp. 116–122.
Summer 1866	Near Cypress Hills.	Piegan.	Gros Ventres and Crow.	Piegan charged, routed and chased enemy on horseback. Greatest defeat in Gros Ventres history.	360 to 400 enemy killed; ca. 10 Piegan killed.	Grinnell, 1895, pp. 134 ff.; Schultz, 1907, pp. 197–199; Kroeber, 1907, pp. 216–221.
Fall 1870	Near present Lethbridge, Alberta.	Blood and Piegan.	Cree.	Cree attacked Blood camp at daybreak; Piegan came to rescue, using repeating firearms.	240 or more Cree killed.	Schultz, 1907, p. 379; Dixon, 1913, pp. 112–115; Hughes, 1911, p. 196.

1855, Blackfoot scalp raids may have averaged one every 2 years over a half-century period. Although horse raiding continued unabated for three decades after 1855, scalp raiding was not pursued with the same frequency or fury as in earlier years. None of my elderly informants had fought in a large-scale intertribal battle. In discussing scalp raiding they relied heavily on what they had been told rather than on their personal experiences.

THE RIDING BIG DANCE

An impressive preliminary to the departure of a scalp-raiding party was the riding big dance, referred to by Wissler (1913, pp. 456–458) as the "horseback dance or big dance." The warriors who volunteered to join the party first rode out of camp for some distance. There they changed to their war clothes, painted themselves in their war paint, painted pictographic representations of their coups on their war horses and decorated them with masks, bells, martingales, and feathers in their tails. Then they mounted and converged upon the camp from the four cardinal directions, carrying their weapons. As a number of old men and women stood in the center of the camp beating drums and singing a song with a lively rhythm, the warriors circled the camp on horseback. Then they shouted, dismounted, and danced on foot, imitating the prancing of their horses, which stepped along beside them to the beating of their drums.

Informants said there were no leaders in this dance. All warriors planning to embark on the expedition took part. The "riding big dance" was also given in former times at the Sun Dance encampment. Thus it survived as a spectacle after its discontinuance as a prelude to a war party. Informants said the Piegan had not observed the riding big dance since about 1900. Two of them expressed the wish that this picturesque and exciting dance might be revived that younger Indians might learn of the splendor of their tribal past. In buffalo days, however, the riding big dance had as its "chief function . . . the arrousal of courage and enthusiasm for war," as Wissler (ibid., p. 456) has reported.

THE WAR HORSE

While the Blackfoot horse raider usually started for the enemy camp afoot, the scalp raider uniformly rode to war. Warriors generally employed their best buffalo horses as war horses. The same qualities of speed and endurance, intelligence, sure-footedness and courage required of the buffalo runner were demanded of the war horse. The winter hunting horse was a favorite mount for war when snow was on the ground. Through experience in hunting a rapport was established between man and mount that enabled the rider to know the

peculiarities and capabilities of his mount and the horse to understand the wishes of his rider under trying conditions that required
their close cooperation.[40]

Buffalo runners used in war were trained to run at a steady pace
while the rider slipped to one side using the horse as a shield. They
were trained to stop quickly, to carry men riding double, and to stay
close to their masters when the latter dismounted. Both Weasel Tail
and Chewing Black Bones stressed the importance of the last attribute.
If the horse became panicky and ran away when the rider dismounted
one or both might be killed. In training a horse to stand still near its
master the rider stopped his running horse, jumped off, holding a
slack line tied to the horse's neck, and when the horse started to move
away be gave the line a violent jerk. After repeated experiences with
this treatment the horse learned to stand still when its master dismounted without use of the line.

In order to spare the valuable war horse as much as possible and
to save its strength for the action in which it was most needed, the
Blackfoot warrior rode a common saddle horse to the field of battle,
leading the war horse.[41]

EQUIPMENT: CLOTHING

The clothing carried by scalp raiders in the 19th century differed
from that taken by horse raiders, although there was great disparity
between the clothing of individual members. All generally set out
wearing their undecorated, everyday clothes, but carried bundles tied
to their saddles or suspended over their shoulders containing their
war medicines and any articles of war costume they possessed. Men
of wealth and distinction as warriors carried elaborately worked war
shirts and leggings. Some owned straight-up feather bonnets decorated with strips of winter weaselskin which they carried in cylindrical rawhide cases.

When the enemy was sighted the war medicines and war costumes
were donned before attacking, if time permitted. Sometimes the
enemy attacked before this could be done. In that case the warriors
carried their fine clothing into battle, for those articles also were

---

[40] Opler (1936, pp. 210–211) distinguished between the Jicarilla Apache horse raid
starting out afoot and the scalp raid proceeding mounted. Even among the relatively
wealthy Comanche, Marcy (1937, p. 157) found that the war horse was ridden in the
buffalo chase as well as for "going into battle" and "on state occasions." The Flathead
war horse was also "used exclusively for bison hunting and fighting" (Turney-High, 1937,
p. 109).

[41] Hamilton (1905, p. 36) who accompanied a Teton Dakota party against the Pawnee in
1842, noted that the Teton led their war horses and did not mount them until they were
ready to charge the enemy. Smoky told me it was Kiowa custom to ride to war on a less
valuable horse and save the war horse for the charge. This was also Cheyenne practice
(Grinnell, 1923, vol. 2, p. 17).

thought to possess protective powers or powers to bring success in battle. Weasel Tail said that since neighboring tribes with whom the Blackfoot fought had the same attitude toward war medicines, both sides often stopped to dress for the fight before going into action.

The majority of Blackfoot warriors, however, did not possess sufficient wealth to afford fancy war costumes. They went into battle wearing only their war medicine feathers, bandoliers or necklaces, face and body paint, breechcloth, and moccasins. Maximilian, who witnessed the battle between the Piegan and a large Assiniboin-Cree force outside Fort McKenzie in the summer of 1833, "saw the Blackfeet ride into battle half naked, but some, too in their fine dresses, with the beautifully ornamented shield obtained from the Crows, and their splendid crown of feathers, and on these occasions they all have their medicines or amulets open and hung about them" (Maximilian, 1906, vol. 23, p. 118). Maximilian did not comment on the wealth factor as a determinant of war costume, although his description portrays it very well.

TACTICS IN MOUNTED WARFARE

The Blackfoot were deficient in the employment of planned and coordinated cavalry tactics under fire. They seemed capable of organizing an initial charge in force. If it was not successful, fighting usually disintegrated into a large number of contests between individual Indians at close range. If the first charge was repulsed the Blackfoot rarely regrouped for another assault on horseback. In their most successful recorded battle, that against the combined Gros Ventres and Crow in the summer of 1866, the Blackfoot, maddened by the murder of their great chief Many Horses, charged with such ferocity that the enemy became demoralized, broke and ran. The Blackfoot followed and cut them down man by man in an extended series of individual actions. In the Piegan fight with the Flathead in the summer of 1810, the former charged the latter, who were protected by a rude rampart composed of their baggage. Failing to break through the Flathead rampart, the Piegan retreated. Two more mounted charges were made "but in a weak manner," after which the Piegan dismounted and advanced in a series of ineffective assaults on foot until evening put an end to the battle (Thompson, 1916, pp. 423-425).

Father Mengarini witnessed a fight between the Flathead and the Blackfoot in the spring of 1846. He described the action:

Firing had already begun on both sides, and the plain was covered with horsemen curvetting and striving to get a chance to kill some one of the enemy. An Indian battle consists of a multitude of single combats. There are no ranks, no battalions, no unified efforts. "Every man for himself" is the ruling principle, and victory depends upon personal bravery and good horsemanship. There is no random shooting, every Flathead always aims for the waist. [Mengarini, 1938, p. 17.]

Blackfoot informants also mentioned their practice of aiming at the mounted enemy's waist as the surest target, because mounted men constantly wove their bodies from side to side to confuse the enemy and prevent his taking accurate aim.[42]

Wissler (1910, p. 155) was informed that the Blackfoot charge on horseback was a "rush in a compact body, scattering along the front of the enemy as they passed, in order to deliver their fire." Informants claimed the charging force sometimes formed a line scattered over a considerable distance. The riders bent low over their horses' necks. If the enemy were afoot they tried to ride them down. Lazy Boy claimed some Piegan were expert at somersaulting backward over their horses' tails, landing on both feet, weapons in hand ready to fight a hand-to-hand combat. Upon overtaking a mounted enemy the Blackfoot tried to unhorse him with his shock weapon. Then, if the enemy was still active, the Blackfoot dismounted and sought to finish him off afoot.

I asked Lazy Boy why the Piegan did so much hand-to-hand fighting when they possessed weapons that would effectively dispose of an enemy from a distance. He made the expected reply, "A man made a name for himself as a brave warrior by killing his enemy close up where everyone could see it."

Sometimes the Blackfoot attack was directed at the enemy's herds of loose horses, in an attempt to run them off and throw the enemy into a panic. The Flathead chief Pelchimo won a signal honor in a battle with the Blackfoot in 1840, while saving the Flathead horses from capture by the enemy (De Smet, 1905, vol. 1, pp. 319–320). Again in an attack upon a Kutenai village on the move, October 27, 1858, the Blackfoot attempted to stampede the defenders' horses, but without success (Hamilton, 1900, p. 83).

USE OF FIRE WEAPONS

The fire weapons employed by scalp-raiding parties were those used by horse raiders—the gun and bow and arrows. Even in my informants' youth many Indians did not own guns. Certainly, prior to their time the bow and arrow was the most common fire weapon.

Rifles were uncommon among the Blackfoot prior to the introduction of the breech-loading, repeating rifle in 1870. The typical fire-

---

[42] Linderman (1930, pp. 145, 155) told of the Crow practice of aiming at a mounted enemy's body "where it sits on his horse" and of a Teton horseman throwing his body from side to side in a running fight. These data suggest these two practices were common in the mounted warfare of the northern Plains.

arm in use before 1870 was the Northwest Gun, a light smooth-bore, flintlock of ⅝-inch bore firing a lead ball. Most Northwest Guns were made in England (some in Pennsylvania) and were traded to the Indians by both American and Canadian companies. They were generally supplied with a barrel length of 2 feet 6 inches to 3 feet 6 inches, but the Indians commonly filed off a piece of the barrel to shorten the gun and make it easier to use on horseback. Governor Stevens, in 1854, termed this weapon "an inferior kind of shot gun." He said this gun and the bow and arrow were the "principal arms of the Blackfeet" at that time (U. S. Comm. Ind. Affairs, 1854, p. 205).

Difficulty of loading the flintlock while in action on horseback made it of limited usefulness in mounted warfare. It seems to have been used primarily in firing at a distance of 100 yards or more before closing with the enemy for combat with shock weapons. It was more valuable as a foot soldier's weapon. This was a factor in causing many battles to be fought on foot. Thus, when the Flathead and Piegan fought an engagement on the Plains in the summer of 1812, horses were used only to watch each other's movements. The Flathead took their position on a grassy ridge with sloping ground behind it. The Piegan advanced on foot in a single line, members of the party about 3 feet apart, until they came within about 150 yards (i. e., within gun range). Then they rushed forward rapidly to make contact with the enemy (Thompson, 1916, pp. 551–552).

Both Thompson (ibid., p. 411) and Maximilian (1906, vol. 23, p. 109) said the Blackfoot were not good marksmen with the gun. The latter acknowledged, however, that they were "expert in the use of the bow." This greater skill in marksmanship, plus greater ease in reloading, encouraged the retention of the bow and arrow as the principal fire weapon employed by the Blackfoot in mounted warfare until the introduction of breech-loading firearms. Only one large-scale battle was fought by the Blackfoot after the acquisition of breechloaders. That was against the Cree, who at that time did not have the advantage of the new weapons. In earlier times it was not uncommon for a Blackfoot warrior to carry both gun and bow and arrows.

USE OF SHOCK WEAPONS

The three principal shock weapons employed by Blackfoot scalp raiders in the 19th century were the lance, war club, and knife. Of these the war club and knife were almost standard equipment. Neither the lance nor war club was carried by horse-raiding parties.

The lance was less favored by the Blackfoot as a shock weapon than was the war club. That it is of ancient use as a weapon cannot be doubted. Informants cited traditions of its employment before the acquisition of horses. In the fall of 1754, Hendry (1907, p. 335) met a small party of "Archithinue" warriors with "Bows and Arrows, & bone spears and darts." Informants described the war lance as 5 or more feet in length, consisting of an iron head 6 inches to 12 inches long, bound to the end of a wooden shaft. At intervals the shaft was wrapped with otter fur to serve as grips, and pendent feathers were attached to the end of the pole. Warriors criticized others who used long lances, saying they were cowards.[43] By grasping the shaft with both hands the warrior brought it down with a quick, oblique downward stroke, which combined thrusting and swinging. The weapon could kill or cripple an opponent if skillfully used (fig. 29). Inform-

FIGURE 29.—Method of wielding the lance by a mounted warrior, Blackfoot.

ants said the lance was last used in warfare by the Piegan in their battle with the Gros Ventres and Crow in 1866.[44]

War clubs, generally carried under the warrior's belt at one side when not in use, were of several types. Although both wooden and elkhorn clubs were used by the Blackfoot in my informants' youth,

---

[43] Weasel Tail was told the Crow had a similar attitude. He cited the instance of a brave Crow warrior taking the long lance of a fellow tribesman, breaking it in two and returning it to him, saying that half that lance was sufficient for a courageous man.

[44] The literature reveals that southern Plains tribes made more extensive use of lances in mounted warfare than did the Blackfoot. Direct contacts with Spanish-Mexican soldiers, who were trained and skilled lancers, may have encouraged greater use of this weapon by those tribes. Pfefferkorn (1949, p. 146) observed that the Apache, who raided into Sonora in the middle 19th century, used many lances taken from slain or captured Spaniards. He noted the Apache could "guide the spear more skillfully when they are on foot than when they are mounted, for, because they are not practiced in delivering the thrust except with both hands and raised arms, they cannot manage the reins of the horse at the same time, and hence often miss the mark." Yet Pike (1810, pp. 10–11), writing of the Apache use of the lance a half century later, observed "they charge with both hands over their heads, managing their horses principally with their knees. With this weapon they are considered an overmatch for the Spanish dragoons single handed, but, for want of a knowledge of tactics, they can never stand the charge of a body which acts in concert." These descriptions show that the Apache employed the lance as did the Blackfoot, using a two-handed, overhand thrust that probably was a survival from the Indian method of lancing in pre-horse times. It is apparent the Indians did not derive their technique of wielding the lance on horseback from the Spaniards. Burnet (1851, p. 236) claimed the Comanche used the "javelin" with great dexterity on horseback ca. 1820. Emory (1857, vol. 1, p. 89) noted that Comanche and Kiowa, raiding into Mexico in midcentury, left their guns behind and depended "alone upon the lance."

the most common club was one consisting of a round stone sewn in a skin cover, an extension of the cover forming the sheathing of a wooden handle. The type is figured in Wissler (1910, p. 164). Until the introduction of breechloaders the war club was in common use for fighting both on foot and horseback. Warriors tried first to cripple the enemy with the club, then proceeded to kill him with another well-aimed blow or with the knife. Weasel Tail described the use of the club in fighting on foot, "If an enemy tries to stab you with a knife, hit him on the arm or wrist and make him drop it. Then hit him over the head with your club." [45]

Both single and double-edged knives were employed in hand-to-hand combat. The broad, sharp, double-edged knife, known to the Blackfoot as a "stabber" or "beaver tail knife" was a favorite of many warriors for hand-to-hand fighting. The warrior grasped the handle so that the metal blade protruded from the heel of his fist. He used a powerful downward chopping motion to penetrate the opponent's body above the clavicle or a sidewise sweep to strike him between the ribs or in the stomach. It was a deadly weapon for close infighting afoot, of little use in opposition to a mounted enemy armed with war club or lance. It was a favorite weapon for finishing off a wounded or disabled enemy and served as the scalping tool. [46]

THE SHIELD

The principal defensive weapon used by scalp raiders in historic times was the shield. Shields were never taken on horse raids by the Blackfoot. Their use in warfare by the Piegan goes back to pre-horse times. Saukamappee told Thompson (1916, pp. 328–329; 330–332) of the use of shields by both sides in two large-scale battles between the

---

[45] The most common Blackfoot war club type was observed among the Lemhi Shoshoni by Lewis and Clark in 1805 (Coues, 1897, vol. 2, p. 561), and among the Crow by Charles McKenzie in the same year (Larocque, 1910, footnote p. 22). However, the elder Henry (1809, p. 298) described a quite different stone-headed weapon in use among mounted Assiniboin in 1776. "In using it the stone is whirled round the handle, by a warrior setting on horseback, and attacking at full speed. Every stroke which takes effect brings down a man, or horse." Carver (1838, p. 188) was told of a handleless shock weapon similarly employed by mounted warriors of the northeastern Plains a decade earlier. He called it "a stone of middling size curiously wrought, which they fasten by a string, about a yard and a half long, to their right arms, a little above the elbow. These stones they conveniently carry in their hands till they reach their enemies, then swinging them with great dexterity, as they ride full speed, never fail of doing execution." Whether the mounted Shoshoni who "dashed at the Peeagans, and with their stone Pukamoggan knocked them on the head," in the earliest encounters of the Blackfoot with a mounted enemy, used a weapon of this kind or a true war club cannot be determined from this brief statement in Thompson (1916, p. 330). The weapon variantly described by Henry and Carver, appears to have resembled the bola perdida of the mounted Tehuelche of Patagonia more closely than the war clubs employed in later warfare on the northern Plains. I have found no indication of its survival among the 19th century Plains Indians.

[46] Informants claimed that these knives were first traded to the Blackfoot by Canadian traders. An excellent example of the type, obtained from the Blackfoot by George Gibbs prior to 1862, is in the U. S. National Museum (Cat. No. 729).

Piegan and Shoshoni before the former obtained horses. He mentioned that the Shoshoni shields were fully 3 feet across, and those of the Piegan, similarly employed to hide the entire seated warrior from the enemy, must have been of about the same size. However, the shields used for the Blackfoot in the period of mounted warfare were nearer half that size, suggesting that the use of horses in war influenced the reduction in shield size. My informants said Blackfoot shields were made from the thick rawhide of the neck of the buffalo bull, shrunken over a fire to a thickness of a half inch or more, trimmed into circular form, and ornamented with painted protective designs and a border of eagle feathers. In native belief the shield's power resided primarily in the medicine paintings and the blessings bestowed upon the shield by medicine men when it was made. However, it was sturdy enough to stop an arrow and to deaden or deflect the force of a ball from a muzzle-loading flintlock. The horseman carried the shield on his left arm (if he was right-handed) in such a way as to cover his vital parts, leaving his left hand and right arm free to handle his offensive weapons.

Although Bradley (1923, p. 258) termed the shield "an indispensable part of every warrior's equipment," informants said that poor men did not possess them. It cost at least a horse to obtain a shield, ceremonially blessed by medicine men. In lieu of a shield the poor man sometimes carried a buffalo robe (with the hair) folded several times, over his left arm. Bradley (ibid., p. 258) learned that the American Fur Co. at one time attempted to introduce polished metal shields among the Blackfoot. This action "was opposed by the medicine men, who would thus have been deprived of an important source of revenue, and the superstitious feelings of the Indians induced them to prefer their own which alone could undergo religious dedication and enjoy the favor of the Great Spirit." [47]

EARLY USE OF PROTECTIVE ARMOR

Shimkin (1947 a, p. 251) found that the modern Wind River Shoshoni referred to the Blackfoot as "Hard-clothes (armor) people." Wissler reported Blackfoot traditions "implying that buckskin shirts of two or more thicknesses were worn as protection against stone and bone points" (Wissler, 1910, p. 163). Weasel Tail cited a tradition regarding Blackfoot use of long shirts, reaching below the knees, made of three thicknesses of buckskin in fighting battles during the pre-

---

[47] The use of a rawhide shield by the Spanish horsemen of old Mexico may have encouraged Plains Indians to employ the shield as a weapon for mounted men. However, there can be no doubt that the Indians were familiar with the rawhide shield before contact with Spaniards. Pfefferkorn (1949, p. 291) described the Spanish soldier's shield of the period 1756-67 as "egg-shaped" and made of three or four layers of rawhide riveted together. The Plains Indian shield was circular, of a single thickness of shrunken buffalo rawhide.

horse period. He claimed this armor was adequate protection against arrows but was unable to ward off bullets from early firearms. Consequently the Blackfoot abandoned its use after their enemies became armed with guns.

There are no contemporary descriptions of the use of this leather body armor by the Blackfoot specifically, although there are descriptions implying its general use in the theater of warfare in which the Blackfoot participated in the 18th century. In December 1772, Cocking (1908, p. 111) saw several horsemen in the Gros Ventres camp wearing "Jackets of Moose leather six fold, quilted, & without sleeves." He was also shown "a Coat without sleeves six fold leather quilted, used by the Snake tribe to defend them against the arrows of their adversaries." Umfreville (1790, pp. 188–189) stated that the Cree and their enemies (who certainly would have included the Blackfoot) wore "coats of mail, made of many folds of drest leather, which are impenetrable to the force of arrows" in their intertribal battles of the period ca. 1775.

There is no indication in either traditions or early contemporary writings that the Blackfoot used horse armor in the warfare of that period or in later years. The only reference to horse armor used by any of the common enemies of the Blackfoot appears in Lewis and Clark's description of the Lemhi Shoshoni in 1805, "they have a kind of armor like a coat of mail, which is formed of a great many folds of dressed antelope-skins, united by means of a mixture of glue and sand. With this they cover their own bodies and those of their horses, and find it impervious to arrows" (Coues, 1893, vol. 2, p. 561).[48]

---

[48] The earliest known description of the use of armor by any Plains Indian tribe refers to both body and horse types. In 1690, Tonty (Cox, 1905, p. 55) found the Caddo on Red River wore "body-coverings of several skins, one over the other, as a protection from arrows. They arm the breasts of their horses with the same material, a proof that they are not very far from the Spaniards." The French explorers Du Tisne and La Harpe found the Wichita and their neighbors on the Arkansas wore hide body armor and decked their horses with breastplates of tanned hide in 1719 (Margry, 1886, vol. 6, pp. 294, 312). Five years later Bourgmont (ibid., vol. 6, p. 446) remarked that the Paduca (Apache) went to war dressed in "specially tanned buffalo skins with which they protect themselves. They also hang them around their horses to protect them against arrows." A Ponca tradition refers to their fights with mounted Comanche, before the Ponca themselves obtained horses, in which the Comanche employed horse armor "of thick rawhide cut in round pieces and made to overlap like the scales of a fish. Over the surface was sand held on by glue. This covering made the Ponca arrows glance off and do no damage." Some Comanche men also wore "breastplates made like those on their horses" (Fletcher and La Flesche, 1911, p. 79). Joseph La Flesche had no knowledge of Omaha use of armor, but he credited the Pawnee with former use of body armor comprising a coat of elkskins, two skins forming the front and two the back, with sand between each pair of skins (Dorsey, 1896, pp. 287–288). In 1775 Peter Pond (1908, p. 354) reported that Yankton Dakota warriors, both mounted and afoot, wore a "Garment Like an Outside Vest with Sleves that Cum down to thare Elboes Made of Soft Skins and Several thicknesses what will turn an arrow at a distans." In the Southwest, the Navaho were reported to have employed two types of buckskin body armor of several thicknesses, one of which was specially designed for use on horseback. It reached to the knees and "was slit at the bottom both in front and behind, in order that the horse might be straddled" (Hill, 1936, p. 9). Teit recorded traditions among

USE OF THE HORSE AS A SHIELD

Wissler (1910, p. 155) reported that the Blackfoot, when fighting mounted "protected their bodies by hanging on the sides of the horses." My informants said boys learned this difficult feat in preparation for their careers as warriors, but that it was rarely employed in actual combat. The rider slipped to one side of his running horse, leaving only one leg over the back of the animal with which to take a heel hold over the horse's hipbone. With one hand the rider held his shield and reins and at the same time firmly grasped his horse's mane. With the other hand he fired his gun under the horse's neck. Both Weasel Tail and Lazy Boy pointed out the danger of this maneuver under combat conditions. It exposed the full side of the horse to the enemy, affording him a very sizable target which, if hit, might result in the horse's fall and death or serious injury to the rider. Only if the enemy possessed a stronger desire to capture the rider's horse than to destroy it would they be deterred from shooting at it. If the enemy were hard pressed, fighting defensively for their lives, they would have no qualms about shooting their opponents' horses.

A survey of the use of this maneuver by other Plains Indian tribes confirms my informants' testimony as to its impracticality as an

the Coeur d'Alene, Okanagon, and Flathead of the wearing of elkhide body armor by warriors of those tribes. He found the Flathead discarded this armor "after the introduction of the horse as cumbersome and inconvenient in mounting and riding" (Teit, 1930, pp. 117, 256, 359).

The foregoing data testify that the wearing of body armor of several thicknesses of skin was virtually Plains-wide in the 18th century, and was customary among some if not all of the neighboring horse-using tribes farther west at that time. There can be little doubt that this armor was of native origin and was not adapted from the Spanish. As early as 1540 Spanish members of the Coronado expedition adopted native armor in preference to the heavy metal armor of European design. Aiton (1939, pp. 558–559) concluded his study of the equipment of that expedition with the statement, "The great majority wore native buckskin suits of armor, cueras de anta, which were much more comfortable on the march and quite effective against Indian weapons." Two centuries later (ca. 1760) the Spanish soldiers of Sonora still wore knee-length, sleeveless jackets of six or eight layers of well-cured deerskins as armor against the arrows of their Apache enemies (Pfefferkorn, 1949, p. 155).

Horse armor, however, had a much more restricted distribution among the horse-using Indian tribes. Contemporary sources tell of its use only by Indians of the Southern Plains and the Shoshoneans (Shoshoni and Comanche). Most probably its use was suggested by Spanish example. Horse armor did not spread far beyond those tribes which were in direct contact with the Spanish in the late 17th and early 18th centuries.

The Plains Indians appear to have abandoned the use of leather armor before the close of the 18th century. Lewis and Clark's account of the Lemhi Shoshoni in 1805 provides the last contemporary mention of the use of horse and body armor by any horse-using western tribe. Probably the ineffectiveness of this armor as protection against gunfire was the primary cause of its abandonment. However, the need for greater mobility and freer use of arms and legs both afoot and on horseback may also have encouraged Indian warriors to discard their bulky and weighty skin armor. The Indians must have noticed also that the English and French traders who supplied them with guns during the 18th century wore no armor. Their example may have been a third influence on the abandonment of armor by the Plains Indians.

offensive tactic. It was a display of horsemanship, tremendously impressive in sham battles to entertain visiting white men, but recklessly ineffective under fire.[49]

POSTRAID CEREMONIES

The ceremonies following the return of a successful scalp raid also differed materially from those that followed the return of a party that had been successful in stealing enemy horses. In 1833, Maximilian (1906, vol. 23, p. 119) described the return of a Blackfoot war party with enemy scalps:

When the warriors come near their camp, after a battle, they sing; and one rides or runs before, often in serpentine lines, backwards and forwards about the tents, holding up and shaking the scalp, and displaying it at a distance. If any one has taken a weapon, he displays it in the same manner, loudly proclaiming his name as having taken it. After a successful engagement, the men sing the song which they call aninay, that is "they are painted black." On these occasions, they assemble in the open air about their tents, with their faces painted black, and then sing, without the accompaniment of an instrument, nor are the scalps displayed. There are no words to this song, which consists only of the usual notes.

---

[49] George Catlin, who witnessed this tactic in a Comanche sham battle in 1834, left both a description and a drawing of it that helped to make this practice well-known to his many readers (Catlin, 1841, vol. 2, pp. 65–66 and pl. 167). However, numerous other writers, both before and since Catlin's publication reported its wide use among the Plains Indians. In 1805, Larocque wrote of the Crow, "In their wheelings and evolutions they often are not seen, having one leg on the horse back and clasping the horse with their arms around his neck, on the side opposite to where the enemy is" (Larocque, 1910, p. 64) ; Lewis and Clark, that same year, noted Lemhi Shoshoni use of this tactic (Coues, 1893, vol. 2, p. 563). Leforge (Marquis, 1928, p. 92) cited an example of its use by the Teton Dakota ; Hamilton mentioned its employment by the Cheyenne (Hamilton, 1905, p. 83) ; Wilson (1924, p. 154) by Hidatsa : Kendall (1844, pp. 212–214) by Kiowa ; and Tixier (1940, p. 167) by Osage. Captain Marcy (1937, p. 156) confirmed Catlin's description of Comanche employment of this tactic. However, Tixier (1940, p. 268), whose information on the Comanche was derived from the experienced trader, Eduard Chouteau, wrote, "They knew better than the others how to hide behind their horse's body, but they scorn this method ; they charge upon the enemy with their chest exposed and their arms outstretched, shouting a war cry."

The use of the horse as a shield was a trick riding act that greatly impressed white traders, explorers, and military men who saw it demonstrated by Indians at frontier forts or under peaceful conditions in Indian camps. The great majority of the writers who described this "war tactic" saw it employed only in sham battles, as had Catlin. William Hamilton (1905, p. 83), the old Indian fighter, said he had never seen this tactic employed in Indian warfare. My extensive readings in the literature on intertribal battles between Plains Indians, written by observers of these conflicts, have revealed just two descriptions of the employment of this tactic in actual warfare. Leforge (Marquis, 1928, p. 92) told of a fight between the Teton Dakota and Crow. As a prelude to the battle daring Crow and Teton riders took turns riding in this fashion at some distance from and parallel to the enemy line while their respective enemies vainly fired at them. It was an act of bravado on the part of these men that in no way affected the later course or outcome of the battle. On November 21, 1834, the trader Zenas Leonard, witnessed a battle between the Crow and Blackfoot. The latter and numerically inferior force occupied a fortified position on the brow of a hill. Crow riders rode in single file along the top of the hill. As each rider approached the Blackfoot breastwork he fired, then threw himself on the side of his horse leaving only one leg exposed, until he rode out of range of enemy fire. The Blackfoot shot and killed so many of their horses and men that the Crow were forced to abandon this unsuccessful maneuver. They made a direct, frontal assault, took the enemy position, and killed every Blackfoot defender (Leonard, 1904, pp. 263–264).

The highlight of the postraid celebration was the scalp dance which Bradley has described:

When scalps were taken they were turned over to the squaws upon the arrival of the war party at the village, to be prepared for the scalp dance. This was done by stretching each scalp upon a hoop, the hoop being attached to a small pole, six or eight feet long, a separate pole for each scalp. Each pole is borne by a squaw, usually a relative of the warrior who took it, who leads in the dance, the warriors and squaws all arrayed in their best attire following her in single file in a circle of a size proportioned to the number of dancers. The step of the dance is little more than a march in quick time, to the music of a song peculiar to the dance. Where the number of dancers is considerable several rings are formed in different parts of the tent and the dance is frequently kept up with intervals of rest for twelve or fourteen days. [Bradley, 1923, pp. 269–270.] [50]

If a member of a raiding party had had a brother, a son, or other close relative killed by the enemy tribe engaged, he mutilated the body of any enemy he killed on the raid, as part of his revenge. Informants said it was common for such a man to cut off the hand of the enemy, pierce a hole in it, pass a cord through the hole and tie the trophy to the bridle of his horse. Thus he carried it back to camp. The hand was carried in the scalp dance as a symbol implying that revenge had been taken for the loss of his relative. After the scalp dance the hand was buried or thrown away. It had served its purpose.

DEFENSIVE WARFARE

DEFENSE OF THE CAMP

Blackfoot camp defenses ordinarily were woefully inadequate. The competent military observer, Lt. James Bradley, has said of them:

Like most nomadic tribes, the Blackfeet never fortified their camps, and it was rare that they chose them with any reference to their possibilities of defense . . . It was not their custom to maintain a guard about the camp either day or night, so that, contrary to popular belief, the surprise of a village was not difficult . . . When no danger was apprehended, bands of horses were sometimes driven to a secluded place and left for days together without a guard. It is thus seen why a daring war party could successfully approach within the vicinity of a village and drive off the outlying bands of horses which were ever such a temptation to the enterprising and adventurous brave. [Bradley, 1923, pp. 286–287.]

With Bradley's criticism in mind, I discussed Blackfoot camp defenses with my two eldest male informants, Lazy Boy and Weasel Tail. They acknowledged that neither the Piegan nor Blood tribes normally posted night guards. They did picket their best horses nightly in front of their lodges. They also relied heavily upon their dogs to bark and waken them if enemy raiders entered the camp at night.

---

[50] Both Maximilian (1906, vol. 23, 115) and Schultz (1907, p. 223) have written accounts of the Blackfoot scalp dance based upon their personal observations.

Weasel Tail said the Indians could distinguish between a dog's snorting at night (which the people termed "barking at spirits") and its barking at approaching strangers. The Blood Indians also knew that Cree raiders had a custom of signaling to each other by coyote howls on approaching their camps at night. He claimed clever Blood Indians could distinguish the imitation coyote howl from the real one.

Blackfoot reliance upon dogs for protection appears remarkable in view of the fact that their warriors were well aware of the ineffectiveness of dogs in enemy camps as obstacles to their own raids. Weasel Tail said that if the enemy dogs started barking when a Blackfoot horse-raiding party approached the camp, the raiders backtracked, circled the camp and approached from another direction after the dogs had quieted down. They threw bits of meat to the dogs to quiet them. He said he had never heard of any man of his tribe having been bitten by a dog while attempting to take horses from an enemy village.[51]

If young men had been out scouting for game during the day and found signs suggesting that an enemy war party might be near, the Blackfoot were more careful. Some band chiefs made a practice of sending out scouts in winter to look for enemy signs. They reported any suspicious signs observed to the chief, who announced them to the people. One or more of three precautionary measures could then be taken: (1) the setting of an individual lodge watch, (2) construction of a corral or corrals for horses, and (3) organization of an ambush.

THE INDIVIDUAL LODGE WATCH

This was a guard, organized on a family basis, usually employed if the danger of attack was felt to be relatively slight. The men and women of each lodge owning picketed horses took turns staying awake and listening for any unusual movement on the part of the horses picketed close by or any noise that might indicate the presence of the enemy. If any suspicious noise was heard the men of the lodge were roused and they rushed out guns in hand. This precaution was only effective in guarding the picketed horses and would not, of course, prevent the enemy from running off the range herds grazing at a distance. Yet enemies were killed as a result of these watches.

---

[51] My informants claimed that the camps of the enemy tribes from which they captured horses were normally no more closely guarded at night than were their own. Weasel Tail said the Crow habitually drove their horses a long distance from camp before dusk, which made it easy for a Blackfoot raiding party, watching from a hill or other secluded spot, to go directly to those horses after nightfall. The Omaha were reported (1819) to have used no "regular sentinels" at night (James, 1823, p. 292). Captain Bonneville, who, camped on the Plains with a large, combined village of Flathead, Nez Percé and Pend d'Oreille in the winter of 1832–33, was impressed by the lack of provision made by those tribes for night protection of their horses and the camp. "They merely drive them (horses) at nightfall to some sequestered dell, and leave them there, at perfect liberty, until morning . . . Even in situations of danger, the Indians rarely set guards over their camp at night, intrusting that office entirely to their vigilant and well-trained dogs" (Irving, 1851, p. 119).

THE HORSE CORRAL

Bradley (1923, p. 287) wrote of the Blackfoot: "Horse corrals were sometimes made of small poles by the united labors of the squaws of the village within which the horses of the whole village were nightly assembled." Maximilian (1906, vol. 23, p. 123) saw a horse corral in the Piegan camp near Fort McKenzie in August 1833, which he described as "a kind of fence of boughs of trees, which contained part of the tents and was designed to confine the horses during the night." Informants said horse corrals were most commonly built in winter. In summer they were constructed only when the chief was convinced that the possibility of a raid was great. Often corrals were made of posts set in the ground to a height of about 6 feet, lashed or nailed to crossrails and provided with a crude gate. Two guards were stationed at the corral during the night. Sometimes other guards were placed at a little distance from the corral. The guards were ordered to ask the name of any man who approached the corral at night. If he refused to answer they were to shoot him. Lazy Boy recalled that Woman Shoe, while guarding a corral in the camp of his band near present Choteau, saw a man approach, take down a gate pole, and rope a horse inside the corral. Woman Shoe challenged him, but the man made no reply. Woman Shoe shot and killed him. Upon close examination the intruder was found to be a Flathead bent on capturing Piegan horses. Lazy Boy believed the Blackfoot obtained the idea of horse corrals from Whites. Indeed the whole procedure of guarding these corrals is suggestive of white influence. Nevertheless the use of horse corrals by Plains Indians was widespread and can be traced back to the early years of the 19th century.[52]

---

[52] Denig (1930, pp. 546–547) claimed horse corrals were built by all the Upper Missouri tribes during the second quarter of the 19th century. Kroeber (1907, p. 147) mentioned the winter horse corrals of the Gros Ventres. Marquis (1928, p. 149) wrote of Crow corrals made of brush piled between the lodges to enclose the center of the camp. Lowie's statement that the Northern Shoshoni kept their horses inside their camp circles would imply some form of corral (Lowie, 1908, p. 208). Although Mandan and Hidatsa customarily stabled horses inside their lodges as protection against theft, those owners who had too many horses to keep in the lodge built corrals of posts and poles under the drying stage beside the lodge, to hold their excess horses (Wilson, 1924, p. 156). In 1840 Tixier (1940, p. 238) noted that the Osage buffalo hunting party built horse corrals when fearing night attacks by the Pawnee. In 1821, Capt. Bell observed the "large, circular pen" adjacent to each lodge, in which the Loup Pawnee placed their horses for safety during the night (Morse, 1822, p. 240). In 1844 Carleton (1943, p. 70) described the corrals of the Grand Pawnee as "made by planting pickets in the ground, the same as we do in building a stockade; are circular, with a hole on one side for the ingress and egress of the animals, which is securely fastened by bars tied by thongs." At the Republican village known as the Hill site and believed to have been the village visited by Pike in 1806, the post mold pattern of a probable horse corral was found by archeologists (Wedel, 1936, pp. 56–57, fig. 6). Near the end of the year 1821, Fowler (1898, p. 60) observed that enemies stole between 400 and 500 horses from "pens" in the center of the village of more than 700 lodges of Kiowa, Comanche, Arapaho, and Cheyenne on the Arkansas, indicating the early employment of horse corrals by the Southern Plains Indians.

THE AMBUSH

"In times of apprehended danger the young men would lie in concealment upon the outskirts of the camp, and were vigilant and effective sentinels" (Bradley, 1923, p. 287). Weasel Tail told of young men taking positions in the tall grass surrounding the camp when they believed an enemy raid was imminent. They remained motionless, flat on their stomachs, concealed from view by the tall grass, with their loaded guns beside them. When the unsuspecting enemy approached they jumped up and opened fire at close range. Sometimes the men in ambush went so far as to picket a fine-looking horse near them to lure some horse-crazy enemy into their trap. (Schultz (1907, pp. 218–222) described in detail a Piegan ambush of a Crow raiding party which resulted in the killing of 7 Crow warriors.[53]

Weasel Tail said it was customary for the chief of a Blood band, on hearing a gun shot near camp, to order a count of all members of the camp to determine if anyone was missing. If all were present he ordered the horses to be brought in close and a guard set in anticipation of a possible attack.[54]

OWNERSHIP OF HORSES RECOVERED FROM THE ENEMY

When the Blackfoot discovered some of their horses had been stolen, hastily organized parties of volunteers usually set out after the raiders. They traveled mounted as rapidly as possible in the tracks of the enemy. Sometimes they were succesful in overtaking the culprits and recovering the captured horses. A horse retaken

---

[53] Schultz (1907, p. 30) described a similar Gros Ventres ambush witnessed by him ca. 1880. Tixier (1940, p. 204) told of an Osage ambush prepared for expected Pawnee raiders who withdrew before entering the trap set for them. Possibly James referred to this type of ambush when he wrote of the Omaha in 1819, "If the nation have reason to believe that the enemy is near at hand, or that there is a probability of an attack, they are necessarily vigilant; young warriors volunteer to look out at different points, or are requested to do so by the chiefs" (James, 1823, vol. 1, p. 292).

[54] Several references in the literature refer to a more cautious employment of sentinels among other tribes than was customary among the Blackfoot. However, the references may not refer to the normal procedure in those camps but to periods of feared attack, when the Blackfoot also took greater precautions. Hendry (1907, p. 339) observed that the chief of the "Archithinue" camp in 1754 ordered "a party of Horsemen Evening and Morning to reconitre." Larocque (1910, p. 65) noted that the Crow in the summer of 1805, "Keep an excellent look out and have always Young men night and day at 2 or 3 miles from Camp upon the watch, besides they often send parties of young men on a two or three days scout on the road they intend to take." Yet part of the time Larocque traveled with the Crow they were in daily fear of an attack by Gros Ventres known to have been in the neighborhood. One night their fear reached such a pitch that 2 hours before daybreak they saddled their horses, tied their small children in the saddles, loaded pack horses with their most valuable property, and sat arms ready in their lodges awaiting an attack that did not materialize (ibid., p. 40). Captain Marcy (1937, p. 164) claimed the Comanche guarded their horses "both day and night" and "even in times of profound peace." If Marcy's observation is correct, it indicates a greater recognition of the importance of constant guard than was found among the tribes of the northwestern Plains. The usual laxness of security provisions among the Blackfoot and their neighbors certainly encouraged horse thievery and increased the incidence of successful raids in that theater of warfare.

from the enemy was considered the property of the man who recaptured it, for he had risked his life to reclaim the animal. He might generously return the animal to its former owner, but he was not obliged to do that. If the owner was a close friend or relative he would be more likely to return the horse to him. In some cases the owner bought his horse from the man who had retaken it.

DEFENSIVE WARFARE IN THE FIELD

It is not possible to estimate the number of relatively small-scale actions involving horse-raiding parties which were inadvertently confronted with enemy parties while en route to capture horses, or were overtaken by the enemy on their return journey. The literature and many accounts of horse raids told by Blackfoot informants indicate clearly that such actions were relatively frequent. Over the years the casualties resulting from these encounters must have greatly exceeded those suffered in the much less frequent battles involving sizable forces.

Defensive measures taken by small parties surprised by the enemy differed according to the relative numbers of the opposing forces and the terrain. The first impulse of the members of a small party on sighting a superior force seems to have been to run for shelter in timber or thickets if such localities were near. In woods or thick brush they could hold off a superior enemy force and escape when darkness came on. Informants' testimony included numerous references to successful defenses under these conditions. The enemy was loath to pursue a smaller force into wooded areas where the men could not be clearly seen. In heavy timber the defending force sometimes threw up hastily built breastworks of logs and brush to further strengthen their position.

If the smaller force was overtaken on the open Plains at a distance from timber it hastily dug shallow pits in the ground using knives for excavating. If there were only a few men in the party they made only a single pit. If forced to defend themselves in open, rocky country, rock fortifications were prepared.[55]

The larger force usually took the offensive. In approaching a fortified position on foot the members of the attacking party moved forward, keeping constantly in motion, jumping from side to side to prevent their enemy from taking careful aim. Generally each mem-

---

[55] None of these defensive measures were peculiar to the Blackfoot. They were commonly employed by the neighboring tribes with whom the Blackfoot were at war. Mention of log forts made by Indians on the Arkansas River appears in Jacob Fowler's Journal of 1821 (Fowler, 1898, pp. 28–29). In the summer of 1820 the Long Expedition saw numerous Indian forts of logs in the central and southern Plains (James, 1823, vol. 2, p. 122). The same source (vol. 1, p. 304) mentions the Omaha practice of digging pits for defense. On the prairies of the Upper Mississippi in 1805, Pike saw round holes in the ground about 10 feet in diameter, dug by the Sioux for defense against attack (Pike, 1932, vol. 2, p. 9).

ber of the attacking force acted on his own.   Men who had the greatest confidence in the protective powers of their war medicines led the attack.   Losses in these assaults were heavy considering the small numbers of men engaged.   Sometimes the attacking force managed to storm the fortification and wipe out the defenders, but not without considerable loss to their own party.

INFLUENCE OF WARFARE ON BLACKFOOT POPULATION

Throughout the historic period prior to 1885, warfare caused a heavy drain on Blackfoot population.   Although the numbers killed in single actions usually were small, the ratio of losses to tribal populations was high compared with the ratios between casualties in modern warfare and national populations.   There must have been a number of years in which more than 1 percent of the total Piegan population died in battles large and small.

The demonstrable effect of war losses was to unbalance the proportions between the sexes.   David Thompson (1916, p. 352) noted of the Piegan ca. 1800, "The grown up population of these people appear to be about three men to every five women, and yet the births appear in favour of the boys."   In 1847, Father Point reckoned the women in the Blackfoot tribes outnumbered the men two or three to one, and attributed this disproportion to war losses (De Smet, 1905, vol. 3, p. 952).   Eleven years later Agent Vaughan estimated 2,060 men and 3,100 women in the four Blackfoot tribes (including the Gros Ventres).   He attributed this disproportion between the sexes to losses of men in war and hunting accidents, and added, "This difference in the number of the male and the female doubtless suggested and sustained the prevailing custom of polygamy among them, many of the men having more wives than one, the number reaching to five or more, according to the caprice or wealth of the man" (U. S. Comm. Ind. Affairs, 1858, pp. 432–433).   Thus warfare, which was to a large extent initiated and perpetuated through raiding for horses, influenced both population trends and family organization among the Blackfoot.[56]

WAR HONORS

In the 1870's, Lieutenant Bradley wrote of the Blackfoot:

The various exploits of war are denominated coups and reflect honor upon their performers according to a certain fixed scale of merit.   To capture an enemy's arms is a coup of the first class; to touch him alive, of the second; to touch his dead body or secure his scalp, of the third; to make a successful theft of an enemy's horses, of the fourth.   [Bradley, 1923, p. 267.]

---

[56] Population losses due to warfare were proportionately greater among some of the enemies of the powerful and aggressive Blackfoot.   The small Flathead tribe was greatly reduced by 1855 (Ewers, 1948 a, p. 23).   The Crow, attacked by the more numerous Teton Dakota from the east as well as by the Blackfoot from the north, suffered such losses that fur traders who knew them feared the Crow would be exterminated (Denig, 1953, p. 71).

My older informants agreed that the taking of a weapon, especially a gun, from the enemy was the highest Blackfoot war honor. They were inclined to omit Bradley's second honor, claiming that to take an enemy scalp was the honor of second rank, and to capture a horse from the enemy was one of the third rank. Some Indians claimed the killing of an enemy warrior should rank ahead of taking the scalp, others did not mention killing as a recognized honor.

The Blackfoot system of grading war honors appears to have been based upon both the degree of daring displayed by the warrior and upon the relative commonness of performance of the several classes of deeds. This is borne out by the fact that in the early 1940's there was no man living on the Blackfeet Reservation in Montana who had taken a gun from an enemy in a hand-to-hand combat. There were three veterans of the intertribal wars who had taken scalps. More than a dozen elderly men had captured enemy horses.

Whether the taking of an enemy's weapon ranked as the highest war honor before the introduction of firearms is not known. However, the Saukamappee account of early Blackfoot warfare shows clearly that the scalp was regarded as a valuable war trophy before the introduction of firearms or horses (Thompson, 1916, p. 333). The addition of horse capture to the hierarchy of war honors was a historic innovation. Possibly it replaced the capture of an enemy woman or child in the series.

While the capture of articles other than weapons from the enemy was considered of sufficient significance to be memorialized in the painting of a warrior's robe, their capture was not ranked in importance with the deeds above mentioned. It was considered only a minor honor for a man to be wounded in battle. Nevertheless, a maimed or disabled warrior was well cared for by his people. Lazy Boy told of a young Piegan who was shot in the leg in a fight with the Crow. An Army surgeon at Fort Benton found it necessary to amputate the leg. When the amputee returned to camp his friends gave him horses and a lodge. Fellow members of his band brought food to him when they returned from hunts thereafter.[57]

---

[57] Capture of enemy horses received recognition as a war honor among other Plains Indian tribes in the first half of the 19th century, although the relative ranking of this act as a war honor differed from tribe to tribe. Tabeau (1939, pp. 204-206) observed that the Arikara, in 1803, considered the theft of horses an act of sufficient importance to admit the perpetrator to the ranks of braves. He was permitted to wear hair on his leggings and a string on his arm symbolic of his achievement. Lewis and Clark (Coues, 1893, vol. 2, p. 559) understood that the Lemhi Shoshoni regarded "stealing individually the horses of the enemy" of nearly equal honor to leading a successful war party or scalping an enemy. The Omaha, in 1819, considered horse capture an honor of the fourth rank, preceded by the capture of a prisoner, striking a live enemy, and striking a dead or disabled opponent (James, 1823, vol. 1, p. 295). Maximilian (1906, vol. 22, p. 310) claimed the Teton Dakota regarded the theft of an enemy horse "as an exploit, and as much, nay more honored than the killing of an enemy." Tixier (1940, p. 138) observed that the Osage (1840) limited the wearing of eagle feathers "to those who have stolen at least a horse from the enemy."

PICTOGRAPHIC REPRESENTATION OF WAR HONORS

Successful warriors were privileged to picture their war honors on their buffalo robes, lodge linings, or lodge covers. A warrior might call upon another man more skilled in painting than himself to execute the pictures. On the whole the Blackfoot were much less interested in the aesthetic than in the symbolic qualities of their recordings. As Wissler has noted, the taking of a picketed horse was sometimes illustrated merely by a representation of a picket pin, while horses taken in an open fight were portrayed by geometric symbols of horse hoofs (Wissler, 1911, p. 41, figs. 4, 5). When horses were portrayed in the old days they were crude, stiff figures, which Lazy Boy aptly likened to the forms of the bent willow horses made as children's toys (pl. 12). They were always painted in profile, and generally in solid colors without outlines. The color was that of the captured horse depicted. Red paint signified a bay or sorrel, yellow a buckskin, blue a blue horse, black a black, etc. Pintos were first painted black, then white spots were added. The figures were executed in earth paints. Willow sticks about 4 inches long, "pointed at one end like a pencil" served for brushes. Informants believed the more detailed horse figures painted on skins in the 1880's and later years at the request of white men were the work of Indian artists whose styles had been influenced by the art of white men.[58]

THE BLACKFOOT WARRIOR IDEAL

Individual participation in either horse or scalp raids was always voluntary. Yet so great was the value placed upon warlike deeds in Blackfoot culture, and so obvious were the rewards of successful theft of enemy horses, that few able-bodied young men refrained from participation.

When a boy was born it was customary for his father to hold him up toward the sun, and pray, "Oh Sun! Make this boy strong and brave. May he die in battle rather than from old age or sickness." As he grew older the boy's father and other male relatives pointed out to him the most distinguished warriors at the Sun Dance encampments and recited their deeds of valor to him as an encouragement to the lad to emulate their worthy actions. Ambition to distinguish themselves served to minimize young men's fears of the hazards of warfare. Certainly the warpath offered the surest road to fame. As one elderly informant said, "A young man's best way to get his name up was through war."

---

[58] Blackfoot paintings of horses never evidenced the lively action and decorative quality of the outlined, polychrome figures rendered by Teton Dakota and Cheyenne artists (Ewers, 1939, pp. 32–35). In recent years Victor Pepion, a Blackfoot artist, painter of the murals in the Museum of the Plains Indian at Browning, has been recognized among the number of capable young Plains Indian painters.

Few young men could resist this strong cultural compulsion toward participation in warfare. Only the physically handicapped, the craven, and some favorite sons of wealthy men whose parents tried to spare them the dangers of the warpath, never took part in raids. But young men of wealth who were ambitious to maintain the family prestige and to follow in the footsteps of courageous forebears, joined the sons of poor and middle-class families in raiding the enemy.

THE HORSE IN TRADE

Let us examine the frequently repeated generality that the horse was the standard of value in the barter of the Plains Indians in historic times, as it applied to the Blackfoot tribes.

INTERTRIBAL TRADE

References to Blackfoot trade in horses with alien tribes are exceedingly rare in the literature. Teit (1930, p. 358) obtained traditions from the Flathead to the effect that "long ago" they traded watertight baskets, shells, pipes, pipestone, flat wallets, and horses, and probably bows and saddles to the Blackfoot. In the fall of 1846, Father De Smet made a peace between the Flathead and Piegan. During the brief period this peace was in effect there apparently was considerable trade between the two tribes. Father Nicholas Point, who remained with the Blackfoot for several months after conclusion of the peace, made a drawing of Blackfoot-Flathead trading operations, the original of which is in the collections of the Jesuit Provincial House, St. Louis, Mo. In October 1858, the River Crow, temporarily at peace with the Piegan, visited the Piegan camp to trade (Hamilton, 1900, pp. 63–64). Doubtless horses were exchanged at that time.

However, it is certain that the Blackfoot engaged in no extensive, annual intertribal horse-trading activities such as were typical of the Crow and village tribes on the Upper Missouri in the early years of the 19th century. (See pp. 7–8.) Blackfoot hostility to nearly all neighboring tribes made regular, large-scale trading operations impossible.

Nevertheless, fractions of the Piegan appear to have traded fairly regularly with the Flathead from at least as early as the 1840's, when the visits of "Blackfeet" Indians to the Flathead were noted by Catholic missionaries at St. Mary's, on the Bitterroot. These Piegan were primarily members of the Small Robes band, a group traditionally friendly to the Flathead, despite the hostility of other Piegan bands toward that tribe (Ewers, 1946, pp. 398–401). Individuals from other Piegan bands, some of whom had intermarried with Flathead, joined them on their journeys over the mountains. The friendly Piegan, informants said, had scouts out ahead to inform the Flathead of the approach of friendly Indians. Sometimes the Flathead repaid the friendly visits of the Small Robes at their village, generally located south of the other Piegan bands, near the Musselshell River. Jim Bridger noted that there were several Flathead Indians living with the Small Robes when he visited them near the Judith Mountains in July 1860 (Raynolds, 1868, pp. 163–164).

Informants claimed these Piegan got Flathead horses in exchange for skin lodges, guns, Hudson's Bay blankets, and quilled or beaded, weaselskin fringed suits. The Piegan gave a 12- or 14-skin lodge for the best Flathead horse. Usually they received by preference unbroken, 1- or 2-year-old horses, which the Piegan trained themselves.

There was also some trade between Piegan and Nez Percé in the last decade of buffalo days, during which those tribes were at peace. The Nez Percé were reluctant to trade their fine Appaloosas, but did part with a few for buffalo products. They were in need of buffalo robes and gave a horse for as few as four robes. They gave 5 or 6 horses for a buffaloskin lodge, and 1 horse for a braided rawhide rope, or for 2 parfleches filled with dried meat plus a buffalo calfskin.

INTRATRIBAL TRADE

Trade with surrounding tribes was limited compared with the lively exchange of horses between individuals of the three Blackfoot tribes.

THE HORSE AS A STANDARD OF VALUE

Actually the horse was a very flexible standard of value. The worth of each animal was determined by its individual qualities and its particular usefulness. A fine racer or buffalo runner was worth several pack animals. Weasel Tail recalled an exchange of seven good horses, one a race horse, for one swift, handsome, long-winded buffalo horse. Weasel Head recalled the trade of a stud horse for another good horse and a pipe.[59]

Horse values also varied over the years because of changes in the relative commonness of horses and of articles offered in exchange for them. In 1809, Alexander Henry (Henry and Thompson, 1897, vol. 2, p. 526) found "a common horse can be got for a carrot of tobacco, which weighs about three pounds, and costs in Canada four shillings." Later, as trade goods became increasingly more common, their value decreased. Still later, after buffalo were gone and the Blackfoot set-

---

[59] Undoubtedly all other horse-using tribes of the Plains and Plateau made similar qualitative distinctions in horse trading. In 1790 Mackenzie (1927, p. 78) reported that an Assiniboin packhorse could be purchased for a gun costing no more than 21 shillings in Great Britain, but a fine buffalo runner could not be obtained for as many as 10 guns. In 1856, Major Owen told of an outstanding race horse purchased by a Pend d'Oreille from the Spokan for 6 horses. This animal was so fast its owner could get no other Indians to race against it (Owen, 1927, vol. 1, pp. 125–126).

tled down to reservation life, horse values decreased markedly in comparison with other items.

A third factor encouraged flexibility in horse values. Rich men, as a rule, were expected to pay more dearly for what they received in trade than were men of average or little wealth. Thus, while the average Blackfoot might give no more than 2 horses for a dress shirt and leggings in the youth of my informants, a rich man would be expected to show his generosity by offering 3 to 9 horses for the same outfit.

JUDGMENT OF HORSES

The Blackfoot were keen and careful horse traders. In many instances they were well aware of the capabilities and past performances of animals offered by their fellow tribesmen. In purchasing an untried colt or an adult animal unknown to them, they examined it closely. Some Indians claimed to be able to select a potential buffalo runner by examination before it was 3 years old. A horse with a long, thin tail bone and fine, small veins was thought to be a fast and valuable one. The horse with a broad-boned tail and large, open veins was considered of little value as a runner. Straight legs and thin hocks were other criteria of value. In watching a horse ridden prospective traders noted its actions. A good, vigorous horse held its head high, threw its legs out as it walked and swung its tail. Some men thought a horse with white spots in the iris of its eyes was a good, tough animal. Most Blackfoot shied away from the horse with light-colored hoofs, believing it to be a tender-hoofed animal. Short Face said that when there was sufficient light for horse raiders to distinguish the colors of horses' hoofs, they tried to take dark-hoofed horses from the enemy.[60]

EXAMPLES OF HORSE VALUES IN INTRATRIBAL TRADE

From aged informants I obtained detailed information regarding the exchange value of horses in the period of their youth, and prior to the depreciation of horse values that took place after the extermination of the buffalo and settlement on reservations. In view of the flexibility of the value of horses themselves, we should consider the following data as examples of transactions known to have taken place during the period, rather than as standards of exchange.

HORSE VALUE IN BUFFALO ROBES

Like the horse, the Indian tanned buffalo robe was extensively employed by the Blackfoot as a medium of exchange in the historic

---

[60] In 1797 David Thompson (1916, p. 214) observed of the northern Plains Indians in general, "As the Horses of this country have no shoes, the colour of the hoof is much regarded; the yellow hoof with white hair is a brittle hoof, and soon wears away; for this reason, as much as possible, the Natives take only black hoofed Horses on their War expeditions."

period. It was the principal unit of value in trade with fur traders in the United States and was employed in intratribal transactions as well. Lazy Boy recalled that his father obtained 2 good horses in exchange for 16 head and tail buffalo robes. Several informants regarded the value of 8 robes for 1 horse as fairly common in the late sixties and seventies. Yet Weasel Head remembered a trade of two large thin, well-tanned robes for a "good horse." [61]

HORSE VALUE IN WEAPONS

Chewing Black Bones claimed a "good horse" was exchanged for a "good bow, 20 or more arrows, and a quiver" in his youth. Yet Maximilian, in 1833, reported the Blackfoot valued a cougarskin quiver at a horse (Maximilian, 1906, vol. 23, p. 119).

I have mentioned the equation of the horse and flintlock gun in the early historic intertribal trade of the Plains Indians. (See pp. 13–14.) Among the Blackfoot, in my informants' youth, some even exchanges of Northwest Guns for horses were made. However, informants said a good horse was worth more than a flintlock. An exchange of "a colt that seemed to have the makings of a buffalo runner" for "a muzzle-loading gun, a filled powder horn, and a shot bag" was mentioned. Another trade involved the exchange of a "muzzle loader, powder horn, and breechclout" for "a good, well-formed, lively horse." [62]   A heavy rawhide shield could be obtained by ceremonial transfer for as little as a single horse or as much as several horses, depending upon the reputed power of the shield and the interests of the negotiators.

HORSE VALUES IN ARTICLES OF MEN'S CLOTHING

In my informants' youth the Piegan gave a horse for a horned bonnet obtained in ceremonial transfer, while three sets of eagle tail

---

[61] The great Padouca chief told Bourgmont, in 1724, his people received a horse for 3 buffalo robes in their trade with the Spaniards (Margry, 1886, vol. 6, p. 440). In 1786 Governor Anza of New Mexico set the value of a "horse of ordinary quality" at 13 buffalo robes in the trade with the Comanche and Ute at Pecos (Thomas, 1932, p. 306). In the Cree and Assiniboin trade of the mid-19th century a horse was valued at 10 robes (Hayden, 1862, p. 247 ; Denig, 1930, pp. 421, 589).

[62] A Kiowa informant told me that in his youth a muzzle-loading gun was valued at a horse among his people. Among tribes poorly supplied with horses guns had relatively less value. In 1719 Du Tisne gave three guns, powder, axes, and several knives to the Osage for 2 horses and a mule marked with a Spanish brand (Margry, 1886, vol. 6, p. 314). In 1805 Lewis and Clark gave a pistol, 100 balls, some powder, and a knife for one Shoshoni horse, and exchanged a musket for another, at a time when the Shoshoni were suffering a temporary scarcity of horses due to recent thefts by the enemy (Coues, 1893, vol. 2, p. 574). Alexander Henry, at the Hidatsa villages in 1806, found it "impossible to purchase a common packhorse for less than a new gun, a fathom of H. B. red strouds, and 200 balls and powder" (Henry and Thompson, 1897, vol. 1, p. 353). A horse was valued at two Northwest Guns among the horse-poor Cree in 1854 (Hayden, 1862, p. 247).

feathers, enough to make a feather bonnet, were worth "the best buffalo horse," or several common horses.[63]

A man's dress shirt and leggings of skin, decorated with hair fringes or weaselskin strips was worth two or more horses to the Piegan in the period 1865–80.[64] The Piegan then valued a striped, blanket-cloth breechclout obtained in trade from the Nez Percé at one horse. A very good horse was paid for a well-tanned, painted buffalo robe.

HORSE VALUES IN ARTICLES OF WOMEN'S CLOTHING

Grinnell stated that the Blackfoot valued a woman's dress profusely decorated with elk teeth at two good horses (Grinnell, 1892, p. 197). This value was expressed by my informants as "the best buffalo horse" or "the best horse you have." The elk teeth alone were very highly valued.[65]

Lazy Boy said that a beaded woman's dress of buckskin or elkskin was considerably less valuable. Some Piegan paid as much as a horse for this type of dress, others as little as five robes. He said a woman might be given two robes to bead a plain woman's dress.

HORSE–PIPE RELATIVE VALUES

Weasel Head and others claimed the Piegan sometimes exchanged a horse for a handsomely carved, evenly blackened pipe bowl and ash stem. However, pipes frequently were obtained at lower prices.[66]

HORSE PAYMENTS IN TRANSFER OF CEREMONIAL PARAPHERNALIA

Undoubtedly considerable misunderstanding has arisen regarding the value of Blackfoot medicine bundles in terms of horses because of

---

[63] Tabeau (1939, p. 90) reported that the Mandan gave a horse for the plumage of an eagle in 1804. Three decades later Maximilian (1906, vol. 23, p. 289) found the Mandan frequently gave "one or two horses for a feather cap." In midcentury Hayden (1862, p. 430) quoted the value of two eagle tails at one horse among the Mandan. In the 1870's the Hidatsa valued a single set of eagle tail feathers at "a buffalo horse" in their trade with neighboring tribes (Mathews, 1877, p. 27). However, Denig (1930, p. 589), writing of the Upper Missouri tribes in general in 1854, stated "Usually the value of the tail feathers of this bird among any of the tribes of whom we write is $2 each in merchandise of this country, or 15 feathers for a horse." But when made into a bonnet "two tails of 12 feathers each would be worth two horses." Kurz (1937, p. 269) reckoned a Crow head-dress of 36 eagle feathers at three packhorses in 1851.

[64] Denig (1930, p. 589) said that 10 weaselskins alone would "bring a horse" among the Crow ca. 1854. He reported a skin shirt and leggings garnished with human hair and porcupine quills was then worth one horse, while a suit trimmed with weaselskins was worth two horses (ibid., p. 589).

[65] In 1805 Laroque (1910, p. 71) observed that the Flathead exchanged a horse for 70 or 80 elk teeth. In 1833 Maximilian (1906, vol. 23, pp. 289, 262) reported Mandan trade of a horse for 100 to 150 elk teeth. Kurz (1937, p. 80) found the Crow valued 100 elk teeth at the price of a packhorse. Denig gave the same Crow evaluation and listed a Crow woman's dress of "fine bighorn skin cotillion adorned with 300 elk teeth" at 25 robes, or a little less than three horses in value (Denig, 1930, pp. 587, 589).

[66] Kurtz claimed the Crow exchanged a packhorse for a catlinite pipe bowl in 1851 (Kurtz, 1937, p. 275).

the very inflated prices paid for these bundles in the early Reservation Period when horses were much more plentiful and much less valuable than in buffalo days. Prolonged discussion of these purchases with informants revealed that the fabulously high prices paid for these bundles were almost without exception confined to the Reservation Period. Even the wealthiest purchasers did not pay such prices in buffalo days. In recent years medicine bundles have been kept in the families of their owners or have been transferred at more modest prices.

The three most highly valued Blackfoot medicine bundles were and still are the medicine pipe, the natoas (or Sun Dance) bundle, and the beaver bundle. Bradley (in the 1870's) stated that medicine pipes were valued at "about nine horses" (Bradley, 1923, p. 265). This figure is in line with payments for medicine pipes in the youth of my informants. They recalled medicine pipe transfers involving payments of as little as 1 horse and a number of buffalo robes and as much as 10 horses. Green Grass Bull claimed the owner of one medicine pipe had been told in a dream to ask no more than 7 horses for it. However, at the turn of the century it was not uncommon for a Piegan to give 30 or more horses to gain possession of a medicine pipe bundle. Informants' testimony corroborated Wissler's statement of three decades earlier, "whereas . . . medicine pipes formerly required but two or three horses, they now often go for thirty head" (Wissler, 1912 a, p. 277). Thirty-nine horses was remembered as the top price paid for a medicine pipe bundle by a Piegan. However, Goldfrank (1945, pp. 29, 45) was told that the Long Time Pipe of the Blood sold several times for 100 horses during the period 1894–1910, although it was transferred for 20 horses and other goods in 1939.

Lazy Boy claimed there were but two beaver bundles owned by Piegan Indians in his youth. These bundles had nearly the same value as medicine pipes at that time. In the Reservation Period the Piegan have purchased beaver bundles from the Canadian Blackfoot. Shorty White Grass was said to have paid 20 horses for one of them.

The natoas bundle was valued at 4 or 5 horses in buffalo days. After the Blackfoot tribes settled down it rose in value to over 30 horses. Goldfrank (1945, p. 45) reported a payment of 10 horses, 1 heifer, a set of harness and a saddle for the Blood natoas bundle in 1929.

BLACKFOOT USES OF HORSE MATERIALS

The horse, unlike the buffalo, was of much greater value to Indians alive than dead. The Blackfoot rarely killed horses for food and virtually never killed them to obtain materials for the manufacture of utilitarian or ceremonial objects. Dead horses furnished some materials utilized by the Blackfoot. The list is meager compared with the list of buffalo uses given on pages 150–151.

THE HORSE AS FOOD

Most aged informants at first denied the Blackfoot ate horse meat, although they were not averse to attributing that practice to the neighboring Gros Ventres and Cree. They claimed their people loved horses too much to kill them for food. Further investigation revealed limited eating of horse meat under conditions of food scarcity. Weasel Tail recalled that Blood raiding parties returning from successful horse raids west of the Rockies sometimes strangled a captured colt and ate it rather than risk being overtaken by the enemy while hunting game or giving away their location by the noise of gunfire in shooting it. Short Face also recalled instances of hungry Piegan raiders killing and eating colts under similar circumstances. During the starvation winter of 1879, the Canadian Blackfoot are said to have eaten horses (Hughes, 1911, p. 246). Some Piegan informants mentioned the eating of dogs in their camps during rare periods of extreme food scarcity in buffalo days, but they denied that horses were killed for food at such times.[67]

USE OF HORSEHIDE

Deerhides and horsehides were favored by the Blackfoot for making drumheads. Both materials were tough and would not soften through use or stretch out of shape to the same extent as the

---

[67] Other Upper Missouri tribes resorted to horse meat more or less reluctantly in emergencies conditioned by scarcity of their usual animal foods. The Cree ate horse meat "although horses were never purposely killed for food" (Mandelbaum, 1940, p. 196). The Assiniboin, also poor in horses, ate both horses and dogs in times of food scarcity, and as a last resort turned to cannibalism to avert starvation. Denig (1930, p. 583) reported cannibalism in but one season during the 21 years of his knowledge of that tribe. Two contemporary accounts tell of Teton Dakota eating of horses in the mid-19th century to prevent starvation (Kurz, 1937, p. 332; Boller, 1868, p. 209). The Cheyenne preferred other meat to horseflesh (Grinnell, 1923, vol. 1, p. 256). Maximilian (1906, vol. 23, p. 277) claimed the Mandan ate "all kinds of animals . . . except the horse."
The relatively wealthy southern Plains tribes, who could better afford to kill horses for food, were less averse to eating horse meat. Pfefferkorn (1949, pp. 144–145) claimed the Lipan Apache, in the mid-18th century, liked nothing better to eat than the fleshy upper neck of a horse, mule, or burro. A century later Bartlett (1854, vol. 1, p. 327) mentioned Apache fondness for mule meat. Tixier (1940, p. 266) reported that the Comanche ate some of their horses when buffalo were scarce or war prevented their hunting. Marcy (1937, p. 174) said the Comanche "often make use of (horses and mules) for food when game is scarce." Mooney reported that the Kiowa had "to eat their ponies to keep themselves from starving, for lack of buffalo" in the summer of 1879 (Mooney, 1898, p. 344). Grinnell (1923, vol. 1, pp. 256–257) claimed the Kiowa preferred fat colt to fat cow. A Kiowa informant told me his people sometimes killed and barbecued an 8- or 10-month-old colt. They regarded its meat as a light, easily digested food.
Attitudes of the horse-using tribes toward eating horse meat varied greatly. The Ute, who had "quite a number of good horses and mules" in 1854, "frequently, when hard pressed, kill(ed) them for food." Okinagon claimed their ancestors made considerable use of horse flesh for food (Teit, 1930, pp. 237, 249). However, Lowie (1924 b, p. 216) reported that Wind River Shoshoni ate horses only to avert starvation. Haines (1939, p. 38) marveled that the Nez Percé, who excelled as horse breeders, failed to use their poorer animals for food, even in time of famine.

hide of the buffalo calf. The belly of the horse furnished the preferred drumhead substance.[68] In my informants' youth older people skinned and tanned the hide of a year old colt that had died for use as a medicine bundle wrapping. They believed this wrapping would bring them luck in acquiring horses.

USE OF HORSEHAIR

Maxmilian (1833) observed Blackfoot use of horsehair "dyed of various colors," as well as human hair, for decorative fringes of men's dress suits (Maximilian, 1906, vol. 23, p. 101). Short Face said the hair of the mane was preferred for these trimmings. The asperger used for shaking water on hot rocks to produce steam in the Blackfoot sweat lodge was made of a horse's tail bound to a wooden handle (fig. 30, *a*). Horse tails served as tipi decorations only if the owner "dreamed" of them as part of the ornament of his lodge. Informants claimed that horsehair ropes were late introductions among the Blackfoot, although they were common among the Plateau tribes in earlier times (p. 75).

HORSE-CHESTNUT PERFUME

The callosity from the inside of the horse's leg, known as the chestnut, was cut away, powdered, and mixed with powdered plant materials to make a perfume which was rubbed on clothing to give it a pleasant odor.[69]

HORSE-TOOTH NECKLACES

Maximilian (1906, vol. 23, p. 100) observed Blackfoot use of horse teeth as necklaces. Short Face said some men believed it would bring them luck and good health to wear a necklace of horse or elk teeth.

USE OF HORSE HOOFS

The Blackfoot did not make glue from horses' hoofs. Their favorite glue, much used in making bows and arrows, came from the boiled phallus of a buffalo bull. In the collections of the Museum of the Plains Indian is a horse hoof, painted, and strung as a neck pendant worn by a weather dancer in the Piegan medicine lodge (fig. 30, *b*). This, however, was an uncommon Blackfoot usage.

---

[68] Use of horsehide for drumheads has been reported for the Plains Cree (Mandelbaum, 1940, p. 216) and Cheyenne (Grinnell, 1923, vol. 1, p. 203). The latter preferred horsehide to other materials for drumheads.

[69] Kroeber (1907, p. 227) mentioned the use of this perfume by the neighboring Gros Ventres.

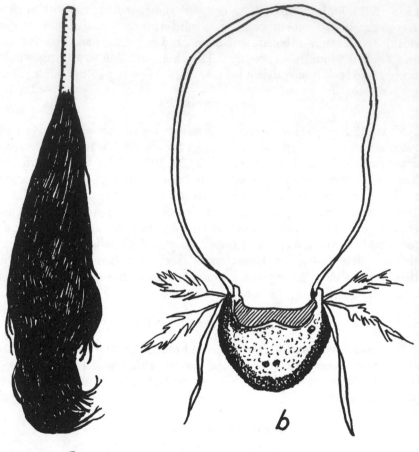

FIGURE 30.—Objects made of horse materials, Blackfoot. *a*, Horsetail asperger
used in sweat-lodge ceremonies; *b*, horsehoof necklace worn by a weather
dancer in the Piegan Sun Dance.

USE OF HORSE MANURE

The manure of a newborn colt was used as a yellow paint rubbed
over the sinew back of a bow or on arrow shafts. It dried hard and
shiny, like glue, and would take a high polish.[70]

---

[70] Wilson (1924, p. 146). reported the use of this substance as an arrow paint by
Hidatsa boys.

THE HORSE IN RECREATION

The horse played a prominent role in the leisure time activities of Blackfoot children and adults in 19th century buffalo days.

THE HORSE IN CHILDREN'S PLAY

Some of the toys of Blackfoot children were designed to help them imitate the daily activities of their elders in their play. Bradley (1923, p. 275) reported that girls "built miniature lodges, collected bundles of wood and made travails." The little lodges, travois and other small-scale reproductions of camp equipment were packed on toy horses in playing "moving camp." The conventionalized horse was a forked stick, the basal end of which was pushed into the ground to support the travois and equipment when not being moved (fig. 31). Girls aged about 6 to 9 years engaged in this play, as recently as ca. 1910.

Figure 31.—Blackfoot girl playing "moving camp," with a conventionalized stick horse, doll, and miniature lodge and household equipment.

Lazy Boy recalled that when he was a small boy he and his sister played with little willow horses. Each was simply but cleverly fashioned by splitting one end of a willow branch and bending the split portion to make the head and forelegs, and splitting the other end of the same piece and bending them to form the tail and hind legs of the horse. Boys about 8 to 12 years of age made and played with these crude horse toys. Indians born since buffalo days were familiar with the pattern. They had played with these toys themselves. In 1942, a middle-aged Piegan woman made two of these willow horses for my small daughter. One of them is shown on plate 12. It measures 14¼ inches long by 10¼ inches high. The saddle is not typical of the woman's saddle of buffalo days.

Wissler (1911, p. 54) was informed that "small boys often played at owning, stealing and tending horses, using rude images of mud or selected stones of appropriate form." Informants recalled that boys 8 to 12 years of age, made miniature horses of clay from a river bank in summer. They would place sticks in the end of each leg while the clay was soft. When the clay dried they could stand the horses in the earth by means of these sticks. Some of the clay horses were as much as a foot long. Boys who had been in swimming in summer sometimes collected flat stones and set them up in the sand beside the river, pretending the stones were horses. They would move them about, make little corrals of sticks for these horses, etc.

An ingenious hobbyhorse, known as "crooked buttocks shape," was made from a fairly heavy tree having a double bend in it. Adults procured these pieces, peeled off the bark, and placed the heavy end in a hole in the ground. The small boy or girl would mount astride it and pretend to ride it. Sometimes a carved wooden horse head was attached to the front of it and a stick or bundle of horsehair tied to the rear to make it look more like a horse. The child might throw a piece of buffalo hide or an old saddle on it and tie reins of rawhide to the upward projection. Sometimes an adult presented one of these hobbyhorses to a favored child of a prominent man and received property in return (fig. 32). Wissler (1911, p. 53) apparently referred to this type of hobbyhorse, although his description is lacking in detail.[71]

---

[71] Similar types of children's play were common among other Plains Indian tribes. Cheyenne and Arapaho girls played moving camp with miniature horses made of forked sticks (Michelson, 1932, p. 3; 1933, p. 598). In 1840, Tixier (1940, p. 235) was amused by the play of little Osage girls. "One walked on all fours like a horse loaded with luggage; after unloading her, her friends helped her to build a small lodge with stakes and a blanket; then all together, horses and horsewomen, going in laughing. On other occasions they drove some pegs in the ground, making a sort of horse with it, and practiced climbing on its back." Teton Dakota boys rode wooden hobbyhorses. Sometimes they placed a saddle on a fallen tree and pretended to ride it. Teton boys and girls pretended to be horses and carried packs, while boys of those tribes carried one another on all fours (i. e., "horse-back"). (Dorsey, 1891, pp. 329, 343). Both Teton and Cheyenne boys played with mud images of horses (Dorsey, 1891, p. 335; Grinnell, 1923, vol. 1, p. 65).

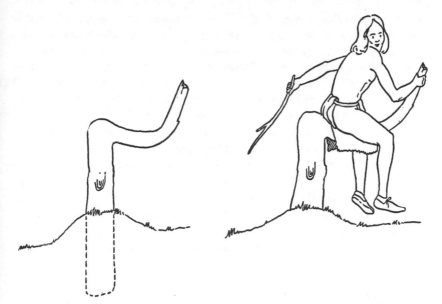

FIGURE 32.—Construction and use of a child's hobbyhorse, Blackfoot.

Lazy Boy said that by the time Blackfoot boys were 10 or more years of age they abandoned play with toy horses for the more serious and responsible activity of tending their families' horse herds.   Girls also had little time for such play after they were called upon to help their mothers with household chores.

At the Heart Butte Sun Dance encampment on the Blackfeet Reservation, Mont., in the summer of 1944, I watched three small boys, aged about 10 years, playing at bull dozing and calf roping in imitation of these modern rodeo events.   In the game of calf roping one boy played the part of the calf, another the horse, and the third the rider. The horse carried the rider after the "calf."   When the rider roped the "calf" he jumped off and bound the "calf's" hands and feet together with a small rope (pl. 12, b).   In the game of bull dozing the rider attempted to grab the "steer" around the neck and shoulders and wrestle him to the ground.   Such play is of recent origin, of course. However, in spirit it is akin to the "horse play" of Blackfoot children in buffalo days.

HORSE RACING

David Thompson wrote of the Piegan ca. 1800, "They have also sometimes horse racing, but not in the regular manner; but bets between individuals in running down animals, as the Red and Jumping Deer, or the killing of so many Cow Bisons at a single race" (Thompson, 1916, p. 359).   It is possible Thompson had not been in Blackfoot encampments in late summer, the traditional horse racing season. Lazy Boy claimed the Piegan began racing horses in his great-grandfather's time, soon after they acquired their first horses. The earliest description of a Blackfoot horse race refers to one held in the combined Blackfoot, Blood, Piegan, Sarsi, and Gros Ventres camp, seen by Paul Kane on June 1, 1848 (Kane, 1925, pp. 295–296). Kane's painting of that race, now in the Royal Ontario Museum of Archeology, is reproduced as plate 13, *b*. The trader William T. Hamilton briefly described a match race between horses of the Crow and Piegan witnessed by him in 1858 (Hamilton, 1900, pp. 66–68). J. Willard Schultz described a match race between horses owned by Piegan and Kutenai ca. 1878 (Schultz, 1907, pp. 134–136). These descriptions are exceedingly fragmentary compared with the wealth of detailed information on old-time Blackfoot horse racing supplied by my informants.

RACE HORSES

A winning race horse was the most valuable horse a Blackfoot Indian could own. In trade a fast race horse would bring several other good horses. Nearly all racers were males, either stallions or geldings. Because courses were generally long, horses were not raced until their third or fourth year. Racers were considered in their prime from their fourth to ninth year. After that they would serve as buffalo runners for a number of years. The ideal race horse was an animal of small size and unprepossessing appearance, whose speed and endurance belied its looks. Indians liked to match a horse of this description, whose ability was not generally known, against a large, finer appearing animal, in the hope of encouraging their rivals to bet heavily and to win large stakes for themselves.

Men carefully watched boys riding year-old colts chasing buffalo calves. If they saw a colt that seemed to outdistance the others they examined it carefully. If they thought it had possibilities of becoming a good racer they trained it until it was ready to race at 3 or 4 years. The potential racer was allowed to run with the range herd much of the time. It was not used for general riding or packing. There was a decided taboo against packing meat or getting blood on a race horse.

INTRATRIBAL AND INTERTRIBAL HORSE RACES

Although the Blackfoot participated in both intratribal and intertribal horse races in buffalo days those races best remembered, and probably most common, were the ones between two societies of the same tribe. Generally men of the same society did not race against each other, even though several men of a society might own fast horses. Intertribal races were held between the Blackfoot tribes (such as Piegan contra Blood), or between the fastest Blackfoot-owned racer and the swiftest horse owned by a neighboring non-Blackfoot tribe.

INTERSOCIETY RACES

At the Sun Dance encampment in late summer there was keen competition between the various Blackfoot men's societies in games and sports. These included the hoop and pole game, the hand or stick game, foot racing, and horse racing. Although there was no established order for these competitions the horse race generally came late in the series. If, for example, members of one society lost to another in a hand game one evening, they might challenge the winning society to a horse race the following day. Detailed descriptions by five informants (both Piegan and Blood) revealed that the challenge was issued according to a set procedure. The society wishing to make the challenge selected one of its members who had been successful in war. He dressed just as he had dressed when he counted coup on an enemy and decorated his horse as it had appeared at that time. He made a round of the camp on horseback, rode up to the lodge of the leader of the rival society, sang his personal war song, lifted his gun and fired at the lodgepoles just above their crossing. Then he shouted his society's challenge to a horse race. The rival society's leader, upon hearing the challenge, rushed out of his lodge, gun in hand, and fired his weapon in the air, shouting his acceptance of the challenge with some such boast as, "I killed an enemy, knocked him down and scalped him. You are not going to scalp me." The challenger then circled the camp again, stopping at the lodge of the leader of his society to formally report the acceptance of his challenge.

The challenge generally was issued early in the morning. Later that day the leader of the challenged society called a meeting of its members. They chose a delegation to visit the leader of the challenging society in his lodge. At this meeting between leaders of the two societies there generally was a great deal of joking and bantering back and forth before they settled down to the business of discussing detailed plans for the race. Then they decided upon the location and distance of the course, time of the race, the horses to be run, and the starters and judges.

Intersociety races were almost always match races, one horse entered by each society. Weasel Tail recalled one race in which each society agreed to enter two horses with the understanding that the winning horse would win all the bets. The course usually was a fairly level stretch of plain near the encampment, permitting the running of the race on a straightway. However, occasions were remembered when no straight course was convenient to the camp, in which case the race was run from the starting point around a low distant hill and back to the starting point again. In that case two judges, one man from each competing society, were stationed on top of the hill to see that neither jockey took an unfair advantage of the other while rounding the hill out of sight of the crowd at the start and finish mark. The distance to be run always was measured by eye. The most frequently mentioned straightway distance was "about as far as you could barely see a horse on the open plain." Some courses were longer. Races were recalled in which the horses at the starting point could be seen from the finish only through a spy glass. Generally the distance was from 2 to 4 miles, very rarely shorter. Informants' statements thus tallied closely with Bradley's reckoning (in the 1870's) that Blackfoot horse races generally were run over a course of "three or four miles" (Bradley, 1923, p. 276).

There was a strict rule requiring each horse entered by a society to be the property of a member of that society. Usually each society had held trials some time prior to the race in which the fastest horses were run to determine the intersociety race entrant for that year. These trials were held in secret at some distance from the encampment. On the day of the race the two horses entered were watched carefully by members of the respective societies who were warned to keep other people away from the competing horses. The greatest precaution was taken to prevent a horse medicine man from coming near the race horses for fear that he might use his secret power to make one of the horses tire or falter in the stretch. (See p. 272, on the powers of Blackfoot horse medicine men.)

Informants did not agree on the method of selection of the jockeys. Some said a jockey was selected by the owner of the race horse. Others claimed the society as a body chose the jockey. However, it is clear that jockeys usually were relatives of the horse owners. They were light, thin, adolescent boys or young men who knew how to handle horses in races. Jockeys usually wore only breechclouts and tied their hair behind their heads to keep it from blowing in their faces. Generally they rode bareback with only a war bridle (a two-reined rawhide rope looped once about the horse's lower jaw) and a whip to control the horse.

The finish line of the race was sometimes just a furrow scraped in the earth across the course. At other times it was marked by two piles of rocks, each about 3 feet high, erected some 60 feet apart. Each pile was set up by members of one of the competing societies. They were men who had used rock fortifications in the defense against the enemy.

Shortly before the race the two competing horses were brought to the finish line where the crowd gathered to view them and place bets on their favorites. Betting usually was heavy, by nonmembers as well as members of the rival societies. Horses were commonly wagered, the horses bet against each other were tied together and held by some lad. Guns, robes, blankets, and food were common stakes. A man might wager his pad saddle against another's bow, arrows, and

quiver. Even painted lodges, together with all their sacred paraphernalia, were bet on the outcome of races. However, the winner
of a painted lodge was required to submit to the ceremony of transfer
before he could gain possession of that lodge. Even though he won
the lodge, he was expected to give the former owner a horse at the
time of formal transfer. On the other hand, if it was discovered that
the loser of a painted lodge attempted to hold back any sacred article
belonging to that lodge, the winner might rub his face in manure and
the loser would have no cause for anger. Before race time great piles
of articles wagered stood near the finish. A man might risk any or
all of his material possessions. Although Wilson (1887, p. 192)
claimed the Blackfoot wagered their wives on horse races, both
Bradley (1923, p. 276) and my informants denied this was ever done.
My informants claimed a man did not bet any of his wife's personal
property. Women, of course, bet among themselves.

As the jockeys walked their horses toward the starting point (assuming the race was to be run on a straightaway) members of the
competing societies drummed, sang their society songs, and engaged
in good-natured horse play, pretending to reinact their coups against
members of the rival society. A man who had taken a scalp in war
would run up to a member of the rival society, knock him down, and
pretend to scalp him. If a man had stolen a horse of the same color
and appearance as one entered in the race by the rival society he might
cry out, "I stole a horse like that one of yours; I had complete power
over it. This horse of yours will be tamed too."

Two leading men, one selected by each society, served as starters.
As the jockeys neared the starting point on their way down the course,
they walked their horses in a wide circle, side by side, around the
starters. As they came abreast of the latter, facing the finish, the
starters gave the verbal signal "Ok'i" (now), and the jockeys whipped
their horses into a run. Lazy Boy said races sometimes were started
by a shot from a gun instead of a verbal signal. The starter, in that
case, must have been a man who had shot an enemy in warfare. If the
starter lied in his claim to that distinction, it was believed one of the
horses in that race would fall.

In order to let the spectators, gathered around the finish, know how
the race was progressing, two horsemen, one on a dark- and one on a
light-colored horse, each representing one of the competing societies,
were stationed at one side of the course about midway of its length.
As the racers came abreast of them the horseman representing the
society whose horse was in the lead at that point would weave his
horse back and forth.

There were two judges at the finish, one representing each society.
Usually, however, there was nothing to judge, for the winning horse
was a hundred yards or more in the lead. Not infrequently one horse

played out and was unable to finish. Rarely was it a close race all the way. Then it was the judge's duty to determine the winner. They might agree upon a winner, disagree and start an argument, or declare the race a tie. In the last instance, the leaders of the two societies decided whether or not they would re-run the race that day after the horses had rested for a while, or whether the race would be re-run at some later date.

After the race was ended the gleeful winners claimed the articles they won in the betting. If a loser became angry because he thought the race had not been honest, men of the winning society knocked him down and rubbed dirt or manure on him. With the winning horse in the lead, members of the winning society formed a procession back to camp. They proceeded once around the camp circle to the lodge of that society's leader. There the winning horse was entrusted to the care of an old man, who tied it outside the lodge and sang to it. That night members of the winning society sang, danced, and rejoiced until a late hour. When all returned to their lodges after this post-race celebration the performance was over.

The losing society might challenge the winning one to a foot race or other contest. That challenge was less formal than the horse-race challenge. Members of a society who had just lost a horse race considered it a good time to organize a raiding party in quest of a better horse in an enemy camp—one that would enable them to turn the tables on their rivals the next year. Chewing Black Bones told of the persistent attempts of one society to capture a fast race horse. The action occurred in his youth.

A member of a Piegan society that had been beaten in a horse race told his friends, "I am going to get a horse from the enemy that will beat that winner." He took a big, fast bay from the Crow. But it was beaten the next year. Then he went to the Gros Ventres and captured a little gray horse. When the returning party was far enough from the Gros Ventres camp to rest and divide the horses, they raced the horses they had captured. The little gray easily outdistanced all the others. It was small but very fast. Next summer in the secret trials to select that society's race horse, the little gray horse finished far ahead of all his competitors.

At the sun dance encampment this society challenged the one that had beaten them the two preceding years. When members of the rival society saw the little gray they made fun of it. Arrangements for the race were soon made. The society entering the little gray suggested, "Last year you beat us. You set the distance." Their rivals, thinking a long course would tire the little gray horse, proposed a longer distance than was usually run. Most Piegan thought the course was too long for the little gray. Betting was heavy against it. But one old man said, "Don't make fun of that little horse. It is small but it may have great power." The race started. At about the half-way point the jockey on the little gray horse was still holding him back, while his rival on a big bay was whipping his mount hard. Then the rider on the little gray horse gave him the whip. He won by a long distance.

HORSE RACES BETWEEN BLACKFOOT TRIBES

Lazy Boy described a race between horses owned by a Piegan and a Blood Indian which was run in his youth:

A Blood Indian who owned a fast race horse named Almost Baldy wanted to challenge Burnt-a-Tree-Down, a Piegan owner of a fast racer, Little Buckskin. The Blood rode up to Burnt-a-Tree-Down's lodge and fired at the lodgepoles above the crossing. Burnt-a-Tree-Down told Big Snake, the camp announcer, to tell the Blood Indian he would race next day. The following morning Big Snake announced the race to the whole camp, which at that time included both Piegan and visiting Bloods. Two men were assigned to arrange the bets. As they were made, the announcer called them out. All bets were between individuals. Horses, guns, robes, and other articles were wagered. Then the contestants agreed upon the course and distance. They raced beside a big lake. About the center of the length of the course were stationed a Blood and a Piegan horseman on a hill. Each had a gun. As the riders passed them the Blood fired his gun as a signal to the watchers that the Blood horse, Almost Baldy, was in the lead. As soon as the gun was fired the Piegan jockey, who had been holding his horse in check, let Little Buckskin go. There were one Blood and one Piegan judge at the finish. But there was nothing to judge. Little Buckskin was far ahead. We Piegans took everything from the Bloods. We were sure happy after that race.

This description indicates that in the intertribal horse races involving only Blackfoot tribes the procedure was like that of the intersociety races, previously described, and with which members of all Blackfoot tribes were familiar.

OTHER INTERTRIBAL HORSE RACES IN WHICH BLACKFOOT PARTICIPATED

Horse races pitting the best Blackfoot-owned horse against the best racer of a neighboring non-Blackfoot tribe were not common in buffalo days, due primarily to the traditional hostility of the Blackfoot toward their neighbors. No detailed descriptions of these races were obtained from informants. Lazy Boy mentioned a race between a horse owned by visiting Nez Percé and the best Piegan racer in which the latter was beaten handily. He thought the Nez Percé horse was the swiftest one he had ever seen.

The two contemporary descriptions of intertribal races in which the Blackfoot participated are brief. Hamilton (1900, pp. 66–68) witnessed a race between Crow and Piegan in 1858. Betting was heavy in ponies and robes. The course was about a half mile in length. Horses were held at the head by men on the ground until the starting signal was given. Jockeys were boys "stripped naked." Little Dog, the Piegan Chief and a Crow chief were the judges. The Piegan won the race and the Crow "departed soon after the race, sullen and silent. All the young Piegans had a great time dancing and singing that night until a late hour."

Schultz (1907, pp. 134–136) described a match race between a Piegan-owned horse and one belonging to a Kutenai in the summer ca. 1878. The betting was excessive, horses bet against each other being held by some nonbetting boy. The course was a level stretch of about 500 yards. The youthful jockeys, naked except for the breech-clout, raced from a standing start across a finish line marked by a furrow scraped across the dusty course. The horses finished in a dead heat and precipitated a fight, both Piegan and Kutenai claiming they had won.

These two cases suggest that intertribal horse races were not con-ducive to friendly relations between the tribes involved. In most respects the race procedure appears to have been similar to that of the intratribal Blackfoot races. However, the standing start was not typical of the latter races, and the distances run appear to have been shorter than was usual in intratribal races.

LATER HISTORY OF BLACKFOOT HORSE RACING

The popular intersociety horse races ended with the breakdown of the Blackfoot men's societies in the 1870's. Curtis (1911, vol. 6, pp. 20–29) reported that with the exception of the Raven Bearers and the Brave (or Crazy) Dogs all Piegan societies became ceremonially inactive before 1880. In 1894, Captain Cooke, Acting Agent, Black-feet Reservation, Mont., reported that he had prohibited gambling among the Indians in his charge and had discouraged "other pernicious practices, such as horse racing" (U. S. Comm. Ind. Affairs, 1894, p. 159). However, this did not put a stop to Blackfoot horse racing. Informants remembered a number of exciting match races in the early years of this century, and McClintock witnessed horse races in the Sun Dance encampment of the Piegan prior to 1910 (McClintock, 1910, p. 278).

In recent years horse races have appeared on the program of the Blackfeet Rodeo at Browning each July. In the summer of 1941, during my residence at Browning, a new oval track was built at the rodeo grounds immediately west of the Museum property. Horse races were held each day of the rodeo. So popular were these races that in succeeding years race meets were held on the same grounds on Memorial Day and again on Labor Day, as well as during the July rodeo period. The spring and fall races were attended primarily by Indians, who showed marked enthusiasm for them. However, the older men among my informants opined that the horses were not as fast as they used to be in their youth. Frank Red Crow had the same opinion of race horses on the Blood Reserve in recent years. "They are too big. Their legs are too heavy."

HORSE RACING AMONG OTHER PLAINS AND PLATEAU TRIBES

Although horse racing was an exceedingly popular sport among the horse-using tribes of the West, the literature affords very fragmentary information on this topic.

George Catlin witnessed a Mandan horse race in the summer of 1832. He termed horse racing "one of the most exciting amusements, and one of the most extravagent modes of gambling" of that tribe. His description is barren of factual details, closing with the erroneous thought that "a horse race is the same all over the world" (Catlin, 1841, vol. 1, p 143). His painting of the Mandan horse race (U. S. N. M. No. 386416) shows that it was a match race, with two lances set in the ground to mark the finish, beside which stood two judges. Maximilian's treatment of Mandan horse racing was still briefer. He stated simply, they "often practice riding on horseback without a saddle, and very swift horse-racing" (Maximilian, 1906, vol. 23, p. 291). These comments are fairly typical of the slight assistance offered by the literature in attempting a comparative study of Plains Indian horse racing.

There is sufficient data in other sources to suggest that Blackfoot horse races had features in common with those of other tribes. Members of Crow societies vied with each other in horse racing and athletic contests (Marquis, 1928, p. 196). In the Northern Shoshoni race course "riders often return to the starting point after going around a stick marking the half goal" (Lowie, 1908, p. 197). Kiowa informants' brief descriptions of the horse races of that tribe revealed that the course usually was on level ground, well over a mile in length, either in a straightaway or circling two men at the half-way mark and return to the finish. Kiowa horse races were usually match races. One Kiowa was remembered who possessed the power of the horse medicine man to cause one of the horses to fall or falter and thus lose the race. Everywhere heavy betting seemed to have accompanied Indian horse races.

In respect to the distance of the course, Blackfoot horse racing had more in common with early horse racing in Europe and in the American Colonies than with modern horse racing in this country. In 1740 English races were over a distance of 4 miles and the racing of 2-year-olds was unknown. In the American Colonies 4 miles was the approved racing distance (Encyclopaedia Britannica, 1944 ed., vol. 11, pp. 763, 768). It is of interest also that the Tehuelche Indians of Patagonia raced their horses "for long distances, four miles or a league being the average" (Musters, 1871, p. 131). This naturally suggests the possibility of Spanish influence on the distances favored in both Tehuelche and Plains Indian horse races. However, it is not necessary to infer such influence to explain the Indians' preference for long races. Endurance was a quality the Plains Indians required of their war and hunting horses. It should not seem strange that they expected the same attribute of their race horses. Consequently Plains Indian horse races were tests of the competing horses' endurance rather than their sprinting ability. As Ferris noted of Flathead horse races, they "generally terminate[d] in favor of bottom rather than speed" (Ferris, 1940, pp. 95–96).

HORSE SYMBOLISM IN INTERSOCIETY HOOP AND POLE GAMES

The series of competitions between rival Blackfoot men's societies during the Sun Dance encampment included hoop and pole games in which horse symbolism played a prominent role. One society challenged another by sending tobacco to its leader. If the challenged society feared the prowess of the other at this game their leader sent the tobacco back and the challengers presented it as a gift to the sun. If the tobacco was accepted the challenge was also.

The game was played on a level stretch of ground about 30 feet long, across each end of which a log was placed at right angles to the length of the course. Before game time members of one society gathered around the log at one end of the course and sang their ceremonial songs. Men of the other society sang around the other log. Each society selected a member with a brilliant war record who was especially adept at this game to represent it.

The hoop used in intersociety contests was fashioned of the neck cord of a buffalo, burnt and shrunk to make it hard. It was about 3 inches in diameter, with 5 or more spokes and an open center. Each spoke was strung with a different color of large necklace beads. Each color represented a different-colored horse. A red bead symbolized a sorrel, white a white, black a black, copper a bay, yellow a buckskin, etc. The poles were of arrow form with metal heads and feathering, but considerably longer than the war or hunting arrow shot from a bow. On plate 13, *a*, is shown a North Piegan hoop (3.2 inches in diameter) and two poles (34.2 inches long), collected in 1901 (cat. No. 69351, Chicago Mus. Nat. History). My Blood informant, Heavy Head, owned a similar set, made ca. 1907.

The spectators, many of whom had bet on the outcome of the play, lined the sides of the course. They were silent as the two players stepped upon the course. Each competitor (usually one man represented each society, although by mutual agreement each society might enter two men) in turn raised his pole toward the sun and offered a short prayer in such words as, "See me. See this arrow. See how it is painted. That is how my arrow was painted when I killed a Crow. I shall shoot to win because what I say is true." Each contestant then verbally declared his target on the hoop in terms of his own past war deeds. One might call out, "I took a white horse from the Flathead. I shall shoot for the white beads." The other might declare, "I took a sorrel horse from the Crow. I shoot for the red beads." It was thought that if a player lied in declaring his coup he would surely lose.

Generally the players agreed upon which of them was to roll the hoop. Some men preferred to roll it so they would have a better knowledge of its speed and course. Others preferred to let their opponent roll the hoop and concentrated their attention upon throwing the pole with accuracy. If the players couldn't agree upon which was to roll the hoop, the one with the better war record was given his choice. Before rolling, each man spat upon the head of his arrow. Then the roller lifted the hoop to the sun and rolled it toward the log at the far end of the course. Both men ran after it and cast their poles before the hoop struck the log. If the pole of one player pierced the center of the ring he won. If neither pole passed into the hoop center that man won whose pole was in contact with the colored beads of his choice when the hoop stopped after rebounding from the log barrier. The game continued until one man either pierced the center hole with his pole or scored his declared point. Usually it was not necessary to roll the hoop more than twice before the winning point was scored. Each society had a judge stationed at each end of the course, to determine the winner.

Curtis (1928, vol. 18, p. 187) briefly mentioned the horse symbolism of beads in the hoop and pole games played between Blackfoot societies. He also claimed the beads might have represented guns or other objects taken from the enemy. If objects other than horses were symbolized, the several informants (both Piegan and Blood) who described this game to me did not know of that fact. Blackfoot traditions claim that the hoop and pole game was known to these Indians long before the introduction of horses. Elderly informants told the story of the game between Napi, the Blackfoot trickster and creator, and a Kutenai on the Oldman River in the dateless past. They played for control of the buffalo. Napi won, and "that is why there were no buffalo west of the Rockies." Certainly Thompson (1916, p. 359) reported the playing of the hoop and pole game by the Piegan before 1800, although he made no mention of horse symbolism in the hoop or of intersociety competitions. In my informants' youth many young men played hoop and pole simply as a gambling game. Such games were less formal than the intersociety contests. There was no counting of coups prior to play, and the contestants simply denoted their targets by the color names of the beads. It would appear that the introduction of horse symbolism into the intersociety hoop and pole game was a historic modification of a game played by the Blackfoot before the introduction of horses.[72]

SHAM BATTLES

In buffalo days Blackfoot warriors on horseback performed sham battles as entertainment for visiting Indians and important Whites. Sir Cecil Denny described the sham battle that followed the making of the Blackfoot Treaty in Canada in 1877, which was so realistic as to cause considerable trepidation among the white officials present.

The Indians had been in a state of excitement all the morning, and while we were atending to our duties five or six hundred mounted warriors, stripped with the exception of a blanket round the loins and in war paint and feather headdresses, staged a mounted war-dance round our camp. These men armed with loaded Winchesters and on the dead run, circled the tents, their rifles exploding and the bullets whistling over our heads. The blood-curdling whoops accentuated the unpleasantness.

They were only half in fun, and had fear been shown by us it is hard to tell what would have occurred; the sham battle might easily have become one of grim earnestness. [Denny, 1939, p. 117–118.]

Capt. W. P. Clark (1885, p. 68) witnessed a Piegan sham battle in the summer of 1881, which "consisted in circling, charging, shouting, firing of guns etc." Sham battles survived as spectacles in the summer Sun Dance encampments of the Piegan after the end of intertribal warfare. McClintock (1910, pp. 277–278) observed and described this mock warfare in the first decade of the present century.

Undoubtedly these dramatic displays afforded active warriors considerable personal satisfaction in showing off their best horses and their own skill as horsemen as well as their fine costumes and athletic ability. Sham battles were common to many, if not all of the Plains tribes as means of entertaining and impressing visiting Indians and Whites in buffalo days. [73]

---

[72] Culin (1907, pp. 420–527) has indicated the very wide distribution of the hoop and pole game among the North American Indians, another suggestion of its antiquity. He does not mention horse symbolism in this game. Ferris (1940, pp. 94–95) said the Flathead employed a small hoop "two or three inches in diameter, having beads of various colors fastened to the inside" in their hoop and pole game prior to 1835. He did not mention the significance of the colored beads.

[73] The earliest reference I have found to a Plains Indian sham battle appears in Alexander Henry's account of his visit to the Mandan in the summer of 1806. "The Mandans assembled in great numbers on horseback, and rode about three miles below the village, where all mustered. They set out in a body, pell-mell, whipping and kicking their horses, directing their courses along the foot of the hills, and made a long circuit at full speed around the village. . . . On their arrival they performed their warlike maneuvers on horseback, feigning their different attacks upon the enemy, giving their strokes of the battle axe and thrusts of the spear, and defending themselves in turn by parrying blows and covering themselves with their shields" (Henry and Thompson, 1897, vol. 1., pp. 362–363). George Catlin was much impressed by the sham battles he witnessed during his travels among the Plains Indians. He described a sham battle executed by Crow warriors on their visit to the Hidatsa in the summer of 1832, and made a sketch of one of the participants in full dress mounted on a richly decorated horse. Two years later he saw a similar performance in the Comanche village visited by Col. Dodge's dragoons (Catlin 1841, vol. 1, pp. 191–193, pl. 76; vol. 2, pp. 65–66).

HORSES AS STAKES IN GAMBLING

Games and gambling were almost synonymous among the Blackfoot. Participants and/or spectators bet on the outcome of nearly all games of skill or chance. Small boys wagered their arrows and wooden tops in their games. As they grew older and acquired more valuable possessions they bet more heavily. In describing the gambling of Piegan men ca. 1800, David Thompson (1916, p. 361) wrote: "The stakes are Bison Robes, clothing, their tents, horses, and Arms, until they have nothing to cover them but some old robe fit for saddle cloths. They have some things they never gamble, as all that belongs to their wives and children, and in this the tent is frequently included; and always the Kettle, as it cooks the meat of the children, and the Axe as it cuts wood to warm them. The dogs and horses of the women are also exempt."

In my informants' youth horses were common stakes in gambling on horse races, foot races, the hoop and pole game, and the stick or hand game. Some young men were both luckless and inveterate gamblers, who lost all their horses and were forced to return again and again to enemy camps to recoup their losses. Their love of gambling kept them poor and at the same time kept them active as horse raiders.[74]

---

[74] Boller (1868, p. 160) mentioned Hidatsa-Mandan betting of horses on hoop and pole games ca. 1860. He added "I have frequently seen Indians play until they had lost everything." Denig (1930, pp. 567–569) wrote that gambling of horses was common among all the Upper Missouri tribes, saying "There are some who invariably lose and are poor all their lives." Even the Flathead, whose numerous "Christian virtues" were recognized by fur traders, missionaries, and Government officials, loved to gamble and employed horses as common stakes (Ewers, 1948 a, pp. 18–19). Certainly gambling was one of the common media by which horses changed hands among the horse-using tribes of the West.

THE HORSE AS A FACTOR IN SOCIAL RELATIONS

SOCIAL STATUS

A century and a half ago David Thompson (1916, p. 363) observed that the Piegan possessed "an inherent sense of the rights of individuals to their rights of property, whether given them, or acquired by industry, or in hunting. All these belong to the person who is in possession of them; and which gives him the right to defend any attempt to take them from him." Individual ownership of all property other than land was the rule among the three Blackfoot tribes. Even sacred bundles, such as the natoas or Sun Dance bundle, the beaver bundle, and the medicine pipe bundle, which were manipulated for the good of the whole community, were individually owned and were transferred from one individual to another through elaborate ceremonies. Individual ownership of horses followed the Blackfoot pattern of ownership of other property.[75]

Blackfoot social stratification was grounded in respect for the right of the individual to own and to accumulate property. In historic times social stratification followed the economic status of the family head, whose wealth was determined primarily in terms of horse ownership. Three Calf stated that in his youth there were three classes among the Blackfoot: the rich, the poor, and the "in between" (middle class). Other informants frequently mentioned the two extremes without naming the middle class specifically. The classes may be briefly characterized as follows.

THE RICH

A man who owned some 40 or more horses was considered wealthy. This number of animals was more than ample to meet his normal family needs for horses to move his possessions and obtain food through hunting. His horses provided the means of acquiring a plentiful food supply, either through his own efforts or through those of other men to whom he loaned horses for buffalo hunting. Moreover, he obtained sufficient food surplus to enable him to entertain through feasts following a successful hunt and still permit his women folk to prepare extensive supplies of pemmican and dried meat in the fall

---

[75] Goldfrank's (1945, p. 6) informant who spoke of "band horses," either was misinformed or did not mean what he was reported to have said. The concept of community ownership of horses was foreign to Blackfoot economic theory and practice.

for winter subsistence. His many horses were the means of transporting surplus foods, one or more large lodges, and many other bulky possessions. His surplus of robes were exchanged at the trading posts for the most improved weapons, metal tools and household utensils, ornaments and trade cloth. He and members of his family dressed well. They owned several changes of clothing including expensive and elaborately decorated dress outfits. Their saddles and riding gear were well made and showy. He possessed the means to purchase membership in men's societies, to obtain important sacred bundles through ceremonial transfers, and to pay leading medicine men to care for sick members of his family. If his favorite wife had the moral qualifications she could reasonably anticipate an opportunity to play the role of medicine woman in the Sun Dance of the tribe. He and his sons could marry well, could have a large choice of mates and could support several wives. Before he died he could make a verbal will dividing his wealth among his children to provide for their continued enjoyment of his many advantages.

Through careful management of his breeding stock he could increase his horse herds and hence his wealth. Yet he lived in constant fear of losing his horses from an enemy raid. Three Calf told of his father's loss of his entire herd through capture by an enemy raiding party. His father died not long afterward and friends said his death was due to his grief over the loss of his horses. Whether the grief was due primarily to his love for the stolen animals or to his feeling of loss of status and lowered standard of living after the horses were gone, is not clear. Probably both factors were involved.

There is evidence that wiser heads saw the folly of storing up treasure in horses alone. Buffalo Back Fat, head chief of the Blood tribe at the time of George Catlin's visit to Fort Union in 1832, handed down this sage advice to members of his family. It was remembered by Three Calf, a descendant of that chief:

Don't put all your wealth in horses. If all your horses are taken from you one night by the enemy, they won't come back to you. You will be destitute. So be prepared. Build up supplies of fine, clean clothing, good weapons, sacred bundles and other valuable goods. Then, if some enemy takes all your horses, you can use your other possessions to obtain the horses you need.

Call in the son of a man who owns a lot of fine horses. Offer the lad something valuable—a shield, a beautiful suit of clothes or some sacred object. The boy may not want it for himself but he will tell his father. When his father hears of your offer he will bring fine horses to obtain transfer of title to the proffered object. You can continue in this way to rebuild your herd by disposing of other valuable possessions.

Furthermore, you will be sure of acquiring horses of the very best quality with which to start your herd anew. You know that when a man seeks to obtain a bundle or other valuable object every one in camp, his rivals as well as his relatives, knows about it and watches to see what he is offering in exchange.

So he will make a show of liberality by offering the best horses he has. Any other property he may offer along with the horses will be of the best quality—blankets, robes, guns or other articles.

Wissler (1912 a, p. 276) found that the prestige gained from ownership of sacred bundles was never lost. "Even though one may fall a victim to utter poverty, he may still, if the ex-owner of many bundles, be spoken of as wealthy and powerful." The wealthy man who was also kind and generous need never fear reduction to abject poverty through loss of his horses. His many friends and relatives would give him horses to care for the needs of his household.[76] However, the wealthy man who was stingy was genuinely disliked by his fellow men. Generosity was felt to be a responsibility of the wealthy. They were expected to loan horses to the poor for hunting and moving camp, to give food to the poor, and to give away horses occasionally. They were expected to pay more in intratribal barter than were Indians who were not well to do. If the man of wealth had political ambitions it was particularly important that he be lavish with his gifts in order to gain a large number of followers to support his candidacy.

In numbers the wealthy comprised by far the smallest of the three Blackfoot social classes. It is doubtful if they totaled 5 percent of the Blackfoot population in buffalo days.

THE MIDDLE CLASS

The middle-class Blackfoot owned from 5 to less than 40 horses. He was economically independent, possessing enough horses to hunt buffalo and move camp. Generally he could obtain adequate meat for his family, although many middle-class families could prepare and transport little winter reserve. He lived in a smaller lodge and entertained much less frequently or lavishly than the rich man. He had fewer robes to trade and consequently received less of the trader's desirable goods. Yet he tried, to the best of his ability to follow the styles set by people of wealth in clothing, ornaments, weapons, tools, household utensils, riding, and transport gear. But his possessions were fewer and, unless his wife or wives were expert and industrious craftswomen, his possessions usually were less elaborate than those of wealthy men. With the help of relatives he could muster horses and other costly items necessary to purchase a valuable sacred bundle. But, as Wissler (1912 a, p. 277) has stated, it was only the wealthy who could purchase large or important bundles without help.

In numbers the middle class comprised the largest of the three Blackfoot classes, and the majority of the population. This class

---

[76] Denig said of the Crow, "If a man has all his horses stolen or killed, he can generally find friends to give him others, tho the giver expects payment when the receiver shall have retrieved his horses or be able to pay in some way" (Denig, 1953, p. 32).

graded almost imperceptibly into the wealthy class at the top and the poor class at the bottom. Loss of a portion of their herd from an enemy raid could reduce many a middle-class family to poverty.

THE POOR

At the bottom of the economically determined social scale were the poor. They were far more numerous than the wealthy, but less numerous than the middle class. At times they may have numbered 25 percent of the total population. Poor families were dependent upon their relatives or band leaders for even the economic essentials. They borrowed horses to move camp or used dogs for transport animals. They borrowed horses to hunt or received food from the more fortunate. Even their small homes often were the tops of old lodges discarded by wealthy owners, cut down to a size the poor people could transport. The poor family, owning less than 5 horses, had few other possessions. This family was easily recognized by the smallness of its lodge and the shabby appearance of its clothing, transport gear, household utensils, and weapons. Generally the poor owned no fancy dress clothing. Their parfleches were old, worn, and greasy; their rectangular rawhide bags unfringed. The poor man's gun, if he owned one, was generally an old muzzle-loader, broken and tied together with buckskin cord.

Undoubtedly, if the poor man had pride or ambition, he suffered greater mental anguish than physical discomfort. Fellow tribesmen saw to it that he did not starve. Yet he realized that he made a poor appearance among his people and that he owned none of the desirable possessions of members of the upper and middle classes. His self-respect suffered through inability to participate actively in many facets of Blackfoot life. He could not purchase important sacred bundles or membership in a society. His desires and opinions carried no weight in decisions involving band and tribal movements. His marriage prospects were very limited. The aged poor were sometimes left behind when camp was moved owing to lack of adequate transport facilities.

Yet the lot of the poor in horses was no worse among the Blackfoot than among the majority of other nomadic tribes and the horticultural tribes as well.[77]

Ferris (1940, p. 300) writing of the Indians of the northern Rockies prior to 1835, stated:

[77] Dorsey and Murie (1940, p. 115), estimated that the poor among the Skidi Pawnee comprised "less than one-half the members." They were "without influence or power, their lodges were smaller and not so completely furnished, they had few or no ponies, and were often the objects of charity." In 1840, Tixier (1940, p. 135) observed that among the Osage "there are poor people; and those who are poor have no horses, no means of hunting the bison in order to secure meat. They own neither huts nor blankets; they live, so to speak, at the expense of the community."

Some of the poorer classes, who do not possess horses, and are consequently unable to follow the buffalo in the prairies, ascend the mountains where deer, and sheep are numerous, and pass their lives in single families—are never visited by' the horsemen of the plains, but sometimes descend to them, and exchange the skins of those animals for robes, and other articles of use and ornament.

Probably Ferris was referring to horseless Shoshoneans. Nevertheless, Alexander Henry (Henry and Thompson, 1897, vol. 2, p. 723) in describing the Piegan in 1811, observed:

There are 30 or 40 tents who seldom resort to the plains, either in summer or winter, unless scarcity of animals or some other circumstance obliges them to join their countrymen. This small band generally inhabit the thick, woody country along the foot of the mountains, where they kill a few beavers, and being industrious, they are of course better provided for than those Piegans who dwell on the plains.

My informant, Richard Sanderville, believed these were the ancestors of the North Piegan who now reside on a separate reserve west of Macleod, Alberta. The "North Piedgans" were named as a distinct band in 1850 (Culbertson, 1851, p. 144). In late buffalo days they still held their own Sun Dance and were recognized as skilled hunters and trappers of small game. Although by Henry's time these Indians were profiting from the fur trade and no longer appeared poor in comparison with the other Piegan, it is possible that their semiseparation from the main Piegan tribe may have been caused by poverty in horses at an earlier date, which made it difficult for them to live by hunting buffalo on the Plains in competition with other Piegan bands better supplied with horses.

CHANGES IN SOCIAL STATUS

In so far as the individual was concerned the Blackfoot system of social status was not crystallized. It offered no positive security to the wealthy. Overnight, as result of an enemy raid or a severe winter storm the rich man might lose his wealth in horses. There was always opportunity for the poor boy, who was also courageous and ambitious, to better his status. As Wissler (1912, pp. 288–289) observed, "the rich young dandies" did "not always turn out the greatest war chiefs, for it has often happened that poor young men have gone on the warpath, captured horses, bought fine clothes, and medicine bundles and become leaders among their people." Informants said ambitious boys of poor families generally started to war at an early age, were frequent participants in horse raids, and were inclined to take the most desperate chances. A few of these men became wealthy, many became respected members of the middle class, some never were successful in acquiring many horses, and others lost their lives in skirmishes with the enemy. The road from rags to riches via the horse-capture route was a long and perilous one.

Another avenue of advancement for the poor boy was through service to a wealthy man, in caring for his horses, and helping him in hunting in return for his own food and care. Orphans commonly were taken into this service (Grinnell, 1892, p. 219).

Adoption into a family of wealth and distinction offered another means of advancement for the poor boy. Three Calf cited the case of a little boy found by Boy, a chief of the Small Robes band of Piegan, in an abandoned Gros Ventres camp. Although Boy had children of his own, he adopted the homeless waif. When the lad grew older he cared for Boy's horses. Later he helped in hunting and went on horse-raiding parties. He was successful in taking enemy horses and once took a gun from an enemy. He began to raise a herd of his own. He married a girl of good family, set up a medium-sized lodge, and raised fine pinto horses. He began to acquire the best of clothing and horse gear. Finally, after he had acquired 2 wives and some 30 or more horses, he became a subchief of the Small Robes band. As an old man he took the name of his Piegan benefactor, Boy.

The practice of medicine offered a specialized medium of advancement for young women as well as men. A number of highly respected women practitioners were remembered by informants. Through their own visions and/or the teachings of established doctors young people learned the use of various medicinal plants and techniques of their administration. The person who could cure the sick or foresee the future was able to demand payments for his services in horses and other valuables.

Some men and women were able to better their condition through their skill as craftsmen. No individual was remembered who attained wealth solely on the basis of his or her skill in crafts. However, there were men and women of the middle class whose incomes were materially enhanced through their ability to manufacture bows and arrows or pipes of high quality (in the case of men), or lodges, clothing, riding and transport gear (in the case of women). Many fine craftsmen were older men whose age prevented their active participation in hunting or horse raids.

POLITICAL ORGANIZATION

THE BAND

Wissler (1911, p. 22) properly considered the band "the social and political unit" among the Blackfoot. In 1856, Blackfoot Agent Hatch stated, "Each tribe is divided into bands, which are governed or led by either a chief or a band-leader, the former office is hereditary, the latter depends upon the bravery of the individual and his success in war" (U. S. Comm. of Ind. Affairs, 1856, p. 625). Bradley's ex-

planation of the Blackfoot chieftancy in the 1870's, is more exact
and detailed:

The position of a chief was neither hereditary nor elective, but wholly self-
creative. The young man ambitious of this distinction sought to be conspicuous
for energy and daring in war, intelligence in council, and liberality in giving
feasts and providing tobacco for the guests of his lodge. The exhibition of
these qualities in more than ordinary degree would win him the respect and
confidence of one after another of his band, who were ready to follow his guidance
and accept his council. When this point was reached he began to have influence and be regarded as a leader or chief. Practice in obtaining popularity
was usually productive of skill in retaining it, and once a chief the distinction
was pretty certain to attach for life. The greatness or authority of a chief
depended wholly upon his popularity, upon the proportion of the tribe whose
confidence could be won and adhesion secured. The number of chiefs that might
be in a band was dependent simply upon the number who could secure this
following. This system did not necessarily array the members of a band into
opposing factions, for several chiefs might enjoy the equal consideration of
all.

But besides the general respect in which a chief was held he had his purely
personal followers, consisting usually of his relatives and nearer friends. [Brad-
ley, 1923, pp. 280–281.]

Discussions of the band chieftaincy by later investigators among the
Blackfoot, Grinnell (1892, p. 219) and Wissler (1911, pp. 22–23), confirm Bradley's keen analysis, as does the testimony of my informants.
The latter insisted that the major requirements for band leadership
were (1) an outstanding, proved war record and (2) a reputation for
generosity. Some contended that no man was recognized as a band
chief unless he had taken a gun from the enemy in hand-to-hand
combat, the highest war honor. Lazy Boy could recall a single exception to this requirement among the Piegan. Night Shoot was an
experienced horse raider, although his record of coups was not outstanding. He brought home many horses and distributed them liberally among the members of his band. He was very generous and
well liked, and became a band chief by popular demand.

It is certain that the requirement of outstanding war achievement
for band leadership had social value. It insured that men who rose
to power in the band were brave and experienced warriors qualified
to lead in the formulation of plans for the protection of the band and
revenge of enemy action against it. In an atmosphere of almost constant warfare with neighboring tribes it was necessary that political
leaders be warriors of proved mettle.

Informants insisted that the requirement of generosity was by no
means of secondary importance in the selection of a band chief. A
stingy warrior was not recognized in spite of his war record. In
discussing the loaning of horses to the poor, Lazy Boy volunteered,

"That is how you get your leadership. When people want a chief they select a good hearted man." [78]

To dispense patronage the ambitious man required a degree of wealth. Probably this helps to explain why some early writers found that the chieftaincy appeared to run in families. Provided a member of a chief's family had a good war record he possessed a distinct advantage in the reputation of his family for past favors granted to members of his band. Other band members had confidence in his ability to use his inherited wealth to maintain the standard of generosity toward them set by his father or elder brother.

The Blackfoot band, the social and political unit throughout the greater part of the year, was a fluid organization. Both the number of bands and the membership of each was subject to almost continual change. Father Point, who spent the winter of 1846–47 with the Piegan claimed there were only "seven or eight fractions of the Piegan tribe" (De Smet, 1905, vol. 3, p. 952). Yet Wissler (1911, p. 21) listed 23 Piegan bands. While it is possible Point may have missed some Piegan bands in his calculation it is more probable that the bands named by Wissler were not all contemporaneous. Heavy losses attendant upon war casualties and severe epidemics necessitated combinations and regroupings of bands, to provide camps of sufficient strength to withstand and revenge enemy attacks. Population growth tended to encourage division of larger bands into smaller units requiring less buffalo for subsistence. Grinnell believed the existence of bands bearing the same name among two Blackfoot tribes was due to persons leaving one tribe to live with another who chose to preserve the name of their former band rather than unite with an existing band in their new tribe. He also claimed that "within the last forty or fifty years (i. e. since ca. 1840–50) it has become not uncommon for a man and his family, or even two or three families, on account of some quarrel or some personal dislike of the chief of their own gens (band), to leave it and join another band. Thus the gentes (bands) often received outsiders" (Grinnell, 1892, p. 210). Although Blackfoot bands may originally have been composed of groups of blood relatives, it is certain that, by processes such as described above, they became mixed long ago. In my informant's youth band exogamy was preferred but not obligatory. Both parents of some of my older informants were of families of the same band affiliation.

Informants indicated that poor people were the most migratory in their band affiliations. They became camp followers of the leader

---

[78] Opler indicated the situation was similar among the Southern Ute, "A man would be wanted for chief if he gave away horses to all those poor people" (Opler, 1940, p. 165).

who seemed to be most able and willing to supply them with their basic needs, food and/or horses for hunting and moving camp. Sometimes these mendicants became so numerous that their demands were too great a drain upon the resources of the band chief. Should he fail to provide for them he would surely lose some of his followers, who would either champion the candidacy of another leader within the band or find residence in another band led by a man who appeared to be more affluent. Care of the poor was a recognized responsibility of the band chief. Should he fail in this his leadership was seriously threatened.[79]

In the fall of 1855, James Doty (MS., p. 23) met a Blood chief, "The Man who sits by the Eagle's Tail," on Bow River. He was chief of a small band of 18 lodges which was at that time so poor "they had only dogs to move with and could not go so far" as to the Council at the mouth of the Judith, where the 1855 treaty was made. Doty does not mention the cause of this band's poverty. It is noteworthy that the chief commanded relatively few followers.

TRIBAL CHIEFTAINCY

As Wissler (1911, p. 25) stated, each of the three Blackfoot tribes, Piegan, Blood, and North Blackfoot, possessed a head chief. In the 1780's, according to David Thompson (1916, pp. 346–347), the Piegan had a civil chief whose office appeared to Thompson to be "hereditary in his family, as his father had been civil Chief, and his eldest son was to take his place at his death and occasionally acted for him." They also had a war chief who "acquired his present station and influence from his conduct in war." Later the functions of civil and war chiefs tended to be combined in one man. The tendency for the head chieftaincy to be handed down in families seemed to persist among the Piegan in the first half of the 19th century. De Smet, in 1846, found that the aged head chief had resigned his office in favor of his younger brother, Big Lake (De Smet, 1905, vol. 2, p. 595). I find no substantiation for Wissler's claim that "most of" the Piegan head chiefs "have been members of the Fat-roasters" band (Wissler, 1911, p. 25). The Piegan head chieftaincy changed hands many times in the period 1855–1903. The office tended to shift from one band to another. Furthermore there were intervals during this period when the head chieftaincy was in doubt because of competition for this office by rivals, each backed by powerful band factions.

---

[79] Fluidity in band membership was characteristic of horse-using tribes as widely separated as the Plains Cree (Mandelbaum, 1940, p. 221), Assiniboin (Rodnick, 1937, pp. 408, 410), Northern Shoshoni (Steward, 1938, p. 251), and Kiowa (Mishkin, 1940, pp. 26–27). Mishkin attributed frequent changes in composition of Kiowa bands to the introduction of horses.

The tendency for the head chieftaincy to run in families has been more marked among the Blood Indians. Since ante-1869 the tribal head chieftaincy has descended in the family of Seen-from-Afar and Red Crow to the present (1951) chief, Shot-on-Both-Sides. Weasel Tail claimed that Buffalo Back Fat, head chief of the Blood Indians in 1832, fathered another tribal head chief who bore the same name. It is certain that the head chief rose to office through distinction gained as a prominent band chief. The basic requirements of outstanding war record and generosity, therefore, were essential to his advancement.

Blackfoot recognition of social status upon the basis of horse ownership served indirectly to limit the power of both tribal and band chiefs in intertribal relations. Older chiefs, who had amassed considerable wealth, and who no longer went to war themselves, would lose more than they could gain through continued warfare. Often they looked with favor upon peace with some neighboring tribe. But their desires were thwarted by ambitious young men who could not be deterred from horse raids against the neighboring tribes in order to gain status for themselves. Father Point (in 1847) found Piegan young men willing to listen to his exhortations to cease stealing from neighboring tribes only if he "could immediately make 'Great Men' of them" (De Smet, 1905, vol. 3, p. 954).

MARRIAGE

The institution of marriage among the Blackfoot offered men of wealth opportunities for wide selection of women for wives, while the marital opportunities of the poor were restricted. A boy of a poor family, who was not very ambitious, had little chance of marriage except to a girl of his own social class. However, the father of a girl of rather loose morals, "who chased around with one fellow after another," might tell her, "You marry that poor fellow, and settle down." There were also orphan girls in camp, some of whom were flighty in their affections, available to marry poor boys. On the whole marriages tended to be contracted between persons of nearly equal status. A poor young man who had been successful in amassing a herd of 8 or 10 horses might be recognized as a young man with a future and might marry into a family of higher status. On the other hand, a wealthy man was besieged with offers of the daughters of ambitious parents of lower status.

Informants resented any implication of bride purchase in the Blackfoot marriage ceremony, insisting there was an exchange of gifts between the families of the bride and groom. This exchange of gifts has been mentioned in accounts of Blackfoot marriage by Bradley

(1923, pp. 272–273) and Grinnell (1892, pp. 211–216). The initial proposal could be made by parents of either the young man or woman. In either case it was a matter of pride for the family receiving the first gifts to return gifts of greater value than those received. Horses were virtually always among the valuable gifts exchanged. Bradley (1923, p. 272) wrote that "two or three horses or their equivalent in other goods constitute the customary offering in cases of intended marriage." Green Grass Bull recalled one marriage in which the groom's folks received over 40 horses from the bride's relatives. Yet he said that he gave his wife's father only one horse when he married, although later, when he returned from horse raids, he presented horses to her father and her two brothers. Three Calf recalled a rare instance of a father's offer of his daughter to a young man in return for a certain horse that man owned which he coveted.[80]

POLYGAMY

In buffalo days the number of Blackfoot women far exceeded that of men due primarily to heavy male war losses. (See p. 212.) At the same time many hands were needed by successful hunters to prepare their robes and skins for the fur trade and to manage their households on the move and in camp. It was usual for wealthy men to have several wives. Men of the middle class, in many instances, were polygamous. Poor men generally were monogamous. There were notable exceptions to this rule. One Piegan was known to have possessed three wives and but one horse. He and his family had a very difficult time moving their few belongings. On the other hand, the wealthy Stingy had one wife. Many parents offered him their daughters, but he refused, saying that more than one wife meant trouble.

There seems to have been a common belief that the practice of the sororate reduced the possibilities of jealousy and friction in polygamous marriages. Double Victory Calf Robe, an aged Blood woman, told me she was a wife in a polygamous union. Her two older sisters were married to Iron Horn. One day her father told her, "My son-in-law is very good to us. You better marry him and be with your sisters." Her parents outfitted a horse and travois and she rode over to Iron Horn's lodge. He accepted her, and gave horses to her father. The exchange of gifts in this marriage of a third daughter to a son-

---

[80] Early references to the exchange of gifts, primarily of horses, in the marriage ceremonies of other Plains and Plateau tribes appear in the literature. Lewis and Clark noted this procedure among the Lemhi Shoshoni in 1805 (Coues, 1893, vol. 2, p. 557). Say reported gift exchanges in the Kansas marriage ceremony in 1819 (James, 1823, vol. 1, pp. 123–124); and Maximilian found them customary among the Mandan in 1834 (Maximilian, 1906, vol. 23, pp. 279–280).

in-law followed the procedure customary in monogamous or first marriages among the Blackfoot.[81]

THE HORSE IN PUNISHMENT OF CIVIL AND CRIMINAL OFFENSES

Bradley (1870's) reported that with the exception of punishments meted out by the police for disobedience of the restriction against premature hunting of the buffalo by individuals—

all crimes of whatever grade were purely private wrongs for which the Blackfoot code provided no penalty but such as the injured party, himself, or his friends, was able to inflict. And if we accept as crimes only those offenses for which custom had in some degree regulated the penalty, we find ourselves reduced to a list of ridiculously small proportions, comprehending in fact only larceny, adultery, and homicide. There were other wrongs which the individual might sustain as assault and battery, or slander, but the injured party was left to inflict upon the offender such punishment as he chose or was able to inflict." [Bradley, 1923, pp. 286–287.]

Cases of larceny were generally settled by restoring to the owner the stolen goods, whether horses or other possessions (ibid., p. 287). In cases of homicide and adultery, the two major offenses against the individual, exaction of fines in horses was common. The relatives of a murdered man generally felt duty bound to revenge his death by killing the murderer. However, that might in turn lead to an extended blood feud between the families of the two dead men, resulting in a series of deaths on both sides. As an alternative the killer's relatives might be able to satisfy the family of the murdered man through payment of a heavy fine in horses and/or other valuables. Informants stated that this alternative was resorted to most commonly if the murderer was of a higher social status than the murdered man, or if the murderer was a member of a large family whose vengeance would surely fall upon his killers. Maximilian told of the resort to this alternative in a case involving the killing of a nephew of a Piegan chief by a Blood Indian in the summer of 1833. After some shots were exchanged between Piegan and Blood the murder was commuted through presents (Maximilian, 1906, vol. 23, p. 159). In 1838, traders at Fort Benton killed a troublesome Blood Indian who had threatened their lives. The Blood in council agreed that the case could be settled by presents of a horse to each of the dead man's brothers (Bradley, 1900, pp. 227–230).

At the Blackfeet Agency in Montana, Indian Agent John S. Wood, in council with the chiefs of the Blackfoot, Blood, and Piegan, adopted

---

[81] Tixier's comment on the Osage, "Any man may marry as many wives as he can take care of," may be regarded as typical of Plains Indian tribes in general (Tixier, 1940, p. 183). Plural marriages probably were more common among wealthier tribes than in poorer ones. Of the wealthy Crow, prior to 1856, Denig (1953, p. 34) wrote, "About one half the nation have a plurality of wives, the rest one each." My Blackfoot data suggests the proportion of plural marriages was smaller among them.

a written code of laws, April 23, 1875. A copy of this code is in the National Archives. It provides that "If any Indian shall kill another, he shall be arrested and tried, and if found guilty of murder, shall be hanged by the neck until dead." This represented an imposition of the white man's punishment upon the Indians. No provision was made for the alternative of payment of horses and goods to the family of the deceased sometimes exacted by the Blackfoot prior to that date. However, it is noteworthy that the Mounted Police continued to recognize the alternative in their dealings with the Canadian Blackfoot as late as 1881. In that year Denny (1939, p. 155) was sent to settle a dispute resulting from the killing of a Cree by a North Blackfoot. "Following a solemn smoke all round I advised the Blackfeet to settle with the family of the slain Cree by payment of so many horses."

The Blackfoot did not recognize adultery on the part of a husband as a crime. However, the punishment of an adulterous woman was severe. In a fit of rage her husband might kill her, or he might permanently disfigure her by cutting off her nose. Maximilian (1906, vol. 23, p. 136) had observed "a great many women with their noses cut off" in the Blackfoot camps near Fort McKenzie in the summer of 1833. Bradley (1923, p. 271) claimed that women with cut noses were common among the Blackfoot in 1833, but gradually this punishment was discontinued. As late as ca. 1920 there was a Piegan woman living on the Montana Reservation whose face had been disfigured as a punishment for adultery. Informants claimed that if the adultress had children the husband, in pity for them, might prefer cutting off his wife's nose to killing her. The adultress might be turned over to the members of her husband's society for their common sexual gratification also (Maximilian, 1906, vol. 23, p. 100, also mentioned that punishment).

From his adulterous wife's partner the husband generally sought redress by dispossessing him of his horses and other property (Maximilian, ibid., p. 100; Bradley, 1923, pp. 271-272). This punishment was reported among other Plains Indian tribes as early as ca. 1800.[82]

The 1875 code of laws for the Blackfoot (mentioned above) specified no penalty for adultery. The offenses specifically listed along with their punishments reflect strongly the imposition of the white man's moral code upon the Indian in other respects. The practice of polygamy, previously sanctioned by the Blackfoot, was forbidden.

---

[82] Thompson (1916, p. 236) noted of the Hidatsa in 1798, "adultery is punishable with death to both parties; though the woman escapes this penalty more often than the man; who can save his life by absconding which, if the woman does not do, she suffers a severe beating, and becomes the drudge of the family. But those living in the villages I was given to understand have relaxed this law to the man in favor of a present of a Horse, and whatever else can be got from him." Lewis and Clark (Coues, 1893, vol. 1, p. 243) reported Mandan and Hidatsa employment of the less severe punishment of horse payments seven years later.

Rape, selling of a daughter, wife, mother, sister or other woman to another Indian or white man; beating one's wife, assault, threat to kill another Indian; theft or sale of horses stolen from a white man; and the buying, selling, or keeping of intoxicating liquors were listed as offenses punishable by fine or imprisonment in this first written code of laws for the Blackfoot. For some offenses (theft, assault, threat to kill) payment of the fine in "horses, robes and peltries" was specified. These were the Indian possessions that had the greatest monetary value in the white man's culture. Probably that fact, rather than desire to follow Indian tradition in the payment of fines, influenced the Government in spelling out its punishments in that revolutionary legal document.

THE HORSE IN SOCIETY ORGANIZATION AND CEREMONIES

Green Grass Bull cited a Piegan tradition to the effect that the custom of purchasing membership in a society originated shortly after the organization of the first men's society in that tribe, when another group of men sought to obtain this society from its organizers. Of Blackfoot societies Maximilian (1906, vol. 23, p. 117) wrote in 1833, "New members are chosen into all these unions who are obliged to pay entrance; medicine men, and the most distinguished men, have to pay more than other people."

Green Grass Bull gave a generalized description of society purchase, minor details of which differed from society to society.

A group of men all about the same age, decided to join a society. They selected a wealthy young man for a leader. Each man took a pipe filled with tobacco. The leader gave his pipe to the leader of the society into which the group wished to buy. Other young men of the group each offered a pipe to a member of the society. If accepted, each society member also received presents from the petitioner who offered him his pipe. Sometimes these gifts were horses, but they might be something else.

The Blood Indian women's society, Matoki, formerly erected a lodge, open at the top and surrounded by horse travois implanted in the ground with their upper extremities tied to the lodge framework. Scraping White said that he had been told the Matoki used dog travois around their lodge in the same way prior to the acquisition of horses. He was unaware of the symbolism. However, if the Matoki ceremony of driving buffalo into the park (lodge) seen by Maximilian in 1833 (Maximilian, 1906, vol. 23, pp. 112–115) dates back to pre-horse days, the symbolism is clear. It was a ceremonial enactment of the driving of buffalo into a pound surrounded with upended dog travois, reported by Weasel Tail as traditional hunting procedure in pre-horse days. In the course of its history the Matoki Society apparently substituted the more recent horse travois for the older dog travois in the construction of their lodge.

PERSONAL NAMES

McClintock (1910, p. 396) in an extended discussion of Blackfoot personal names, stated, "The use of horses and the capture of horses from other tribes having been a prominent feature of their life, it was but natural that the word horse was used in a great variety of name combinations." Actually a study of two extended lists of names of male signers of important documents reveals a limited use of personal names including the word "horse" or with horse connotations.

The list of Blackfoot Indians of the Montana Reservation (largely Piegan) who signed the Land Agreement of 1895, includes the names of some 80 percent of the adult male population of the Reservation at that time. Of the 305 names listed only 11 appear to have horse associations. They are:

Albert-Buffalo-Horse
Black-Horse-Rider
Bobtail Horse
Fast-Buffalo-Horse
Day Rider
Double Rider

First Rider
Many-White-Horses
Ride-in-the-Middle
Rides-at-the-Door
Rupert Rider

The same list includes 94 names referring to birds and animals other than the horse, including 22 buffalo names and 17 bear names. Bird names alone totaled 33. Eighteen names referred to guns and/or their use (Agreement etc., 1896, pp. 23–27).

Of the 200 male residents of the Blood Reserve who signed the memorial presented to the Canadian Government by R. N. Wilson, May 31, 1920, only 9 bore names with horse associations. They were:

Many-White-Horses
Riding-in-the-Door
Owns-Different-Horses
Charles Goodrider
Many Mules

Bob-Riding-Black-Horses
Day Rider
Black Horses
Mike-Mountain-Horse

Percentagewise the horse names in this list are but little commoner than those of the Piegan list, comprising 4.5 percent of the total compared with 3 percent in the Piegan list. The Blood list includes 70 names referring to birds and animals other than the horse, including 16 buffalo names, 12 wolf, and 11 eagle names (Wilson, 1921, pp. 38–40).

Both of the lists of names mentioned above were recorded after Agency rolls were established and family surnames were fixed in the early Reservation Period. Doubtless in buffalo days, when many men possessed several names in the course of their active lives, the total number of names associated with horses was greater. Nevertheless, the Blackfoot preference for reemployment of names of family members of earlier generations was a check upon the coining of new names and tended to perpetuate the old ones from generation to generation (Wissler, 1911, p. 17). One name, Boy, can be traced back to the 18th century. It was the name of David Thompson's principal informant among the Piegan in 1787, an aged Cree who had lived among the Piegan since his young manhood. The name was borne by one of the Piegan chiefs whom Maximilian (1906, vol. 23, p. 157) met at Fort McKenzie in the summer of 1833. It was the name of a band chief in the mid-19th century, and was assumed by the Gros Ventres boy whom that chief adopted. The latter was the paternal grandfather of the young artist, Calvin Boy, who executed a number of the illustrations in this publication.

There is evidence that some wealthy horse owners received names denoting that fact. Examples were Many Horses and Many White Horses, prominent Piegan. It appears certain, however, that Blackfoot acquisition and use of horses did not strongly influence their pattern of name selection. Names referring to wild animals and birds of the Blackfoot Country have continued to predominate over horse names among the full-blood population to the present day.

HORSES AS GIFTS

Because of its value and usefulness the Blackfoot considered a horse one of the most desirable of gifts, bringing satisfaction to the recipient and honor to the donor for his generosity. One of the surest ways for a man to "get his name up," to rise to a position of leadership in his band, was through frequent and liberal gifts of horses to needy band members. Poor people sometimes took advantage of this custom by offering a wealthy man's child a present of little value or praising the man loudly in public in the hope of obtaining the gift of a horse in return. A poor woman owning nothing but a little pemmican or dried meat might take it to the lodge of a wealthy man and offer it to his child. The man, touched by her apparent generosity, might give her a horse a hundred times more valuable than her gift. [83]

More formal give-aways took place at the annual Sun Dance encampment. Visitors usually were present from friendly tribes (primarily other Blackfoot tribes). They were called upon by name and given gifts of horses, blankets, weapons, parfleches, or articles of clothing by the wealthy men and warriors who danced in the medicine lodge. The give-away has survived among the Indians of the Blackfeet Reservation, Mont. In the period of my residence on that reserva-

---

[83] Tixier (1940, p. 200) observed a similar action among the Osage in 1840. When a visiting Kansa noticed a number of excellent horses in front of an Osage lodge he found out the owner's name then went about the village proclaiming the virtues of that man until he gave him one of his horses.

tion it was customary for the people of one community (Starr School, Old Agency, Browning, etc.) to give a social dance periodically to which those of other communities were invited. Presents were made to visitors. Gifts included small amounts of money as well as useful articles. The reservation social worker was perturbed by the fact that some of the donors were from families on relief. Yet those people had received gifts when visiting other communities and felt duty-bound to make presents in return. [84]

It was customary among the Blackfoot to make gifts at stated occasions. Horses commonly were given at these times by wealthy and many middle-class men. Relatives presented gifts to the first child of a marriage. Presents were given to the man or woman who named the child. Wealthy men gave away horses when their sons killed their first buffalo. The man who first called the rich father's attention to the fact that his son had learned to ride was the recipient of a horse, a robe, or other gifts. It was customary for warriors after returning from successful horse raids to give away some of the animals captured. A warrior whose name was changed following a successful scalp raid commonly gave a horse to the older man who performed the naming ceremony in his honor. A specialized form of give-away by relatives of a deceased man is described on page 288.[85]

Payments to medicine men were made in the form of advance gifts to secure the doctors' services. Grinnell (1892, pp. 283–284) described the Blackfoot procedure in some detail, indicating that in cases of prolonged illness virtually all the family's possessions might pass to the doctor or doctors who attended its sick member. Green Grass Bull recalled that payments of one to three horses for the services of Indian doctors were not uncommon in his youth. A stingy man who had paid for the treatment of a relative might demand his horses back if the patient died.[86]

---

[84] The give-away was a widespread Plains Indian custom. Tixier (1940, p. 203), witnessed one among the Osage in 1840; Kroeber (1902–7, p. 18) remarked that the Arapaho considered it a greater honor to present a horse to a stranger than to another Arapaho.

[85] Grinnell (1923, vol. 1, p. 118) mentioned Cheyenne rich men's gifts of horses to the poor in celebration of their sons' killing of their first buffalo. Kroeber mentioned Arapaho presents of a horse to the man who pierced a child's ears (Kroeber, 1902–7, pp. 18–19).

[86] Le Forge, who lived among the Crow in the 1870's, claimed men of that tribe boasted of liberal payments they had made to Indian doctors. This liberality was encouraged by Crow belief that should a person be niggardly in his payments the patient would linger in ill health or die (Marquis, 1928, p. 187).

THE HORSE IN RELIGION

THE HORSE MEDICINE CULT

Horse medicine (ponokâmita saám) was and still is considered the most secret and one of the most powerful medicines of the Blackfoot. Wissler (1912 a, pp. 107–111) included a brief description of horse medicine and its uses in his study of Blackfoot ceremonial bundles. That description was based upon information obtained from the aged Piegan, Red Plume, by D. C. Duvall, Wissler's mixblood assistant. All my older informants had great respect for the power of horse medicine. Some of them were afraid to discuss it. One man claimed that if he were to talk of horse medicine he would become paralyzed. Another said if he told me what he knew of horse medicine harm surely would come to both of us. Nevertheless eight of my older informants, including both Piegan and Blood Indians, were willing to discuss this subject with me. In addition, Wallace Night Gun, leader of the horse medicine cult on the Blackfeet Reservation, Mont., during the 1940's, proved a willing and exceedingly helpful informant. His portrait appears on plate 15, *A*. Wallace Night Gun died in the fall of 1950, aged ca. 78 years. In December of that year his horse medicine bundle was purchased by the Smithsonian Institution. It is catalog No. 387744 in the United States National Museum collections.

Wissler (1912 a, p. 110) was informed that there were "less than twenty horse medicine men." My informants named 21 Piegan, 8 Blood, and 3 North Blackfoot Indians who possessed objects sacred to the horse medicine cult. All were not horse medicine practitioners. Judging from the frequency of their mention by informants the following seem to have been the most prominent and/or most active horse medicine doctors in buffalo days: the Piegan Indians Wolf Calf, Fish Child, White Antelope, Boy, and Generous Woman; the Blood Indians Water-Old-Man, Owner-of-Sacred-White-Horse, Many-Spotted-Horses, and Ghost Woman; and the North Blackfoot Indian, Yellow Lodge. Ghost Woman was the only female known to have possessed horse medicine powers.

Among the South Piegan, at least, the horse medicine men comprised an organized cult, the members of which attended the cult ceremony, the horse dance, in a body, interchanged secrets of the uses of specific medicines, and throughout much if not all of the cult's known history had a recognized leader. In the middle and late 19th century Wolf Calf was the leader. In recent years, and until his death, Wallace Night Gun held that position.

ORIGIN AND HISTORY OF THE PIEGAN HORSE MEDICINE CULT

Wallace Night Gun and most older informants regarded Wolf Calf, Wallace's maternal grandfather, as the originator of the horse medicine cult among the Piegan. Wolf Calf, also known as Pemmican Maker, died shortly before 1900. He was a friend and informant of George Bird Grinnell, who was inclined to credit Wolf Calf's claim to membership in the Piegan party that met and fought Capt. Meriwether Lewis' small force on or near the present Blackfeet Reservation in 1806. Grinnell reckoned Wolf Calf's age at 102 in 1895 (Wheeler 1904, vol. 2, pp. 311–312; Grinnell's photograph of Wolf Calf, p. 313).

Wallace Night Gun said Wolf Calf was a young man when he began to dream of horse medicine. As Night Gun recalled Wolf Calf's explanation of the origin of horse medicine, it happened in this way:

In Wolf Calf's youth the Piegan owned horses and had lost all fear of these animals. Nevertheless, they had never been able to capture any of the wild horses with long manes and shaggy tails which they saw in their country. Whenever they got close to the wild horses they ran away. One day, while Wolf Calf's band was moving camp, members saw some wild horses in the distance. A party of men (including Wolf Calf) rode after them and chased them for miles. They caught up with one of the wild ones, roped it and threw it. They put a war bridle on it and led it back to camp. When it was tied, all the people gathered around it. The horse was quiet. It stood still and looked around. Members of the group who had captured the animal agreed to give it to Wolf Calf to keep with his herd. Wolf Calf necked the horse with one of his mares. For 3 days the wild horse was well behaved and remained beside the mare. On the fourth day Wolf Calf decided to let it run with his herd. That night the wild horse disappeared and did not come back.

Later Wolf Calf had a troublesome stallion in his herd named Gone-in-Different-Brush. It had a habit of leaving the herd, mixing with the horses of other owners and biting them. One day a man came to Wolf Calf and told him, "Take that stallion, throw him and cut him, so he won't bother our herds." Wolf Calf asked his boy to get the horse. "We shall halter break him, throw him and I'll castrate him." The boy went after the horse but it got away from him and again bothered the other man's herd. Then that man told his boys, "I'll fix him." He roped the stallion, threw him, and tied bones to his forelock and around his neck. After the stallion was untied he ran away bucking and jumping as fast as he could go. "Now," said the man, "he will never come back." But after a while he saw the horse returning. The bones were gone from its forelock and neck. Again and again the man tried to keep the bothersome bones on the stallion, but without success. Finally, in desperation, the man threw the horse down, roached his mane, cut his tail short, and tied rawhide tightly in his short tail. Again he released the stallion, saying, "Now he will never come back." But next morning the man found Wolf Calf's stallion back in his herd. His tail and mane had grown long. On his head was paint—red and white clay. Then the man told his boys, "Let that horse alone. We can do nothing with him."

All this time Wolf Calf didn't know how his stallion had been treated by his neighbor. One night his stallion, Gone-in-Different-Brush, appeared to him in his dream, and said, "Father, tell that man to let me alone. Don't let him abuse me any more. Help me and I shall give you great power that you can use all your life." Wolf Calf then told his neighbor, "Don't harm that horse any more. I'll catch him and break him." Wolf Calf broke the stallion and always was careful to treat him well, petting him and giving him special attention.

About a year later the stallion again appeared to Wolf Calf in a dream. "Father," he said, "I am grateful for your kindness to me. I want to repay you. You will always have a lot of horses. Wherever you are I shall be with you to help you. Now I shall give you the sacred dance of the horses. We dance it. It will be your secret. Let your people keep it from generation to generation."

Each time Wolf Calf caught his stallion after that he saw paint on it. The horse grew old and Wolf Calf continued to dream of it. It became so old grass dropped from its mouth when it fed. Finally it died. Then Wolf Calf cut some of the dead horse's mane and the soft chestnut from one leg and kept them in a bundle in his lodge as a remembrance of his favorite horse.

Wolf Calf felt badly and continued to think of that horse. A few months later he had a dream in which the wild horse he had kept in his herd for 4 days some years before appeared to him. The wild horse said, "I know you miss your favorite horse. I want you to know I appreciate what you did for me too. You didn't kill me, but let me go. Father, I am Sitting-on-a-Hill. I shall give you my power. I'll give you all the roots that grow in the ground that we horses like to eat. They will be your medicine."

Later Wolf Calf, in another dream, saw people dancing the horse dance. They were arguing. One said, "What shall we do?" Another said, "We shall give him secret power to cure the people?" The first one said, "No, we shall give him secret power to cure horses." Finally they agreed, "Let us throw these powers together. Let us give him power to do both."

Then Wolf Calf told his friends of his dreams for the first time. "I have dreamed of this power a long time. Through my horses and these men I was given secret power. I am going to dance the dance just as I saw it. I shall call it the horse dance." The people gathered to watch Wolf Calf dance the horse dance.

Some time later Wolf Calf was watching horses grazing beside a river. As he approached he saw them pawing with their forefeet, digging up roots. He found a root partly unearthed and picked it up. It was about 6 inches long. When he started home with it the horses followed him. That night he was told in another dream, "This root you found will be good for many things. If a horse is sick take some of this root, grind it into a powder and mix it with sage. Then give it to the sick horse. Put it in water, throw the horse down and let him drink it. The horse will be able to eat and you will save it." Then Wolf Calf gave another dance and gathered the people around. He told them of his new power. They agreed, "This is a very powerful dance."

Wolf Calf tried all the medicines he was told of in dreams. Some were for sickness. If a man couldn't eat, a certain root would restore his appetite. If someone felt lazy a little powdered medicine would make him feel energetic again. There was also a medicine to turn a fine day into a raging blizzard or to make rain come on a dry day.

Then Wolf Calf told the people, "If anyone is sick we shall give the secret horse dance. It will pull him through. If a war party is surrounded by the enemy and one of that party vows to give me a feast and invite me to dance, that man will escape unharmed."

Night Gun said Wolf Calf transferred some of his horse medicine power to his son-in-law, Fish Child. Fish Child then began to have dreams of horse medicine. He and Wolf Calf decided to pool their knowledge. Lazy Boy claimed Fish Child's primary contribution was his discovery of a medicine for stimulating an exhausted horse. Lazy Boy credited Wolf Calf with originating the use of horse medicine for influencing the actions of race horses. Fish Child transferred horse medicine to Boy (born ca. 1848), the Gros Ventres brought up by a Piegan chief. Boy dreamed of a whip and a rope. These sacred articles were added to the leader's bundle and have been employed in the horse dance ceremony ever since.

Night Gun mentioned no other Piegan who made any significant contribution to the elaboration of the sacred paraphernalia, ritual, or medicinal practices of Piegan horse medicine men. He was familiar with the history of some of the transfers of this power among the Piegan. Fish Child transferred some of his power to Stingy, the blind man renowned as a breeder of horses, who in turn transferred at least a part of his paraphernalia, "the double whip," to Eagle Child, who died near Starr School in 1941. Fish Child also transferred some of his power to White Grass, a band chief. In his last illness Fish Child gave his power to his son, Black Coyote (born ca. 1831). Weasel Head (who died in 1943) received some horse medicine from Boy.

Tracing the transfers from Wolf Calf since the time of his exchange of medicines with Fish Child, Night Gun told of at least one occasion on which Wolf Calf aided White Quiver, the most successful of all Piegan horse raiders, by giving him one of the plumes from his bundle and explaining how it could be used to bring stormy weather when White Quiver approached an enemy camp to capture horses. Wolf Calf also gave some medicine and a plume to Iron Shield. Little Plume received some of Wolf Calf's medicine, and shortly before his death gave it to his brother, Yellow Kidney (still living). The gift included two horse medicine songs.

Night Gun said his grandfather, Wolf Calf, carefully taught him the songs and ritual of the horse dance and the uses of some horse medicines. Wolf Calf intended for Night Gun to be his successor as leader of the cult. However, when Wolf Calf died, his son White Antelope (born ca. 1860) claimed the sacred horse medicine bundle. There was an argument and Mike Short Man and White Antelope split the bundle. White Antelope lost interest in horse medicine, but noted that Phillip Arrowtop was becoming interested in it. On his death White Antelope left the bundle to Wallace Night Gun with the provision that Phillip Arrowtop (still living) should be given some of the paraphernalia and medicines. This was done. When Mike-

Short-Man was near death he offered his horse medicine to Night Gun, but the latter requested that it be transferred to Herman Dusty Bull, who wanted it. On Herman's death, his brother, Charles Dusty Bull (still living) acquired this bundle, said to contain paints, feathers, and some horse medicines.

These data indicate that the Piegan horse medicine cult originated in the visions of one man, Wolf Calf, and was elaborated by the contributions of at least two others, who willingly pooled their knowledge with Wolf Calf. Since their time nothing has been added to the ritual, materia medica, or medicinal practices of the cult. Horse medicine powers were transferred to many other men. There was a tendency for them to be transferred in fullblood families from brother to brother or father to son. In the process much knowledge of the employment of horse medicines was lost. In recent years the possession of horse medicine songs and paraphernalia, entitling the owner at attend and participate in the horse dance, has been coveted, while there has been little interest in the use of horse medicine to cure or influence the actions of horses. It is certain that the uses of many specific medicines are no longer known. In the early 1940's, only Wallace Night Gun and Phillip Arrowtop were thought to be capable of using horse medicines. In recent years the primary function of the cult has been the observance of the traditional horse dance for the purpose of curing sick humans.

That this is not a comprehensive history of the Piegan horse medicine cult is apparent from the fact that elderly informants named other horse medicine men active in that tribe in buffalo days. While it is probable these men obtained their powers from Wolf Calf they may have made some independent discoveries.

My eldest male informants, Lazy Boy and Weasel Tail, claimed that Water-Old-Man, a Blood Indian, older than Wolf Calf, possessed and used horse medicine before Wolf Calf originated the cult among the Piegan. If that is true, Wolf Calf's dreams may have been conditioned by his knowledge of Water-Old-Man's practices. In the Blood tribe, as among the Piegan, there was a tendency for horse medicine power to be transferred within families. However, Weasel Tail could not recall two members of the same family possessing this power at the same time. No one now living on the Blood Reserve has knowledge of the use of horse medicine in the opinion of all Blood informants questioned on this point. The bundles of the best-remembered practitioners in that tribe, Water-Old-Man and Owner-of-a-Sacred-White-Horse, were said to have been buried with them. Ghost Woman, the last Blood Indian known to have made extensive use of horse medicine, died about 1925. Knowledge of its use was lost on her death although her bundle remained in her family. Although my informants had knowledge of the existence of the horse medicine cult among the North Blackfoot, I obtained no history of that cult.

Older informants said that in their youth some horse medicine men were regarded by laymen of that tribe as possessors of much greater powers than others. Some horse medicine men also were recognized as specialists in the use of horse medicines for specific purposes. There was rivalry between horse medicine men of the three Blackfoot tribes.

Scraping White told of a contest between Water-Old-Man, the noted Blood practitioner, and Berry Eater, a leading North Blackfoot horse medicine man, which took place in his father's time (i. e. probably before 1860). They decided to test their respective powers by racing on horseback over the ice of a frozen river. Members of both tribes placed bets on the outcome of the race. Water-Old-Man rode a buckskin, Berry Eater a sorrel. Neither horse was an experienced racer. Before they started each rider invoked the aid of his medicine. They ran their horses at full speed over the slippery river ice. As they neared the opposite shore, Berry Eater's horse slipped just enough to throw it off stride. Water-Old-Man's horse finished strong, won the race, and the Blood Indians collected their winnings. Probably this was the contest referred to by Wissler (1912, a, p. 111).

TRANSFER OF HORSE MEDICINE POWER

The common procedure for obtaining horse medicine, in the lifetime of my informants (both Blood and Piegan), was for a person seeking this power to go to a recognized horse medicine man and offer him gifts of horses, robes, blankets, money or other valuables, along with a pipe, saying, "I want some of your horse medicine," and naming the use the seeker wished to make of it. If the horse medicine man did not wish to grant the request, either because the payment did not appear adequate or for any other reason, he refused to accept the pipe. Then he sang some of his horse medicine songs to avoid bad luck coming his way because of his refusal. If the horse medicine man accepted the pipe he called all the other members of his village who possessed horse medicine power to a horse dance for the purpose of making the transfer and explaining to the neophyte how to make use of the medicine. If, after receiving the medicine, the recipient should still be doubtful regarding any detail of its use, he returned to the man from whom he had secured the power, made an additional payment and requested further instruction.

Weasel Tail recalled his own failure to obtain horse medicine. His experience furnishes a first-hand account of the transfer procedure:

When I was a boy about 17 years of age, I met an old Blood Indian named Rain Maker one day while I was returning to camp with two buffalo I had killed. I told the old man to take them both. Rain Maker prayed for me, then he said, "My boy, you will live to be an old man like I am." He then told me to kill two more buffalo so that he might have four tongues. I killed the buffalo and took him the tongues. The old man, who was known as a horse medicine man, then invited me to a feast at which other horse medicine men were present. During the ceremony Rain Maker got down on all fours in front of me singing. He held his fists tightly clenched and moved his hands back and forth in imitation of a horse pawing with his forefeet. When Rain Maker finished his singing and pawing the ground in front of me he said, "Now, my boy, you are foolish. I have just offered you this medicine and you didn't take it. I wanted to help you. The medicine in my right hand is for doctoring horses. The one in my left hand is for horse racing. They are very powerful." Then the old man told me that since I had not grasped one of his hands while he was pawing and singing I could not have any of his medicine.[87] I realized then that I had made a great mistake. But before that I knew no better. Never again did I seek horse medicine.

In former times the horse medicine man did not relinquish his own right to make use of medicines after transferring the right to another. However, in recent years Indians have transferred horse medicine songs and paraphernalia, relinquishing all title to them, but retaining the right to attend the horse dance. Perhaps the recent concept of transfer of title has been applied only since the Indians became thoroughly familiar with the white man's concept of property rights in reservation days, and since the decadence of the employment of horse medicines as means of influencing the actions of horses.

THE HORSE DANCE: CEREMONY OF THE HORSE MEDICINE MEN

Wallace Night Gun said the ceremony of the horse medicine cult was properly termed "the horse dance." In the old days it was held primarily on occasions of transfer of horse medicine powers. On occasion Wolf Calf employed the ceremony as a means of testing the knowledge of other horse medicine men. After he had assembled the horse medicine men, he took one of his medicines from his bundle, for example, a certain root used in his practice. He chewed it, rubbed some dirt on it, then called upon any other man who possessed the power to make use of that root to prove it. The medicine was passed among the assembled horse medicine men until it reached one who had knowledge of its use. He drummed and sang the songs appropriate to its use, threw the medicine on his body, and caused it to disappear. He then removed it from some other part of his body and threw the root back to Wolf Calf. In a gathering of horse medi-

---

[87] A parallel procedure occurred in the Blackfoot ceremony of transfer of the bear knife. Informants said that near the close of that ceremony the owner, after imitating the antics of the bear, threw this dangerous weapon at the prospective owner. If he failed to catch the knife he did not gain possession of this sacred object.

cine men there might have been as many as three or four who possessed the secret of the use of the designated medicine. Each in turn gave proof of his power by singing the songs of that medicine and the sleight-of-hand performance just described. In recent years, however, the horse dance has served primarily as a ceremony for curing sick humans.

Invitations to attend the horse dance were extended to recognized horse medicine men and to medicine pipe men who possessed horse medicine songs by presenting each with a feather from the leader's bundle (pl. 16, A, a). The person who requested the ceremony was responsible for delivery of the feathers. Before the leader handed the feathers to him for distribution he chewed some of his horse medicine and blew some of it on the feathers, then toward the messenger. Then he told him who was to receive each feather and reminded him that on presenting the feather he was to tell the recipient only the place and time of meeting. If a man failed to attend after receiving a feather, he must, on the next day, tie a rock to it and throw it into a lake or stream to avoid bad luck. The leader later added a new feather to the bundle to replace the one thus destroyed. Each man who attended the ceremony gave his feather to the leader as he entered the lodge. The leader returned the feathers to his bundle.

Wallace Night Gun claimed he observed the horse dance just as Wolf Calf, who taught it to him, had practiced it. As leader of the cult on the Blackfeet Reservation in Montana he kindly invited me to attend one of the ceremonies. The description of this ceremony that follows is based upon my own observations of the horse dance plus interpretations of the esoteric aspects of the ritual furnished by Wallace Night Gun a few days later.[88]

The horse dance was performed on that occasion in the combined living room and kitchen of the frame home of my interpreters, Reuben and Cecile Black Boy, in the Moccasin Flat section of Browning on the evening of March 29, 1943. Neither Reuben nor Cecile attended, stating that they were not cult members and hence did not think it proper that they should attend the ritual. Night Gun told me, however, there was no prohibition against nonmembers witnessing the ceremony, but children were excluded for fear they might later try to imitate some of the songs or gestures employed in the ritual. It was considered very bad luck to employ these songs or gestures outside their proper ceremonial context.

There were less than a dozen witnesses other than the participants. Among them was a young woman who had been in poor health all

---

[88] This description may be compared with Clark Wissler's short paragraph on the ceremony published in 1912 (Wissler, 1912 a, pp. 109–110). My informants said that Red Plume, Wissler's informant, was not a member of the horse medicine cult.

winter, in whose honor the ceremony was given. Nearly all the other witnesses were relatives of this woman or of the two male assistants to the cult leader, both of whom had also been sickly that winter. I was the only white person present.

The room in which the ceremony was held was roughly 12 feet wide by 25 feet long, extending in a general north-south direction. Wallace Night Gun, the cult leader, sat on the floor in the center of the south end of the room. He was flanked by members of the cult, 6 in number, and one medicine-pipe owner who had been invited to attend. They formed a wide arc facing north. In the center of the west wall stood the wood stove, and opposite it on the floor in front of the east wall sat the wives of the cult members. Witnesses were provided with chairs ranged in two rows at the north end of the room.

The horse dance ritual consumed more than 7 hours, beginning at 9:30 p. m. While the leader began to open his medicine bundle on the floor in front of him, one of his two assistants, both of whom were middle-aged men learning the ceremony, began the construction of the ceremonial altar on the floor about 3 feet in front of Night Gun. The assistant first spread a square piece of cloth on the floor and emptied a sack of fine gray earth upon it. Following the leader's instructions he smoothed the earth into a flat circular area about 30 inches in diameter with a cylindrical red-painted stick, 7 inches in length, from the leader's bundle (pl. 16, A, f). He then carefully picked out all the bits of stone remaining in the earth. Next, the leader told him to draw the outline of a square in the earth with the stick. He marked out a square a little over a foot on a side and ran a line in a north-south direction down the center of the square dividing it into two equal rectangles. He then extended from each corner of the square a zigzag furrow in the earth more than 6 inches long. Next he made a small depression in the earth about 4 inches north of the square. Night Gun requested the second assistant to take a live coal from the fire in the wood stove and place it in the depression. This he did with the wooden fire tongs shown on plate 16, A, c. Then he placed sweetgrass on the coal to make a sweet-smelling smudge. Night Gun then handed the first helper a packet of charcoal which he sprinkled evenly over the rectangle comprising the west half of the square so as to blacken it completely, and extended black lines in the two zigzag furrows on the west side. Similarly he colored the east rectangle and the two zigzag furrows on that side with red earth paint. Next Night Gun handed the assistant two red and two black plumes, and he inserted them upright in the four corners of the square, beginning with the northwest corner (black) and continued in a clockwise order, i. e., northeast (red), southeast (red), and southwest (black).

Construction of this ceremonial altar was slow and deliberate. Wallace Night Gun told me Wolf Calf had explained to him that he had been told how to make the altar in one of his dreams. It was important that it should be made in just that way for every horse dance ceremony. Night Gun said the red rectangle symbolized day and the black one night. The zigzag furrows represented "the thunder's lightning." The plumes were also required by Wolf Calf's dream. Wolf Calf used to give them to persons who requested his help. Hence they were renewed from time to time (pl. 16, A, b). The completed altar appeared as sketched in figure 33.

While the men rested, the wife of one of the cult members began to cut up three beef tongues on the floor near the center of the room. In front of her was a smudge in a tin pan. She made two passes with one hand toward the smudge before drawing longitudinal black lines with charcoal on each tongue, followed by the drawing of similar lines in red paint on each. Then she cut each tongue into small pieces each about 2 inches square. Wallace explained that only a woman who had been given this power could cut the tongues. If no such woman was in attendance at a horse dance, the leader would paint the face of one of the cult member's wives and instruct her in the ritual of tongue cutting. At any later ceremony that woman would be privileged to cut the tongues.

While this woman was at work, Night Gun called the young woman who had been in poor health, and for whose benefit the ceremony was given, to come to him. She knelt before him, as he uttered a prayer for her welfare. Then he painted her entire face and a band about one-half inch wide around each of her wrists with red paint, applying the paint with his thumbs. Next he prayed for and painted each of his two assistants and the owner of the medicine pipe bundle who was present. All of them I knew had been sickly that winter. The aged medicine pipe owner had been treated by several white doctors. (He died in the fall of 1947.)

Night Gun later told me it was customary for those who were blessed and painted to give him presents either before the ceremony or just prior to the painting. Unless the leader was satisfied that he was well paid he would not proceed with the ceremony. If satisfied, he instructed the other cult members present to remember these givers in their ritual prayers. The leader might also call upon any other witness, not a member of the cult, to come forward to be blessed. That witness need not pay for the privilege unless he was so disposed. Painting gave him the right to attend future horse dance ceremonies. Through witnessing the ceremony, listening to the songs, and studying the ritual he might eventually desire to buy into the cult.

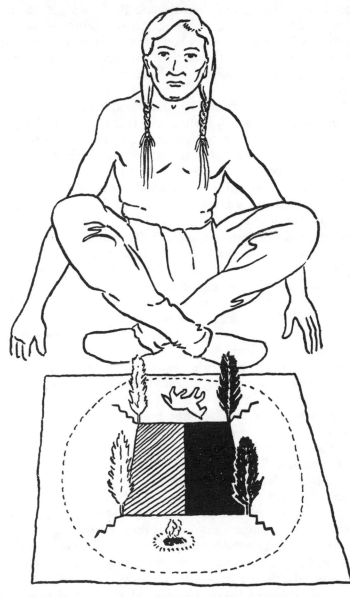

FIGURE 33.—Altar for the South Piegan horse dance ceremony.

Before the painting was finished the leader's second helper, seated on the floor northwest of the altar, began preparing tobacco for the cult members. He placed his knife on the smudge near the altar, then shaved a plug of commercial tobacco and mixed it with dried bear-berry leaves (a common Blackfoot smoking mixture). The cult members then passed a pipe, consisting of a plain stem and a small blackstone bowl from the leader's bundle (pl. 16, *B*, *c*). Meanwhile the woman who had cut the tongues painted three stripes of red paint on the inside of a large kettle and placed the tongues in it, making two feints toward the kettle with the first handful of meat before dropping it in the kettle. Water was added and the kettle was placed on the stove to boil.

The leader then drew from his bundle a little rawhide cutout figure of a horse in profile, 6½ inches long (pl. 16, *B*, *a*). He placed it on the earth south of the rectangular altar. He gave his second assistant a red-painted rock about the size of a fist, which the man carried to the front door of the house, made two passes at the door frame, then hit it with a resounding rap with the rock, and returned to his place. Night Gun said this was a caution to the horse medicine men never to fall over or bump a rock.

There followed praying, singing, and drumming by the horse medicine men. This was the most prolonged portion of the ritual. First the leader offered a prayer to the spirit of the rawhide horse, then sang three of his ritual songs, accompanied by the beating of three drums held by himself and the two members of the cult nearest him on the left. When he had finished he passed his drum to the man on his left who in turn gave a prayer and sang three medicine songs owned by him. This combination of praying, drumming, and singing was continued until each cult member had performed individually. Then the entire cycle was continued twice more, until each member had sung his three songs three times. Night Gun said that if one of the singers was a new member who possessed only one song he was privileged to sing it three times each cycle. Meanwhile he tried to learn another song, which he might later purchase, by listening carefully to the others. The leader might loan a fellow member one of his songs for a particular ceremony, but it "went back to the bundle" when the ceremony ended. Men who had owned the same song as one being sung by another were permitted to join in the singing. The wives of some of the male singers also joined their husbands, singing softly from their stations near the center of the floor. The songs were wordless tunes in which the same stanzas were repeated many times. Some singers inserted a prayer between each song.

At the conclusion of this ritual a meal was served to all persons present. It consisted of bread, crackers, boiled ribs, and coffee. It was then well past midnight. There followed a second session of singing, by the cult members, and after a brief rest, a third session. These were exact duplicates of the session described in detail above. In each of the three sessions each member sang three songs on each of three passings of the drums.

Then came the ceremonial climax. Wallace Night Gun, the leader, covered his head with a blanket and sang three songs. Then, pipe in hand, he prayed to the spirits of Wolf Calf's horses, Sitting-on-a-Hill and Gone-in-Different-Brush, the horses that had given Wolf Calf his secret power. Night Gun then took from his bundle the mane and chestnut of Wolf Calf's sacred stallion and prayed for the sick who had requested the ceremony. Then, as other cult members drummed, he rose and danced, holding a braided rawhide rope, noosed at one end, and a whip over his wrist. Both were taken from his bundle (pl. 16, B, b, e). Three times as he danced he made gestures toward the little rawhide horse in front of the altar as if to rope it, holding the rope in his right hand. Then he repeated these gestures with his left hand, and again with his right hand extended. Night Gun danced in place, always facing the altar.

The leader then sat down and called upon the tongue cutter to ask if the tongue soup was ready to serve. Receiving an affirmative reply he began to dismantle the altar. First he picked up the rawhide horse and wrapped it. Then his first assistant removed the plumes from the altar, one at a time, handed them to him, and he wrapped them. Finally he asked for volunteers to destroy the remainder of the altar. His first assistant and one of the cult members stepped forward with blankets wrapped about their waists. Night Gun gave each of them a bit of horse medicine which they chewed and rubbed on the soles of their moccasins. The leader told them, "Now, dance up to the painting three times; on the third time step on it and smash it down flat." In accompaniment to the beating of drums, the two men danced side by side toward the altar. Twice they retreated, rearing backward like skittish horses. Then they boldly advanced with pawing steps, stepped upon the altar, turned their feet upon it and destroyed the painting.

Next the leader addressed the women sitting on the floor opposite the stove. Two women rose, each with a cup in hand, and danced toward the kettle on the stove, which had been boiling for hours. Twice they retreated. The third time they placed their cups in the kettle. The leader then told them to place three pieces of the tongue in a cup and to set it in front of him. With a stick covered with red paint he speared a piece of tongue, prayed for the sick woman, and gave her the first piece. In succession he removed the other pieces and gave one to each of his assistants.

The leader then instructed the women to take the earth that had composed the altar and the remains of the smudge outside, pray to them, and bury them where people would not step. Next he picked up the painted rock, prayed no one would be hurt by stepping on a rock on the way home and that none of their horse's feet would be harmed by rocks. He gave it to one of the sick men and told him to take it to a stream on leaving the house, pray to it, and throw it into deep water. Then the tongue soup was distributed to all those present. Having consumed it, they went home.

In many respects the horse dance may be regarded as a typical Blackfoot ceremony. Wissler (1912 a, pp. 248–271) has pointed out that singing, drumming, dancing with sacred paraphernalia, praying, the passing of the pipe, face painting, the recognition of taboos, and the following of strictly formalized and prolonged ritual patterns were common characteristics of Blackfoot bundle ceremonies. Even the employment of dry-painted altars appeared in other important bundle ceremonies (ibid., pp. 255–257). R. N. Wilson (1909, pp. 16–20) in his detailed description of the use of a dry-painted altar in the Sun Dance ritual, noted that this altar was destroyed before the medicine woman's party left her lodge. In that painting black symbolized night, and yellow day.[89]

Aside from the horse symbolism characteristic of the horse dance, the most distinctive feature appears to be the repeated and consistent employment of the ritual number 3. To my knowledge this is the only Blackfoot ceremony in which that ritual number occurs. In fact Wissler regarded 4 as the ritual number of all Blackfoot ceremonies, including the horse dance (Wissler, 1912 a, pp. 110, 247). In this detail his account of the ceremony is in error.

USES OF HORSE MEDICINE

The powers of Blackfoot horse medicine men, as explained by informants, were many and varied. Not only were they credited with the ability to control the health and actions of horses but they were thought to have been able to influence the movements of buffalo and to cure and aid the activities of humans.

Horse medicine was most commonly employed in the treatment of sick, injured, wounded, or exhausted horses. Curing of sick horses generally involved the administration of medicine by nose or mouth as a part of the ritual. Owners of valuable horses generally entrusted their treatment to experienced horse medicine men when these animals were ill. The medicine men were paid for their services.

Three Calf recalled that Wolf Calf frequently was called upon to doctor horses that were staggering and near death. Wolf Calf rubbed his medicine on the horse's nose, back, and kidneys, then shook its tail four (three?) times. If the horse made no move Wolf Calf told the owner there was no hope for it. If it moved it would get well.

---

[89] Wissler (1912 a, p. 257), has pointed out the occurrence of dry painting among the Dakota, Cheyenne, and Arapaho of the Plains, as well as among the Southwestern tribes.

Wallace Night Gun said Wolf Calf mixed his medicine with sage for use in doctoring horses. Lazy Boy recalled that Wolf Calf was especially successful in treating horses with colic or distemper. Three Calf had observed Wolf Calf's methods in treating distemper. He first told a young man to throw the afflicted horse down. Then the old man placed a slim wire in a fire until it became red hot and touched it to the horse's nose. Meanwhile his medicine was boiling. He threw the horse's head back and poured the medicine down its nose. When the horse was turned loose it sneezed, pus ran from its nose, and it recovered.

Wolf Calf did not attempt to treat horses with broken bones. However, Calf Tail, a Blood horse medicine man was a specialist in that treatment. Weasel Tail recalled that Calf Tail once was called upon to doctor a fine horse with a broken leg. He asked the owner to bring him the shank of a buffalo or horse. After receiving the shank, Calf Tail sang a song and rubbed dirt on it. Then he tied the shank to the horse's broken leg and told the boy not to bother it for four (three?) days. At the end of that period Calf Tail washed the horse's leg and the bone tied to it. He untied the bone and rubbed dirt on it. The horse rose and walked away "without even a limp."

Weasel Tail recalled two instances of the curing of battle wounds by horse medicine men:

Yellow Lodge, a North Blackfoot horse medicine man, rode his horse through the lines of the Cree enemy three times. The Cree shot and wounded the horse in the chest. After the battle Yellow Lodge dismounted, burned some sage, making a great deal of smoke, rubbed some horse medicine on the horse's mouth, then rubbed some on both sides of the wound where the bullet had entered and left the horse's body. Then he rubbed medicine on his hands and slowly tapped the horse on the kidneys four (three?) times. Each time the animal appeared to improve. The last time it pulled away from its rope and began eating grass. The horse recovered completely.

Many-Spotted-Horses had a fine animal, Double-Blue-Horse, shot above the kidneys in a battle with the Gros Ventres. Many-Spotted-Horses got the horse home alive. His old father went to the horse and said to it, "You are a fine horse, but I am more powerful than you. It looks like you are going to die, but you will not die. I shall doctor you." The old man painted the horse's breast with red earth paint. He tied a plume to the horse's forehead and a rabbit's tail to its tail. Then he rubbed his horse medicine on the horse's nose. Next he rubbed the medicine on his hands and tapped the horse four (three?) times on the back. The horse was cured and lived many years longer.

Despite the miraculous powers credited to horse medicine men, informants agreed they were powerless to avert the disastrous mange epidemic of 1881–82. Horse medicine men did not employ their secret powers to facilitate or condition the breeding of horses.

Probably the second most common use of horse medicine was in doctoring humans. The procedure employed has been described in my detailed account of the horse dance (pp. 264–270).

Horse medicine was employed by some specialists to influence the outcome of horse races. The medicine was always used to handicap one of the competing horses, never to give a favored horse unusual speed or stamina. This use of horse medicine was always dangerous to the horse medicine man. If the owner of a horse that had lost a race learned that horse medicine had been used against his animal he might punish the medicine man severely if he learned his identity. Yet Wolf Calf, Generous Woman, Ghost Woman, and Head Carrier, the latter a North Piegan, were well known as persons who were notably successful in handicapping race horses through their horse medicine powers. Night Gun said that if the owner of a race horse came to Wolf Calf and asked him to use his medicine against his opponent's horse, Wolf Calf painted a rock with his medicine, prepared the ceremonial altar and placed his rawhide horse upon it. He asked the man, "What do you want to happen to the other horse? Do you want it to fly the track, buck, or kick up?" If the man wished the horse to fly the track, Wolf Calf placed the rock on the rawhide horse's head before continuing his ritual. If he wished it to buck, he placed it on the horse's shoulders; if he wanted it to run a short distance, kick up, and refuse to run, he put the rock on the horse's hind legs. Wolf Calf might also give the jockey of the horse belonging to the man he was helping a willow stick with horse medicine on it, with instructions to touch the other horse with this stick when he was alongside it in the race to make that horse drop behind. If the other horse gained the lead the jockey was to drop the stick in its tracks and that horse would surely falter. Informants credited both Head Carrier and Ghost Woman with use of the medicine-covered-stick method of influencing horse races.

Wolf Calf also was able to assist contestants in other sports. If a young man came to him for help in playing the hoop and pole game, Wolf Calf told him to shout a certain phrase when he cast his pole. His opponent's pole would be sure to strike the ground and break. Wolf Calf gave a foot racer who sought his aid some of his medicine and told him to chew it, rub it on his feet just before the race, always run to the right of his opponent, and he surely would win.

Horse medicine had a number of important uses in war. Wolf Calf sometimes was petitioned to help a young warrior in horse raiding. If Wolf Calf accepted the man's pipe and gift when offered, he gave him a plume from the ceremonial altar and explained, "If you can't get near the enemies' horses take this dirt (from the ceremonial altar) and mix it with water. Dip the plume in the mixture. It will rain, the enemy will stay inside their lodges and you will have no trouble taking their horses." Or he would give the man some plant medicine and tell him to rub it on his rope just before entering the enemy camp. "The enemy's horse will come right up to you and you can rope it." He might offer further help, stating, "If the horse you have taken plays out on the way back, or the horse of someone else in your party plays out, dismount, sing these songs I give you, take some of this medicine I give you and rub it on the horse's nose or teeth or place it in its mouth. Then go around to the rear of the horse, tap it on the tail bone three times, with the medicine rubbed on your hand. The exhausted horse will perk up and move along." Wolf Calf expected that the recipient of such favors would give him the best horse he stole from the enemy on his return. If the man did not use all the medicine he received, Wolf Calf told him to keep it and use it as long as any remained.

In a running fight, a man who possessed horse medicine might rub some of it on his whip, point the whip at his enemy, and drop it in the tracks of the enemy's horse. "That horse was sure to falter or fall."

Fish Child, Calf Tail, and Ghost Woman also were said to have employed horse medicine for war purposes. Ghost Woman gave it to her son to rub on his rope and body when on horse raids. She is also credited with having escaped capture by the enemy through the use of her medicine. One day she was traveling alone when an enemy party surprised her. She sang a song, took some medicine from a pouch at the side of her dress, threw it on the ground, and the enemy was unable to overtake her. However, the most miraculous escape is credited to the Blood horse medicine man, Owner-of-a-Sacred-White-Horse. Once he was chased by the enemy. He employed his medicine to enable his mount to leap a wide, washed out coulee (estimated by various informants at from 10 to 40 feet across) and escaped death at the hands of a superior force.

Some men were credited with power to use horse medicine in hunting buffalo. Short Face cited the case of Black Plume, a member of a hunting party which sighted a white buffalo but could not catch it. He asked the party to stop while he took a piece of black root, laid it on a rock, and placed the rock on one of the footprints of the white buffalo. That buffalo slackened its speed. Black Plume remounted, caught up with the buffalo, and killed it. The white robe was dressed and given to the sun. Black Plume was a medicine pipe man rather than a horse medicine man. Wissler's informant may have had this case in mind when he stated that medicine pipe men could use horse medicine in hunting buffalo (Wissler, 1912 a, p. 111).

In winter, when the footing was snowy or icy so as to make buffalo hunting on horseback treacherous, one who had the power sang his medicine songs and prayed that the horses of his party would not fall. He took a black root, chewed it, and sprinkled it on the horses of his party. Then they could chase buffalo without mishap, no matter how bad the footing.

A man who possessed horse medicine for use in catching wild horses rubbed it on his hands, feet, and rope. Then he circled the wild horse up wind so that the odor of the medicine would be carried to the nostrils of the wild one. When the wild horse smelled the medicine it came to him. He roped it by the front feet and threw it down. Only horse medicine men were said to have had success in capturing wild horses. Apparently few of them exercised this power.

To keep a horse that had a tendency to stray in its proper herd, one who possessed horse medicine might neck it together with a gentle horse, and rub horse medicine on its nose. After a time it was untied and permitted to graze unfettered. "It would never stray again."

Lazy Boy mentioned one more use of horse medicine. If a horse medicine man became jealous of another Indian's fine horse he might employ his medicine to render that horse "no good for buffalo hunting, war or anything else." [90]

TABOOS RECOGNIZED BY HORSE MEDICINE MEN

Wallace Night Gun said that Wolf Calf had been warned in his dreams of a number of actions he should avoid and which should be avoided in his presence. These taboos have been recognized by Piegan horse medicine men since Wolf Calf's time.

Ribbones or shinbones must not be broken in the horse medicine man's lodge or home. Any one who ignored this taboo would suffer a broken leg or rib.

If anyone places a knife or other sharp object upright in the ground inside a lodge when a horse medicine man is present he will surely get a sliver in one of his feet or one of his horses will suffer a foot injury.

No child should play at riding a wooden stick horse in a lodge while a horse medicine man is present, or the child will suffer misfortune.

If a horse medicine man should go into any home and see a child carelessly throwing a feather around, he must tell him to stop it at once or the family will surely have bad luck.

For anyone to sing any of the horse dance songs or to imitate the gestures of the horse dance except in their proper ceremonial context would bring misfortune to him. The only exception to this rule applied to owners of medicine pipe bundles who had been given horse medicine songs which could be sung in the medicine pipe ritual. The Blackfoot considered some horse medicine songs very attractive.

---

[90] Wissler (1912 a, pp. 108–111) mentioned Blackfoot use of horse medicine to cure horses of the colic, revive exhausted horses, cause a horse to lose a horse race, capture enemy horses, catch wild horses and to hunt buffalo.

They were tempted to sing them for pleasure at times when they were forbidden to do so.´ They believed that if one who had not the horse medicine power should sing a horse dance song while on horseback his horse would fall.[91]

IDENTIFICATION OF HORSE MEDICINES

Identification of the substances employed by the Blackfoot as horse medicines poses a difficult problem. It is certain that some of the medicines formerly employed by noted horse medicine men were not known to the Piegan or Blood Indians of the early 1940's. Wallace Night Gun acknowledged that he knew neither the substances nor the specific uses of some of the medicines in the bundle he inherited from Wolf Calf. In deference to his desire to keep those medicines secret which he did employ, I did not question him as to their identity. Nevertheless, his voluntary recital of the origin and use of Wolf Calf's horse medicines (related above) makes general mention of botanical medicines, primarily roots.

Dr. V. E. Rudd, division of botany, United States National Museum, compared the fragments in the seven skin pouches in Wallace Night Gun's horse medicine bundle (pl. 15, *B*) with herbarium specimens. She found that the large, single pouch contained ground fir needles, probably *Abies lasiocarpa.* McClintock (1910, p. 524) reported Blackfoot use of sweet pine in poultices for fevers and colds in the chest in the treatment of humans. One of the small pouches on the buckskin cord contained rootstocks of baneberry (*Actaea eburnia*). McClintock (1910, p. 526) stated that the root of this plant was boiled as a Blackfoot medicine for coughs and colds. Each of the other five pouches contained bracts of flower heads of sagebrush (*Artemisia* sp.). However, each of these pouches was marked with a different-colored bead. It is possible that some of the finely powdered material in these pouches comprised bits of other plants used in conjunction with the sagebrush. McClintock (1910, p. 526) listed *Artemisia frigida* tops as a Blackfoot remedy for heartburn and mountain fever.

A century and a half ago David Thompson (1916, p. 365) observed that the Indians of the Plains collected "scented grasses, and the gums that exude from the shrubs that bear berries and a part of these is for giving to their horses to make them long winded in the chase." Presumably he had reference to botanical medicines administered by laymen rather than by horse medicine men. Short Face, who was not a member of the horse medicine cult, believed some of the secret medicines used by horse medicine men were the same ones administered to

---

[91] Wissler (1912 a, pp. 108, 111) cited the taboos against breaking a shinbone in the lodge and singing of horse medicine songs out of context.

horses by laymen. One of these was the root of *Townsendia excapa*, which laymen boiled and poured into the mouths or noses of tired horses to revive them. He believed a root similar to baneberry, and known to the Blackfoot as "strong root," which laymen smashed and fed to horses at any time of year to make them hardy, was another horse medicine ingredient. He claimed (and as we have seen above, correctly) that the root of the baneberry, frequently found in medicine pipe bundles, was one of the secret horse medicines.

Other informants who did not possess horse medicine power, but who had carefully observed the grazing habits of horses, made conjectures as to the identification of some horse medicines. Three Calf understood that the roots of a plant that grew around alkali lakes and of which horses were very fond (possibly the mat muhly, *Muhlenbergia squarrosa*) (U. S. Forest Service, 1937) was a horse medicine ingredient. Weasel Tail thought a weed that grew on the Plains which horses often pawed up while grazing was ground to a powder and mixed with the ground heart and feet of a beaver to form a horse medicine. Another informant knew of a medicine used by the Kutenai for attracting wild horses, which he believed was employed by Blackfoot horse medicine men for the same purpose. It was prepared from the lachrymal glands of the elk, which have a strong odor, especially if the animal is taken in rutting season.

These are the only suggestions of possible use of animal materials in Blackfoot horse medicines. Certainly the bulk of the evidence points to the employment of plant materials in these medicines. When I discussed horse medicine with E. C. Moran of Stanford, Mont., a collector of Montana drug plants for commercial uses, he suggested that the locality furnished two plants, known for their drug properties, *Clematis* and *Equisetum*, which would be likely ingredients in Blackfoot horse medicines. *Clematis* has been reported as a horse medicine among both the Nez Percé and Teton Dakota, but I have no evidence of its use as such by the Blackfoot.

COMPARATIVE DATA ON HORSE-MEDICINE IDENTIFICATION

Table 8 summarizes information on plant medicines known to have been used as horse stimulants by other horse-using tribes of the West. I am indebted to Edith V. A. Murphy, botanist, employed by the United States Indian Bureau, for field data on Arapaho, Nez Percé, and Ute usages. Eugene Barrett, forester, Rosebud Reservation, kindly supplied the Teton Dakota data. It is noteworthy that *Thalictrum* sp., which grows in the Blackfoot habitat, was employed as a horse stimulant by more than one other tribe. *Paeonia brownii*, though not reported from the Blackfoot country, was available in Wyoming and Idaho, at no great distance from the Blackfoot range.

Data regarding horse medicines used as depressants are scarce. Mrs. Murphy informed me that Ute medicine men placed a root (unidentified) in the mouth of an opponent's race horse to make it logy. She also reported that the Ute formerly fed sleepy grass to a horse as a depressant, although details of this usage were not obtainable. The Montana ranges contain a number of stock-poisoning plants injurious to horses, including larkspur, locoweed, lupines, and death camass. However, we have no proof that Indian horse medicine men employed any of these plants in concocting depressant medicines.

TABLE 8.—*Plant medicines used as horse stimulants by other tribes*

Tribe	Plant	Use
Arapaho	"Hiwaxuhaxhiwaxu" (native name). Probably wild peony (*Paeonia brownii*).	Root rubbed on nose of tired horse to refresh it (Kroeber, 1902–7, p. 424). Probable identification by Mrs. E. V. A. Murphy.
Cheyenne	*Anaphalis margaritacea* var. *subalpina*.	Dried and powdered flowers placed on sole of each hoof and blown between horse's ears to make it long-winded and untiring (Grinnell, 1923, vol. 2, pp. 187–188).
	Thalictrum sparsiflorum	Dried and ground to fine powder, administered by mouth to make horse spirited, long winded, and enduring (ibid., pp. 141, 173–174).
	(?)	Unidentified root obtained from Kiowa-Apache, administered by mouth to make horse long winded and stimulate a tired horse (ibid., p. 139).
Gros Ventres	Niitsican (native name), "hollow root." Unidentified.	Given horses to strengthen and refresh them (Kroeber, 1908, p. 226).
Nez Percé	*Clematis douglassii*	Scraped end of root held in nostrils of a fallen horse. Immediate stimulating effect. (U. S. Forest Service, 1937, p. B58.)
	Paeonia brownii, wild peony	Chewed root placed in horse's mouth and mouth held shut until horse swallowed to stimulate exhausted horse (Mrs. E. V. A. Murphy).
Omaha	*Laciniaria scariosa*	Corn chewed and blown into horse's nostrils to make it long winded. Flower heads mixed with shelled corn fed to horses to make them swift (Gilmore, 1919, pp. 133–34).
Pawnee	*Ionoxalis violacea*, sheep sorrel; and *Xanthoxalis stricta*, yellow wood sorrel.	Bulbs pounded and fed to horses to make them fleet (Gilmore, 1919, p. 98).
Sarsi	(?)	An herb or root administered to give horse surpassing power (Jenness, 1938, p. 74).
Teton Dakota	*Clematis douglassii*	Dried and powdered root administered by nostrils to stimulate tired horses when hard pressed by enemy (Eugene Barrett).
Ute	"Ewuhigare" (native name). Unidentified.	Pounded and rolled with grass and administered to revive an exhausted horse (Lowie, 1924 b, p. 311).
	Paeonia brownii, wild peony	Root chewed and placed in horse's mouth to give it long wind (Mrs. E. V. A. Murphy).

RELATIONSHIP OF HORSE MEDICINE TO OTHER BLACKFOOT MEDICINES

Wissler (1912 a, pp. 107–108) pictured and described an attachment known as "a thing to tie on the halter" as a Blackfoot ceremonial bundle. My informants referred to this object as "horse bridle." Three Calf recalled that Generous Woman, a prominent Piegan horse medicine man, made one of these bridles of a thin stick about 18 inches long, covered with red flannel, with feathers pendent at the ends and small bags of horse medicine tied to the stick. Other "horse bridles" were similar save that they were trimmed with strips of white weaselskin. Although these objects were made and used primarily by horse medicine men they were wrapped in separate bundles when not in use. Wallace Night Gun said that men who were not horse medicine cult members were known to have dreamed of one of these bundles. If the lay dreamer wished to make a bundle like the one seen in his dream he went to a horse medicine man and asked for help. The latter then told him to make the bridle just as it appeared in his dream and to bring it to him to give it power. Upon payment the horse medicine man gave the owner several little packages of horse medicine to tie to the "horse bridle," together with instructions for the use of these medicines. The owner attached this "horse bridle" to his horse when he rode to war or rode in the riding big dance. It was believed to make the horse lively, to keep it from falling, and to keep enemy bullets from hitting it. Night Gun said men who dreamed of these bridles also received songs in their dreams which were added to the collection of horse medicine cult songs. He claimed there were few of these bridles among the Piegan in buffalo days. The only one I saw on the Blackfeet Reservation was owned by a cult member.

Wissler (1912 a, p. 111) noted the introduction of horse medicine ritual into the medicine pipe ceremony of the Blackfoot. Night Gun said it was common practice for a medicine-pipe owner to ask a horse medicine man to insure that the horse used to carry the medicine pipe would not fall or be harmed while camp was on the move. The horse medicine man used his sacred rope and whip in the ceremony of blessing the horse of the medicine pipe man. He sang and transferred three horse medicine songs to the pipe owner. He also transferred some of his power to the whip and rope of that man. It is noteworthy that a whip and rope are among the objects in the typical Blackfoot medicine pipe bundle, and that horse medicine songs appear in that ceremonial ritual. McClintock (1948, pp. 56–60) described a medicine pipe transfer he witnessed in which not only the whip and rope but also the saddle, bridle, and horse used to transport the pipe were transferred. In that transfer ceremony four (three?) horse songs were sung with great care "lest misfortune befall their horses." There were restrictions that the horse employed to carry the medicine pipe must be used only by its owner "lest some of his horse-herd sicken and die," and that the medicine pipe owner "must not strike a dog or horse, nor cut a horse's tail." The medicine-pipe owner who had purchased three horse medicine cult songs was privileged to attend the horse dance and to sing those three songs during the ceremony.

Less certain is the relationship between horse medicine and the horse-painted lodge formerly found among the Piegan. Wissler and Duvall (1908, p. 94) have published Head Carrier's version of the origin legend of the horse-painted lodge. It is noteworthy that Head Carrier was a North Piegan horse medicine man. John Old Chief claimed Wolf Call formerly owned the horse-painted lodge and transferred it to a North Blackfoot medicine man before he died. Other informants denied this. One man claimed the horse-painted lodge of the Piegan was of Gros Ventres origin.

THE SOUTH PIEGAN BLACK HORSE SOCIETY

Jim Walters said that Mountain Chief (who died in 1942) originated a dancing society known as the Black Horse Society. Mountain Chief preserved the head of a black horse he had stolen from the enemy. During his dance he carried this head on a stick, and gave away horses. Jim's father obtained the horsehead from Mountain Chief and gave the dance, giving away good horses and receiving poor ones in return. Jim told his father it wasn't worth keeping. His father gave the head to John Two Guns, who kept it for a while, then gave it to someone else, who probably threw it away. At the Christmas dance at Starr School in 1942, a dance by members of the Black Horse Society was requested. Only one man came out to dance. There seems to have been no direct connection between this short-lived society and the horse dance of the horse medicine men, although the existence of the powerful horse medicine cult may have inspired the organization of the Black Horse Society.

EVIDENCES OF THE HORSE MEDICINE CULT AMONG OTHER TRIBES

Respect for the supernatural powers of horse medicine men was widespread among the Plains Indians. Although most comparative data on this subject relate to the nomadic tribes, the earliest reference to the existence of the cult appears in an account of the horticultural Arikara written by the fur trader Tabeau in 1803-04. Tabeau regarded Kakawita, chief of the Male Crow division of the Arikara, in whose lodge the trader resided, as the most influential and highly respected man in the tribe. Kakawita possessed a medicine bundle containing a little whip "which makes a famous courser out of a draught horse, and, when he hangs it on his wrist, while singing a certain song, all the horsemen who accompany him fall from their horses." Among the chief's taboos was the belief that his "powder [sic] was weakened if some one broke a bone in his lodge" (Tabeau, 1939, pp. 185–186). Three decades later Maximilian (1906, vol. 23, p. 394) noted an Arikara taboo against breaking a marrow bone in a hut. "If they neglect this precaution, their horses will break their legs in the prairie." Skinner (1914, p. 532) heard of the Plains Cree horse dance but was unable to obtain detailed information regarding it. He believed, perhaps erroneously, that it was "presumably . . . a mimetic dance to obtain increase of the herds." The anthropological literature lacks information on Kutenai, Flathead, and Nez Percé horse medicine concepts and procedures.

Informants claimed the Cree, Sarsi, Gros Ventres, Kutenai, Nez Percé, and Flathead, neighbors of the Blackfoot, all had horse medicine men in buffalo days. Jenness briefly described the Sarsi concept and practice of horse medicine. The spirit of a horse that had been treated particularly well might appear to its owner in a vision and reveal to him an herb or root that would give horses great speed or cure horses, together with appropriate songs. Among the standard paraphernalia of the Sarsi practitioner were a whip and a rope (Jenness, 1938, p. 74). These are all factors in Blackfoot belief and practice.

Although Jenness claimed the Sarsi obtained horse medicines from the Cree, Mandelbaum (1940, pp. 195–196, 277) reported that the one Cree ceremony in which the horse figured prominently, the horse dance, was as much for weasel spirit as for horse. His description of the overt actions in this dance fails to reveal their underlying significance.

Lowie (1924 a, p. 329) found that the Assiniboin horse dance ranked "on a par with the Sun Dance," but was unable to obtain an adequate account of it because of "its esoteric character." However, Rodnick (1938, pp. 50–52) obtained a description of the Horse Dance Society from Medicine Boy, an elderly Assiniboin, residing on Fort Belknap Reservation, who had been a cult member. Rodnick termed this society's ceremony "second in secretness to the Sun-Dance." It was performed at the time of initiation of new members about once every 2 years. All members were invited and the neophyte gave presents to them before and during his initiation. Although the total ceremonial complex contained many elements foreign to the Blackfoot cult, some elements resembled those of the Piegan ceremony. The leaders (two in number) made long prayers, which included prayers to the spirit of the horse, sang, and drummed. Members danced in imitation of horses and demonstrated their individual supernatural powers. They traced "figures on the ground," sang ceremonial songs, and finally covered the traced figures with dirt. Members observed the taboo against breaking a marrow bone and one against burning feathers. The powers of Assiniboin cult members, as described by Rodnick, included those of freshening a tired horse, curing horses with broken legs and other afflictions, making a horse gentle, and setting broken bones of humans. Rodnick found the Assiniboin society was no longer active in 1935.

Lowie (1924 a, pp. 329–334) published a detailed account of the Crow horse dance. He was told the River Crow derived their ceremony from the Assiniboin within the lifetime of his informants and that the Assiniboin in turn attributed its introduction to the Northern Blackfoot. Crow horse dancers formed a loose association of less than 6 to more than 30 men with their wives. Members of this group owned powerful medicines whose ingredients were secret, used for reviving tired horses and curing sick horses and humans. In former times the horse medicine bundle was opened only when outsiders gave a feast in honor of the medicine. An account of Crow acquisition of this ceremony from the Assiniboin mentioned the necessity for the Crow to seize the medicines of the Assiniboin dancers before the conclusion of the singing or they would not be able to secure the rites. (Note the similar Blood Indian custom described by Weasel Tail on p. 263.) Important points of resemblance between the Crow and Blackfoot cults appear to confirm Lowie's traditional information on the historical relationship of the horse medicine cults of these tribes. Analysis of available information on Assiniboin and Crow horse medicine cults indicate that the former was more closely related to the Blackfoot cult than was the latter.

Wissler (1912 b, pp. 95–98) described the horse medicine cult of the Oglala Dakota, which was composed of persons who had dreamed of horse medicines and who held ceremonies in a tipi followed by a spectacular parade around camp. One of Wissler's informants claimed his great-grandfather originated the cult among the Oglala and recited the origin tale. The Oglala ceremony included the element of dancing in imitation of horses. Oglala used horse medicine to make horses swift, to cure sick and wounded horses, to revive exhausted horses, to calm a balky horse, and to influence the outcome of horse races. Brood mares were also treated to produce fine colts.

My Oglala informants (1947) recalled the use of horse medicine to handicap an opponent's race horse. Lone Man, brother of one aged informant, was said to have possessed power to doctor both horses and people. Eugene Barrett (letter of Sept. 21, 1943) wrote me that he was told a Nez Percé Indian, who formerly lived with the Brule Dakota, employed horse medicine to assist in breaking wild horses. He built a fire and placed some of his secret herbs in it to produce a smoke that had a soothing effect upon the horse to be broken. Densmore (1948, p. 181) reported that a Teton named Jaw carried little bags of horse medicine attached to his war whistle. He employed his medicine in curing sick horses and tied one bag to his horse's bridle before going in battle. On horse-stealing raids he chewed horse medicine, approached the horses from windward, and caused them to prick up their ears and be attracted to him. The available evidence on Teton Dakota uses of horse medicine is sufficient to indicate both its extensive employment and its many similarities to Blackfoot concepts and usages.

Kroeber (1902–7, pp. 424, 431–432, 436) does not mention any ceremonial organization of horse medicine men among the Arapaho.

"An old man who had horse-medicine taught it to his son and several other young men. In teaching it to them, he drew on the ground, with red paint, another horse or mule, somewhat smaller, facing the north. While this medicine was in the tent no peg or other part of the tent might be removed, lest there be a storm." The Arapaho used horse medicine to cause mares to have colts of certain desired colors, as well as to cure sick horses and to revive exhausted ones. Other medicines were used to rub on the body of a man who was about to break a horse, or to moderate the swelling caused from being kicked by a horse. Perhaps if we had more detailed data on Arapaho horse-medicine practices their relationship to those of the Blackfoot cult would appear more numerous.

Mooney (1907, p. 414) learned that the Cheyenne had "several sets of 'horse medicine' doctors, each set having its own special secret for the treatment of ailing horses, together with special taboos, and special costume, face paint, and songs for use during treatment." Unfortunately Mooney did not elaborate upon this general statement. Grinnell (1923, vol. 2, pp. 139–143) denied there was a guild of horse doctors among the Cheyenne, claiming that men who possessed powers to heal men also had powers to cure horses. He found that Cheyenne doctors recognized a number of taboos, including the one against breaking a bone in their lodge (unless upon arising the woman of the lodge first struck the important lodgepole four times). The Cheyenne employed horse medicine to revive exhausted horses, to make horses long winded, to cure sick horses, to prevent men or horses from being hurt in war or in the buffalo hunt, to treat persons thrown from horses, and to handicap an opponent's race horse. Grinnell's description of the treatment of sick horses recalls Blackfoot methods previously described. Although the Cheyenne procedure involved ritual rubbing, blowing, and moving about the horse, medicine was administered by mouth and/or nose in the course of the ceremony. Grinnell stated that Gland, a very old medicine man in 1862, claimed to possess the original medicine of Minhik, a celebrated Cheyenne medicine man of an earlier period. This suggests that the practice of horse medicine among the Cheyenne originated well before the middle of the 19th century.

Grinnell also claimed the Cheyenne method of employing horse medicine in influencing horse races was adopted by the Kiowa, Comanche, and Apache. Two Kiowa informants told me of the former use of horse medicine by certain Kiowa men to handicap race horses. Alice Marriott has informed me that Kiowa horse shamans did not form a society. Each acted in obedience to his own dreams. They possessed a wide variety of paraphernalia and songs. She said that among the Kiowa only horse medicine men castrated horses.

Mooney (1898, p. 253) laconically reported that the Kiowa-Apache "have a 'horse medicine' of their own of considerable repute." Miss Marriott learned that a famous Kiowa-Apache horse medicine man was active during the period of Mooney's field work among the Kiowa (early 1890's).

The Chiricahua Apache believed a mistreated horse had supernatural power to cause the owner sickness which could be cured only by a doctor who specialized in the horse ceremony (Opler, 1941, pp. 239–240). The same source (pp. 294–300) cites examples of horse power transmitted to humans who were able to cure sick horses as well as persons hurt in falls from horses. The ceremony also was conducted to bring luck to horse raiders. Songs and prayers were included in the ceremony. Horse doctors also were called upon to perform rites to make horses run fast in races. This is the only reference I have found to the use of horse medicine to assist rather than to handicap a race horse. As among the Kiowa, these Apache brought their horses to the horse medicine men to be castrated.

Far to the northwest, among the Puyallup-Nisqually of northwestern Washington, Marion Smith (1940, p. 68) found vestiges of a horse medicine cult. The man possessing horse power "was good with horses. They liked him. He doctored them and made saddles for a business."

In view of the geographically widespread, scattered evidence of belief in and practice of horse medicine among the horse-using tribes of the Plains and Plateau summarized above, it would be strange indeed if such beliefs and usages were not known to other tribes of the Plains and to many Plateau tribes concerning whose practice of horse medicine no reports are available. I am inclined to believe that lack of information from these tribes is probably due to incomplete reporting rather than to absence of the horse-medicine complex in the cultures of those tribes. The fact that horse medicine tended to be veiled in secrecy probably discouraged Indian informants from volunteering information about it to ethnologists who were not well known to them or who showed no marked interest in the function of horses in their cultures. It appears certain that the horse-medicine cult was much more widely diffused among the Indian tribes of western North America than was the much studied and much better known Sun Dance. It may not be too late to obtain valuable data regarding its occurrence among some of the tribes of the Plains and Northwest, from which reports of horse medicine are not available, through field work with aged informants.

The assembled comparative data indicate that tribal differences in the nature and degree of organization of practitioners, in ceremonial rituals, in associated taboos, and in specific uses of horse medicines existed. Nevertheless the available data from the Blackfoot, Sarsi, Assiniboin, Crow, Arikara, Teton Dakota, Arapaho, Cheyenne, Kiowa, and Chiricahua Apache indicate a common substratum of beliefs and usages which strongly suggests that the horse medicine cults of these tribes were historically related. Native testimony to the effect that the Assiniboin and Crow derived their horse-medicine cults from the Blackfoot suggests that the Blackfoot were at least a secondary center of diffusion of the cult. However, native traditions also suggest that the Oglala and Cheyenne as well as the Blackfoot possessed active horse-medicine cults early in the 19th century. I have cited proof of the existence of the cult among the Arikara as early as 1803–4. It is probable that some tribes of the Great Plains possessed horse medicine cults in the 18th century, although the evidence is insufficient to enable me to name them.

The horse-medicine cult certainly appears to have been a native invention. Possibly it began to develop shortly after the acquisition of horses in response to the need for the services of veterinarians to care for these precious possessions. Their actions clothed in secrecy, blessed with supernatural sanctions, and embellished with elaborate ritual, their powers feared by their fellow tribesmen, these primitive horse doctors may have extended their activities to include the control of the actions of horses in the hunt, in war, and in horse races, and added some of the functions of the earlier cult of healers of sick humans. On the other hand, the first horse medicine men may have been persons who had previously treated humans and/or dogs, and who already possessed considerable knowledge of the medicinal plants of their tribal habitats. Through processes of trial and error they may have discovered additional medicines which proved efficacious in the treatment of horses. Although ritual and magical factors played prominent roles in the use of horse medicines, there was an empirical element in the selection of plant materials administered in the curing rituals.

SACRIFICE OF HORSES AFTER THE DEATH OF THEIR OWNERS

A Blackfoot Indian felt a strong attachment for his favorite horse, his trusted companion on the buffalo hunt and scalp raid. If this animal died it was not unusual for his proud owner to weep publicly. The owner might request his family to have his favorite horse killed beside his own burial place, if that horse survived him. Thus the close companionship between man and horse might continue in the spirit world. However, poor families, who could not afford to sacrifice a horse, more commonly cut short the mane and tail of the deceased owner's favorite mount. Green Grass Bull explained that the horse was then considered to be in mourning for its owner in much the same way as was the mourning wife who cut the hair of her head. Sometimes the mane and tail of a woman's favorite pack or travois horse were cut after her death. Horses so treated could be used without any period of delay after the owner's death.

Maximilian (1906, vol. 23, p. 121) was told of instances when "twelve or fifteen horses were killed . . . at the funeral of a celebrated chief." However, his mention of 150 horses killed following the death of "Sacomapoh" probably is an exaggeration. Weasel Tail said the greatest number of horses he had seen killed at one burial was 10. The Piegan continued the custom of killing horses as grave escorts until about the year 1895. Among the Canadian Blackfoot the custom was followed sporadically for several years after that date.

Upon the death of an important leader the sacrifice of horses was coupled with an elaborate ceremony of burial in a death lodge. Among the great chiefs honored with death-lodge burial were Lame Bull, first signer of the 1855 treaty with the United States Government (who died in 1858) and Many Horses, the wealthiest Piegan (who died in 1866). Lesser chiefs and prominent warriors received this honorary burial on a less grandiose scale.

When one of these leaders died his lodge was arranged on the inside just as it had been when he was alive, with beds and backrests in place and his favorite equipment displayed as it had been when he used to entertain prominent guests in his lodge. His body was dressed in his finest clothing and laid on a bed in the lodge, or preferably on a pole platform erected in the center of the lodge, built high enough to prevent predatory animals from molesting the body. The body was laid upon the platform with feet facing the doorway (east). Then the deceased's close relatives prepared the horses to be killed, decorating them with elaborate and costly riding gear. The dead man's favorite horse was painted with pictographs representing the owner's coups. That horse's tail was braided and tied in a ball, and a feather pendant was tied in it. His mane was braided and feathers were tied in it also.

Everyone in camp attended the funeral. The horses to be sacrificed were led to the door of the death lodge. Each horse in turn was shot with a gun, pressed against its head and fired by a relative of the deceased. After all the horses were killed the riding gear of the dead man's favorite horse sometimes was stripped off and placed inside the death lodge. At other times the people of the camp were privileged to strip the dead horses of their gear for their own use. Green Grass Bull explained the Blackfoot belief that the spirit of the horse joined that of its owner, wearing the gear it bore at the time it was killed. After the horse's spirit had departed the actual trappings had no more value to the dead Indian than did the carcass of the sacrificed horse itself.

After the horses were killed in front of the lodge, rocks were piled in lines extending outward from the death lodge in the four cardinal directions. Each pile of rocks represented one of the departed leader's coups. Usually these death lodges were erected in out of the way localities at some distance from camp. Occasionally the lodges were looted by passing enemy war parties. But none of the valuable articles in the death lodge were disturbed by members of his camp for fear the dead man's spirit would haunt them. The bodies of the dead horses were left to decay where they fell.[92]

COMPARATIVE DATA ON HORSES AS GRAVE ESCORTS

The literature reveals that the custom of killing horses after the owner's death was followed by other Plains and Plateau Indian tribes. The destruction of horses appears to have been greatest after the death of a wealthy member of a tribe that was relatively rich in horses. Thus over 70 horses were said to have been killed after the death of a leading Kiowa chief (Yarrow, 1881, p. 143). On the other hand, the Plains Cree, notoriously poor in horses, were content to clip the manes and tails of the horses of the deceased (Mandelbaum, 1940, p. 250). Some Central Plains tribes killed the horses by strangling them (Omaha—Fletcher and La Flesche, 1911, p. 83; Kansa—Bushnell, 1927, p. 53; Oto and Missouri—Yarrow, 1881, p. 96). Chiricahua Apache either stabbed or shot the horses (Opler, 1941, p. 474). While the Assiniboin, Cheyenne, Arapaho, and Teton Dakota shot them, as did the Blackfoot (Denig, 1930, p. 572; Grinnell, 1923, vol. 2, p. 160; Michelson, 1933, p. 606; Bushnell, 1927, p. 40; Yarrow, 1881, p. 180), most tribes simply left the dead bodies under the burial scaffold or tree, or beside the grave. However, the Coeur d'Alene skinned the dead horses and hung the skins at the grave. If the skins were needed they suspended only the horse's hoofs (Teit, 1930, pp. 173–174). On occasion the Nez Percé skinned and stuffed the horses and set them up as grave monuments (Spinden, 1908, p. 252).

Other tribes reported to have killed horses as grave escorts were the Sarsi (Jenness, 1938, p. 39), Crow (Denig, 1930, p. 479; Lowie, 1912, p. 227), Arapaho (Kroeber, 1902–7, p. 17), Sisseton Dakota (Yarrow, 1881, p. 109), Wichita (ibid., p. 103), Comanche (Neighbors, 1852, vol. 2, p. 133; Yarrow, 1881, p. 99), Wind River and Lemhi Shoshoni (Lowie, 1909, p. 215; 1924 b, p. 282), Bannock (Marquis, 1928, p. 105), and Flathead (Mengarini, 1871–72, p. 82). This custom of the Plains Indians appears to have been an expression of the widespread

---

[92] Denig (1930, p. 573) wrote that very brave and renowned Assiniboin warriors sometimes requested that their bodies be placed inside their lodges after their death. The-Iron-Arrow-Point, noted chief of the Rock Band of Assiniboin, received a death-lodge burial ante-1850.

primitive custom of providing the dead with objects thought to be useful to them in the afterlife.

Cropping the mane and tail of a dead man's horse or horses provided a method of honoring the dead without sacrificing valuable property. Probably it was much more common among Plains and Plateau tribes than the few, scattered references in the literature indicate. The wealthy Comanche and the Chiricahua Apache cut the manes and tails of those horses of the deceased man which had not been killed at the grave (Parker, 1855, p. 685; Opler, 1940, p. 474). Sarsi clipped the hair of horses that belonged to a warrior killed in battle (Jenness, 1938, p. 39). Flathead considered their mourning period for the dead ended when the clipped mane and tail of the dead man's horse grew out (Turney-High, 1937, p. 146). Other tribes reported to have cut the manes and tails of dead men's horses were the Plains Cree (Mandelbaum, 1940, p. 250), Assiniboin (Lowie, 1909, p. 42), Crow (Leonard, 1904, p. 271), Teton Dakota (Dorsey, 1894, p. 487), and Lemhi Shoshoni (Lowie, 1909, p. 215).

DISPOSAL OF HORSES AFTER THE DEATH OF OWNER

If the head of a Blackfoot family knew he was about to die he called his relatives together and told them how he wished his horses and other property divided among them, designating which items were to be received by each relative. If a man died without a verbal will procedures differed. His eldest son, or other close relative might take charge of the distribution of the property. However, a distant relative, angered at being left out of consideration, might help himself to a horse without its being reclaimed by the one to whom it was allotted.

I asked particularly about the distribution of the great herd of Many Horses, wealthiest of Blackfoot horse owners, after he and his favorite wife were murdered by the Gros Ventres in the summer of 1866. Lazy Boy said that after the battle between the Piegan and Gros Ventres, which followed shortly after the discovery of Many Horses' body, the Piegan erected a death lodge for Many Horses, and his eldest daughters selected more than 10 of his favorite horses to be killed before the burial lodge. Later Lazy Boy's father, Calf Looking, a band chief in the Piegan camp, took charge of the distribution of Many Horses' herd. Many Horses' eldest daughter instructed him to divide the horses among the three surviving wives, the several daughters, and one son of the deceased chief. After each received a sizable herd, she asked that the rest of the horses be given to the people. Every member of Many Horses' band received a horse and some persons outside the band also got one.

This orderly distribution of horses following a death intestate was possible only in cases where the deceased was a man of prominence who had been well liked and highly respected by his people during his life. In many instances of death intestate members of the camp, whether or not they were related to the deceased, made a run for his property as soon as they learned of his death through the loud weeping and wailing of his close relatives. Men of the camp ran for his horses, while women went to get his household furnishings. The men might take all the good horses in his herd and leave the poor ones for the widow. Close relatives of the deceased, preoccupied with their mourning, did not attempt to prevent this raid, and custom decreed that they should not do so. The raiders were not permitted to take horses or other property belonging to the dead man's wife or other members of his family before his death, even though horses belonging to those people ran with the dead man's herd. On a woman's death people might raid her horses and other property. Informants recalled that these raids were made with particular relish upon the property of a man of some wealth who had had a reputation for stinginess. As one informant stated, "Even his wife would be glad to be rid of him, and she would remarry shortly after his death."

Wissler (1911, pp. 26–27) claimed these raids were limited to relatives of the deceased. However, our informants' contentions that anyone in the village might share in the raid were based upon personal observations. They are corroborated by the brief description of Culbertson (1851, p. 126), penned a century ago.[93]

SECONDARY ASSOCIATIONS OF THE HORSE IN BLACKFOOT RELIGION

IN BUNDLE TRANSFERS

Wissler (1912 a, pp. 253–254) expressed the opinion that the association of horse payments with the transfer of Blackfoot medicine bun-

---

[93] Recognition of the legality of a verbal will made before death seems to have been widespread in the Plains. Kiowa informants spoke of this custom in their tribe. Cheyenne also recognized it (Llewellyn and Hoebel, 1941, pp. 214–215). Inheritance customs in cases of death intestate varied widely, with preference given to different relatives by different tribes. Tixier (1940, p. 184) found that the Osage recognized a form of primogeniture by which the eldest son inherited all his father's horses, while the eldest daughter became owner of the lodge. The Plains Cree father's horses were distributed by the eldest son among his brothers and sisters, reserving one horse for the widow (Mandelbaum, 1940, p. 251). The Cheyenne widow's right to her husband's horses was "law" (Llewellyn and Hoebel, 1941, p. 216), while the Gros Ventres' wife inherited nothing from her husband, his property generally being divided among his father, mother, brothers, sisters, and children (Kroeber, 1908, pp. 180–181). Kroeber found no fixed customs of inheritance among the Arapaho. The death of a wealthy man resulted in considerable competition among his relatives, although his brothers and sisters generally acquired much of his property (Kroeber, 1902–7, p. 11). I have the distinct impression from reviewing the literature that inheritance patterns in other Plains Indian tribes may have been no more standardized than they were among the Blackfoot. However, I have found no description in the literature of the raid on property by nonrelatives of the deceased among tribes other than the Blackfoot.

dles was "so fixed that one must suspect the present system of transferring bundles to have developed in its present form since the introduction of the horse." Lack of information on the occurrence and transfer of bundles in early times makes it impossible to check Wissler's hypothesis. Native tradition claims the Sun Dance and beaver bundle originated before the introduction of horses. There is also a tradition that the Blood Indians' Long Time Pipe was transferred through dog payments before horses were known to these Indians. It is possible that horses may have replaced slaves, dogs, robes, or whatever other valuables may have been given to insure the transfer of sacred objects in pre-horse times. The fact that horses, after their introduction, were recognized as valuable media of exchange in secular transactions probably would have encouraged their use as payments for medicine bundles as well. Whatever the origin of the close association of horse payments with bundle transfers, it is certain that it existed in 19th-century buffalo days. The owner of an important sacred bundle received the petitioner who wished to obtain title to it with mixed feelings. He weighed his loss of sacred power through the relinquishment of his bundle against his gain through the acquisition of a number of fine horses offered in payment.

IN THE SUN DANCE CEREMONY

The influence of the horse made itself apparent at various stages of the Sun Dance, the most important Blackfoot tribal religious ceremony. I have described (p. 128) the care given to the transport of the medicine woman's sacred paraphernalia to the Sun Dance encampment on a horse travois. War honors, most commonly acquired on horse raids, were required of both the cutter of the tree to be used for the center pole, and by men who cut the thongs to bind the rafters to the posts in the construction of the lodge. The latter rite was transferred through payment of a horse and other property. Before cutting the hide the cutter was required to raise his knife and publicly declare four personal coups, which commonly included the capture of enemy horses. In recent years older men who have counted coups have stood as sponsors for younger men or women who paid to cut the hide. Plate 17, *a*, portrays Makes-Cold-Weather (ca. 1866–1950), one of the last of the Piegan veterans of intertribal horse raids, counting his coups before his protege cut the hide in the Sun Dance near Browning in 1943.

Men who underwent the excruciating self-torture in the Sun Dance lodge (pl. 17, *b*), did so in fulfillment of vows, made before going into dangerous action, to submit to the torture if they came through safely. The two accounts of personal experiences in self-torture, which I obtained from elderly Blood Indians, indicate that the vows of both men were made shortly before they entered enemy camps to steal horses. There is a possibility that the Blackfoot tribes borrowed the Sun Dance torture from the Arapaho in the historic period, and hence since the introduction of horses (Ewers, 1948 b, pp. 167–168, 171–172).

Three quarters of a century ago Bradley (1923, pp. 267–268) wrote of the warriors who entered the Blackfoot Sun Dance to count their coups during the closing days of the ceremony.

Those who desire the privilege of recounting their coups must first present a horse to someone at the door of the medicine lodge (an irrevocable gift), when he may enter the lodge and in his turn relate his exploits, illustrating them by gestures indicating the manner of their performance.

The horse stealers, however, are not required to make the gift of a horse at the door but bring with them a bundle of sticks, and casting one into a fire kept burning in the lodge, say: "At such a time I stole so many horses at such a place, from some enemies." Then casting in another stick describe another occasion.

If the Blackfoot observed the Sun Dance before they obtained horses, as was uniformly claimed by informants, it was none the less influenced by the presence of the horse in historic times. The data cited above show that even the details of this most sacred tribal ritual were colored by Indian regard for and preoccupation with horses.

BELIEFS CONCERNING THE SUPERNATURAL POWERS OF HORSES

There was a general belief among the Blackfoot that horses possessed supernatural powers. Just as they believed some humans possessed stronger supernatural powers than others, so they thought the sacred powers of some horses were more potent than those of ordinary horses. I have referred (p. 259) to the two horses which were credited with having bestowed horse medicine powers upon their owner, Wolf Calf, in his dreams. Horses that performed deeds of unusual strength or endurance, that miraculously escaped from battle without a scratch, or received wounds thought to have been mortal yet recovered, were spoken of by informants as animals possessing potent "secret power." Their remarkable deeds were proof to the Indians of their possession of that power.

Weasel Tail cited a case which will prove this point.

Heavenly Colt was a strong, gray horse born of a mare stolen from the Flathead by a Blood Indian. He was broken for riding at 3 years of age and proved to be an excellent war horse. After Heavenly Colt gained a wide reputation among the Indians, the Gros Ventres stole him. In the battle between the Piegan and Gros Ventres in the summer of 1866, Heavenly Colt was ridden by Sitting Woman, Gros Ventres head chief. During the action the horse was shot through the neck. Three Suns, a Piegan chief, ran to the horse and said, "It is too bad such a fine horse must die. I shall claim him until he dies." Then the horse dropped. But the next morning the Piegan saw a gray horse on a distant hill.

They went after him and found he was Heavenly Colt. He was alive and in good condition. Heavenly Colt was returned to his rightful Blood owner. That horse had great secret power.

Like humans, horses were believed to survive death as spirits possessing the power to return and make their spirit presences known to the living. Weasel Tail illustrated his own strong belief in horse spirits by relating a personal experience.

About 50 years ago I visited the lodge of Steel, a Blood Indian. I knew Steel thought his father's spirit was near him at all times. I asked Steel, "Where is your father, Many Spotted Horses?" While I talked I heard a horse whinny far away. Then I heard a horse at the back of the lodge shaking and its stirrups rattling. Then I heard someone talking behind Steel. I could see no one there. It was Steel's father's spirit, come to visit him on his spirit horse.[94]

BELIEFS REGARDING THE ORIGIN OF HORSES

The beliefs of the great majority of aged, fullblood Blackfoot Indians regarding the origin of horses are embodied in their mythology. In the course of my field work on the Blackfeet Reservation, Mont., elderly Piegan informants recited three different myths explaining the origin of horses. One was told by Short Face, recognized by his fellows as the most accomplished storyteller on the reservation, in the fall of 1943. In the summer of 1947, my interpreters, Reuben and Cecile Black Boy, said that during the intervening years Dog Child, a North Piegan, had told them another version of this myth. Short Face's version, which I have given a title to, follows.

THUNDER'S GIFT OF HORSES

Many years ago, when people used dogs for moving camp, there lived a Piegan named Wise Man. He and his wife were a handsome couple, but they wore very plain buckskin clothes. One day Wise Man said to his wife, "I have been thinking about something. If my plans work out we shall have very fine clothes. Let's move away from here and make camp in the woods. I'll collect all the wood you need, but you must not break any of the sticks I bring in."

Wise Man and his wife moved to the woods. After he had brought in wood, he told his wife, "Now I shall go up the hill and catch some eagles." He ascended the hill, dug a pit, found a dead coyote and cut it open, placed a roof of sticks over the pit after he had climbed into it, and tied the coyote on the roof. When eagles saw the coyote they swooped down and began pecking at the carcass. Wise Man grabbed each eagle in turn as it ate, pulled it into the pit and wrung its neck. He caught eight eagles. Then he returned to camp and told his wife, "I shall make myself a bonnet from these feathers." He made his bonnet—

---

[94] Wilson (1924, pp. 144–145) reported Hidatsa belief that all horses had supernatural powers, and that if horses were not properly cared for they would not increase in numbers and might leave their negligent owners. A Hidatsa informant also claimed the Assiniboin considered their horses sacred and sang sacred songs to them (ibid., p. 142). Dorsey (1894, p. 499) mentioned the Dakota custom of praying to horses. The existence of their horse medicine cults is evidence of belief in the supernatural powers of horses among other Plains and Plateau tribes.

a circle of feathers standing straight up, with a feather trailer down the back. Then he fashioned some weasel snares and went about the countryside snaring weasels. He took them to his wife and said, "Now, tan these." She replied, "But what are you going to do with them?" "I shall use them to decorate my suit," said Wise Man. She tanned the weaselskins and sewed them on his plain buckskin suit as a fringe, just as he requested. Then he donned his new costume and asked her, "How do I look? Take a good look at me." She looked him up and down admiringly and replied, "You are very handsome looking man." Wise Man then said, "I am completely dressed. Now I shall show you how to dress."

He went into the woods and found an elk lick with many elk around it. With bow and arrows he killed a large number of them. From each he took only two teeth. He carried them to camp and drilled a hole near the base of each tooth. Then he showed the elk teeth to his wife and told her how to sew these teeth on her plain elkskin dress. When she had done that, she put on her dress, stood before her husband and asked him, "Now, how do I look?" Wise Man replied, "You are certainly a very beautiful woman. That is how I want you to look when you have occasion to wear your best clothes."

The couple then returned to the camp of their people. When the others saw their fine clothes, all the young men and women wanted their garments. They offered to barter their most valuable possessions for them. But Wise Man refused, saying, "I will not sell these clothes. You must hunt and make them for yourselves just as we have done. But I am going back to the woods and I shall make up another outfit which I shall trade you."

So Wise Man and his wife returned to their former camping place in the woods. There he met a man. The stranger said to him, "I shall help you. You haven't fixed that bonnet right. You should have quills on the feathers. You should have quills on your leggings and shirt too." Wise Man had never heard of quills and he asked, "But how shall I get these things you call quills? How shall I learn to fix them on my bonnet and shirt?" "Thunder will show you how to do that," the man replied. "But I have never seen Thunder," said Wise Man. "Where is he?" The stranger explained, "He lives above. You follow along the mountains to the end of the earth. There you will find a way to go to him."

Wise Man went to his wife and told her of his talk with the stranger. "A man came to me who told me how I can make my clothes even prettier by putting quills on them. He named someone who could help me to do this. I don't know who that is, but he told me how to find him." His wife answered, "All right, go look for him."

So Wise Man loaded his dog and went away, following the foot of the mountains. He passed mountain lions, bears and other large animals but they did not harm him. Some of them turned into persons. Finally he reached the end of the mountains. Ahead was nothing but water. The shore was thick with brush. Wise Man climbed a cliff and looked down. In the brush he saw a lodge. He descended and entered the lodge. It was empty. After a long time a man entered and spoke to him. "Where are you going? You can't go any farther." Wise Man replied, "I am going to find Thunder." The man said, "He is in the sky. You can't go there. But I shall help you, my boy. Climb this cliff and you will find some goats. Kill one, cut off the ends of his horns and bring them back here."

Wise Man did as he was told. When he returned with the pieces of horn the man told him, "I will give you my moccasins. Fasten these goat horns to them and they will help to hold you up. I shall help you. Follow me." They began to ascend, Wise Man following in the footsteps of the stranger, who had told him to look only ahead. After they had climbed a long time they reached a level place. It was another world.

Then the stranger turned to Wise Man and said, "This is Thunder's home. After you have walked a way you will be surrounded by horses. They are dangerous animals, but they will not hurt you. I shall leave you here. Go on to Thunder's camp. The first animals you meet will be Thunder's horses."

Wise Man walked on until he saw the horses. One of them spied him, and all came toward him and surrounded him. At first Wise Man was afraid. But the strange animals did not harm him. He soon lost his fear and began to pet them. They were so thick around him he could not proceed. But when night came they all lay down and went to sleep. Then Wise Man crawled away from them and walked on toward the lights of two camps in the distance. When he came near them he saw that they were beautifully painted lodges, each with a medicine pipe in front of it. He walked inside one of them. Thunder was there.

When Thunder saw Wise Man he told him to sit down. Then Thunder made a smudge and began to show Wise Man the ritual of the medicine pipe. Wise Man told him, "I came here to find out how to look good in my clothes. I want you to tell me what to do and how to do it. That is what is on my mind." Thunder replied, "My boy, come with me and I shall show you." Outside the lodge Thunder pointed to a porcupine and told Wise Man, "Kill it." This Wise Man did. Then Thunder showed him how to remove the quills, how to flatten them, to dye them different colors and to sew them on garments. When he had finished, Thunder said, "My boy, you have been good. You didn't frighten my horses. They didn't hurt you. They are the animals I ride. Because you did not frighten my horses and they were not afraid of you I shall give you some of them. I'll show you the songs of my pipe and my painted lodges and give them to you also. I'll show you how to pack the pipe on a horse's back. But before I give you all these things you must pay me." Wise Man asked, "What shall I give you?" Thunder said, "Give me a woman from your people, and give me a white buffalo robe." Wise Man asked, "How are you to get the woman?" Thunder replied, "My boy, I can do it with your help." Wise Man then said, "I shall get you a woman. But the white buffalo is very fast. I'll try to get you a white buffalo robe, but it will be very difficult."

Then Thunder went to his herd and selected 10 head of horses, and gave them to Wise Man saying, "Now, my boy, take these. They will raise colts for you and increase. I shall put a porcupine on earth. It too will increase. You can kill porcupines, eat them, and use their quills. Generation after generation of your people will use these things. There will be no end to them. I want you to take the medicine pipe, and in the spring of the year when the leaves begin to come out you will hear me rumbling. Gather your friends quickly and dance to the medicine pipe as I have shown you. I shall see you then and know that you have heard my call. Until the end of the world you will have these things. Not until then shall I take them back."

Thunder then said, "Now, my boy, I'll take you down. Tie the tails of two old mares together. When you have done that you will be on earth again. To-night there will be a strong wind. If your lodges fall down or if your horses become frightened, I'll take them back. Otherwise you may keep them. In future times many of your old people, to whom I shall give the power, will dream of animal-painted lodges and sacred pipes."

The night after Wise Man's return to earth there was a storm and a very high wind. But the horses were not frightened and the lodges did not fall. Wise

Man kept the things Thunder gave him. Until this day the Indians have porcupines, painted lodges, medicine pipes, and horses.

In March 1943, Chewing-Black-Bones recited another myth explaining the origin of horses. He claimed that Head Carrier, who died half a century earlier, told him the following story, which I have named.

WATER SPIRIT'S GIFT OF HORSES

A long time ago there was a poor boy who tried to obtain secret power so that he might be able to get some of the things he wanted but did not have. He went out from his camp and slept alone on mountains, near great rocks, beside rivers. He wandered until he came to a large lake northeast of the Sweetgrass Hills (Lake Pakowki). By the side of that lake he broke down and cried. The powerful man who lived in that lake heard him and told his son to go to the boy and find out why he was crying. The son went to the sorrowing boy and told him that his father wished to see him. "But how can I go to him?" the lad asked. The son replied, "Hold onto my shoulders and close your eyes. Don't look until I tell you to do so."

They started into the water. As they moved along the son told the boy, "My father will offer you your choice of the animals in this lake. Be sure to choose the old mallard and its little ones."

When they reached his father's lodge, the son told the boy to open his eyes. He did so and was taken into the father's lodge. The old man said to him, "Son, come sit over here." Then he asked, "My boy, why did you come here?" The boy explained, "I have been a very poor boy. I left my camp to look for secret power so that I may be able to start out for myself." The old man then said, "Now, son, you are going to become the leader of your tribe. You will have plenty of everything. Do you see all the animals in this lake? They are all mine." The boy, remembering the son's advice, said, "I should thank you for giving me as many of them as you can." Then the old man offered him his choice. The boy asked for the mallard and its young. The old man replied, "Don't take that one. It is old and of no value." But the boy insisted. Four times he asked for the mallard. Then the old man said, "You are a wise boy. When you leave my lodge my son will take you to the edge of the lake. When it is dark he will catch the mallard for you. When you leave the lake don't look back."

The boy did as he was told. At the margin of the lake the water spirit's son collected some marsh grass and braided it into a rope. With the rope he caught the old mallard and led it ashore. He placed the rope in the boy's hand and told him to walk on, but not to look back until daybreak. As the boy walked along he heard the duck's feathers flapping on the ground. Later he could no longer hear that sound. As he proceeded he heard the sound of heavy feet behind him, and a strange noise, the cry of an animal. The braided marshgrass turned into a rawhide rope in his hand. But he did not look back until dawn.

At daybreak he turned around and saw a strange animal at the end of the line, a horse. He mounted it and, using the rawhide rope as a bridle, rode back to camp. Then he found that many horses had followed him.

The people of the camp were afraid of the strange animals. But the boy signed to them not to fear. He dismounted and tied a knot in the tail of his horse. Then he gave everybody horses from those that had followed him. There were plenty for everyone and he had quite a herd left over for himself.

Five of the older men in camp gave their daughters to him in return for the horses he had given them. They gave him a fine lodge also. Until that time the people had had only dogs. But the boy told them how to handle the strange horses. He showed them how to use them for packing, how to break them for riding and for the travois, and he gave the horse its name, elk dog. One day the men asked him, "These elk dogs, would they be of any use in hunting buffalo?" The boy replied, "They are fine for that. Let me show you." Whereupon he showed his people how to chase buffalo on horseback. He also showed them how to make whips and other gear for their horses. Once when they came to a river the boy's friends asked him, "These elk dogs, are they of any use to us in water?" He replied, "That is where they are best. I got them from the water." So he showed them how to use horses in crossing streams.

The boy grew older and became a great chief, a leader of his people. Since that time every chief has owned a lot of horses.

The third horse origin myth was told by Mrs. Cecile Cree Medicine in July 1947. She explained that her father, Running Crane, chief of the Lone Eater's Band of the Piegan, had told it to her. This myth I have also named.

HOW MORNING STAR MADE THE FIRST HORSE

Before the Piegan had horses they had dogs. Then everything was flint. There was no iron.

One night a Piegan invited all the chiefs to his lodge. He told his wife, "You sit outside with the baby." Her sister saw her sitting there and asked her what she was doing outside alone. She replied, "My husband does not want me to be in the lodge with the chiefs." She was very unhappy. Later she looked into the sky and saw the bright morning star. She said, "I wish 1 could be married to that pretty star up there."

Next morning she went to pick up buffalo chips for fuel. She saw a young man approaching her. He said, "Now I have come for you." But she replied, "I will have nothing to do with you. Why do you want me to go away with you? I'm married." Then the young man reminded her, "Last night when you were sitting outside your lodge you said you wanted to marry me, the bright star. I heard you and now I have come for you." She replied, "Yes, that's right. Let's go."

The young man said, "Take hold of my back. Follow me, but keep your eyes shut." She did as she was told. After a time the young man told her to open her eyes. When she did she saw that the country was strange to her. Young Morning Star then asked her into his lodge where an old man was sitting. He was Sun, Morning Star's father. Sun said, "My son, why did you bring this girl here?" The young man answered, "It was the girl's wish. So I went after her."

After a time Morning Star and this woman had a little boy. Old grandfather Sun said, "I shall give the boy something to play with." He gave him a crooked tree which was every bit the shape of a little horse, and said, "Now, my boy, play with this." When Morning Star saw his son playing with the wooden toy he said to his wife, "Wouldn't it look better if this plaything had fur like a deer?" She agreed. So they put fur on it. Then Morning Star said, "Another thing it should have is a tail." So he put a black tail on it and added some ears as well. Then he said, "Now let's take some black dirt and rub its hoofs so they will shine." So it was done.

Then his wife said to the Morning Star, "Now you are finished. Are you satisfied?" "No," replied Morning Star, "Put the boy on the animal's back. Let him ride it." When the boy was astride the toy, Morning Star said, "Now I shall make it go. I shall call sh-sh-sh-sh four times. The fourth time it will start like an animal." The first time Morning Star called, the horse began to move its legs. The second time, the horse began to move its tail. The third time it moved its ears. When he called sh-sh-sh-sh the fourth time the horse shied. Then Morning Star called "ka-ka-ka-ka," and the horse stood still. Morning Star cut a piece of rawhide for a bridle. The boy had great fun with his little horse.

Later, when the boy's brothers and sisters went to dig wild turnips, his mother asked Morning Star, "Why can't I do that?" He told her she might go with the others, but she must not dig the turnip with the big leaves. So she joined the party. She saw the big-leafed turnip and began to dig around it. At last she dug it up. Dust came up through the hole. When the dust cleared away she looked into the hole and way below she saw her own camp and her parents. She began to cry.

When she returned to Morning Star's lodge he saw her swollen eyes and knew what had happened. He asked her, "Why are you crying?" She told him that she was lonesome for her parents. Morning Star then told her she could return to them. He instructed his people to cut rawhide rope. They made a great pile of it. Then he told his wife, "I'll take you down the rope first. Then I'll take the horse down by my own power." He wrapped his wife and son in buffalo robes, tied them to the rope, and lowered them through the turnip hole.

Two young fellows lying on their backs near the camp of the woman's parents saw a strange object descending from the sky. They were frightened and started to run away when the bundle reached the earth. But the woman called to them, "Untie me." They untied her and went to camp to tell the woman's husband that she was back. When her husband saw the little boy he told his wife, "I don't want him here. Don't feed that boy. Don't give him any bedding. Let him sleep by the door." The woman was watched so closely she couldn't help her son. A half-brother took pity on the little boy. He hid some of his own food and gave it to the little boy to keep him from starving.

Morning Star saw how badly his son was treated on earth. One day when the half-brother took the boy into the brush hunting they saw a strange man. They were afraid and started to run when the man called, "Stop!" They halted and sat down beside the man. He told the little boy, "You are my son. I know your brother loves you and has fed you. But I have come after you because you have been abused." The little boy began to cry. "No, I want to stay with my brother." Then Morning Star explained, "Three of us cannot go. I can only take you. But I promise you I'll give your brother some great power here on earth."

Before he departed Morning Star told the older boy, "Go to that lake yonder. Sleep beside it for four nights. I'll give you power. The man in that lake will help you too. But I warn you that before sunrise, while you are sleeping, animals like I gave your little brother will come out of the lake. When you wake, pay no attention to the other horses. Just try to catch the little, shaggy, buckskin colt. If you catch that colt all of the other horses will stop beside him. If you don't catch him, all will run back into the water."

The morning after the older brother's first night by the lake he tried to catch one of the pretty colts rather than the ugly little buckskin Morning Star had told him to get. All of the horses ran back into the lake. The second morning the older brother tried again and failed. The third morning all of the horses got away once more. During the fourth night Morning Star came to the boy in his dream and said, "Now, my boy, I told you to catch that shaggy buckskin colt. If you don't catch him tomorrow you will not have my power."

Next morning, when the boy awoke he saw the horses again. This time he singled out the little colt and roped him with a rawhide line. All the other horses stampeded toward the lake. As the leading ones reached the shore the little buckskin whinnied. They all turned and ran back toward him. On the fifth night Morning Star again appeared to the boy in his dream, saying, "Now, my boy, when you return home with those horses give everyone but your father a horse. Because he abused you, he shouldn't have any."

When the boy returned to camp and distributed the horses, his father became very angry. "Why didn't you give me one of them?" he raved. The boy, with Morning Star's power, struck his father and killed him.

Morning Star then told the boy, "From now on your people will have horses. You will no longer need to use dogs. In time you will have many horses. Your horses will never disappear. You need never walk any more."

The principal chief of the camp sent word to the boy that he wanted him for a son-in-law. He gave the boy his two daughters and offered him his place as head chief.

More than 40 years ago Duvall obtained a condensed version of this third myth, which was said to have been told by Head Carrier many years before. As published (Wissler, 1912, pp. 285–286), this story links the origin of horses with the woman-who-married-a-star episode, although details of the creation of horses by the star differ from Mrs. Cree Medicine's version, and the episode explaining the later acquisition of horses by the older brother is lacking.

Two other Blackfoot myths explaining the acquisition of the first horse from the waters of a lake have been published. One account was told to George Bird Grinnell by Almost-a-Dog, a Piegan. It most nearly approximates the episode of the acquisition of horses from a lake by the elder brother contained in Mrs. Cree Medicine's version (Grinnell, 1895, pp. 166–168). The other myth, told Rev. Edward F. Wilson by the North Blackfoot chief, Big Plume, purports to explain how the Shoshoni first obtained horses from the waters of a large, salt water lake "away south" (Wilson, 1887, p. 185).

The number and variety of Blackfoot myths explaining the origin of horses may be due to the tendency for each narrator to elaborate the basic theme as he sees fit and to link the story of the origin of horses with portions of other myths. It is significant that the five recorded Blackfoot mythological accounts of the origin of horses credit the first horses either to sky spirits or to underwater spirits. In this respect the horse origin myths follow the tribal pattern of imputing the origin of their most sacred possessions to one or the other of these spirit sources. The Sun Dance and medicine pipe are represented in Blackfoot mythology as gifts of Sun and Thunder, two of the most feared and revered sky spirits. The beaver bundle and buffalo painted lodges are represented as gifts of the underwater people, also held in great awe by the Blackfoot. These myths constitute evidence that to the native mind the horse was a godsend of importance comparable to that of their most sacred ceremonies, created by the same supernatural powers who gave the Indians their traditional ceremonial institutions.[95]

---

[95] In the 1870's Lieutenant Bradley recorded a Crow myth to the effect that their first horses came out of the water (Bradley, 1923, pp. 298–299). Possibly Crow and Piegan myths relating to the water origin of horses developed from a common source. In 1947, Enoch Smoky recited to me a Kiowa myth, which he claimed his grandfather had told him. "It used to be that the Kiowa used only dogs for pack animals. Then one time an old medicine man had a dream in which he saw a strange animal. He began thinking about how he could make it. He took some mud and made a body, covered it with the hair of a prairie dog, gave it the eyes of an eagle, hoofs made from a turtle shell and wings to make it travel faster. But the horse flew away up into the air and did not return. There it remained to bring cyclones. Later the old man made another animal just like the first, but without wings. It was successful. From that time on the Kiowa have had horses."

THE INFLUENCE OF THE HORSE ON BLACKFOOT CULTURE

THE PRE-HORSE BLACKFOOT INDIANS

In the preceding pages I have described the many functions of the horse in Blackfoot Indian life of the Horse Culture Period. To evaluate properly the influence of the horse on Blackfoot life greater historical perspective is needed. We must try to characterize the culture of these tribes in the period immediately preceding their acquisition and use of horses, a period which, for purposes of contrast with the Horse Culture Period, I shall term the Pedestrian Culture Period. No European is known to have visited the Blackfoot during that period. Therefore, the literature contains no first-hand observations of Blackfoot life at that time. We must infer the conditions of that life from other sources.

It seems to me there are four types of source materials which may prove helpful in this reconstruction. These are: (1) the testimony of aged Piegan and a Cree Indian living among the Piegan regarding conditions and events of the Pedestrian Culture Period, in the late years of which they had lived, as recorded by David Thompson in 1787; (2) the traditions regarding life in the Pedestrian Culture Period surviving among aged Blackfoot Indians as reported in the literature or obtained by word of mouth in the field; (3) contemporary descriptions of the life of other buffalo-hunting tribes in the Pedestrian Culture Period written by white observers of those tribes; and (4) apparent survivals of Pedestrian Culture traits among the Blackfoot, and/or neighboring tribes to the eastward, who were relatively poor in horses in 19th-century buffalo days, as reported by 19th-century observers and more recent ethnologists. Our picture of Blackfoot life before the acquisition of horses must be a composite based upon a careful and logical weighting of the information derived from these four sources. At best this is an interpretation, not an exact portrayal.

Before we consider specific changes wrought in the culture of the Blackfoot as a result of their acquisition and use of horses, we must locate them and characterize their Pedestrian Culture economy in general terms. We need not concern ourselves here with the problem of the remote origins of the Blackfoot. Our interest lies in their geographical and cultural position in the years immediately preceding their acquisition of horses.

Kroeber (1939, p. 82) regarded the Blackfoot as "ancient occupants of the northern true plains or rather of the foothills of the Rockies and the plains tributary thereto." However, David Thompson, in 1787, found that the testimony of elderly Piegan (born and raised in the Pedestrian Culture Period) clearly pointed to that tribe's residence on the Saskatchewan Plains, near the Eagle Hills, some 400 miles east of the Rockies, in the early 18th century. It was not until after the Blackfoot tribes obtained both horses and guns that they pushed southwestward to the foothills of the mountains and the area that became their historic homeland (Thompson, 1916, pp. 327–329, 348).

Blackfoot traditions support this interpretation of the southwestward movement of these people in early historic times. This movement is also attested by traditions of the Flathead and Kutenai, whom the Blackfoot drove from the eastern foothills of the Rockies in present Alberta and Montana (Ferris, 1940, pp. 90–92; Thompson, 1916, pp. 304, 327–344, 463; Teit, 1930, pp. 316–321).

Assuming that the Piegan lived near the Eagle Hills and the Blood and North Blackfoot resided at no great distance from them to the northward or eastward in the period immediately preceding their acquisition of horses, it follows that the Blackfoot tribes were on the grassy plains well within the range of the buffalo at that time. This locality was north of the known limits of aboriginal maize cultivation in the Great Plains. Although the Blackfoot probably grew small plots of tobacco, it is improbable that they raised food crops. They were hunters of buffalo and smaller game and collectors of wild plant foods in season.

Thompson also found that elderly Piegan had "no tradition that they ever made use of canoes" (Thompson, 1916, p. 348). It appears clear, then, that the pre-horse Blackfoot of the early 18th century were pedestrians. Presumably they walked over the Plains, carrying their possessions by dog transport and on their own backs, in quest of buffalo, in warmer weather and retreated to timbered river valleys or to marginal forested areas in winter. The basic economy of the historic Blackfoot, characterized by dependence upon the buffalo for food, some clothing, and shelter (lodge covers), antedated the Horse Culture Period.

HORSE ACQUISITION AS A STIMULUS TO CULTURAL INNOVATION

The horse differed both physically and behaviorly from the dog, which had been the Indian's only domesticated animal and only beast of burden in the Pedestrian Culture period. This fact alone required extensive adjustments in the daily habits of Indians who undertook to acquire, breed, care for, and use horses.

The fact that the horse was a grass- rather than a meat-eater (as was the dog) compelled the Indians to pay close attention to pasturage requirements. Good grass for the horses became a determining factor in the selection of campsites and the duration of occupation of those sites. When horses consumed the grass in the neighborhood of a camp, that camp had to be moved. Eventually the Indians gained practical knowledge of the grasses and tree bark affording the best horse feed. They endeavored to locate their more settled winter camps in places where the best winter forage could be found. Thus the feeding habits of horses conditioned Blackfoot nomadism. In addition, the need to protect farflung grazing herds of horses increased the area of camps to be defended against enemy attacks.

The fact that the horse was too large to keep inside the skin lodge with the family, that it habitually strayed if not restrained or carefully watched, and that it did not bark (as did the dog) in the presence of strangers, presented problems in the care and protection of domesticated animals such as were unknown to Indians of the Pedestrian Culture Period. Methods of herding, hobbling, picketing, corralling, and specialized winter care were developed in attempting to solve these problems posed by the very nature of the horse itself. The daily care and breeding of sizable herds of horses gave to the old hunting culture something of a pastoral quality unknown to the cultures of most primitive hunting peoples.

The fact that the horse was larger and stronger than the dog and that it could be taught quickly to drag or bear heavy burdens or to carry a grown man on its back served to condition its functions in Indian culture. Methods of training horses and of teaching Indians to ride and manage these lively animals had to be perfected. These methods necessitated the learning of new motor habits on the part of the Indians. The manufacture of riding and transport gear became a new home industry requiring specialized manual skills. Adapting horses to the three primary uses of hunting, moving camp, and warfare presented numerous problems of varying complexity which challenged Indian ingenuity and stimulated thought. Whether the Blackfoot found answers to these problems for themselves or whether they borrowed the methods and techniques of other horse-using tribes, it is certain that every Blackfoot born and raised in the Horse Culture Period was required to learn motor and manual habits, owing to the presence of the horse in his cultural environment, of which Indians of the Pedestrian Culture Period were entirely ignorant.

Through careful observation of horses, while living in daily contact with them, the Blackfoot Indians gained remarkable understanding of these animals. Their knowledge is illustrated by their ability to distinguish their own horses from those of other owners on sight, without recourse to brands or other identifying marks; by their keen judgment of the relative values and merits of horses; and by their discrimination of some 10 types of horses on the basis of their ability and/or training to perform specialized services, i. e.: (1) the primary charger (buffalo hunting and war horse), (2) the winter hunting horse, (3) the common saddle horse, (4) the travois horse, (5) the pack horse, (6) the pole-dragging horse, (7) the race horse, (8) the stud, (9) the brood mare, and (10) the lead mare of a grazing herd.

That the horse, which literally lifted the Indian off his feet, broadened his concepts of area and distance, shortened his concepts of travel time, altered his opinions of the difficulties of moving camp and making a living, and that it quickened the tempo of his life and made that life more exciting, cannot be denied, even though we lack precise techniques for evaluating the psychological influences of the acquisition and use of horses upon the Indians.

INFLUENCE ON HUNTING

Blackfoot traditions point to the surround on foot as the favorite method of hunting buffalo before their ancestors acquired horses. Grinnell (1892, p. 234) obtained a tradition to that effect more than 60 years ago. Weasel Tail described a method of surrounding the buffalo which he had been told was employed by the Blood Indians before they had horses:

After swift-running men located a herd of buffalo, the chief told all the women to get their dog travois. Men and women went out together, approaching the herd from down wind so the animals would not get their scent and run off. The women were told to place their travois upright in the earth, small (front) ends up. The travois were spaced so that they could be tied together, forming a semicircular fence. Women and dogs hid behind them while two fast-running men circled the buffalo herd, approached them from up wind, and drove them toward the travois fence. Other men took their positions along the sides of the route and closed in as the buffalo neared the travois enclosure. Barking dogs and shouting women kept the buffalo back. The men rushed in and killed the buffalo with arrows and lances.

After the buffalo were killed the chief went into the centre of the enclosure, counted the dead animals, and divided the meat equally among the participating families. He also distributed the hides to the families for making lodge covers. The women hauled the meat to camp on their dog travois. This was called surround of the buffalo.

It is certain that Blackfoot traditions of the surround on foot are in keeping with similar traditions among the Cheyenne (Grinnell, 1923, vol. 1, pp. 264 ff.) and Kiowa (Mishkin, 1940, p. 20). Furthermore, contemporary writers furnished definite proof of the employment of the surround by pedestrian tribes farther east in hunting buffalo prior to 1700.

Sieur Pierre Deliette, who accompanied a village of the Illinois on a buffalo hunt in 1688, not only described their surround of the buffalo on foot, but observed that guards prevented the disruption of the communal effort by attempts to hunt alone in advance of the village. These guards punished offenders through destruction of their property "without the man or woman saying a single word" (Pease and Werner, 1934 b, pp. 307–311).

Henry Kelsey, the first white man known to have met Indians on the northern Plains, described the buffalo surround on foot of the Assiniboin or Cree in 1691:

> Now ye manner of their hunting these Beasts on ye Barren ground is when they seek a great parcel of them together they surround them with men which done they gather themselves into a smaller Compass Keeping ye Beasts still in ye middle and so shooting ym till they break out at some place or other and so get away from ym. [Kelsey, 1929, p. 13.]

Nicholas Perrot noted that some of the eastern marginal tribes fired the prairie grass to prevent the surrounded buffalo from escaping the pedestrian hunters (Blair, 1912, vol. 1, pp. 120–122).

Blackfoot traditions also refer to the impounding of buffalo and driving them over cliffs. They credit the mythological character, Blood Clot, with the initiation of the buffalo fall. We know that impounding buffalo was practiced on the Plains before the Indians acquired horses, for Spanish explorers witnessed the construction and use of a cottonwood corral by a village of 50 lodges of foot Indians near the Canadian River in 1599 (Bolton, 1916, pp. 227–228). The survival of impounding among the Assiniboin and Cree, eastern neighbors of the Blackfoot, until the end of buffalo days was due primarily to their relative poverty in horses.

Granted that the Blackfoot employed one or more methods of communal buffalo hunting before they acquired horses, we then have a clue to their community organization at that time. Surrounding or impounding of buffalo by footmen could not have been successfully accomplished by camps composed of relatively small family groups. The cooperative hunt necessitated a band or village organization of 10 or preferably more lodges. Saukamaupee told David Thompson of "small camps of ten to thirty tents" of Piegan which were obliged to separate for hunting in pre-horse times, as well as a large gathering of some 350 warriors who feasted and danced for several days before starting to battle against the Shoshoni ca. 1723 (Thompson, 1916, pp. 328–329). This suggests that pre-horse buffalo-hunting techniques were efficient enough to permit seasonal convocations of several bands or whole tribes. That, of course, was the seasonal pattern in the 19th century. Alexander Henry, in 1811, noted that the Piegan dispersed into small camps of 10 to 20 lodges in winter and united in large camps of 100 to 200 lodges in summer (Henry and Thompson, 1897, vol. 2, p. 723). Apparently the basic pattern of the Blackfoot yearly round was established before the introduction of horses in response to the requirements of buffalo hunting and ceremonial practices.[96]

Nevertheless, buffalo hunting on foot in the Pedestrian Culture Period must have been exceedingly dangerous, arduous, time consuming, and sometimes unsuccessful. Early historic accounts of impounding and falling buffalo told of repeated failures to lure the game into the traps prepared for them (Bolton, 1916, pp. 227–228; Cocking, 1908, pp. 109–112; Henry and Thompson, 1897, vol. 2, pp. 576–577).

If buffalo were nearly as plentiful on the Saskatchewan Plains in pre-horse times as they were known to have been in 1754 and later years, the early hunters occasionally must have slaughtered many more animals than their immediate needs required. This must have encouraged feasting on choice morsels and waste of considerable quantities of less desirable meat after a very successful hunt. On the other hand, the migratory habits of the buffalo and the limited mobility of the pedestrian Indians must have caused periods of food scarcity, reduced rations, and occasionally, perhaps, starvation. Probably famine was most common in winter in those days, just as periods of relative scarcity were experienced in later years when deep snows or icy ground prevented the use of horses in hunting. In the severest winter weather historic Blackfoot buffalo hunters enjoyed no advantage over their prehistoric ancestors. They were forced to revert to methods of stalking buffalo on foot which must have been practiced by their forebears long before horses reached the Blackfoot country.

In the matter of food supply the greatest advantage horse users enjoyed over their pedestrian ancestors lay in their ability to transport quantities of dried provisions to their winter camps in the fall of the year as insurance against hunger and starvation during the most inclement winter months. Not only could horsemen follow the buffalo more closely and keep within striking range of fresh meat throughout most of the year, but they could save a portion of their fair weather surplus for consumption during periods of foul weather scarcity.

Probably horses were first adapted to hunting buffalo in the communal hunt. In the mounted surround the Indians simply took advantage of the horse's greater mobility to expedite the kill. Horsemen also replaced footmen in driving and luring buffalo into pounds or over cliffs. The buffalo drive with the aid of horses survived until after the middle of the 19th century among the Blackfoot. Probably it was retained longest by those bands who were relatively poor in horses.

---

[96] La Vérendrye's (1927, pp. 311, 313) observations of the pedestrian, buffalo-hunting Assiniboin in 1738, mention their organization into sizable bands. In the fall of that year he met a village of 40 lodges, and visited another of 102 lodges.

It was the chase on horseback that fully exploited the horse's ability to run faster than the swiftest buffalo. This new hunting technique was more efficient and adaptable than any method previously employed. Not only did it require a fraction of the time and energy but it was less dangerous and more certain of success than other methods. It could be employed by a single hunter or the men of an entire village. Within a few minutes a skilled hunter, mounted on a fleet, intelligent, buffalo horse could kill at close range enough buffalo to supply his family with meat for months. Yet the chase required no new weapon. The bow and arrow, and lance, both certainly known to their pedestrian ancestors, remained the favorite weapons of Blackfoot buffalo hunters until the introduction of breech-loading rifles, barely a decade before the extermination of the buffalo. The effectiveness of the chase on horseback was due primarily to the employment of carefully selected, trained, long-winded, buffalo horses. Consequently these horses were prized possessions. Their selection and training became important men's activities.

Once a considerable number of tribal members acquired buffalo hunting horses, hunting on foot became obsolete as a warmer weather technique. As the trader, Nathaniel J. Wyeth, shrewdly observed a century ago, "It is a well-established fact that men on foot cannot live even in the best game countries, in the same camp with those who have horses. The latter reach the game, secure what they want, and drive it beyond the reach of the former" (Wyeth, 1851, vol. 1, p. 208). Police regulation of the tribal summer hunt, which we have noted was a characteristic of pre-horse communal buffalo hunting, preserved the fiction of equal opportunity for all. Actually it enabled the owner of the fastest running horse to get first chance at the herd. It deprived the poor man, who owned no buffalo horse, of the right to hunt. It is obvious that under such conditions the poor would have been much worse off than they would have been under pre-horse conditions, when every family in the camp participated actively in the hunt and shared of its spoils, unless special provisions were made for their benefit. The Blackfoot adopted two measures necessary for the welfare of the poor: (1) the loaning of buffalo horses to the poor by the wealthy, and (2) the presentation of outright gifts of meat to the poor by successful hunters.

Undoubtedly the quickness and ease with which buffalo could be dispatched by mounted hunters released active men's time and conserved their energies for other activities such as warfare, feasting, and ceremonies. A relatively small number of hunters could supply meat for a band while other young men of the camp journeyed on prolonged horse raids. Certainly the ease with which mounted hunters could kill buffalo encouraged the slaughter of many more animals than the Indians needed for subsistence and hastened buffalo extermination.

INFLUENCE ON CAMP MOVEMENTS AND POSSESSIONS

"In the old days, before the Blackfoot had horses, they were moving camp with dog-travois." So reads the start of a Blackfoot tale describing the origin of the Bear Lodge (Wissler and Duvall, 1908, p. 92). Many Blackfoot origin tales begin with references to the use of dogs as beasts of burden in the days before these Indians acquired horses. (See pp. 291, 295, this bulletin.) There can be no serious doubt of the historical validity of such initial statements. Probably use of dogs as beasts of burden was common to all Plains Indian tribes in pre-horse times. We know that Spanish explorers saw southern Plains tribes moving camp via dog transport in the 16th century (Winship, 1896, pp. 504–527; Onate *in* Bolton, 1916, pp. 226–227); that Bourgmont saw pedestrian Kansas traveling with loaded dogs in 1724 (Margry, 1886, vol. 6, p. 414); and that La Vérendrye witnessed the use of dog travois by horseless Assiniboin, near neighbors of the Blackfoot, in 1738 (La Vérendrye, 1927, pp. 317–318).

Both dog packing and the dog travois survived among the Blackfoot in historic times. William Gordon (in Chardon, 1932, p. 342) and John Work (1923, p. 129), fur traders, saw Blackfoot war parties packing moccasins, ammunition, and provisions on the backs of dogs in the early 19th century. In March, 1824, Alexander Ross (1913, p. 373) met "eight Piegan and a drove of dogs in train with provisions and robes for trade at the Flathead post." My aged informants recalled that even in their youth, in the waning years of buffalo hunting, families poor in horses made extensive use of dog travois, while heavy winter snows sometimes rendered horses useless for carrying or dragging loads, causing whole bands to revert temporarily to the use of dog transport.

Compared with the horse the dog was a bearer of relatively light burdens. Assuming that the dog employed by the Indians in pre-horse times was the same size and strength as the Indian dog of the 19th century, described by Bradley (1923, p. 278) as "very similar in appearance to the large gray wolf," I estimate a strong dog was capable of packing a load of approximately 50 pounds or of dragging 75 pounds on the travois.[97] Although early descriptions of the number of dogs seen under load in moving camps of Plains Indians mention as many as several hundred animals, the proportion of dogs to

---

[97] These estimates are based upon a survey of numerous estimates of the weight of dog loads appearing in the Plains Indian literature, as well as testimony of older informants.

families, when given in the literature, does not exceed 6 to 12. The necessity for feeding dogs (which were meat eaters like their masters)· must have placed practical limits upon the number of dogs owned in pre-horse days. Difficulties of managing dogs on the move must have been other factors limiting their numbers as burden bearers. Informants frequently mentioned the penchant of travois dogs for chasing rabbits or female dogs, for fighting among themselves, and for running into streams to drink while in harness. To prevent dog fights travois had to be spaced some distance apart while on the move. To supplement the services of the dogs, women of the camps had to carry heavy burdens on their backs. I have pointed out the survival of this custom among horse-poor tribes in historic times (pp. 142–143). Dog transport was wholly inadequate for conveying the aged, sick, or infirm adults. Informants estimated that a train of heavily loaded dogs would travel no more than 5 or 6 miles a day.

Limited transport facilities inevitably restricted the weight of baggage that could be carried by the pre-horse nomads, and thus limited their possessions. In 1599, Onate observed that the lodge covers of the southern Plains Indians met by his expedition were transported by medium-sized dogs and weighed less than "two arrobas" (50 pounds) (Bolton, 1916, p. 227). Unless the buffalo-cowskins of which those covers were made were dressed thinner, and therefore were lighter in weight than the buffaloskins used for lodge covers in later years, the covers seen by Onate must have comprised no more than six or seven skins. Six or seven skin lodges are attributed to the Blackfoot of the Pedestrian Culture Period in tribal traditions. Larger covers could have been used if they were made in two pieces, each transported on the back or travois of a single dog. But the necessity for dragging the lodgepoles, which increased in length and weight with the size of the lodge, must have encouraged the use of small lodges in the years before horses were available for pole dragging services.

One aged Blackfoot informant had heard a tradition to the effect that some of his pre-horse ancestors did not use a tipi at all but stretched buffaloskins over upended dog travois to form a shelter. The use of such a shelter would have eliminated the necessity of transporting tipi poles when camp moved. Grinnell (1923, vol. 1, p. 50) reported Cheyenne traditions of their former use of this type of shelter. Wilson (1924, pp. 223–224, figs. 51–55) described and pictured this type of structure as employed by Hidatsa in the third quarter of the 19th century when suitable tipi poles were not available. It provided sleeping quarters for as many as 11 people. Maximilian (1906, vol. 23, p. 16) actually saw horse-poor Assiniboin erecting temporary traveling huts of poles, dog travois, and brush near Fort Union in 1833. There is, therefore, ample proof of the use of a dog travois foundation shelter by northern Plains Indians. However, I am inclined to believe that the tipi probably was the primary dwelling of the Blackfoot of the Pedestrian Culture Period. All available information, both traditional and comparative, points to the relative smallness of the homes of the pre-horse Blackfoot.

Nevertheless, it is possible that two or more families may have shared a single lodge in order to minimize the load to be transported. In 1700, Le Sueur (1902, p. 187) noted that "two or three men with their families" lived in one buffaloskin lodge among the pedestrian Sioux near present Mankato, Minn. Three quarters of a century later the elder Henry (1809, p. 309) observed that two to four families resided in a lodge among the horse-poor Assiniboin.

The baggage that could be carried by dogs and women, over and above the lodge itself, must have been very limited. Elaborate lodge furnishings, numerous changes of clothing, extensive supplies of fresh or dried meat, wild fruits and vegetables would have been excess baggage to the pre-horse Blackfoot. So probably would have been large and bulky medicine bundles, such as the natoas, medicine pipe, and beaver bundles of the late 19th century represented in museum collections today. If such bundles existed they probably were of less complex, more rudimentary form. The great bulk of the baggage must have consisted of articles essential to daily living. In the meagerness of its possessions the average Blackfoot family of the Pedestrian Culture Period must have resembled the poor family of 19th century buffalo days, and for the same basic reason—lack of facilities for transporting heavy loads when camp was moved.

The application of horse power to camp movement enabled the Blackfoot to move farther and faster with heavier loads. The horse, packing 200 pounds on its back or hauling 300 pounds on the travois, could move four times the load of a heavily burdened dog twice as far in a day's march. Thus, animal for animal the horse was eight times as efficient as the dog as a burden bearer. Horse transport permitted the manufacture, use, and movement of lodges with larger and heavier covers and longer poles—larger Indian homes. Not only could the family of average means have a home of its own, but the wealthy family often possessed more than one lodge. Not only could essential possessions be moved, but bulky or heavy articles of only occasional use could be taken along. Women no longer were compelled to carry backbreaking burdens, but rode horseback and conserved their energies for other tasks. The aged and the physically handicapped could be carried on travois, and were no longer in danger of abandonment on the Plains by their able-bodied fellows.

Possession of a herd of horses was the prime requisite of the family that would enjoy these advantages of a higher standard of living. In historic Blackfoot culture that meant families of wealth and of the middle class. Poor families not only lacked these advantages but were handicaps to the more fortunate. When camp was moved the latter were faced with the problem of slackening their pace to that of the poor pedestrians, of leaving the poor families behind, or of furnishing the poor with enough horses to move their meager possessions at a more rapid rate. Enlightened self-interest motivated wealthy families in loaning some of their surplus horses to the poor for moving camp.

It is noteworthy that the dog travois did not become entirely out-moded after the acquisition of horses. The dog travois remained a useful contrivance for gathering wood near camp and for auxiliary transport in carrying light articles when camp moved. Lightly bur-dened dogs could keep pace with the more heavily burdened horses. Finally, possession of a number of dogs trained for travois duty served as insurance against some evil day when a family horse herd might be stolen by enemy raiders or lost through disease or winter storms, as well as against the hard winter when dogs might travel over crusted snows in which burdened horses would have bogged down.

INFLUENCE ON WARFARE

Saukamappee told David Thompson (1916, pp. 328–332) of large-scale battles between the Piegan and Shoshoni in pre-horse times, in which the opposing forces, although ostensibly seeking enemy scalps, were content to form lines facing each other, barely within arrow range, protecting themselves behind large rawhide shields (3 feet in diameter), while shooting arrows at their opponents from their long bows (the length of which came to their chins). This was a fire fight which continued until darkness put an end to the battle. Casualties were few and there was no close contact if the numbers of the com-peting forces were nearly equal. Although the warriors carried lances, knives, and battle axes, they apparently made no use of these shock weapons unless there was sufficient disparity in numbers between the forces to encourage the larger one to close with the enemy.

The acquisition of guns and horses rendered that old, static, pri-marily defensive, pitched battle obsolete. No longer could a warrior hide behind his shield in safety. Accent shifted to offensive mobility. Defensive weapons, the 3-foot shield and body armor, which impeded movement on horseback, were discarded. Only a small, rawhide shield, just large enough to cover the vital organs of a mounted war-rior, was used for protection. Even muzzle-loading firearms were of limited service to the mounted warrior, who found difficulty in reloading them on a running horse. The old reliable bow and arrows (the bow shortened to facilitate its use on horseback) remained the primary fire weapons, while the lance, war club, and knife continued in common use as shock weapons. The mounted charge brought combatants into close contact affording them opportunities for wielding their favorite shock weapons in hand-to-hand conflicts in which the skill, strength, agility, and courage of the individual were of vital importance. Although this man-to-man fighting tended to increase casualties greatly, it also offered much greater opportunities for Indians to achieve individual coups or war honors, which were scaled according to the degree of courage required to win them.

Saukamappee also informed Thompson (ibid., p. 329) that the greatest damage in the scalp raids of the pre-horse period occurred when a larger force surprised, attacked, and massacred a small camp of 10 to 30 lodges, which was obliged to separate for hunting. Probably that type of action was much more common in pre-horse warfare than the indecisive pitched battle between forces of nearly equal size. It also occurred with some frequency in historic times, with the same disastrous results.

The precursor of the horse raid in Blackfoot warfare must have been the slave raid. Girls or young women from neighboring tribes were captured for economic reasons as well as for purposes of sexual gratification. They provided needed assistance in the communal hunt, performed laborious household chores, and carried burdens when camp was moved. The early literature of the northern Plains tells of the practice of slave raiding in the middle of the 18th century. In fact, it was an "Earchethune" (Blackfoot or Gros Ventres) slave, taken to Fort York by her Assiniboin or Cree captors some time prior to 1743, who inspired James Isham to send Anthony Hendry to seek to open trade with the distant tribes of the Upper Saskatchewan in 1754 (Isham, 1949, pp. 113–15). At the "Archithinue" village of 200 lodges Hendry "saw many fine girls who were captives," proving that those people also took female slaves (Hendry, 1907, p. 339). The 50 or more slaves seen by Bougainville (1908, pp. 187–189) at the French posts in present Manitoba and Saskatchewan in 1757, probably included some Blackfoot women. As late as the first decade of the 19th century neighboring Cree still referred to the Blackfoot as "slaves," although by that time horse raiding had largely supplanted slave raiding in the warfare of the area (Henry and Thompson, 1897, vol. 2, p. 523). It seems fair to assume that the capture of female slaves, prominently mentioned by mid-18th-century observers, was a survival from pre-horse times and did not originate in the few years between the acquisition of horses and the first historic mention of slave raiding in and near the Blackfoot country.

We have no detailed description of northern Plains slave-raiding procedures, but the De Gannes memoir (Pease and Werner, 1934 b, pp. 375–388) gives a very clear account of Illinois slave raids against the Pawnee and Quapaw ca. 1700. Many elements of the Illinois slave raid closely resembled those of Blackfoot horse raids of historic times. Particularly noteworthy are the following: (1) the slave raid was distinguished in procedure from that of the large war party seeking scalps, (2) slave-raiding parties were small, not ordinarily exceeding 20 persons, (3) members carried birdskin war medicines, (4) youngest members performed menial tasks for experienced raiders, (5) scouts were sent ahead of the outgoing party to reconnoiter the enemy, (6) inexperienced members remained with the baggage in a concealed location, while (7) experienced men made a dawn attack on the enemy camp to secure prisoners, (8) the raiding party made a speedy departure with their prisoners, marching two days and nights without stopping, (9) the capture of a prisoner was reckoned as a war honor of higher rank than the killing of an enemy.

This slave-raiding pattern may have been an old one, widespread among Algonquian and perhaps other tribes as well, and known to the pre-horse Blackfoot Indians. Certainly, elements of this raid are clearly observable in the pattern of the Blackfoot horse raid of the 19th century as described by my informants and in the literature (see pp. 177–189).

The primary motive for Blackfoot horse raiding in the 18th century, when horses were new to the Blackfoot country, must have been economic—the desire to obtain animals needed for hunting buffalo and transporting baggage. I believe the economic motive remained dominant until the end of buffalo days. Need, not greed or glory, was the major stimulus impelling most young men to engage in the hazardous time and energy–consuming enterprise of the horse raid. Wealthy Blackfoot comprised a small minority. They were generally men of middle or advanced years, many of whom were unusually successful as breeders of horses. The average Blackfoot family found it difficult to meet the needs of its nomadic existence with the number of horses it possessed. There were few young men who did not need more horses than their families could spare them if they were to marry and raise families; while the sons of poor families, who far outnumbered the favored children of the rich, were noted as the most active and inveterate horse thieves. The fact that a captured horse counted as a war honor served as a secondary stimulus to horse raiding. But we must not overestimate the importance of that stimulus. This was a low-grade coup, an impressive assemblage of which alone would not qualify a man for leadership in his band.

It was the continuing economic need for horses, periodically heightened by serious losses of horses from enemy raids, destruction by plagues or severe winter storms, that made horse raiding the most common form of Blackfoot warfare and tended to perpetuate this type of warfare. Once undertaken, horse raiding continued, since its basic cause, an inadequate supply of horses to meet the needs of daily living, persisted. The horse raid remained the average young man's surest road to economic security and social advancement as long as the nomadic life based upon buffalo hunting persisted.

I have found no evidence whatsoever, of either traditional or comparative nature, to suggest that the Blackfoot ever made a practice of raiding neighboring tribes to secure dogs or were forced to defend their camps from attacks by enemy dog thieves. The defensive measures adopted against alien horse raiders, the individual lodge watch of picketed animals, and the corral, must have been developed after horses were acquired in response to the obvious need for their protection. Yet neither the Blackfoot nor their neighbors perfected an adequate, organized, nightly defense against enemy horse-raiding parties, something that could have been easily provided by placing a few armed men on watch each night. In the historic horse raid, as in the scalp raid, emphasis was placed upon offensive operations.

INFLUENCE ON TRADE

The important role of the horse in Blackfoot trade in historic buffalo days was due to this animal's recognized usefulness and the fact that the supply of horses never equaled the demand for them. It is doubtful if any item played a role of such importance in the barter of the Pedestrian Culture Period. In those days dogs must have had a much greater value than they did after horses relegated them to a place of secondary importance as burden bearers. A stronger than average, tractable travois or pack dog must have demanded a good price. However, dogs could have been bred in litters too rapidly for them to have been in short supply. Perhaps female captives (slaves) were the most valuable items of barter in those times. But the demand for them must have been limited compared with the later demand for horses. Probably food, clothing, lodges, ornaments, and weapons were bartered by the early Blackfoot among themselves if not in intertribal trade as well.

Although the historic Blackfoot commonly exchanged horses for buffalo robes, articles of clothing, weapons, and ceremonial bundles, the relative values of these articles in comparison with horses were not fixed. Trading generally involved agreement between the two parties engaged as to a fair exchange. Qualitative differences in horses were recognized.   A good race horse or a buffalo runner was worth several common pack animals.   Consequently the best horses had a premium value in trades involving items other than horses.   Even more subtle distinctions were made between the worth of two race horses or two buffalo horses.   Wealthy men were expected to pay more dearly than were people of modest means.

Live horses were always more valuable to the Blackfoot than were dead ones.   These Indians seldom killed horses for food, and then only in cases of dire necessity.   The hide, hair, teeth, and other horse products made into useful articles were derived from animals which had died of accidental or natural causes.   The number of these items was very restricted in comparison with the great variety of useful articles derived from buffalo.

INFLUENCE ON RECREATION

The prominent role of the horse in Blackfoot children's play during the Horse Culture Period mirrored the importance of that animal in the life of their parents at that time.   Children's play of the Pedestrian Culture Period probably tended to imitate the serious activities of their elders, and so differed from that of later children.   When boys made and played with wood, stone, or mud toy horses, or pretended to ride boldly on hobbyhorses; when girls "moved camp" with conventionalized stick horses equipped with miniature reproductions of riding and transport gear bearing miniature household equipment packaged and packed according to the custom of their culture, they were pleasantly and painlessly preparing themselves for more responsible participation in a culture in which management and use of horses were important aspects of daily life.

Horse racing probably replaced foot racing as the most popular sport of Blackfoot adults.   Buffalo hunting, interband communications, and intertribal warfare in the Pedestrian Culture Period must have placed a premium upon physical stamina and speed of foot. The great Miniconjou chief, One Horn, bragged to Catlin of his former ability to run down a buffalo on foot and kill it with an arrow, as well as his record of having won every foot race he had entered (Catlin, 1841, vol. 1, p. 211).   Yet the ability to run down a buffalo may have been fairly common in earlier times, when everyone hunted on foot.   As late as the middle of the 19th century Denig (1930, p. 566) noted that next to being a good hunter and warrior men of the Upper Missouri tribes prized "the name of being a good runner (fast and long)."   Foot racing survived among the historic Blackfoot in intersociety contests at the Sun Dance encampment, but horse racing surpassed it in popular interest.   Stamina, a quality necessary to the buffalo horse, was the greatest asset of the race horse, for the course, as a rule, was a lengthy one. No other horse was as highly prized by the Blackfoot as was the winning racer.

Indirectly the horse influenced other forms of Blackfoot recreation. I have described (pp. 236–238) the introduction of horse symbolism into the intersociety hoop and pole game. The common employment of valuable horses as stakes in gambling must have encouraged interest in other games of chance even though the games themselves may have been known to the Blackfoot in earlier times.

INFLUENCE ON SOCIAL LIFE

During the Pedestrian Culture Period, when men literally stood on an equal footing, class distinctions must have been less marked than in historic times. The cooperative hunt was an organization of near equals in which the kill was equally divided among participating families. Limited transportation facilities inhibited the accumulation of property and militated against social stratification based upon wealth. Undoubtedly individuals who achieved outstanding war records or possessed supernatural powers to call the buffalo (beaver bundle owners), to cure the sick, or to perform acts of magic attained positions of distinction and leadership which ranked them above the average man.

After the introduction of horses permitted the accumulation of property, social status came to depend less upon a man's physical and mental qualities and more upon the number and quality of his possessions. A class system began to develop in which there were rich, middle-class, and poor families, distinguished primarily on the basis of their relative wealth or poverty in horses.

The rich man owned not only the most horses but generally the best ones as well. Wealth in horses permitted rich men to care for and use their animals so as to increase their numbers and enhance their value. Rich men owned the largest and best-furnished lodges, the finest clothing, and the most sacred and valuable medicine bundles. They also enjoyed certain privileges denied the other classes. They had the widest choice of mates in marriage and could take the most wives. They could even get away with murder by presenting horses to relatives of the deceased man. On the other hand, the rich man was expected to accept responsibilities which men of the other classes did not shoulder. He was expected to assist the poor through gifts of food and horses and loans of horses for buffalo hunting and moving camp. He was expected to be generous in his hospitality and liberal in his barter with others. Probably no one was more genuinely disliked by the majority of the Blackfoot than the stingy man of wealth.

Blackfoot Indians of the middle class shared the advantages of that higher standard of living made possible by the ownership and use of horses. Generally their possessions were more modest in number, size, and/or quality than those of rich people, but they were surely finer and more numerous than those of the average Blackfoot in prehorse times. The middle-class man possessed the means to enable him to participate fully in the social, economic, and religious life of his band and tribe. On rare occasions he might need assistance from his relatives in assembling horses for gifts or purchases.

It is questionable, however, whether the poor were not worse off than they would have been in the Pedestrian Culture Period. Their possessions actually may have been no more meager than were those of the average family in earlier times. But during the Horse Culture Period their lodges, clothing, weapons, etc. were so inferior as to make their living definitely substandard. Lack of horses alone prevented them from hunting buffalo or moving camp with their fellows unless they received assistance through loans of horses by wealthy relatives or band leaders. They became dependent followers of the leader who offered them most in economic security. Their poverty denied them participation in many activities which previous writers have considered typical of Blackfoot culture in general, such as the companionship of polygamous marriage, membership in societies, the wearing of elaborately decorated dress clothing, and the manipulation of complex and powerful sacred bundles.

Yet under the conditions of life prevailing in buffalo days the Blackfoot class system did not become crystallized. Hazards beyond their control prevented members of the wealthy class from becoming permanently entrenched. Enemy horse raiders, winter storms, or disease might wipe out the rich man's herd quickly and without warning. Buffalo-Back-Fat's sage advice to members of his family (pp. 241–242) to invest heavily in valuable other than horses, might have counteracted the damaging effects of such losses upon social status had it been more widely followed. If wealth might be short-lived, poverty need not be permanent for the poor young man who possessed ambition and courage. Through aggressive action, in repeated raids upon enemy camps, he might acquire the horses necessary to raise both his economic and social status. The rise of poor but ambitious young men as well as the fall of unfortunate wealthy families kept the class system fluid.

Women's status was decidedly improved as a result of the acquisition of horses. Women were emancipated from the toil of carrying heavy burdens in moving camp and from active participation in prolonged hunts afoot. Some of the time and energy they saved may have been devoted to the perfection of arts and crafts for which there must have been an increased demand, now that people could transport many changes of clothing and seek handsome gear to show off their horses. The decadence of slave raiding decreased women's fears of being taken captive by alien peoples.

The coming of the horse offered greater security to the aged and the physically handicapped. Whereas their lives were formerly sacrificed because they could not be taken along with the moving camp, these people could live well in the Horse Culture Period if they owned horses which others might use to kill buffalo and move camp for them. Stingy, the wealthy, blind, influential Piegan (frequently mentioned in previous pages), probably would have died in infancy had he been born during the Pedestrian Culture Period.

The band, basic political and residential unit among the Blackfoot, probably was a stable, exogamic organization of blood relatives, led by the most able, mature man in the group in the Pedestrian Culture Period. By the waning decades of buffalo days the Blackfoot band had become a fluid organization, composed both of related and unrelated families, within which marriage was permitted. Necessity for extensive reorganization of bands following serious plagues and war losses in historic times undoubtedly contributed to this change in the character of Blackfoot bands. Dependence of the poor in horses upon the charity of wealthy leaders helped to keep the bands fluid. The poor followed the leader who was able and willing to offer them the greatest security through dispensing gifts of food and gifts or loans of horses. They readily shifted their band allegiance if they thought they could improve their condition thereby.

It is doubtful whether the ability to dispense individually owned property to other band members was a factor of any importance in the selection of a band chief in the Pedestrian Culture Period when, presumably, there were no marked extremes of wealth and poverty. However, in the Horse Culture Period requirements for band leadership came to include considerable wealth and a willingness to employ it for the alleviation of the poor.

INFLUENCE ON RELIGION

If the Blackfoot Indians looked upon dogs as sacred animals in the days when dogs were their only domesticated animals, their descendants appear to have no traditions regarding that attitude. I have found no trace in Blackfoot culture of a dog cult organized for the express purpose of appealing to dog spirits for aid in doctoring or influencing the actions of dogs.

On the other hand, the horse came to occupy a position of considerable prominence in Blackfoot religious beliefs and rituals. The sudden appearance of this animal, whose services did so much to lighten the daily tasks of the Indians and to raise their standard of living, demanded an explanation. The Blackfoot looked upon the horse as a godsend. In their mythology it was represented as a gift of powerful sky or water spirits. Horses were thought to possess supernatural powers. The ability of certain horses to perform feats of unusual strength or endurance was proof to the Indians that those animals possessed those powers to a very high degree.

Some horses were believed to have appeared to their owners in dreams and conferred their powers upon them. Through such transference of powers the secret horse medicine cult was believed to have originated. The relatively few members of this cult carefully guarded their knowledge of the origin of their medicines and restricted their use by outsiders in such a way that their secrets would not be revealed. Members were feared and respected by fellow tribesmen to the extent that many aged Indians still fear to discuss the cult. There are no other Blackfoot ceremonial organizations whose secrets have been so closely guarded, with the possible exceptions of the Horn Society among the Blood and the Tobacco Planters of the North Blackfoot. The influence of horse medicine men's activities pervaded the fields of warfare, hunting, recreation, and curing, as well as the daily lives of their people. Their ritual practices were designed to heal sick and wounded horses and to cure humans, to revive exhausted horses, to assist individuals in capturing horses from the enemy or in handicapping enemy war horses, to prevent hunting horses from falling in slippery winter weather and to retard the movements of buffalo in the hunt, to handicap race horses, to capture wild horses, and to prevent horses from straying from their owner's herds. Their ceremony, the horse dance, followed the generalized Blackfoot ceremonial bundle pattern but had distinctive features. Taboos observed by horse medicine men also were distinctive. There was a close relationship between the horse medicine men and owners of medicine pipes whom the horse specialists customarily aided. These specialists also aided other Indians in the preparation of protective "horse bridles" worn under the heads of war horses on scalp raids.

Indirectly the influence of the horse affected other Blackfoot religious rituals. Horse payments were invariably made as inducements to owners of ceremonial bundles to transfer their power to prospective purchasers. At intervals throughout the tribal Sun Dance ceremony participants were required to recite their coups, most commonly acquired through raiding for horses. In the two cases of self-torture during a Sun Dance that have been recorded in detail, the suppliants are known to have vowed to undergo the torture just before entering enemy camps to take horses.

Finally the horse was given a role of prominence in burial and mourning rites. The favorite horses of a wealthy individual were killed near his grave so that their spirits might accompany his to the afterworld and there continue to be of service. The family that could not afford to sacrifice a horse was content to cut the mane and tail of one or more horses belonging to the deceased. There is a tradition to the effect that dogs were sometimes killed at the graves of their owners before the Blackfoot acquired horses. If such was the case, the substitution of horses for dogs simply indicated Blackfoot recognition of the greater value and usefulness of horses in the afterworld as well as in this one.

THE HORSE AND THE FUR TRADE

It has not been my intention to argue the influence of the horse in Blackfoot Indian culture at the expense of minimizing the influence of the fur trade.[98] Both were powerful catalytic agents which contributed to the reshaping of Plains Indian culture in the historic period. Among the Blackfoot they were contemporary influences. Both the horse and trade goods began to reach the Blackfoot before the middle of the 18th century and remained potent influences until the end of buffalo days. However, it is not easy to isolate the influence of one as opposed to the other. The two influences complemented one another in bringing about radical changes in the tribal way of life. For example, both the horse and the fur trade encouraged Indian destruction of buffalo resources and contributed toward the extermination of the buffalo in the Blackfoot country. Use of horses made it easy for Indians to kill many more buffalo than were required for their subsistence. The fur trade, offering ready markets for excess hides and pemmican, made it profitable for them to do so.

Looking at the question historically, we must recognize that the Blackfoot played a relatively insignificant part in the fur trade prior to 1831. Both Anthony Hendry and Mathew Cocking dejectedly reported the "Archithinue" Indians' lack of interest in traveling to the British posts to trade in the third quarter of the 18th century. Known movements of the Blackfoot during the 18th century were away from the British and French posts on the lower Saskatchewan to the eastward of them, southwestward toward the tribes from whom they captured horses. After British posts were established in their country, on the Upper Saskatchewan, in the late years of that century and early years of the following one, the Blackfoot showed little interest in trapping small and valuable fur-bearing mammals for the trade. They preferred to hunt buffalo on horseback and to remain relatively independent of the traders. They traded primarily horses and pemmican at the forts.

---

[98] I have been a student of the fur trade among the Blackfoot for more than a decade. I am well aware of the influence of that trade on Blackfoot material culture.

It was not until the American Fur Co. established a post on the Missouri (1831) in Blackfoot country, and that company began to accept buffalo robes in trade, that the Blackfoot became important procurers of animal skins for the fur trade. Long before that time the Blackfoot had become experienced in the use of horses. Only through the use of horses for killing and transporting buffalo could the great number of robes supplied the traders by the Blackfoot in the period ca. 1835–80 have been obtained. Only through the exploitation of cheap and accessible land and water transportation could traders handle a sufficient volume of heavy, bulky, and relatively cheap buffalo hides to make trade in them profitable. The mountain men, who continued to collect the furs of smaller mammals and to transport them overland, made as extensive use of horses in their operations as did the Blackfoot, whom they tried to avoid.

Larpenteur's statement (p. 29, this bulletin) equating wealth in horses, polygamy, and extensive trade at the posts clearly shows the correlation between Indian wealth in horses (which permitted the killing of many buffalo), the polygamous union (which provided many female hands to dress robes and skins for market), and large-scale trade at the posts. It was the wealthy Indian who was the primary patron of the trading posts. Poor men had few robes to offer.

The fur trade furnished to the Indians new materials for use in their manufactures, arts, and crafts. Their use of horses influenced the form and function of many of the items made from these new materials. Metal knives obtained in trade greatly facilitated the manufacture of articles of rawhide. But these articles were primarily saddles, harness, and transport luggage especially designed for use in moving camp with horses. The fur trade supplied glass beads, cloth, metal, and shell for use in making and decorating articles of clothing, as well as horse gear. Yet in designing these articles the Indians were mindful of the enhancement of their appearance on horseback. Generally it was the wealthy family that possessed the most elaborately decorated costumes and riding and transport gear. Those who owned no horses had none of them.

Both the horse and the gun influenced Indian warfare, encouraging the abandonment of fighting in closely grouped, static lines, in favor of mobile, spread formations. Both horse and gun encouraged the abandonment of heavy, rawhide body armor which impeded physical movement without providing adequate protection from gunfire. When first employed by the Blackfoot against enemies unfamiliar with the use of firearms, the muzzle-loading flintlock created a panic among their opponents out of all proportion to its true effectiveness as a fire weapon (Thompson, 1916, pp. 330–332). But in later years, after both the Blackfoot and their neighbors were armed, the muzzle-loader proved an ineffective cavalry weapon, because of the difficulty of reloading it on a running horse. The Blackfoot hunter and warrior continued to employ the traditional bow and arrow as his principal fire weapon until the introduction of breech-loading rifles in 1870, a decade before the disappearance of the buffalo.

One change in the material culture of the Blackfoot (and other Plains Indians) that some writers have attributed to the influence of the horse should properly be credited to fur-trade influence. That is the decline and disappearance of pottery making among the nomadic tribes. I do not believe the introduction of horses had anything to do with that change. The earthen pot could have been transported just as safely and more easily on horseback or the horse-drawn travois as on the dog travois. The disappearance of pottery was due to the substitution of the metal trade kettle for the native-made clay vessel (Ewers, 1945 a, p. 296).

It is difficult to see that the fur trade materially influenced Blackfoot social or political organization save through the disastrous epidemics introduced by way of its river craft, which compelled band reorganization after the plagues were spent. Those chiefs who gained in prestige through their close association with the traders generally were men of outstanding accomplishment by Indian standards. Lesser traders who married Indian women may have helped to raise the status of these women's families thereby. However, it is doubtful if the marriage of Alexander Culbertson, the most influential trader in the Blackfoot Country, to the Blood woman, Natawista Iksana, greatly strengthened the position of her brother, Seen-From-Afar. He was the son of the Blood head chief, and a man of ability, so recognized by his own people. He is still remembered as "the great chief" who owned more horses than any other Blood Indian.

SURVIVALS

Many traits characteristic of the Horse Culture Period in Blackfoot history were abandoned in the period 1880–1905. Extermination of the buffalo eliminated the horse's important functions in hunting. Settlement in permanent log houses eliminated the horse's functions in moving camp. Enforcement of intertribal peace brought an end to horse raiding and the use of horses in warfare. In this period, when local authority passed from the native chiefs to the Indian Agent, who attempted to carry out the national Indian policy of the time, i. e., encouragement of Indians to adopt white men's ways, some of the traits most intimately associated with Indian use of horses were drastically modified. The Indians adopted the white man's stock saddle and bridle, his method of mounting, his wagon and harness, his names for horses, and his horse commands. Even the

Indian pony gradually was replaced by larger and stronger animals resulting from the breeding of white men's work horses with the Indians' stock.

Nevertheless, the continuity of Blackfoot culture was not entirely broken by the cultural revolution that followed the disappearance of the buffalo and the abandonment of the nomadic, hunting existence. In the 1940's, six decades after the buffalo were gone, the influence of the Horse Culture Period of buffalo days survived. Survivals were noticeable in Blackfoot work habits, their concepts of wealth, their recreation, social relations, and ideals.

After the buffalo were gone the Blackfoot took readily to cattle raising but showed little interest in or aptitude for farming, which involved techniques and procedures alien to their experience. In the 1940's Agricultural Extension Agents on the Blackfeet Reservation in Montana recognized that the successful Indian farmers were persons of considerable white admixture. The fullblood group showed little interest in settling on the irrigated projects to grow crops. Fullbloods still preferred to make their living by raising livestock, primarily cattle and sheep. This preference is traceable to the tribe's generations of accumulated experience in the care of horses and its lack of crop-growing traditions.

I have pointed out (p. 30) the survival of the concept of wealth in terms of horse ownership among the older fullbloods on this reservation, even though horses in the 1940's had relatively little monetary value. This is definitely a survival from the days when individual wealth was determined primarily in terms of horse ownership.

I have also (p. 234) referred to the survival of interest in horse racing, long a favorite sport among the Blackfoot. In fact their ready acceptance of the entire rodeo complex may be attributed to their background of appreciation of skill in the handling of horses.

There remains an appreciation of the value of ceremonial bundles among the Blackfoot which is out of all proportion to the function of those bundles in the religious life of these people in modern times. A number of bundle owners have neither the knowledge nor the desire to use these sacred bundles ceremonially. Yet they are reluctant to part with them, mindful of the fact that their former owners prized them as equivalent in value to many horses. The horse medicine cult, though limited in function, still holds a respected position in the religious life of the fullbloods.

Blackfoot social relations are still marked by the dependence of poor relatives upon tribal members who have achieved a degree of economic success. This drain of the "have-nots" upon the "haves" has the effect of limiting the economic progress of ambitious individuals, if not actually of inhibiting the desire of fullbloods of extensive family connections to achieve material success. Along with that traditional custom of sharing, the traditional ideal of generosity survives to inhibit the adaptation of the white man's ideals of budgeted expenditures and saving for a rainy day.

The intense patriotism of the Blackfoot in volunteering their services to their country in two World Wars is a survival of the traditional Blackfoot concept of the warrior ideal. During World War II, when the Blackfoot furnished a much greater proportion of their able-bodied population for military service than was required of them, one still heard fullblood parents comforted by the old adage of buffalo days, "It is better for a man to die in war than to die of old age or sickness."

Finally, there survives among the Blackfoot a genuine love of horses that is the heritage of a people whose ancestors' admiration for horses amounted to veneration.

THE PLAINS INDIAN HORSE COMPLEX

ELEMENTS IN THE HORSE COMPLEX OF THE PLAINS INDIANS

In pages 20 through 298 of this work I have described the factors of ownership, care, breeding, training, and use of horses, and beliefs regarding horses that collectively comprised the horse complex of the Blackfoot Indians in 19th-century buffalo days. In the footnotes and brief comparative sections of those pages I have presented comparative data regarding the existence of the same traits among other horse-using tribes of the Great Plains and the Plateau.

Let us now turn to this comparative material in an effort to define as precisely as possible the elements in the basic horse complex of the historic Plains Indians. I should like to be able to present a graphic chart listing the elements of the horse complex for each tribe. However, the comparative material is too fragmentary to make such a detailed comparison of many elements possible. In the absence of more complete comparative data I believe it is legitimate to infer that any traits in the horse complex of the Blackfoot which have been reported for two or more other, geographically noncontiguous tribes of the area were common to a greater number of Plains Indian tribes and may tentatively be considered part of the basic horse complex of the Plains Indians.

I have endeavored to itemize the traits of this basic horse complex as specifically as existing data permit. Undoubtedly, if the literature on the care, breeding, training, and use of horses among other Plains tribes was more precise and more voluminous this list of traits could have been extended. I am of the opinion that, with this study as a guide, reliable information on these aspects of the horse complex can still be obtained from elderly fullbloods of a number of Plains Indian tribes, and that such information would tend to increase the total number of traits listed below (asterisks indicate local variations):

Ownership traits:
  Horses individually owned, private property.
  Wide range in numbers of horses owned by individual tribal members.
  Owner recognized his horses by their appearance and actions (no identifying marks placed upon the animal).

Care traits:
  Color names given to horses.
  *Boys responsible for daily care of family herds.
  Wild grass primary horse feed.
  Horses watered thrice daily.

Care traits—Continued

Horses left to rustle for food in winter snows.

Supplemental feeding of cottonwood bark in winter.

*Picketing choice horses near lodges at night.

Losses of horses in severe winters common (especially among northern nomadic tribes).

Plant medicines used to treat common horse ailments.

Rawhide shoes used to protect sore-footed horses.

Breeding traits:

Many male animals gelded.

Training traits:

Lariat used for capturing wild horses.

Horses broken for riding at an early age (commonly 1 to 3 years).

Horses broken for riding in water (plus other methods).

Children taught to ride by tying them in the saddle.

Children learned to ride alone by 5th or 6th year.

Riding and guiding traits:

Verbal commands used to stop and start but not to turn horses.

Well-trained horses guided without use of reins.

Right side mounting customary for right-handed riders.

Both sexes rode astride.

Use of short stirrups.

Riding-gear traits:

War bridle most common form (2-reined, continuous line, looped around horse's lower jaw).

Use of some form of trailing line to permit rider to recover horse if thrown from the saddle.

Use of a rawhide lashed, wood- or horn-handled whip.

*Saddle making a woman's occupation.

Use of stuffed-skin pad saddle by active young men.

Use of wood frame, rawhide-covered saddle by women.

Use of wood and horn frame saddle for packing.

Small-sized frame saddles made for children's use.

Horses commonly saddled and cinched from right side.

Use of a buffaloskin saddle blanket.

Use of a skin saddle housing.

Use of a rawhide crupper.

Spurs not in common use.

Horses painted to represent valorous acts of owner.

Horses' tails decorated with feathers.

Travois and transport gear traits:

Use of horse travois for transporting infirm.

Makeshift travois of lodgepoles sometimes used for transporting household equipment.

Lodgepoles dragged in two bundles (one each side of horse or mule) by means of a specialized hitch.

Willow-frame sunshades used on true or makeshift travois.

Parfleche (made in pairs) used as packhorse luggage.

Double saddlebag carried on women's riding horses.

Rawhide (rectangular and/or cylindrical) saddlebags carried on women's riding horses.

Camp movement traits:

Main body surrounded by mounted advance, side, and rear guards.

Men rode saddle horses; women saddle or travois horses.

Babies transported on horseback with mothers.

Toddlers and aged or infirm carried on true or makeshift travois.

Small children (learning to ride) tied on horseback.

Lodge cover folded and carried on packhorse (less commonly on the travois).

Meat transported in parfleche.

Women responsible for packing and moving household equipment.

Men carried only arms and accouterments.

Poor in horses borrowed horses to transport possessions, or walked using dog travois.

Drinking water required on march carried in paunch containers.

Winter camp moved when grass inadequate for horse feed.

Average distance of normal day's march, using horses for transport, 10 to 15 miles.

Mules used primarily as pack animals.

Hunting traits:

The buffalo horse, a well-trained animal, used only for hunting, war, and dress parade.

Employment of buffalo surround on horseback.

The chase on horseback favored method of buffalo hunting.

Buffalo horse led to hunting ground to conserve its energy.

Mounted hunters lined up to give them an equal start in the chase.

Preference for bow and arrow, secondary use of lance in mounted buffalo hunting (prior to introduction of breech-loading rifles).

Right-handed bowmen approached buffalo from right.

Right-handed lancers approached buffalo from left.

Maximum kill in a single chase by mounted hunter, four or five buffalo.

Taboo against packing meat on a buffalo horse.

Women cared for buffalo horses after return of hunters.

Loaning of buffalo horses to the poor for hunting.

Strict regulation of summer, tribal hunt by men's societies.

Hunting of buffalo on foot when snow or ice prevented use of horses in winter.

*Mammals other than buffalo rarely hunted from horseback.

Warfare traits:

Need for horses an important cause of intertribal wars.

The horse raid, a distinctive type of military operation.

*Small horse-raiding parties most common.

Horse raiders drummed and sang war songs before departure.

Individual war medicines carried by members of horse-raiding parties.

Packs of equipment carried by horse raiders relatively standardized.

*Horse raiders commonly went to the enemy on foot.

Horse raiders constructed temporary lodges for their protection on outward journeys.

Captured horses distributed among members during return journey.

Raiders encouraged to give away horses on return from successful raids.

The scalp or revenge raid, a military expedition distinct from the horse raid.

The buffalo horse served as a war horse in battle.

Scalp raiders commonly rode common horses, saving their primary horses for battle service.

Warfare traits—Continued

Preference for bow and arrow in mounted warfare (prior to introduction of breech-loading rifles).

Lance and war club principal shock weapons of mounted warriors.

Corrals built to protect horses from capture by enemy raiders.

General laxness in night guarding of horse herds against enemy raids.

Ambushes set to counter expected attacks by enemy raiders.

Capture of enemy horse recognized as a war honor.

Trade traits:

Horses common media of exchange in intertribal and intratribal trade.

Qualitative value distinctions recognized in horse trading.

*Horse not commonly killed for food.

Use of horsehide for drumheads.

Social relations traits:

Social stratification based upon relative wealth in horses.

Wealth in horses a virtual requirement for band chieftaincy.

Size of the portable lodge largely determined by relative wealth in horses.

Positive correlation between number of horses owned and quality and quantity of other family possessions.

Polygamy and wide selection of marriage mates positively correlated with wealth in horses.

Dependence of the poor in horses upon wealthy leaders a factor in band organization and fluidity of bands.

Exchange of horses as gifts in marriage.

Horse payments made in retribution for offenses committed.

Give-away of horses to enhance social prestige of donor.

Recreational traits:

Horse toys used in children's play.

Horse racing a popular sport.

Race horses especially trained and highly valued.

Horse races were tests of endurance rather than sprinting speed.

Sham battles performed on horseback to amuse and impress visitors.

Horses commonly employed as stakes in gambling.

Religious traits:

Secret, powerful horse medicine cult, members of which were believed to have derived their powers from horses.

Use of plant medicines as horse stimulants.

Horses killed as grave escorts on death of prominent owners.

Horses' tails and manes cut in mourning for dead owners.

Belief in the supernatural powers of horses.

Myths explaining the supernatural origin of the first horse or horses obtained by the tribe.

This list of 119 traits in the horse complex of the Plains Indians reflects the unevenness of the available comparative data. Numerous traits are listed in the hunting and warfare categories because the details of the hunting and war practices of many tribes are relatively well known. On the other hand, a single trait appears in the breeding category. Undoubtedly, if we knew more about the horse-breeding customs of other tribes, other entries might be added in this category. But the subject of horse breeding has been neglected to the point that comparative data cannot be found in the literature. This list of traits reflects the current state of our knowledge of the details of the Plains Indian horse complex. It is subject to modification and extension through future research.

Asterisks placed beside several of the traits listed above indicate, as mentioned, that there were local variations in these traits. Thus, while the majority of the Plains Indians seem to have entrusted care of horses to boys, the horse-poor Cree men are reported to have cared for their horses themselves. The horticultural Mandan, Hidatsa, and Arikara picketed their best horses inside their earth lodges at night and fed corn to horses. Among the marginal Chiricahua Apache, men rather than women were the saddlemakers. The Comanche and Kiowa of the southern Plains not uncommonly organized large-scale horse-raiding expeditions which rode into Mexico and carried off large numbers of stolen horses. The wealthy tribes of the southern Plains and the Plateau appear to have made much more use of horses in hunting animals of the deer family than did the great majority of the Plains Indians. The Blackfoot themselves probably were atypical in their relatively weak development of intertribal trade in horses. The list as presented appears to define most precisely the horse complex of those tribes which, like the Blackfoot, were middle class in terms of horse ownership. Variants from this norm certainly occurred among the horse-poor Assiniboin and Cree, the horticultural tribes, and the wealthy Indians of the southern Plains and Plateau.

ORIGINS OF THE PLAINS INDIAN HORSE COMPLEX

Although comparative data on the distribution of elements in the Plains Indian horse complex are far from complete, existing data do show that many traits in this complex were widely diffused over the area from the Apache, Comanche and/or Kiowa in the south to the Assiniboin and/or Cree in the northeast and the Nez Percé and/or Flathead in the northwest. Why should there have been such widespread uniformity?

This brings us to the problem of the origin of elements in the horse complex, a problem made exceedingly difficult by the meagerness of historical information on the early years of horse use in the Great Plains. Certainly no one would suggest that each tribe of this vast region independently invented all the traits in its horse complex. It is equally certain that this complex, which was so well integrated into the buffalo-hunting economy of the Plains Indians, was not borrowed in its entirety from some nonbuffalo-hunting people living outside the Great Plains. Rather the complex appears to have comprised a fusion of traits originating in different sources. It appears that each trait in the complex was derived from one or another of three major sources of origin: (1) customs of horse-using white men which were borrowed by the Plains Indians, with or without modification, (2) adaptations of preexisting Indian traits to new conditions resulting from the use of horses, and (3) Indian inventions following the acquisition of horses in response to specific needs created by the problem of efficient use of the new animals in their native culture.

In considering the diffusion of traits from horse-using Whites I am mindful of the facts that Plains Indian Horse Culture was based upon the use of animals obtained from Europeans, and that this culture developed within the Colonial Period on and beyond the frontiers of white settlement. Opportunities for white influence on the development of the Plains Indian horse complex were numerous in the early years of Indian experience with horses, and during those years which were but poorly covered by contemporary literature. Initial stimulus came from the Spanish of the Southwest, from whom the horses themselves were obtained. There is ample proof that branded Spanish horses and articles of Spanish riding gear were diffused as far north as the Saskatchewan Valley before 1800. We must remember also that English and French traders, who possessed extensive knowledge of European horse usages, were among the Plains Indians in the 18th century. Some of those traders lived in close contact with the central and northern tribes. Through example or suggestion these traders may have contributed to the formulation of the horse complex of the Plains Indians years before many of the traits of this complex were specifically mentioned in the literature.

Nevertheless, in spite of the numerous and in some cases prolonged European contacts with the Plains Indians before 1800, relatively few traits in the horse complex of these tribes in the third quarter of the 19th century can be traced to European influences with any degree of probability. It is possible that the influence of individual white traders on this complex was so subtle as to evade detection, and that this influence was greater than ever can be demonstrated. However, only the following traits can be listed as probably of European origin, on the basis of our present knowledge:

Use of a rawhide-covered, wooden frame saddle.
Use of short stirrups.
Use of a crupper.
Use of a martingale.
Use of a double saddlebag.
Use of horse armor (limited among the Indians).
Use of the lariat.
Use of horse corrals.
Gelding of male horses.

The following additional traits in the Plains Indian horse complex *may* be of European origin:

Color names for horses.
One or more Spanish horse commands.
Use of surcingle method of breaking horses for riding.
Use of mules primarily as pack animals.
Use of a pad saddle.

The use of a mountain-lion-skin saddle housing may have been adopted from Spanish-Mexican practice of the Colonial Period.

It is noteworthy that the majority of the traits suggestive of white influence are concerned with riding gear and transport equipment. Such articles could have been copied or adapted from specimens that fell into the hands of Indians who had no direct contacts with Whites. However, if such traits as use of the lariat, gelding, color names, horse commands, and the surcingle method of breaking were borrowed from Whites, they must have been learned through direct contacts with Europeans and close observation of their customs.

On the other hand, the Plains Indians rejected a number of traits of European horse culture. These were:

Branding as a means of ownership identification.
Use of spurs.
Use of bitted bridles.
Left side mounting.
Use of the sidesaddle by women.
Spanish method of using the lance by horsemen.
Spanish men's preference for riding male animals.

We know also that Indians customarily broke their horses for riding at an earlier age than did the Spaniards. Spanish use of horse armor was imitated by a limited number of Plains Indian tribes. Obviously the Indians were not slavish imitators of European horse usages. They were selective in their borrowing and redesigned equipment or modified practices to suit their particular needs and their own tastes.

By far the greater number of items in the Plains Indians' horse complex inventory appear to have borne the stamp of Indian ingenuity.

A number of traits in this horse complex appear to have been adaptations of customs in common practice among these tribes before the introduction of horses. The inspiration for the adoption of these traits must have come from within Plains Indian culture rather than from outside it. A number of these traits, and the suggested source of inspiration for each, follows:

Use of plant medicines in doctoring horses. (Plant medicines previously used in treating humans and probably dogs.)
Use of the horse travois. (An adaptation of the dog travois for use with a larger and stronger animal.)

Employment of the buffalo surround on horseback. (An adaptation from the prehistoric buffalo surround on foot.)

Use of the bow and arrow and lance as weapons in hunting buffalo on horseback. (Previous use of these weapons in hunting buffalo afoot.)

Regulation of the summer, tribal hunt by men's societies. (Previous regulation of communal hunts afoot.)

Horse raid procedures. (Adaptations from procedures in slave raids afoot.)

Preference for the bow and arrow as fire weapons of mounted warriors. (Previous use of the bow and arrow by warriors afoot.)

Use of the lance and warclub as shock weapons by mounted warriors. (Previous use of these shock weapons by footmen.)

Use of the rawhide shield as a defensive weapon by mounted warriors. (Previous use of the shield by footmen.)

Capture of enemy horses recognized as a war honor. (Capture of slaves previously recognized as a war honor.)

It is most probable that many traits in the horse complex associated with the use of horses in hunting, warfare, and camp movement were continuations of or modifications from similar Plains Indian traits of the Pedestrian Culture Period.

Numerous traits in the Plains Indian horse complex must have been developed by the Indians in response to the necessity for devising measures for the care, training, and use of the new animals after these Indians acquired horses. Others reflect the Indians' peculiar attitude toward the new animal. Perhaps the most distinctive of those traits that appear to have originated de novo among the Plains tribes, without influence from foreign sources or suggestions from any of their own practices of the Pedestrian Culture Period, were:

Boys responsible for daily care of family herds.
Supplemental feeding of cottonwood bark in winter.
Picketing choice horses near lodges at night.
Children taught to ride by tying them in the saddle.
Right side mounting customary for right-handed riders.
Use of the war bridle.
Use of the trailing line.
Parfleche used as packhorse luggage.
The buffalo horse, a well-trained animal, used only for hunting, war, and dress parade.
The buffalo chase on horseback.
Taboo against packing meat on a buffalo runner.
Use of horse as shield by mounted warriors.
Horse toys used in children's play.
Sham battles on horseback to amuse and impress visitors.
Horses commonly employed as stakes in gambling.
Social stratification based upon relative wealth in horses.
Secret, powerful horse medicine cult, members of which were believed to have derived their powers from horses.

It seems apparent that even though the Plains Indians derived their horses from Europeans within the Colonial Period, their own contributions to the development of specific traits in their horse complex were much greater than were those of outsiders. It was the adaptation of the European horse to the service of a nomadic, buffalo-hunting people that gave to the Plains Indian horse complex its distinctive character. It was the Plains Indians, who had hunted buffalo long before the appearance of the horse, who determined the role the new animal was to play in their life, and who were primarily responsible for developing the details of their own horse complex.

THE HORSE COMPLEX IN PLAINS INDIAN HISTORY

THE NATURAL AND CULTURAL SETTING

The vast herds of buffalo that roamed the grassy plains between the Mississippi River and the Rocky Mountains made that area one of the finest natural hunting grounds in the world. From the time of Folsom Man, some 10,000 or more years ago, until the extermination of the buffalo ca. 1880, dependence upon the buffalo was a characteristic of the Indian cultures of this area. In the period immediately preceding the spread of the Spanish horse over the Great Plains the dominant culture of the area was shared by those tribes living along the fertile river valleys, in semisedentary villages, growing crops of corn, beans, and squash. Undoubtedly, these tribes relied heavily upon buffalo meat to supplement their vegetable diet. Presumably they hunted buffalo extensively during those periods of the year when they were not actively engaged in planting, cultivating, or harvesting their crops. The distances traveled in these hunts must have depended upon the relative scarcity or availability of buffalo near their villages. The Mandan in the north, the Pawnee in the Central Plains, and the Wichita in the south were the westernmost of these horticultural tribes. Westward of them, on the High Plains, lived several tribes who were nomads, depending upon the wandering buffalo herds for their livelihood, which they followed on foot carrying their portable lodges and meager possessions with them on dog travois and on their own backs. It seems most probable that these tribes included the Blackfoot in the north, the Shoshoni-Comanche in the Montana-Wyoming area, and the Kiowa, and Apache (Coronado's "Querechos and Teyas") farther south. There may have been other tribes that have since disappeared or were absorbed by known tribes. Compared with the toil and uncertainty of the nomad's life, that of the gardening tribes must have appeared relatively easy and secure to the Indians of the time.

Their experience with dogs as transport animals prepared the Plains Indians for acceptance of the horse as a stronger and more useful "big dog," which would relieve them of carrying heavy burdens and expedite buffalo hunting. The Indians were fortunate also that their grasslands afforded excellent range for horses on which these herbiverous animals would thrive and increase in numbers with relatively little care. Cultural and natural conditions greatly encouraged the ready acceptance of the horse by the Plains tribes and their rapid conversion from pedestrians to horsemen.

I believe the role of the horse complex in the history of the Plains Indians can best be comprehended in terms of three periods, as follows.

1. PERIOD OF DIFFUSION AND INTEGRATION

(From the first acquisition of horses by Plains Indians to about 1800)

In view of the elemental simplicity of Plains Indian methods of breaking horses and teaching individuals to ride, I see no reason to believe that any prolonged period was required for the conversion of pedestrian Indians to horsemen. I believe that the most important determinant of the rate of diffusion of horses from tribe to tribe was the number of animals available, and that the number of horses traded or captured from Spanish or Pueblo Indian sources increased as the 18th century progressed. This increase, combined with the natural increase in the herds possessed by Indians, made possible wider distribution of horses over broader areas. Although tribes on the periphery of the Spanish Southwest may have begun to acquire them as early as 1640, horses were a novelty to the majority of the northern Plains tribes a century later. The great period of horse diffusion in the northern portion of the Great Plains was from ca. 1740 to 1800. A Blackfoot Indian, born ca. 1725, could have witnessed the acquisition of the first horse by his people and lived to see the relative stabilization of tribal horse holdings among them by ca. 1800.

In the northward spread of horses trade appears to have been the most important avenue of diffusion. The primary center of diffusion was the Spanish Southwest from which horses were traded or stolen and driven northward to secondary diffusion centers among the Shoshoni in western Wyoming or Montana, and at or near the horticultural villages on the Missouri. From these secondary centers horses were traded to other tribes of the northern Plains, sometimes passing through tertiary centers of diffusion such as the annual trading fair on the James River where horses obtained by the Teton from the Arikara were traded to other Dakota tribes. The number of tribes engaged as primary intermediaries in supplying the secondary centers gives a clue to the expanding nature of this trade. Presumably the Ute were the earliest suppliers of the Shoshoni center, while the Comanche entered this trade after 1705. The Kiowa and Kiowa Apache seem to have been the earliest suppliers of the horticultural tribes on the Upper Missouri. Sometime after 1750 the Comanche appear to have shifted their trade to the horticultural tribes. Prior to 1800 the Cheyenne and Arapaho had entered the trade between the primary center and the horticultural tribes, while the Crow became active in acquiring horses at the Shoshonean center and trading them at considerable profit on the Missouri.

Raiding for horses appears to have been a secondary avenue of diffusion, necessitated by the inability of Indians to purchase needed horses at prices they could afford to pay for them. Certainly horse raiding was common throughout the area from the Spanish frontier to the Saskatchewan Plains in the last quarter of the 18th century.

The 18th century witnessed the widespread adaptation of horses to their three primary uses among the Plains Indians—i. e., as riding animals in hunting and warfare and as burden bearers in moving camp. Whether the Indians preferred to use horses for riding or for transporting equipment in the early years of their experience with these animals, when their horse holdings were limited, is an interesting question. In 1719 La Harpe (Margry, 1886, vol. 6, p. 279) and Valverde (Thomas, 1935, p. 131) noted that the Lipan and El Cuartelejo Apache transported their lodges by dog traction, while they employed horses in warfare. On the other hand, Hendry (1907, p. 351) observed that the Eagle Hills Assiniboin used horses "for carrying the baggage and not to ride on" in 1755. Although these data are not sufficient to fully justify such a conclusion, they suggest the possibility that those tribes in direct contact with horse-using Spanish peoples may have adopted the horse initially as a riding animal, while some tribes remote from the primary diffusion center preferred to employ their first horses as a replacement for dogs as beasts of burden. Yet Hendry witnessed "Arthithinue" Indians riding horses in the buffalo chase on the Saskatchewan Plains in 1754. We know that the Pawnee of the Central Plains hunted buffalo on horseback before 1700.

Undoubtedly, the hostile pressure from Ojibwa, armed with firearms, was an important factor in the westward movement of Algonquian and Siouan tribes from Minnesota and the eastern Dakotas toward the High Plains. However, once these tribes had become Plainsmen and had acquired horses their greater mobility enabled them to halt the westward movement of their pedestrian enemies at the forest margin. In 1798, an Ojibwa chief explained to David Thompson (1916, p. 264):

While they (Sioux) keep to the Plains with their Horses we are no match for them; for we being footmen, they could get to windward of us, and set fire to the grass; when we marched for the Woods, they would be there before us, dismount, and under cover fire on us. Until we have Horses like them, we must keep to the Woods, and leave the plains to them.

Before 1800 the Arapaho, Gros Ventres, Crow, and Cheyenne, traditionally horticultural tribes, had become nomadic hunters and all except the Gros Ventres had become actively engaged in supplying horses to the secondary diffusion centers on the Upper Missouri. Although the Arapaho-Gros Ventres may have begun to move westward as a result of pressures from the eastward before horses reached the Missouri River area, it appears most probable that they did not relinquish horticultural practices until they became aware of the advantages of hunting buffalo on horseback. I should prefer to look upon the conversion of all those formerly horticultural tribes to nomadism as part of the great movement leading to the concentration of many hunting tribes in the formerly lightly populated High Plains, where buffalo were most numerous, in the 18th century. This movement of tribes proceeded from both east and west, into the High Plains. The powerful Dakota tribes moved westward, with the Teton in the lead. Farther north the Assiniboin and Cree moved in the same direction. From the west, and probably somewhat earlier owing to their earlier acquisition of horses, the Shoshoni, Flathead, Pend d'Oreille, and Nez Percé entered the High Plains only to be later driven back by the southwestward movement of the aggressive Blackfoot. Yet those tribes continued to make periodic hunting excursions in force to the buffalo plains. Within the High Plains there was a general southward movement of tribes toward the primary diffusion center for horses. The Apache were pushed southward by the powerful Comanche and the Kiowa and Kiowa-Apache followed, being in turn forced to move by the advancing Teton. While this movement continued in the 19th century with the southward drift of the Arapaho and Cheyenne as well as the Blackfoot, it was set in motion long before 1800.

Once strange peoples then came into frequent contact on the High Plains. Their meetings resulted in exchanges of objects and ideas among which were traits of the horse complex itself. As might be expected, this close proximity also caused conflicts over hunting grounds and horses. Ambitious young men, needing horses to gain economic and social status among their own people, stole them from neighboring tribes. Horse raiding not only engendered intertribal wars but tended to perpetuate them.

During the 18th century the culture of the nomadic horse-using buffalo hunters became the dominant culture of the Great Plains. Tabeau (1939, pp. 151–153) in 1803, explained the abandonment of horticulture by the Cheyenne on the Missouri a few years earlier as a direct result of their unfavorable competition with the nomadic Sioux.

The Sioux always wandering, left little for capture to the enemy, who often knew not where to find them, and the Cheyennes, settled there were every day exposed, in spite of their superior courage, to some particular catastrophe. To lessen this disparity more, they abandoned agriculture and their hearths and became a nomadic people.

Farther to the southwest a similar drama was being enacted, in which Apache tribes were forced to abandon their fields and flee southward to escape the pressure of the aggressive, better armed Comanche (Thomas, 1940, pp. 58–59).

Before 1800, the stability which the growth of crops had given to the horticultural tribes, and which in pre-horse times had made their way of life more secure than that of the nomadic hunters, had become a handicap. Their sedentary villages were surrounded by mobile horsemen who attacked and insulted them or made peace to obtain garden produce in exchange for surplus products of the chase, at will. Penned up in their compact villages, the horticultural tribes on the Missouri suffered heavy losses from the white man's plagues, beginning with the smallpox epidemic of 1781.

Even though many of the traits in the Plains Indian horse complex were not specifically mentioned in the literature until after 1800, it appears most probable that the great majority of the traits in this complex were widely diffused over the area before that date. Even the distinctive horse medicine cult, first mentioned in Tabeau's description of the Arikara in 1803, was probably an 18th-century innovation.

Whether or not the horse complex was sufficiently well formulated in the minds of members of some of the tribes engaged in supplying horses to the secondary diffusion centers in the middle of the 18th century to permit its being borrowed almost in toto by some of the northern tribes is questionable. However, it does seem reasonable to suppose that ideas regarding the care, training, and use of horses and attitudes toward horses, as well as the animals themselves were exchanged at those primitive market places. Certainly extensive borrowing must have taken place long before the establishment of white men's trading posts on the Upper Missouri or the inauguration of white traders' rendezvous in the Wyoming country. We may even question whether the fur traders' rendezvous itself was not an adaptation of the Indian horse traders' fair in the same general region in protohistoric times.

2. PERIOD OF CRYSTALLIZATION AND MAXIMUM UTILIZATION

(From about 1800 until the extermination of the buffalo)

Before 1800 the use of horses had spread among the Indian tribes to the natural limits of the Great Plains in the northeast and across the Rockies beyond the Plains in the northwest. The first eight decades of the 19th century constituted the heyday of Plains Indian Horse Culture. By and large, traits of the horse complex observed at or near the beginning of the century persisted until the extermination of the buffalo. The horn pommel and cantle pack saddle appears to have been the only material culture trait in the complex invented within this period. It spread rapidly over the Plains and into the Plateau. There was a tendency during this period for horse raiding to replace trading as the most common means of acquiring horses. Among those tribes which were not poor in horses there was a tendency toward the abandonment of the buffalo drive and the surround in favor of the chase. It was probably during this period, after memories of the first acquisition of horses had become dim, that the beautiful mythological explanations of the origin of horses became popular.

The relative wealth in horses of the tribes of the area changed little during this period. No tribe is known to have advanced from poverty to wealth in horses, nor was a wealthy tribe reduced to poverty. Individuals were actively increasing their herds through breeding and capture of enemy horses. Their activities were offset by loss of horses stolen by the enemy and through deaths.

The horticultural tribes of the Upper Missouri continued to decline in numbers and relative importance, offering little in the way of furs to the traders and limited opposition to the advancing frontier of white settlement. The powerful, nomadic, buffalo-hunting tribes, the Teton Dakota, Arapaho, Cheyenne, Comanche, and Kiowa were the principal fighters of the Plains Indian wars aimed at preventing white invasion of their beloved hunting grounds.

3. PERIOD OF DISINTEGRATION

(From the extermination of the buffalo to the present)

With the extermination of the buffalo, settlement of the Indians in permanent dwellings upon reservations, and the end of intertribal warfare, the three primary functions of horses in their traditional culture—their use in hunting, moving camp, and warfare—were rendered obsolete. In their adjustment to a new way of life, with the encouragement of the Government, Indians adopted white men's horse usages. Even the Indian pony has become nearly or entirely extinct. Yet there remain among other tribes, as among the Blackfoot, survivals of customs and attitudes which are remainders of their Horse Culture heritage.

OLD THEORIES AND NEW INTERPRETATIONS

Two opposing theories regarding the influence of the horse upon Plains Indian culture have been presented by able and experienced students of Plains Indian life.

Clark Wissler, in his pioneer study entitled, "The Influence of the Horse in the Development of Plains Culture" (Wissler, 1914), expressed the belief that the traits which he regarded as most characteristic of Plains Indian culture of the historic period (the tipi, the travois, the foot war party, the coup, the Sun Dance, the camp circle, men's societies, and the circumscribed range with summer and winter camps) were, or probably were known to the Plains Indians before they acquired horses. He concluded that "There is no good evidence at hand to support the view that the horse led to the development of the important traits," that "no important traits, material or otherwise, were either dropped or added," and that "from a qualitative point of view the culture of the Plains would have been much the same without the horse." He believed that "as an intensifier of original Plains traits, the horse presents its strongest claim."

Kroeber, in "Cultural and Natural Areas of Native North America" (Kroeber, 1939, pp. 76-77), warned against such an "essentially static conception" of Plains Indian culture history.

> Could any good-sized group have lived permanently off the bison on the open plains while they and their dogs were dragging their dwellings, furniture, provisions, and children? How large a tepee could have been continuously moved in this way, how much apparatus could it have contained, how close were its inmates huddled, how large the camp circle? How often could several thousand people have congregated in one spot to hold a four or eight days' Sun dance? By the standard of the nineteenth century, the sixteenth-century Plains Indian would have been miserably poor and almost chronically hungry, if he had tried to follow the same life. Showy clothing, embroidered footgear, medicine bundle purchases, elaborate rituals, gratuitous and time-consuming warfare, all these he could have indulged in but little—not much more than the tribes of the intermountain or southern Texas regions. [Kroeber, 1939, pp. 76-77.]

These views of both Wissler and Kroeber reflect the paucity of specific information on the details of the pre-horse culture of the Plains Indians which existed when they prepared their statements and still exists (and which is a handicap under which any student of the problem must labor), as well as the lack of a careful analysis of the Plains Indian horse complex as a basis for their reasoning. Kroeber appears to have been unduly skeptical of the possibility of groups of communal bison hunters existing on the Great Plains before the introduction of horses. Rugged as their life may have been compared with that of later horse-using nomads, we have both archeological and early historical proof of its existence. From the time of Folsom Man until the appearance of horticultural practices only a few centuries prior to the introduction of the horse into the area, the inhabitants of the Great Plains were hunting peoples. Spanish explorers in the 16th century met sizable villages of pedestrian hunters dwelling in portable skin lodges, moving camp with the aid of dogs, and impounding buffalo on the southern Plains, whose sustenance "comes entirely from the cows, because they neither sow nor reap corn." The archeologist Waldo R. Wedel (1940, p. 327) cautiously observed, "It does seem possible, though, that the "Querecho-Teyas" type of life in 1541 was already rather old, and furthermore that it was very similar to, if not a direct continuation of, cultural habits deduced by the prehistorian from remains at the few geologically old sites which have thus far been intensively worked in western Nebraska and northern Colorado." [99] It does not seem probable that the numerous buffalo drive sites in Montana and southern Alberta were used entirely by horse-using peoples. I am of the opinion that *the* reason European explorers failed to find a pedestrian buffalo-hunting people on the northern High Plains was that horses had already been introduced to that region before white men reached it.

It is my contention that the horse complex was adapted to a preexisting pedestrian buffalo-hunting economy the bearers of which readily recognized that horses would be of great advantage to their way of life. The culture of the pedestrian hunters may have included most if not all of the traits Wissler has ascribed to it as well as other traits which survived with little modification in the Horse Culture Period. Nevertheless, I cannot believe that Plains Indian life in the Horse Culture Period, which included such elements as the daily care, breeding and training of horses, the teaching of children to ride, the chase, specialized riding and transport gear adapted to the use of horses, new methods of packing and transporting camp equipment, frequent horse raiding and mobile scalp raiding, extensive trade in horses, social status based upon property ownership, important role of the horse in children's play, horse racing, and the horse medicine cult, did not differ qualitatively as well as quantitatively from Plains Indian life in the Pedestrian Culture Period. The use of horses not only enriched the material culture of the tribes who acquired them but it altered their habits of daily life, served to develop new manual and motor skills, changed their concepts of their physical environment and the social relationships of individuals.

Probably the most distinctive new trait of the Horse Culture Period was social rather than material in nature. The adaptation of horses to the Plains Indian economy brought about a change from a relatively classless society to a society composed of three classes, which graded almost imperceptibly into one another, and in which membership was determined largely upon the basis of horse ownership—a privileged but responsible upper class, a relatively independent middle class, and an underprivileged and dependent lower class. The influence of this class system not only was apparent in Indian care and use of horses, but it was active in trade relationships between individuals, in marriage, in legal procedures and religious practices. Failure to recog-

---

[99] Dr. Wedel confirmed and expanded this thought in his article entitled "Some Aspects of Human Ecology in the Central Plains" (Amer. Anthrop., vol. 55, pp. 504–505, 1953).

nize the existence of these classes has, in the past, resulted in an idealized portrayal of Plains Indian culture based primarily upon the activities and attributes of the wealthy.

I find closest analogies to this class system not among the pre-horse cultures of the Great Plains, but among horse-using nomadic peoples of other continents. Patai (1951, p. 410) has briefly described the three-class system, based upon relative wealth in horses within the local groups among the nomads of Central Asia. Murdock (1951, pp. 421–422) recognized "social gradations based upon wealth or military prowess" as a distinctive characteristic of the horse-using nomads of the South American pampean area. Does it not seem probable that a tendency toward a class system based upon ownership of property (particularly in horses) was characteristic of horse-using nomadic peoples, and that this characteristic distinguished their cultures qualitatively from that of pedestrian nomads?

It appears to me that the influence of the horse permeated and modified to a greater or lesser degree every major aspect of Plains Indian life. Considering the rapidity of its adaptation, the number and diversity of the horse's associations in Plains Indian culture was truly remarkable. Edward Sapir, in his brilliant work entitled "Time Perspective in Aborginal American Culture, a Study of Method" (1916, p. 21), has proposed as one test for inferring the relative age of an element in culture that, "The more frequently an element is associated with others, the older, generally speaking, it will be felt to be. . . . One feels that it takes considerable time for an element of culture to become so thoroughly ramified in the cultural whole as to meet us at every step." The application of this test to the case of the horse in Plains Indian culture of the third quarter of the 19th century, when horse associations in the culture greatly outnumbered dog associations, would lead to the totally erroneous conclusion that these Indians had known and used horses for a longer period than they had employed dogs. In the case of the horse, the remarkable number and diversity of its associations must have been due to the readiness with which these Indians accepted this new animal and the remarkable adaptability of the culture and the horse to one another.

My studies of the influence and functions of the horse in Plains Indian culture have impressed me with the need for further research on a number of aspects of the problem. To gain a better understanding of the influence of the horse among these Indians we should have additional historical, descriptive, and comparative studies. There is a need for a careful analysis of the Spanish-Mexican horse complex of the Colonial Period which will afford us a detailed, factual basis for comparison with the horse complex of the Plains Indians. We should have similar studies of the horse usages of English, French, and early American fur traders operating in and near the Great Plains. The search for manuscript materials which may shed additional light on Plains Indian horse usages during the important period of diffusion and integration of the horse complex prior to 1800 should be encouraged. At the same time there is a need for careful analysis of the horse complexes in buffalo days of several additional tribes, based upon field studies with elderly informants as well as published and manuscript materials. When and if such studies are made among one of the southern Plains tribes which was formerly wealthy in horses (Kiowa or Comanche), among one or more of the Plateau tribes which was formerly wealthy also, and among one of the northern nomadic tribes which was poor in horses (Assiniboin or Plains Cree), we should have a much better basis for recognition of the common elements and local variations in the horse complex of the Plains Indians than we have now.[1] Furthermore, detailed comparison of the Plains Indian horse complex with the horse complexes of nomadic groups of southern South America, Central Asia, and the Near East should provide a better understanding of horse nomadism as a way of life.

---

[1] Since the present work was written, the volume entitled "The Comanches, Lords of the South Plains," by Ernest Wallace and E. Adamson Hoebel, has appeared (Norman, Okla., 1952). Although this book contains a chapter entitled "The Horse and the Buffalo," it does not provide the detailed information on Comanche horse culture needed for comparative study.

APPENDIX

USE OF MULES

The Mexican mule, described by Captain Marcy (1859, p. 112) as "square-built, big-bellied and short-legged" in comparison with the larger American mule, reached the Blackfoot country little if at all later than did the horse. Anthony Hendry saw "four Asses" in the "Archithinue" camp on the Saskatchewan Plains which he visited in October 1754 (Hendry, 1907, p. 339). David Thompson wrote of a Piegan raid on a Spanish party far to the southward, which may have occurred as early as 1787, in which these Indians captured many mules as well as horses. He also described another raid by the Piegan on the Shoshoni in 1787, during which the raiders took horses and 15 mules (Thompson, 1916, pp. 370, 341–342). Buffalo-Back-Fat, noted Blood head chief prior to 1850, is said to have been especially fond of mules. He is reputed to have owned as many as 60 mules at one time. His younger relatives and friends gave him any mules they captured from enemy camps. He kept his mules in a separate herd.

The Blackfoot tribes continued to take mules from their enemies until the end of intertribal horse raiding in 1887. Before mid-century they began to obtain the larger American mules which had been stolen or traded from overland emigrants or the United States Army by tribes living to the south of the Blackfoot. Weasel Head, a Piegan informant, claimed to have stolen six mules from the Crow in the days of intertribal warfare.

The Blackfoot tribes never bred mules. Wissler found that "mules were highly prized" by the Blackfoot "as they were thought to have superior powers of various kinds. Their origin was regarded as mysterious" (Wissler, 1910, p. 97). However, Weasel Tail claimed that Blood Indians early learned from the Nez Percé how these hybrids were bred from the union of a mare and a donkey. Informants stated that the Blackfoot valued mules highly because of their strength and smartness.

In my informants' youth the Blackfoot tribes used mules primarily as transport animals. Weasel Head claimed mules' necks were too strong to permit their use as tractable riding animals. They were employed primarily for hauling lodgepoles in moving camp. A strong mule could haul at least a third more poles than could the average Indian pony. Some mules also served for packing meat and camp equipment. Weasel Tail said that in his youth the Blood used

341

a mule to bring in the center pole for the medicine lodge. They lashed two stout lodgepoles to each side of the mule, tied two shorter poles across those poles at the usual position of a travois loading platform, and lashed the butt end of the center pole securely to these cross poles with a broad rawhide rope. The upper end of the center pole dragged along the ground as the mule pulled the load. Piegan informants had no knowledge of their tribe's use of mules for this purpose.

Because of their superior strength mules had a greater trade value than packhorses in intratribal trade among the Blackfoot. A mule owner could ask two horses for his mule and receive them in exchange.

Comparative data on use of mules.—In 1805, Lewis and Clark saw mules with Spanish brands among the Shoshoni which were "the finest animals of that kind we have ever seen . . . . The worst are considered as worth the price of two horses, and a good mule cannot be obtained for less than three and sometimes four horses" (Coues, 1893, vol. 2, p. 559).

In the 1870's the Crow Indians stole mules from the Sioux, many of which bore the United States brand, indicating that the Sioux in turn had taken them from the Army. The Crow "liked to get these animals for dragging lodge poles" (Marquis, 1928, p. 101). Wilson (1924, p. 277) indicated Hidatsa preference for mules as pack animals. My Kiowa informants said their tribe also used mules primarily for packing.

Among the tribes near the Mexican and Texan settlements mules were more common than among the northern tribes. George Catlin, during his visit to a large Comanche encampment in 1834, observed that about one-third of these Indians' herds were composed of mules "which are much more valuable than horses" (Catlin, 1841, vol. 2, p. 62).

It is noteworthy that the Spanish of Sonora in the middle 18th century valued a mule at twice the price of a horse, and used mules primarily for packing heavy loads (Pfefferkorn, 1949, pp. 94–95).

BIBLIOGRAPHY

ABERT, JAMES WILLIAM.
 1846. Journal of Lieutenant J. W. Abert, from Bent's Fort to St. Louis in 1845. U. S. 29th Congr. 1st sess., Sen. Doc., vol. 8, No. 438.

ADAIR, JAMES.
 1775. The history of the American Indians. London.

AGREEMENT MADE WITH INDIANS OF THE BLACKFEET RESERVATION BY COMMISSIONERS APPOINTED UNDER ACT OF MARCH 2, 1895.
 1896. U. S. 54th Congr. 1st sess., Sen. Doc., vol. 4, No. 118.

AITON, ARTHUR S.
 1939. Coronado's muster roll. Amer. Hist. Rev., vol. 44, No. 3, pp. 556–570.

ALEXANDER, HARTLEY BURR.
 1939. The horse in American Indian culture. In "So Live the Works of Men." Albuquerque, N. Mex.

AMERICAN FUR COMPANY PAPERS.
 MS. Manuscript materials in the New York Historical Society Library, New York.

AUDUBON, MARIA R., EDITOR.
 1897. Audubon and his journals. 2 vols. New York.

BANCROFT, HUBERT HOWE.
 1888. California pastoral, 1769–1848. San Francisco.

BARRETT, S. A.
 1922. Collecting among the Blackfeet Indians. Milwaukee Publ. Mus. Year Book for 1921.

BARTLETT, JOHN RUSSELL.
 1854. Personal narrative of explorations and incidents in Texas, New Mexico, California, Sonora, and Chihuahua connected with the United States and Mexican Boundary Commission, 1850–53. 2 vols. New York.

BATTEY, THOMAS C.
 1875. Life and adventures of a Quaker among the Indians. Boston.

BISHOP, MORRIS.
 1933. The odyssey of Cabeca de Vaca. New York.

BLACKFEET AGENCY ARCHIVES.
 MS. Manuscripts in the Museum of the Plains Indian, Browning, Mont.

BLAIR, EMMA HELEN, EDITOR.
 1912. The Indian tribes of the Upper Mississippi Valley and region of the Great Lakes. 2 vols. Cleveland.

BOLLER, HENRY A.
 1868. Among the Indians. Eight years in the Far West: 1858–1866. Philadelphia.

BOLTON, H. C.
 1897. The language used in talking to domestic animals. Amer. Anthrop., vol. 10, No. 3.

BOLTON, HERBERT E., EDITOR.
1916. . . . Spanish exploration in the Southwest, 1542–1706. *In* "Original narratives of early American history." New York.
1949. Coronado, knight of Pueblos and Plains. New York.

BOUGAINVILLE, LOUIS ANTOINE.
1908. Memoir of Bougainville, 1757. The French regime in Wisconsin, 1743–1760. Ed. by Louise Phelps Kellogg. Wisconsin Hist. Soc. Coll., vol. 18. Madison.

BRACKETT, COL. A. G.
1917. A trip through the Rocky Mountains. Montana Hist. Soc. Contrib., vol. 8.

BRADBURY, JNO.
1817. Travels in the interior of America, in the years 1809, 1810, and 1811. Liverpool and London.

BRADLEY, JAMES H.
1896–1923. The Bradley manuscript in the Montana Historical Society Library. Helena, Mont. Publ. in part Montana Hist. Soc. Contrib., vols. 2, 3, 8, 9.
1900. Affairs at Fort Benton. Montana Hist. Soc. Contrib., vol. 3.
1923. Characteristics, habits and customs of the Blackfeet Indians. Montana Hist. Soc. Contrib., vol. 9.

BURNET, DAVID G.
1851. The Comanches and other tribes of Texas . . . *In* Schoolcraft, Henry R., "Historical and statistical information respecting the history, condition and prospects of the Indian tribes of the United States," vol. 1, pp. 229–241. Philadelphia.

BUSHNELL, DAVID I., JR.
1922. Villages of the Algonquian, Siouan and Caddoan tribes west of the Mississippi. Bur. Amer. Ethnol. Bull. 77.
1927. Burials of the Algonquian, Siouan and Caddoan tribes west of the Mississippi. Bur. Amer. Ethnol. Bull. 83.
1940. Sketches by Paul Kane in the Indian country, 1845–1848. Smithsonian Misc. Coll., vol. 99, No. 1.

BUTSCHER, LOUIS C.
1942. A brief biography of Prince Paul Wilhelm of Wurtemberg (1797–1860). New Mexico Hist. Soc. Rev., vol. 17, No. 3.

CABRERA, ANGEL.
1945. Caballos de America. Buenos Aires.

CAMPBELL, FRED C.
MS. Blackfeet industrial survey (1921). Heart Butte and Old Agency Districts. Blackfeet Reservation, Mont. Manuscript in Museum of the Plains Indian, Browning, Mont.

CARLETON, LT. J. H.
1943. The prairie logbooks. Ed. by Louis Pelzer. Chicago.

CARVER, JONATHON.
1838. Travels through the interior parts of North America, in the years 1766, 1767 and 1768. New York.

CATLIN, GEORGE.
1841. Letters and notes on the manners, customs, and conditions of the North American Indians. 2 vols. London.

CHARDON, F. A.
1932. Chardon's journal of Fort Clark, 1834–39. Ed. by Annie Heloise Abel. Pierre, S. Dak.

CHESNUT, VICTOR KING, and WILCOX, E. V.
>   1901. The stock poisoning plants of Montana: A preliminary report. U. S.
>   Dept. Agr., Div. Bot., Bull. 26.
CLARK, CAPT. W. P.
>   1885. The Indian sign language. Philadelphia.
COCKING, MATHEW.
>   1908. An adventurer from Hudson Bay. Journal of Mathew Cocking from
>   York factory to the Blackfeet country, 1772–1773. Ed. by Laurence
>   J. Burpee. Trans. Royal Soc. Canada. Ser. 3, vol. 2.
COOKE, CAPT. P. ST. G.
>   1857. Scenes and adventures in the Army. Philadelphia.
>   1925. Journal of a dragoon march on the plains in 1843. Ed. by Wm. E.
>   Connelley. Mississippi Valley Hist. Rev., vol. 12, No. 1.
COUES, ELLIOTT, EDITOR.
>   1893. History of the expedition under the command of Lewis and Clark . . .
>   4 vols. New York.
COUNCIL OF THE BLACKFEET, BLOOD AND PIEGAN TRIBES OF INDIANS. BLACKFEET
>   AGENCY, MONTANA TERRITORY, APRIL 20–23, 1875.
>   MS. Records, Office of Indian Affairs. Letters Received, 1875. Montana
>   W–847. National Archives.
COX, ISAAC JOSLIN, EDITOR.
>   1905. The journeys of Réne Robert Cavelier, sieur de La Salle . . . 2 vols.
>   New York.
COX, ROSS.
>   1832. Adventures on the Columbia River. New York.
CULBERTSON, THADDEUS A.
>   1851. Journal of an expedition to the Mauvaises Terres and the upper Mis-
>   souri in 1850. Ann. Rep. Smithsonian Inst. for 1850.
CULIN, STEWART.
>   1907. Games of the North American Indians. 24th Ann. Rep. Bur. Amer.
>   Ethnol, 1902–3.
CURTIS, EDWARD S.
>   1909, 1911, 1928. The North American Indian . . . vols. 4, 6, 18. Norwood,
>   Mass.
DALE, H. C., EDITOR.
>   1918. The Ashley-Smith explorations and the discovery of a central route
>   to the Pacific, 1822–1829. Cleveland.
DALY, H. W.
>   1908. Pack transportation. Office of the Quartermaster-General, War Dept.
>   Washington.
DENHARDT, ROBERT M.
>   1937. Grain threshing and horse breaking. Western Horseman, vol. 2, No. 5.
>   1938. The western saddle. From Moslem Spain to Modern California.
>   Westways, vol. 30, No. 2.
>   1947. The horse of the Americas. Norman, Okla.
>   1948. What color is he? Western Horseman, vol. 13, No. 1.
DENIG, EDWIN T.
>   1930. Indian tribes of the Upper Missouri. Ed. by J. N. B. Hewitt. 46th
>   Ann. Rep., Bur. Amer. Ethnol., 1928–29, pp. 375–628.
>   1950. Of the Arickaras. Ed. by John C. Ewers. Missouri Hist. Soc. Bull.,
>   vol. 6, No. 2.
>   1951. Of the Sioux. Ed. by John C. Ewers. Missouri Hist. Soc. Bull., vol.
>   7, No. 2.

DENIG, EDWIN T.—Continued
    1952. Of the Assiniboin. Ed. by John C. Ewers. Missouri Hist. Soc. Bull.,.
        vol. 8, No. 2.
    1953. Of the Crow Nation. Ed. by John C. Ewers. Anthrop. Pap. No. 33,.
        Bur. Amer. Ethnol. Bull. 151.
DENNY, SIR CECIL.
    1939. The law marches west. Toronto.
DENSMORE, FRANCES.
    1918. Teton Sioux music. Bur. Amer. Ethnol. Bull. 61.
    1948. A collection of specimens from the Teton Sioux. Mus. Amer. Ind.,.
        Heye Foundation. Indian Notes and Monographs, vol. 11, No. 3.
DE VOTO, BERNARD.
    1947. Across the wide Missouri. Boston.
DIXON, JOSEPH K.
    1913. The vanishing race. New York.
DOBIE, J. FRANK.
    1941. The longhorns. Boston.
    1952. The mustangs. Boston.
DODGE, COL. HENRY.
    1836. Journal of a march of a detachment of dragoons under the command
        of Colonel Dodge, in the summer of 1835. War Dept. U. S. 24th
        Cong., 1st sess., H. R. Doc. 181.
DORSEY, GEORGE A., and MURIE, JAMES R.
    1940. Notes on the Skidi Pawnee society. Ed. by Alexander Spoehr. Field
        Mus. Nat. Hist. Anthropol. Ser., vol. 27, No. 2.
DORSEY, JAMES OWEN.
    1891. Games of Teton Dakota children. Amer. Anthrop., vol. 4, pp. 329–345.
    1894. A study of Siouan cults. 11th Ann. Rep. Bur. Amer. Ethnol., 1889–90,.
        pp. 361–544.
    1896. Omaha dwellings, furniture, and implements. 13th Ann. Rep. Bur.
        Amer. Ethnol., 1891–92, pp. 263–288.
DOTY, JAMES.
    MS. Letter from James Doty to Isaac Stevens, Governor of Washington
        Territory, December 20, 1854. Records of the Bureau of Indian
        Affairs. Washington Superintendency Field Papers. National
        Archives.
    MS. Report of Secretary Doty upon his mission to the North Camps,.
        Aug. 31st to — 1855. Office of Indian Affairs. National Archives.
DOUGLAS, FREDERIC H.
    1937. A Crow beaded horse collar. Denver Art Mus., Material Culture
        Notes No. 2.
    1942. Parfleches and other rawhide articles. Denver Art Mus. Leaflet
        77–78.
DUNBAR, JOHN B.
    1884. The Pawnee Indians. Mag. Amer. Hist. vol. 4, No. 4; vol. 5, No. 5.
ELKIN, HENRY.
    1940. The northern Arapaho of Wyoming. In Linton, Ralph, ed., "Ac-
        culturation in seven American Indian tribes." New York.
EMORY, WM. H.
    1857. Report on the United States and Mexican boundary survey. 3 vols.
        Washington.
Encyclopaedia Britannica.
    1944. Vol. 11, pp. 763, 768.

EVANS, HUGH.
   1927. Hugh Evans' journal of Col. Henry Dodge's expedition to the Rocky
      Mountains in 1835. Ed. by Fred S. Perrine. Mississippi Valley
      Hist. Rev., vol. 14, No. 2.
EWERS, JOHN C.
   1939. Plains Indian painting. Palo Alto, Calif.
   1943. Were the Blackfoot rich in horses? Amer. Anthrop., n. s., vol. 45, No. 4.
   1944 a. The Blackfoot war lodge: Its construction and use. Amer. Anthrop.
      n. s., vol. 46, No. 2.
   1944 b. The story of the Blackfeet. U. S. Office of Indian Affairs. Indian
      Life and Customs, Pamphlet No. 6.
   1944 c. Food rationing is nothing new to the Blackfoot. Southwest Mus.
      The Masterkey, vol. 18, No. 3.
   1945 a. The case for Blackfoot pottery. Amer. Anthrop., n. s., vol. 47,
      No. 2.
   1945. b. Blackfeet crafts. U. S. Indian Service, Indian Handicrafts No. 9.
   1946. Identification and history of the Small Robes band of the Piegan
      Indians. Jour. Washington Acad. Sci., vol. 36, No. 12.
   1948 a. Gustavus Sohon's portraits of Flathead and Pend d'Oreille Indians,
      1854. Smithsonian Misc. Coll., vol. 110, No. 7.
   1948 b. Self-torture in the Blood Indian Sun Dance. Jour. Washington
      Acad. Sci., vol. 38, No. 5.
   1949. The last bison drives of the Blackfoot Indians. Jour. Washington
      Acad. Sci., vol. 39, No. 11.
FARNHAM, THOMAS J.
   1900. Travels in the great western Prairies, the Anahuac and Rocky
      Mountains. Early Western Travels, vols. 28–29. Ed. by Reuben
      Gold Thwaites. Cleveland.
FERRIS, W. A.
   1940. Life in the Rocky Mountains. Ed. by Paul C. Phillips. Denver.
FLETCHER, A. C., and LA FLESCHE, F.
   1911. The Omaha tribe. 27th Ann. Rep. Bur. Amer. Ethnol., 1905–6.
FOWLER, JACOB.
   1898. The Journal of Jacob Fowler, 1821–22. Ed. by Elliott Coues. New
      York.
GARRAGHAN, GILBERT J.
   1927. Emergence of the Missouri Valley in history. Illinois Catholic Hist.
      Rev., vol. 9, No. 4.
GARRARD, LEWIS H.
   1927. Wah-to-yah and the Taos trail. Ed. by Stanley Vestal. Oklahoma
      City.
GIBBS, GEORGE.
   1855. Report of George Gibbs to Captain McClellan, on the Indian tribes
      of the Territory of Washington. March 4, 1954. *In* Pacific Rail-
      road Survey Report of Explorations and Surveys to Ascertain the
      Most Practical and Economical Route for a Railroad from the
      Mississippi River to the Pacific Ocean. Vol. 1. Washington.
GILMORE, MELVIN R.
   1919. Uses of plants by the Indians of the Missouri River region. 33d
      Ann. Rep. Bur. Amer. Ethnol., 1911–12, pp. 43–154.
GOLDFRANK, ESTHER S.
   1945. Changing configurations in the social organization of a Blackfoot
      tribe during the reserve period. The Blood of Alberta, Canada.
      Amer. Ethnol. Soc. Monogr. No. 8.

GRAHAM, ROBERT CUNNINGHAM.
    1930. The horses of the conquest. London.
GREGG, JOSIAH.
    1905. Commerce of the prairies: or the journal of a Santa Fe trader. *In*
        Early western travels. Ed. by Reuben Gold Thwaites. Vols. 19-20.
        Cleveland.
    1941. Diary and letters of Josiah Gregg. Ed. by M. G. Fulton. Norman, Okla.
GRINNELL, GEORGE BIRD.
    1889. Pawnee hero stories and folk-tales. New York.
    1892. Blackfoot Lodge tales. New York.
    1895. The story of the Indian. New York.
    1923. The Cheyenne Indians, their history and ways of life. 2 vols. New
        Haven.
HAINES, FRANCIS.
    1938 a. Where did the Plains Indians get their horses? Amer. Anthrop.,
        n. s., vol. 40, No. 1.
    1938 b. The northward spread of horses among the Plains Indians. Amer.
        Anthrop., n. s., vol. 40, No. 3.
    1939. Red eagles of the Northwest. Los Angeles.
HAMILTON, WM. T.
    1900. A trading expedition among the Indians in 1858. Montana Hist. Soc.
        Contr., vol. 3.
    1905. My sixty years on the Plains, trapping, trading and Indian fighting.
        New York.
HARMON, DANIEL.
    1903. A journal of voyages and travels in the interior of North America.
        New York.
HATCH, E. A. C.
    MS. Diary. June 7-October 15, 1856. Typed copy in Montana Hist. Soc.
        Libr.
HAYDEN, FERDINAND V.
    1862. Contributions to the ethnography and philology of the Indian tribes
        of the Missouri Valley. Trans. Amer. Philos. Soc. n. s., vol. 12,
        pt. 2. Philadelphia.
HENDRY, ANTHONY.
    1907. York Factory to the Blackfeet country. The Journal of Anthony
        Hendry, 1754-55. Ed. by Lawrence J. Burpee. Trans. Royal Soc.
        Canada, ser. 3, vol. 1, sect. 2.
HENRY, ALEXANDER.
    1809. Travels and adventures in Canada, and the Indian Territories, be-
        tween the years 1760 and 1776. New York.
HENRY, ALEXANDER, and THOMPSON, DAVID.
    1897. New light on the early history of the greater Northwest. Ed. by
        Elliott Coues. 3 vols. New York.
HILL, W. W.
    1936. Navaho warfare. Yale Univ. Pub. Anthrop., No. 5.
HIND, HENRY YOULE.
    1860. Narrative of the Canadian Red River exploring expedition of 1857
        and of the Assiniboine and Saskatchewan exploring expedition of
        1858. 2 vols. London.
HODGE, FREDERICK WEBB, EDITOR.
    1907, 1910. Handbook of American Indians north of Mexico. Bur. Amer.
        Ethnol. Bull. 30, pts. 1·and 2.

HORNADAY, WILLIAM T.
　　1889. The extermination of the American bison. Ann. Rep. U. S. Nat. Mus.
　　　　for 1886–1887, pp. 367–548.
HOUGH, WALTER.
　　1895. Primitive American armor. Ann. Rep. U. S. Nat. Mus. for 1893.
HUGHES, KATHERINE.
　　1911. Father Lacombe, the black-robe voyager. New York.
HYDE, GEORGE E.
　　1937. Red Cloud's folk, a history of the Oglala Sioux Indians. Norman,
　　　　Okla.
INMAN, COL. HENRY.
　　1899. The Old Santa Fe Trail. Topeka.
IRVING, WASHINGTON.
　　1851. The adventures of Captain Bonneville, U. S. A. New York.
ISHAM, JAMES.
　　1949. James Isham's observations on Hudsons Bay, 1743. Ed. by E. E. Rich.
　　　　Champlain Soc. Publ. Hudson's Bay Co., ser. 12. Toronto.
JABLOW, JOSEPH.
　　1951. The Cheyenne in Plains Indian trade relations 1795–1840. Amer.
　　　　Ethnol. Soc. Monogr. No. 19.
JAMES, EDWIN.
　　1823. Account of an expedition from Pittsburgh to the Rocky Mountains
　　　　performed in the years 1819 and 1820. 2 vols. and atlas.
　　　　Philadelphia. London.
JAMES, THOMAS.
　　1916. Three years among the Indians and Mexicans. Ed. by Walter B.
　　　　Douglas. St. Louis.
JENNESS, DIAMOND.
　　1938. The Sarcee Indians of Alberta. Nat. Mus. Canada, Bull. 90.
　　　　Anthrop. Ser. No. 23. Ottawa.
JESUIT RELATIONS AND ALLIED DOCUMENTS.
　　1896–1901. Missionaries in New France, 1610–1791. Travels and explora-
　　　　tions of the Jesuits. Ed. by Reuben Gold Thwaites. 73 vols.
　　　　Cleveland.
KANE, PAUL.
　　1925. Wanderings of an artist among the Indians of North America.
　　　　Toronto.
KELSEY, HENRY.
　　1929. The Kelsey papers. Ed. by A. G. Doughty and Chester Martin.
　　　　Pub. Arch. Canada and Pub. Rec. Office Northern Ireland. Ottawa.
KENDALL, G. W.
　　1844. Narrative of the Texan Santa Fe Expedition. 2 vols. New York.
KOCH, PETER.
　　1896. Life at Muscleshell in 1869 and 1870. Montana Hist. Soc. Contr., vol.
　　　　2.
　　1944. A trading expedition among the Crow Indians, 1873–1874. Ed. by Carl
　　　　B. Cone. Mississippi Valley Hist. Rev., vol. 31, No. 3.
KROEBER, ALFRED L.
　　1902–7. The Arapaho. Bull. Amer. Mus. Nat. Hist., vol. 18.
　　1908. Ethnology of the Gros Ventres. Amer. Mus. Nat. Hist., Anthrop. Pap.,
　　　　vol. 1, pt. 4.
　　1939. Cultural and natural areas of native North America. Univ. California
　　　　Publ. in Amer. Archaeol. and Ethnol., vol. 38. Berkeley, Calif.

Kurz, R. F.
    1937. Journal of Rudolph Friederich Kurz . . . 1846–1852. Trans. by
        Myrtis Jarrell. Ed. by J. N. B. Hewitt. Bur. Amer. Ethnol. Bull.
        115.
Larocque, François.
    1910. Journal of Larocque from the Assiniboine to the Yellowstone, 1805.
        Canada Archives Publ. No. 3.
Larpenteur, Charles.
    1898. Forty years a fur trader on the Upper Missouri. The personal nar-
        rative of Charles Larpenteur. Ed. by Elliott Coues. 2 vols. New
        York.
La Salle, Réne Robert Cavelier, sieur de. See Cox, Isaac Joslin, Editor.
La Vérendrye, P. G. V.
    1927. Journals and letters of Pierre Gaultier de Varennes de la Vérendrye
        and his sons . . . Ed. by Lawrence J. Burpee. Champlain Soc. Publ.
        16. Toronto.
Leonard, Zenas.
    1904. Adventures of Zenas Leonard, fur trader and trapper, 1831–1836. Ed.
        by W. F. Wagner. Cleveland.
Le Sueur, Jacques.
    1902. Le Sueur's voyage up the Mississippi. Wisconsin Hist. Soc. Coll., vol.
        16.
Lewis, Oscar.
    1942. The effects of white contact upon Blackfoot culture, with special refer-
        ence to the role of the fur trade. Amer. Ethnol. Soc. Monogr. No. 6.
Lewis and Clark. See Coues, Elliott.
Linderman, Frank Bird.
    1930. American; the life story of a great Indian, Plenty-coups, chief of the
        Crows. Yonkers, N. Y.
Linton, Ralph, Editor.
    1940. Acculturation in seven American Indian tribes. New York.
Llewellyn, K. N., and Hoebel, E. A.
    1941. The Cheyenne way: Conflict and case law in primitive jurisprudence.
        Norman, Okla.
Long, James L.
    1942. Land of Nakoda; the story of the Assiniboine Indians. U. S. Mon-
        tana Writers Project. Helena, Mont.
Lowie, Robert H.
    1908. The northern Shoshone. Amer. Mus. Nat. Hist. Anthrop. Pap., vol.
        2, pt. 2.
    1909. The Assiniboine. Amer. Mus. Nat. Hist., Anthrop. Pap., vol. 4, pt. 1.
    1912. Social life of the Crow Indians. Amer. Mus. Nat. Hist. Anthrop.
        Pap., vol. 9, pt. 2.
    1915 Dances and societies of the Plains Shoshone. Amer. Mus. Nat. Hist.
        Anthrop. Pap., vol. 11, pt. 10.
    1916. Plains Indian age societies: Historical and comparative summary.
        Amer. Mus. Nat. Hist., Anthrop. Pap., vol. 11, pt. 13.
    1922 a. The material culture of the Crow Indians. Amer. Mus. Nat. Hist.,
        Anthrop. Pap., vol. 20, pt. 3.
    1922 b. Crow Indian art. Amer. Mus. Nat. Hist., Anthrop. Pap., vol. 21,
        pt. 4.
    1922 c. The religion of the Crow Indians. Amer. Mus. Nat. Hist., Anthrop.
        Pap., vol. 21, pt. 2.

LOWIE, ROBERT H.—Continued
  1924 a. Minor ceremonies of the Crow Indians. Amer. Mus. Nat. Hist., Anthrop. Pap., vol. 21, pt. 5.
  1924 b. Notes on Shoshonean ethnography. Amer. Mus. Nat. Hist., Anthrop. Pap., vol. 20, pt. 3.
McCLINTOCK, WALTER.
  1910. The Old North trail . . . London.
  1930. The tragedy of the Blackfoot. Southwest Mus. Pap., No. 3. Los Angeles.
  1948. Blackfoot medicine-pipe ceremony. Pt. 2. The Masterkey, vol. 22, No. 2. Southwest Museum. Los Angeles.
McDONNELL, ANNE, EDITOR.
  1940. The Fort Benton Journal, 1854–1856, and the Fort Sarpy Journal, 1855–1856. In Montana Hist. Soc. Contr., vol. 10.
M'GILLIVRAY, DUNCAN.
  1929. The journal of Duncan M'Gillivray of the Northwest Company at Fort George on the Saskatchewan, 1794–1795. Ed. by Arthur S. Morton. Toronto.
MacINNES, C. M.
  1930. In the shadow of the Rockies. London.
MACKENZIE, ALEXANDER.
  1927. Voyages from Montreal, on the river St. Lawrence, through the continent of North America . . . 1789 and 1793. Toronto.
MACKENZIE, CHARLES.
  1889. The Missouri Indians, 1804–1805. In Masson, L. R., Les bourgeois de la compagnie du Nord-Ouest. Vol. 1. Quebec.
MANDELBAUM, DAVID G.
  1940. The Plains Cree. Amer. Mus. Nat. Hist., Anthrop. Pap., vol. 37, pt. 2.
MARCY, CAPT. RANDOLPH B.
  1859. The Prairie traveller, a handbook for overland expeditions. New York.
  1937. Adventure on Red River. Ed. by Grant Foreman. Norman, Okla.
MARGRY, PIERRE.
  1876–86. Découvertes et établissements des français dans l'ouest et dans le sud de l'Amérique Septentrionale (1614–1754). Mémoires et documents originaux recueillis et publés par Pierre Margry. 6 vols. Paris.
MARQUIS, THOMAS B.
  1928. Memoirs of a white Crow Indian. New York.
MATHEWS, WASHINGTON.
  1877. Ethnography and philology of the Hidatsa Indians. U. S. Geol. and Geogr. Surv. Misc. Publ., No. 7.
MAXIMILIAN, see WIED NEUWIED, MAXIMILIAN ALEXANDER PHILIP, PRINZ VON.
MEAD, JAMES R.
  1908. The Pawnees as I knew them. Kansas Hist. Soc. Trans., vol. 10.
MELINE, JAMES F.
  1868. Two thousand miles on horseback. Santa Fe and back. A summer tour through Kansas, Nebraska, Colorado, and New Mexico, in the year 1866. New York.
MENGARINI, GREGORY.
  1871–72. Indians of Oregon. Journ. Anthrop. Inst. New York, vol. 1.
  1938. Mengarini's narrative of the Rockies. Ed. by Albert J. Partoll. Montana Univ. Historical Reprints. Sources of Northwest History, No. 25.

MICHELSON, TRUMAN.
  1932. The narrative of a Southern Cheyenne woman. Smithsonian Misc.,
      Coll., vol. 87, No. 5.
  1933. Narrative of an Arapaho woman. Amer. Anthrop., n. s., vol. 35, No. 4.
MIRO, ESTEVAN.
  1946. A description of Louisiana. Draft by Miro. *In* "Spain in the
      Mississippi Valley, 1765-1794." Ann. Rep. Amer. Hist. Assoc. for
      1945, pp. 159-167.
MISHKIN, BERNARD.
  1940. Rank and warfare among the Plains Indians. Monogr. Amer. Ethnol.
      Soc., No. 3. New York.
MITCHELL, D. D.
  1855. Blackfeet Indians. *In* Schoolcraft, Henry R., "Historical and statis-
      tical information respecting the history, conditions and prospects
      of the Indian tribes of the United States," vol. 5, pp. 685-687.
      Philadelphia.
MOONEY, JAMES.
  1898. Calendar history of the Kiowa Indians. 17th Ann. Rep., Bur. Amer.
      Ethnol., 1895-96, pt. 1, pp. 129-445.
  1907. The Cheyenne Indians. Mem. Amer. Anthrop. Assoc., vol. 1, pt. 6.
MORA, JOE.
  1949. Californios. Garden City. N. Y.
MORGAN, LEWIS HENRY.
  MS. Journal of a trip up the Missouri River on the steamboat Shreveport
      (Spread Eagle) in 1862. Manuscript in Rush Rhees Library. Univ.
      Rochester.
MORSE, JEDIDIAH.
  1822. A report to the Secretary of War of the United States, on Indian affairs,
      comprising a narrative of a tour performed in the summer of 1820
      . . . New Haven, Conn.
MURDOCK, GEORGE PETER.
  1951. South American culture areas. Southwestern Journ. Anthrop., vol.
      7, No. 4.
MURRAY, CHARLES AUGUSTUS.
  1839. Travels in North America during the years 1834, 1835, and 1836. 2
      vols. London.
MUSTERS, GEORGE CHAWORTH.
  1871. At home with the Patagonians. London.
NASITIR, ABRAHAM P.
  1927. Spanish exploration of the Upper Missouri. Mississippi Valley Hist.
      Rev., vol. 14, No. 1.
NEIGHBORS, R. S.
  1852. The Na-u-ni or Comanches of Texas. *In* Schoolcraft, Henry R., "His-
      torical and statistical information respecting the history, condi-
      tion and prospects of the Indian tribes of the United States," vol. 2,
      pp. 125-134. Philadelphia.
NYE, COL. W. S.
  1943. Carbine and lance, the story of old Fort Sill. Norman, Okla.
OGDEN, PETER SKENE.
  1909-11. The Peter Skene Ogden journals, Snake Expedition, 1825-1826.
      Oregon Hist. Soc. Quart., vol. 10, No. 4; Expedition of 1826-27,
      vol. 11. Portland, Oreg.

OPLER, MARVIN K.
    1940. The Southern Ute of Colorado. *In* Linton, Ralph, ed., "Acculturation in seven American Indian tribes." New York.
OPLER, MORRIS E.
    1936. A summary of Jicarilla Apache culture. Amer. Anthrop., n. s., vol. 38, No. 2.
    1941. An Apache life-way; the economic, social and religious institutions of the Chiricahua Indians. Chicago.
ORDWAY, JOHN.
    1916. Sergeant Ordway's Journal. Ed. by Milo Quaife. Wisconsin Hist. Soc. Coll., vol. 22.
OWEN, JOHN.
    1927. Journal and Letters of Major John Owen, 1850–1871. 2 vols. Ed. by Paul C. Phillips. Montana Hist. Soc. Helena, Mont.
PALLISER, JOHN.
    1863. The journals, detailed reports and observations relating to the exploration by Captain Palliser . . . 1857–1860. London.
PARKER, W. B.
    1855. Manners, customs, and history of the Indians of southwestern Texas. *In* Schoolcraft, Henry R., "Historical and statistical information respecting the history, conditions, and prospects of the Indian tribes of the United States," vol. 5, p. 685. Philadelphia.
    1856. Notes taken during the expedition commanded by Capt. R. B. Marcy, U. S. A., through unexplored Texas in the summer and fall of 1854. Philadelphia.
PATAI, RAPHAEL.
    1951. Nomadism: Middle Eastern and Central Asian. Southwestern Journ. Anthrop., vol. 7, No. 4.
PEASE, T. C., and WERNER, R. C., EDITORS.
    1934 a. La Salle in the Illinois Country, 1680. Coll. Illinois State Hist. Libr., vol. 23. French series, vol. 1. Springfield, Ill.
    1934 b. Memoir of De Gannes concerning the Illinois country. Coll. Illinois State Hist. Libr., vol. 23. French series, vol. 1. Springfield, Ill.
PFEFFERKORN, IGNAZ.
    1949. Pfefferkorn's description of the Province of Sonora. Ed. by Theodore E. Treutlein. Coronado Cuarto Centennial Publ., vol. 12. Albuquerque.
PHINNEY, MARY ALLEN.
    n. d. Jirah Isham Allen, Montana pioneer. Rutland, Vt.
PIKE, ZEBULON M.
    1810. An account of expeditions to the sources of the Mississippi, and through the western parts of Louisiana. Philadelphia.
    1932. Pike on the Mississippi, 1805–1806. Ed. by Wilhemina Stockwell. *In* "New Spain and the Anglo-American West," vol. 2. Los Angeles.
POND, PETER.
    1908. Journal of Peter Pond, 1740–1775. Coll. Wisconsin State Hist. Soc., vol. 18.
RADIN, PAUL.
    1923. The Winnebago tribe. 37th Ann. Rep. Bur. Amer. Ethnol., 1915–16, 560 pp.
RANGEL, NICOLAS.
    1924. Historia del Toreo en Mexico. Mexico City.

RATHBONE, PERRY T.
1946. Charles Wimar, 1828–1862. Painter of the Indian Frontier. Bull., City Art Mus. St. Louis, vol. 31, Nos. 2–3.
RAY, VERNE.
1932. The Sanpoil and Nespelem: Salishan peoples of northeastern Washington. Univ. Washington Publ. Anthrop., vol. 5, No. 1.
RAYNOLDS, W. F.
1868. Report on exploration of the Yellowstone River. Washington.
REMINGTON, FREDERIC.
1889. Horses of the plains. Century Mag., vol. 37, No. 3.
RODNICK, DAVID.
1937. Political structure and status among the Assiniboine Indians. Amer. Anthrop., n. s., vol. 39, pp. 408–416.
1938. The Fort Belknap Assiniboine of Montana. Philadelphia.
ROE, FRANK GILBERT.
1939. From dogs to horses among the Western Indian tribes. Trans. Roy. Soc. Canada. 3d ser., vol. 33, section 2. Toronto.
1951. The North American buffalo. Toronto.
ROSS, ALEXANDER.
1855. The fur hunters of the far West: A narrative of adventures in Oregon and the Rocky Mountains. 2 vols. London.
1913. Journal of Alexander Ross—Snake Country Expedition, 1824. Ed. by T. C. Elliott. Oregon Hist. Soc. Quart.
ROSS, MARVIN C.
1951. The west of Alfred Jacob Miller. Norman, Okla.
SAINT-PIERRE, LEGARDEUR DE.
1886. Journal of Legardeur de Saint-Pierre. Rep. Canada Archives. Ottawa.
SAPIR, EDWARD.
1916. Time perspective in aboriginal American culture. Geolog. Surv. Canada. Memoir 90. Anthrop. series 13.
SCHAEFFER, CLAUDE E.
1950. Bird nomenclature and principles of avian taxonomy of the Blackfeet Indians. Jour. Washington Acad. Sci., vol. 40, No. 2.
SCHOLES, F. V.
1937. Troublous times in New Mexico, 1659–1670. New Mexico Hist. Rev., vol. 12.
SCHULTZ, J. WILLARD.
1907. My life as an Indian. Boston.
1919 a. Rising Wolf. Boston.
1919 b. Running Eagle, the warrior girl. Boston.
SCHULTZ, J. W., and DONALDSON, J. L.
1930. The Sun God's children. Boston.
SHIMKIN, D. B.
1938. Wind River Shoshone geography. Amer. Anthrop., n. s., vol. 40, No. 3.
1939. Shoshone–Comanche origins and migrations. Pacific Sci. Cong., 6th, Berkeley, Calif. Proc., vol. 4.
1947 a. Wind River Shoshone ethnogeography. Univ. California Anthrop. Records, vol. 5, No. 4.
1947 b. Childhood and development among the Wind River Shoshone. Univ. California Anthrop. Records, vol. 5, No. 5.

SIBLEY, H. H.
    1854. Sport of buffalo-hunting on the open plains of Pembina. *In* Schoolcraft,
        H. R., "Historical and statistical information respecting the history,
        condition and prospects of the Indian tribes of the United States,"
        vol. 4, pp. 94–110. Philadelphia.
SKINNER, ALLANSON.
    1914. Political organization, cults, and ceremonies of the Plains-Ojibway
        and Plains-Cree Indians. Amer. Mus. Nat. Hist., Anthrop. Pap., vol.
        11, pt. 6.
    1915. Societies of the Iowa, Kansa and Ponca Indians. Amer. Mus. Nat.
        Hist., Anthrop. Pap., vol. 11, pt. 9.
    1925. Observations on the ethnology of the Sauk Indians. Part 3. Notes on
        material culture. Bull., Milwaukee Pub. Mus., vol. 5, No. 3.
    1926. Ethnology of the Iowa Indians. Bull., Milwaukee Pub. Mus., vol. 5,
        No. 4.
SMET, PIERRE JEAN DE.
    1905. Life, letters and travels of Father Pierre Jean de Smet . . . Chitten-
        den, H. M., and Richardson, A. T., ed. 4 vols. New York.
SMITH, E. WILLARD.
    1913. Journal of E. Willard Smith while with the fur traders, Vasquez and
        Sublette in the Rocky Mountain region, 1839–1840. Oregon Hist.
        Soc. Quart., vol. 14, No. 3.
SMITH, MARIAN W.
    1940. The Puyallup-Nisqually. Columbia Univ. Contr. Anthrop., vol. 32.
SPIER, LESLIE.
    1925. An analysis of Plains Indian parfleche decoration. Univ. Washington
        Publ. Anthrop., vol. 1, No. 3.
SPINDEN, HERBERT J.
    1908. The Nez Percé Indians. Mem. Amer. Anthrop. Assoc., vol. 2, pt. 3,
        pp. 165–274.
STANLEY, JOHN MIX.
    1855. Report of Mr. J. M. Stanley's visit to the Piegan camp at the Cypress
        Mountain. *In* Pacific Railroad Survey report of explorations and
        surveys to ascertain the most practicable route for a railroad from
        the Mississippi River to the Pacific Ocean, vol. 1. Washington.
STANSBURY, HOWARD.
    1852. Exploration and survey of the valley of the Great Salt Lake of Utah,
        including a reconnaissance of a new route through the Rocky Moun-
        tains. Philadelphia.
STEVENS, ISAAC I.
    1860. Isaac I. Stevens' narrative of 1853–1855. *In* Pacific Railroad Survey
        report of explorations and surveys to ascertain the most practicable
        route for a railroad from the Mississippi River to the Pacific Ocean,
        vol. 12, bk. 1. Washington.
STEWARD, JULIAN H.
    1938. Basin-plateau aboriginal sociopolitical groups. Bur. Amer. Ethnol.
        Bull. 120.
    1939. Notes on Hillers' photographs of the Paiute and Ute Indians taken on
        the Powell expedition of 1873. Smithsonian Misc. Coll., vol. 98,
        No. 18.

STRONG, W. DUNCAN.
 1940. From history to prehistory in the northern Great Plains. Smithsonian
      Misc. Coll., vol. 100, pp. 353–394.
STUART, GRANVILLE.
 1865. Montana as it is. New York.
 1896. Historical sketch of Deer Lodge County, Valley and City. Montana
      Hist. Soc. Contr., vol. 2.
SUCKLEY, GEORGE.
 1855. Report of Dr. Geo. Suckley, Assistant Surgeon, U. S. A., of his trip in
      a canoe from Fort Owen . . . to Vancouver. *In* Pacific Railroad
      Survey report of explorations and surveys to ascertain the most
      practicable route for a railroad from the Mississippi River to the
      Pacific Ocean, vol. 1. Washington.
SWANTON, JOHN R.
 1928. Social organization and social usages of the Indians of the Creek Con-
      federacy. 42d Ann. Rept., Bur. Amer. Ethnol., 1924–25, pp. 23–472.
 1939. The survival of horses brought to North America by De Soto. Amer.
      Anthrop., n. s., vol. 41, No. 1.
 1942. Source material on the history and ethnology of the Caddo Indians.
      Bur. Amer. Ethnol., Bull. 132.
 1946. The Indians of the Southeastern United States. Bur. Amer. Ethnol.,
      Bull. 137.
TABEAU, PIERRE-ANTOINE.
 1939. Tabeau's narrative of Loisel's expedition to the Upper Missouri. Ed.
      by Annie Heloise Abel. Norman, Okla.
TEIT, JAMES.
 1900. The Thompson Indians of British Columbia. Mem. Amer. Mus. Nat.
      Hist. vol. 2; Publ. Jesup N. Pac. Exped., vol. 1, No. 4; Anthrop.
      vol. 1, pt. 4.
 1909. The Shuswap. Mem. Amer. Mus. Nat. Hist., vol. 4, pt. 7; Publ. Jesup
      N. Pac. Exped., vol. 2, No. 7.
 1930. Salishan tribes of the western plateau. Ed. by Franz Boas. 45th Ann.
      Rept., Bur. Amer. Ethnol., 1927–28, pp. 23–396.
THOMAS, ALFRED B.
 1932. Forgotten frontiers. A study of the Spanish Indian policy of Don
      Juan Bautista de Anza, Governor of New Mexico, 1777–1787. Nor-
      man, Okla.
 1935. After Coronado. Spanish exploration northeast of New Mexico, 1697–
      1727. Norman, Okla.
 1940. The Plains Indians and New Mexico, 1751–1778. Coronado Cuarto
      Centennial Publ., vol. 12. Albuquerque, N. Mex.
THOMPSON, DAVID.
 1916. David Thompson's narrative of his explorations in western America,
      1784–1812. Ed. by J. B. Tyrrell. Champlain Soc. Publ. No. 12.
      Toronto.
TIXIER, VICTOR.
 1940. Tixier's travels on the Osage prairies. Ed. by John Francis McDermott.
      Norman, Okla.
TROBRIAND, PHILIPPE REGIS DE.
 1951. Military life in Dakota. The Journal of Philippe Regis de Trobriand.
      Ed. by Lucille M. Kane. St. Paul, Minn.
TRUDEAU, JEAN-BAPTISTE.
 1921. Description of the Upper Missouri. Ed. by Annie Heloise Abel. Mis-
      sissippi Valley Hist. Rev., vol. 8, Nos. 1–2.

TURNEY-HIGH, HARRY H.
   1937. The Flathead Indians of Montana. Mem. Amer. Anthrop. Assoc., No.
     48. Menasha, Wis.
   1941. Ethnography of the Kutenai. Mem. Amer. Anthrop. Assoc., No. 56.
     Menasha, Wis.
   1949. Primitive war, its practice and concepts. Columbia, S. C.
TWINING, W. J.
   1878. Report of Capt. W. J. Twining, Chief Astronomer and Surveyor. *In*
     Reports upon the survey of the boundary between the territory of
     the United States and the possessions of Great Britain from the
     Lake of the Woods to the summit of the Rocky Mountains. Wash-
     ington.
UHLENBECK, C. C.
   1911. Original Blackfoot texts. Verh. K. Akad. Wetenschappen Afd. Letter-
     kunde. N. s., vol. 13.
UMFREVILLE, EDWARD.
   1790. Present state of Hudson's Bay, containing a full description of that
     settlement and the adjacent country; and likewise of the fur trade.
     London.
UNITED STATES COMMISSIONER OF INDIAN AFFAIRS.
   1850–1910. Annual reports. Washington, D. C.
UNITED STATES FOREST SERVICE.
   1937. Range plant handbook. 512 pp. Washington, D. C.
VERNON, ARTHUR.
   1941. The history and romance of the horse. Garden City, N. Y.
VILLAR, JOSE ALVAREZ DEL.
   1941. Historia de la Charreria. Mexico City.
WEBB, WALTER PRESCOTT.
   1931. The Great Plains. Boston.
WEDEL, WALDO R.
   1936. An introduction to Pawnee archaeology. Bur. Amer. Ethnol., Bull.
     112.
   1940. Culture sequences in the central Great Plains. *In* Smithsonian Misc.
     Coll., vol. 100, pp. 291–352.
   1946. The Kansa Indians. Trans. Kansas Acad. Sci., vol. 49, No. 1.
WHEELER, OLIN D.
   1904. The trail of Lewis and Clark. 2 vols. New York.
WHIPPLE, A. W.
   1856. Report upon the Indian Tribes. *In* Pacific Railroad Survey report of
     explorations and surveys to ascertain the most practicable route for
     a railroad from the Mississippi River to the Pacific Ocean. Vol. 3.
     Washington.
WHITMAN, WILLIAM.
   1937. The Oto. Columbia Univ. Contr. Anthrop., vol. 28. New York.
WIED-NEUWIED, MAXIMILIAN ALEXANDER PHILIP, PRINZ VON.
   1906. Travels in the interior of North America. *In* Early western travels.
     Ed. by Reuben Gold Thwaites. Vols. 22–24. Cleveland.
WILSON, EDWARD F.
   1887. Report on the Blackfoot tribes. Rep. British Assoc. Advancement Sci.,
     vol. 57.
WILSON, GILBERT L.
   1924. The horse and dog in Hidatsa culture. Anthrop. Pap., Amer. Mus.
     Nat. Hist., vol. 15, pt. 2.

WILSON, R. N.
  1909. The sacrificial rite of the Blackfoot. Royal Soc. Canada Transactions, ser. 3, vol. 3.
  1921. Our betrayed wards. Ottawa.
WINCHELL, N. H.
  1911. The aborigines of Minnesota. St. Paul.
WINSHIP, GEORGE PARKER.
  1896. The Coronado expedition, 1540–1542. 14th Ann. Rep. Bur. Amer. Ethnol., 1892–93, pt. 1, pp. 329–613.
WISSLER, CLARK
  1910. Material culture of the Blackfoot Indians. Amer. Mus. Nat. Hist., Anthrop. Pap., vol. 5, pt. 1.
  1911. The social life of the Blackfoot Indians. Amer. Mus. Nat. Hist., Anthrop. Pap., vol. 7, pt. 1.
  1912 a. Ceremonial bundles of the Blackfoot Indians. Amer. Mus. Nat. Hist., Anthrop. Pap., vol. 7, pt. 2.
  1912 b. Societies and ceremonial associations in the Oglala Division of the Teton Dakota. Amer. Mus. Nat. Hist., Anthrop. Pap., vol. 11, pt. 1.
  1913. Societies and dance associations of the Blackfoot Indians. Amer. Mus. Nat. Hist. Anthrop. Pap., vol. 11, pt. 4.
  1914. The influence of the horse in the development of Plains culture. Amer. Anthrop., n. s., vol. 16, pt. 1.
  1915. Riding gear of the North American Indians. Amer. Mus. Nat. Hist., Anthrop. Pap., vol. 17, pt. 1.
  1927. North American Indians of the Plains. Amer. Mus. Nat. Hist. Handbook Ser. No. 1, 3d ed.
  1936. Population changes among the northern Plains Indians. Yale Univ. Publ. Anthrop., No. 1.
  1938. The American Indian. New York.
WISSLER, CLARK, and DUVALL, D. C.
  1908. Mythology of the Blackfoot Indians. Amer. Mus. Nat. Hist., Anthrop. Pap., vol. 2, pt. 1, pp. 1–163.
WORCESTER, D. E.
  1945. Spanish horses among the Plains Indians. Pacific Hist. Rev., vol. 14, No. 4.
WORK, JOHN
  1923. The journal of John Work. Ed. by William S. Lewis and Paul C. Phillips. Cleveland.
WYETH, NATHANIEL J.
  1851. Indian tribes of the South Pass of the Rocky Mountains; the Salt Lake Basin; the Valley of the Great Säaptin, or Lewis' River, and the Pacific Coasts of Oregon. In Schoolcraft, Henry R., "Historical and statistical information respecting the history, condition and prospects of the Indian tribes of the United States," vol. 1, pp. 204–228. Philadelphia.
WYMAN, WALKER D.
  1945. The wild horse of the West. Caldwell, Idaho.
YARROW, H. C.
  1881. A further contribution to the study of the mortuary customs of the North American Indians. 1st Ann. Rep., Bur. Amer. Ethnol., pp. 87–203.

PLATES

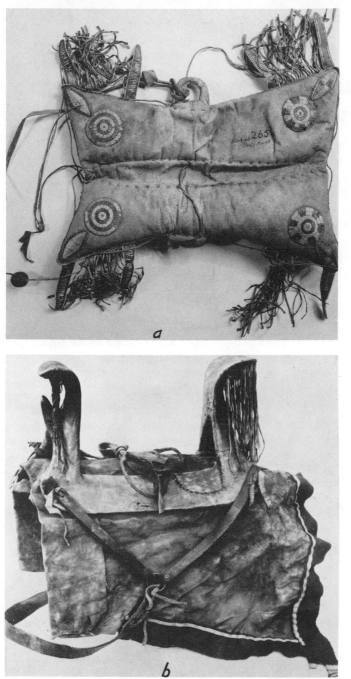

a, Man's pad saddle, Blackfoot. (Collected by Capt. Howard Stansbury, 1849. U.S.N.M. No. 2656.) *b*, Woman's "wood saddle," Blood Indians. (Collected by R. N. Wilson, 1897. Chicago Museum of Natural History No. 51752.)

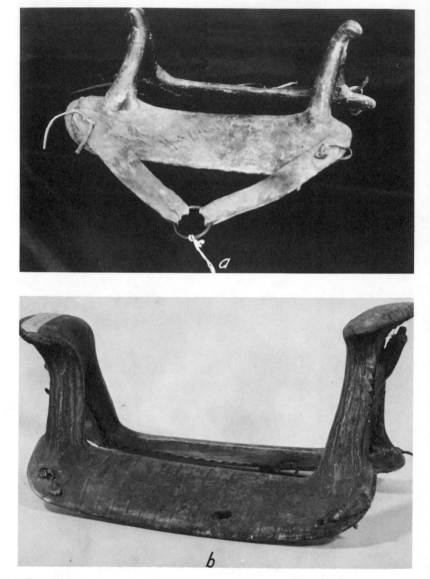

a, ''Prairie chicken snare saddle,'' Piegan. (Museum of the Plains Indian. Cat. No. 187L.) *b*, Wooden frame pack saddle, Sioux. (Collected by Dr. Nathan S. Jarvis, 1833–36. Brooklyn Museum. Accession No. 50–67–62.)

"The Bloods Come in Council." Pencil sketch by Gustavus Sohon in 1855, showing horse equipment of the period. (U. S. National Museum.)

a, Travois with paunch water container attached. (Drawing by a Southern
Cheyenne Indian, collected by H. R. Voth in 1889. U. S. N. M. No. 166032.)
b, Travois used as a litter, Crow Indians. (Photograph taken prior to 1900.)

Saddled Blackfoot Indian Pony. 1852. Pen and ink drawing by Rudolph Friederich Kurz. (Courtesy Berne Historical Museum.)

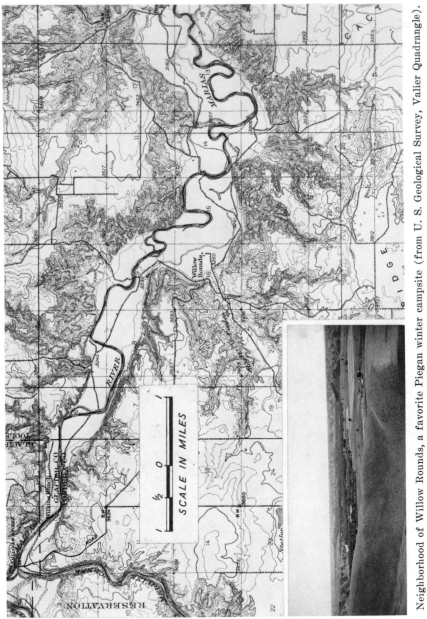

Neighborhood of Willow Rounds, a favorite Piegan winter campsite (from U. S. Geological Survey, Valier Quadrangle). *Insert:* Willow Rounds in 1951, view looking east.

Encampment of Piegan Indians near Fort McKenzie, summer 1833. (Lithograph from original drawing by Carl Bodmer.)

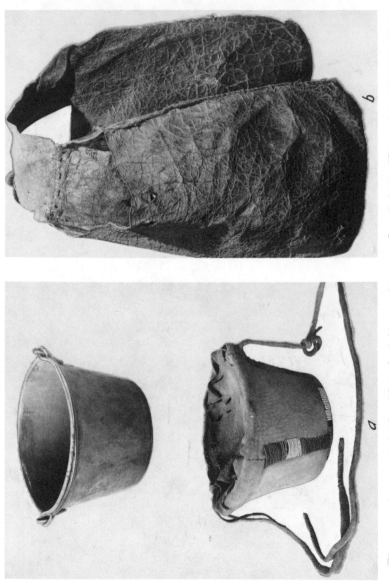

a, Two-quart, brass trade kettle with its buckskin traveling case, Crow Indians. (Collected in 1892. U. S. N. M. No. 154339.) *b*, Buffalohide double-bag, used in transporting food and small household articles on a packhorse, Blackfoot. (American Museum of Natural History No. 50/5381.)

Method of crossing a stream with camp equipment, Flathead Indians. Pencil sketch by Gustavus Sohon, ca. 1855. (U. S. National Museum.)

White Quiver (circa 1860–1931), the most successful Piegan horse raider. (Courtesy Museum of the Plains Indian.)

a, Child's toy horse of bent willow. Made in 1942 after an old Piegan pattern.
  (Courtesy Miss Jane Ewers.) *b*, Piegan boys playing calf roping at Heart
  Butte Sun Dance Encampment, summer 1944. (Courtesy Museum of the
  Plains Indian.)

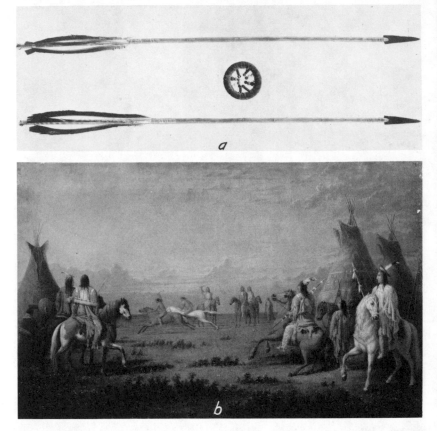

a, Beaded wheel and arrows used in the hoop and pole game, North Piegan. (Collected by R. N. Wilson in 1901. Chicago Museum of Natural History No. 69351). *b*, Blackfoot horse race, June 1, 1848. (Painting by Paul Kane. Courtesy Royal Ontario Museum of Archaeology.)

Piegan Indians chasing buffalo near the Sweetgrass Hills in September 1853. (Lithograph from original illustration by John Mix Stanley.)

A, Wallace Night Gun (ca. 1872–1950), leader of the Piegan Horse Medicine Cult. (Courtesy Great Northern Railway.)   *B*, Portion of Wallace Night Gun's horse medicine bundle in the United States National Museum (No. 387744): Pouch (*a*) contains beaded horse fetish (*b*) and pouches of secret horse medicines (*c* and *d*).

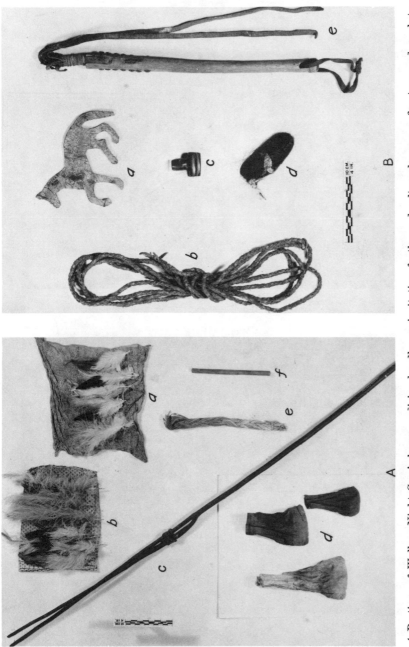

A, Portions of Wallace Night Gun's horse medicine bundle: *a*, invitation feathers; *b*, altar plumes; *c*, fire tongs; *d*, packets of red and black earth colors; *e*, sweetgrass used in making smudge; *f*, altar marking tool. *B*, Portion of Wallace Night Gun's horse medicine bundle: *a*, Rawhide horse fetish; *b*, rawhide rope carried by horse-dance leader; *c*, pipe bowl smoked in horse dance; *d*, horse mane fetish; *e*, whip carried by horse-dance leader.

a, Makes-Cold-Weather, aged Piegan warrior, counting four horse-raiding coups
before cutting the hide in the Sun Dance, 1944. (Courtesy Museum of the
Plains Indian.) *b*, A Blood Indian horse raider expiating his vow to undergo
self-torture in the Sun Dance lodge, 1892. (Photograph by R. N. Wilson.
Courtesy American Museum of Natural History.)

INDEX

Abert, James William, quotation from, 111

Abies lasiocarpa, 275

Actaea eburnia, medicinal use of, 275

Adultery, punishment for, 251, 252

Aged, abandonment of, 142, 243, 308

Agricultural products, traded for horses, 10, 11 (map)

Agriculture, lack of, 122

Aiton, Arthur S., on Coronado's horses and armor, 2, 205

Algonquian tribes, 333

Ambush, war method, 210

American Fur Co., 125, 203, 319

Ammunition, exchanged for horses, 8, 9, 13, 219

Amulets, 198

Anaphalis margaritacea subalpina, medicinal plant, 277

Animal predators, attacks on horses, 51

Antelope, 121, 166, 170

Apache Indians, 3, 4, 7, 331
 eating habits, 222
 horse raids by, 3
 horses received by, 18, 333
 origin of horse complex, 327
 raids by, 177, 185, 197
 raids on, 4, 14, 334, 335
 riding gear, 84–85
 social customs, 282
 transportation gear, 111, 137
 treatment of horses by, 48, 56
 wealth in horses, 24 (table)
 weapons used by, 201
 See also Chiracahua Apache

Arapaho Indians, 9, 23, 139, 171, 270, 276, 336
 conversion to nomadism, 9
 death customs, 286, 288
 games by, 226
 horses obtained by, 18, 332, 333
 hunting methods, 154, 162
 medical plants used, 277
 moves by, 334
 relations with Blackfoot, 173
 religious rites, 290
 role in horse trading, 8, 12, 45
 social customs, 256, 281, 282, 284
 transportation gear, 110, 119, 137
 treatment of horses by, 40, 48, 55
 wealth in horses, 24 (table)

"Archithinue Indians," 145, 154, 169, 201, 210, 310, 318
 horses possessed by, 17, 18, 39, 40, 333
 raids on, 172
 riding gear, 83

Arikara Indians (northernmost Caddoan-speaking people), 4, 8, 23, 279
 enemies of Blackfoot, 173
 food consumption, 168, 169, 170
 horses obtained by, 9, 12, 18, 213
 horses obtained from, 5, 10, 332
 hunting methods, 154
 role in trading, 13
 social customs, 284, 335
 treatment of horses by, 43, 44, 47, 327
 wealth in horses, 24 (table)

Armor, protective, 203–204, 309

Arrowheads, metal, traded for horses, 7

Arrowmaking tools, 136

Arrows, iron-headed, 156
 stone-headed, 156

Artemisia cana, range grass, 41

Artemisia frigida, medicinal use of, 275

Artemisia sp., medicinal use of, 275

Ashley, William H., trader, quotations from, 44

Asperger, ceremonial, 223, 224 (fig.)

Assiniboin Indians, 23, 43, 45, 78, 154
 clothes, 182
 death customs, 286, 287
 eating habits, 222
 guns owned by, 16
 horses acquired by, 5, 10, 12, 17, 18
 horses distributed among, 188
 hunting methods, 303, 304
 lack of horses by, 4, 134, 137, 142, 144, 165, 307, 308, 327, 340
 living conditions. 307–308
 movements of, 123, 130, 142, 144, 334
 origin of horse complex, 327
 packs carried by, 184
 raids by, 172, 174, 185
 raids on, 20, 171, 173, 176, 192
 religious beliefs, 291
 riding gear, 83, 99
 social customs, 280, 284
 social organization, 248
 trade with, 217, 219
 trade with Mandan, 13
 transportation gear, 102, 110, 119, 137
 treatment of horses by, 64
 wealth in horses, 24 (table), 31 (table)
 weapons used by, 202

Atsina Indians, *see* Gros Ventres.

Awls, 182, 184
 metal, traded for horses, 7, 13

Axes, 184
 battle, 309, 310

359

O